SHOOTING DOWN
THE STEALTH
FIGHTER

...For our families...
...and for those, known and unknown,
who were there...

The Kosovo war is slipping down America's impressive memory hole; of course it's never discussed in the endless considerations on the 'War on Terror'. In fact, if we really cared about ending terrorism around the globe, we would explore our own actions. Milosevic claimed he was fighting terrorists. The KLA were considered terrorists by the US and the West, it was explicitly stated before our involvement. Acting to preserve our 'credibility', we armed and supported said terrorists, and demonized not only the Serbian government, but the whole people, wrecking a country that will take decades to recover, if it ever does.

Noam Chomsky

The man who ventures to write a contemporary history must expect to be criticized both for everything he has said and everything he has not said.

François-Marie Arouet Voltaire in
a letter to M. Bertin de Rocheret

SHOOTING DOWN
THE STEALTH
FIGHTER

EYEWITNESS ACCOUNTS FROM THOSE WHO WERE THERE

MIHAJLO (MIKE) S. MIHAJLOVIC &
DJORDJE S. ANICIC

The last war in the twentieth century

*The extraordinary story of the band of maverick missileers and the first
combat downing of the STEALTH aircraft in history*

AIR WORLD

AIR WORLD

SHOOTING DOWN THE STEALTH FIGHTER
Eyewitness Accounts from Those Who Were There

First published in Great Britain in 2021 by
Air World
An imprint of
Pen & Sword Books Ltd
Yorkshire – Philadelphia

ISBN 978 1 52678 042 3

Typeset by SJmagic DESIGN SERVICES, India.
Printed and bound in the UK by CPI Group (UK) Ltd, CR0 4YY.

Pen & Sword Books Limited incorporates the imprints of Atlas, Archaeology, Aviation,
Discovery, Family History, Fiction, History, Maritime, Military, Military Classics, Politics,
Select, Transport, True Crime, Air World, Frontline Publishing, Leo Cooper, Remember
When, Seaforth Publishing, The Praetorian Press, Wharncliffe Local History, Wharncliffe
Transport, Wharncliffe True Crime and White Owl.

For a complete list of Pen & Sword titles please contact

PEN & SWORD BOOKS LIMITED
47 Church Street, Barnsley, South Yorkshire, S70 2AS, England
E-mail: enquiries@pen-and-sword.co.uk
Website: www.pen-and-sword.co.uk

Or
PEN AND SWORD BOOKS
1950 Lawrence Rd, Havertown, PA 19083, USA
E-mail: Uspen-and-sword@casematepublishers.com
Website: www.penandswordbooks.com

MIX
Paper from
responsible sources
FSC® C013604

Contents

CONTENTS

Preface

There are many excellent books covering subjects such as radars, stealth technologies, airplanes and air defence suppression. Most radar and stealth technology books are highly specialized and intended for narrow circles of professionals. Air defence manuals are especially intended for end users who are usually from the military. The NATO air campaign[1] in the Federal Republic of Yugoslavia in 1999 is covered in few books and there is a handful of publications in different languages about parts of this subject together, but none of which pulls all those parts together.

The intention of this book is to describe and enlighten in detail one event that shook, shaped and steered aviation twenty years ago. That event happened when something that was a marvel in aviation had been brought down with something that was, at the time of use, almost obsolete. This book looks firstly through the eyes of missile crews rather than through the eyes of the pilot in the last war of twentieth century, where one small independent country in the middle of Europe was brutally attacked by a mighty alliance for controversial political reasons. But this event was not just the end of an experiment, rather the beginning. Definitely in the future stealth and missile would meet many more times in the sky over other countries.

Both authors participated in that war in the air defence and intelligence roles. Lieutenant Colonel Anicic, as a missile battalion deputy commander and executive officer (XO), was personally involved in downing the F-117A. Because of the necessary requirements of security, both stealth and air defence materials are not widely known and there is much speculation about these events, both in printed material and on the web. Some are pure fantasy, some are close to the truth. The real truth is now known to a very narrow circle of experts but even there some of the finer details are not known.

One of the challenges with this approach is to objectively expose errors without casting the slightest shadow on those who took an oath and fought for their countries. In most books about air warfare, there is an accent on one side

---

1. From the Serbians' point of view, the NATO campaign was an act of calculated aggression.

or the other, depending on who the author is and for which audience the book is intended. Of course, most books are related to the pilots – fighter pilots, bombers or 'wild weasel' crews. This book takes another approach. We have tried to put the reader into the cabin of the missile fire control centre as well as into the aircraft cockpit. All those personnel tried to do was their duty as best as they could and live to fight another day. As the operations of both missile crew and pilot are highly technical, an approach has been made to explain the technology behind their actions so that the ordinary reader, who is not military or educated in engineering, can understand better what went on. Many authentic photos and illustrations are used to support the text and help the reader to better understand the written material.

Why, for example, do American and other NATO pilots fight and sometimes die, or kill enemy soldiers or, worse, innocent civilians, in places far from home which most in their own countries have barely even heard of? The short answer is that they were ordered to, and the military was at the mercy of elected government officials. It was not the decision of men in uniforms where and whom to fight, so, having no real choice, they went, and in future they will do so again. Suits and ties in Washington DC, Wall Street, Tel Aviv or London, for example, make wars for their own interests, sometimes geopolitical sometimes economic, and the soldiers just execute their orders, like them or not. For politicians there are no eternal enemies, just eternal interests. Today's enemy is tomorrow's friend and vice versa. Very often the 'enemy of my enemy is my friend.'

On the other side, there are missile system crews. Ordinary people, professionals, like their opponents in the sky. Their job is to defend the sky over their country. Throughout their military careers they train, over and over again, so that in less than thirty seconds they can bring down an aircraft. That thirty seconds is all they have to do their duty, or to die trying. Only highly trained and motivated crew can do that and live to fight another day.

Pilots and missile crews never actually see the faces of their opponents. The most they will see is maybe a monochrome picture on the screen in the cockpit with the crosshair in the middle of it where the laser bomb will hit, or a blip on the radar screen and another blip of the missile which in a few seconds will intercept the target. Behind that building in the crosshairs or that blip on the radar screen are living creatures – people with families, somebody waiting for them to come home. The feelings in those few seconds before the bomb or missile launches can be understood only by those who have experienced it.

Some may find this book trivial, or too simple, even for an introductory text. Again, please accept our apologies; the simplicity is because we did not include anything we couldn't understand ourselves. Radar and stealth experts may be bothered by some of the approximations, but these approximations have proved adequate for real applications. Some readers will undoubtedly find subjects in the text for which references aren't properly cited. The author apologizes in advance for these errors, but twenty years in the dark makes them difficult to correct. Try as one might, there will always be mistakes that escape into the text; please notify us of any you find, so they may be corrected.

The text is orientated towards the ordinary reader who is interested in the history of warfare and military technology. It may also be of interest for graduate engineers with a background in radar, communications, and basic physics. The intelligence community and military analysts may find interesting some of the attacking aircraft, missile batteries and search and rescue tactics and procedures.

This book is written so that every chapter can be read without reading the previous chapter. The reader may ask: Can this book be used to train somebody to shoot down the aircraft? The answer is of course 'no'. For that a high degree of training is necessary; but this book might shed some extra light on the subject. Another question: Is there a 'magic bullet' with which to shoot down a stealth airplane? The answer is again 'no'. But there are methods and procedures which are here described in a plain way.

This book is a labour of love and passion, and it represents years of work both researching and writing.

Djordje Anicic (left) and Mike Mihajlovic (right) in March 2019, 20 years after the war.

Foreword

Neva against the STEALTH

Since the NATO intervention in Yugoslavia, a considerable number of publications have been written in a number of languages analyzing how the old missile system SA-3 Goa (S-125M1 Neva) was able to track and shoot down the modern aircraft considered almost invisible, the famous US Air Force F-117A, pride of the US aircraft industry and scourge of Saddam's air defences during the Gulf War. In these publications the different aspects of these events are addressed, but not a single one (except maybe some highly classified analyses available only to the designated few) addresses the whole aspect. In this book, the authors, using verifiable information, analyze what happened, before, during and after the event. This is an authoritative work about the technology and tactics involved in the collision which took place in March 1999.

The reader is first introduced to the development and characteristics of radars, the basis of stealth technology and the stealth programme, missile guidance and the development of the SA-3 air defence system, and anti-radiation missiles as the main enemy of the missile units. After that is the story of the combat itself, in which the authors talk about the role of the missile crew as well as the pilot and his views.

F-117A was technologically far more advanced than the missile system and, by all parameters presented before the war, it was considered 'invisible' for the SA-3 system. Previous combat engagements greatly contributed to this aura of invincibility. This myth was crushed on the night of 27 March 1999 when the first missile hit its target. What this event showed was that an obsolete missile system can be very useful if the crew who operates that system is properly trained and experienced. The combat was decided by the missile crew alone, without any support from high command or the air defence network. There was no magic in the downing of the stealth. The missile system worked in its own autonomous way and was able to detect, track, engage and destroy the aircraft which was supposed to be invisible to that very same system.

FOREWORD

A whole chapter is dedicated to the 3rd Air Defense Missile Battalion as the winner in this duel with the Stealth. It covers the role of every member of the combat crew. It also includes training, tactical procedures, modes of readiness prior to combat engagement, regime of operations, tracking, target acquisition and much more. Of particular interest is that Lieutenant Colonel Anicic was one of the commanders in the crew which downed the stealth, which makes the account especially fascinating.

I was personally engaged in the analyses of this engagement and of the behaviour of every crew member, including the support units as well as the pilot (aircraft trajectory, speed, manoeuvre etc). My conclusion was that the combat crew performed all tactical steps brilliantly.

Commands issued to engage and stop the fire control radar in the brief intervals were crucial for the safety of the people and equipment, denying the enemy the use of anti-radiation missiles. On the other hand, the pilot of the F-117A performed masterfully so that the missile hit him almost at the end of its effective range. There are many questions left unanswered, such as: What happened after the radar imitator emitted signals a few hours before the duel? Who picked them up, and how were they processed in the NATO analysis department? Was there any alteration of the preprogrammed flight paths? What happened with the other two blips which Lieutenant Colonel Anicic saw on his screen? Did the pilot get any warning signal that he was being tracked by the fire control radar? And why did the pilot say that he was hit by the second missile when only the first one actually acquired the target?

The US Air Force engaged two F-117A squadrons (12 + 12 +1). After the combat stopped, twenty-two airplanes flew back to the States. What happened with the other three? One was confirmed as a combat loss, but it is unknown (to the public) what happened with the other two. It is evident that they didn't fly to the States on their own.

NATO wanted to destroy the air defence capabilities of the Yugoslav armed forces in the first few days of combat, but they failed, even though they were hundreds of times stronger. Yugoslav air defence and armed forces in general withstood seventy-eight days of bombing. In the end they retreated, but they were not defeated. Its stationary air surveillance units were crippled. Older SA-3 systems also suffered losses, but the other parts of the military were virtually unscathed. NATO tried different approaches. A vast number of aircraft were available to them, including strategic aviation such as B-1B, B-2 and B-52. Was the B-2 bomber engaged? We devote a whole section to this question.

Finally, this book shines new light on the dark world of historical manipulation and speculation, and it will definitely consign many dubious theories to the dustbin.

Vladimir Neskovic, Eng., PhD, Col (ret)

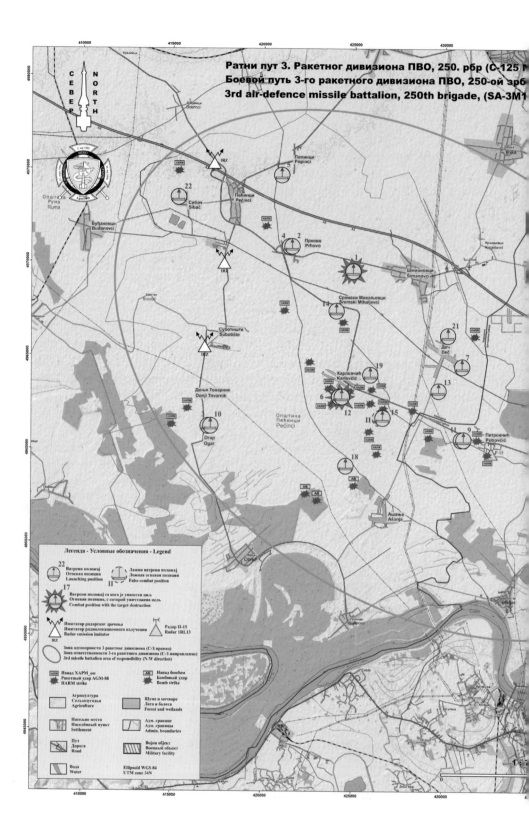

Ратни пут 3. Ракетног дивизиона ПВО, 250. рбр (С-125 N

Боевой путь 3-го ракетного дивизиона ПВО, 250-ой зрб

3rd air-defence missile battalion, 250th brigade, (SA-3M1

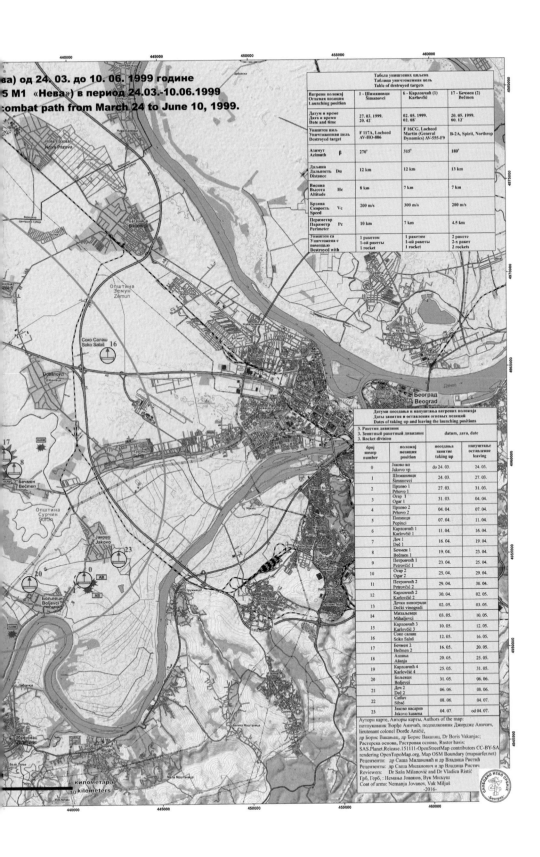

ва) од 24. 03. до 10. 06. 1999 године
5 М1 «Нева») в период 24.03.-10.06.1999
combat path from March 24 to June 10, 1999.

Ватрени положај Огневая позиция Launching position	1 - Шимановци Šimanovci	6 - Карловчић (1) Karlovčić	17 - Бечмен (2) Bečmen
Датум и време Дата и время Date and time	27. 03. 1999. 20. 42	02. 05. 1999. 02. 08	20. 05. 1999. 60. 12´
Уништен циљ Уничтоженная цель Destroyed target	F 117A, Locheed AV-HO-806	F 16CG, Locheed Martin (General Dynamics) AV-555-F9	B-2A, Spirit, Northrop
Азимут Azimuth β	270°	315°	180°
Даљина Дальность Du Distance	12 km	12 km	13 km
Висина Высота Hc Altitude	8 km	7 km	7 km
Брзина Скорость Vc Speed	200 m/s	300 m/s	200 m/s
Периметар Параметр Pc Perimeter	10 km	7 km	4.5 km
Уништен са Уничтожена с помощью Destroyed with	1 ракетом 1-ой ракеты 1 rocket	1 ракетом 1-ой ракеты 1 rocket	2 ракете 2-х ракет 2 rockets

Табела уништених циљева
Таблица уничтоженных цель
Table of destroyed targets

Датуми поседања и напуштања ватрених положаја
Даты занятия и оставления огневых позиций
Dates of taking up and leaving the launching positions

број номер number	положај позиция position	поседања занятие taking up	напуштања оставление leaving
0	Јаково вп Jakovo vp	до 24. 03.	24. 03.
1	Шимановци Šimanovci	24. 03.	27. 03.
2	Прхово 1 Prhovo 1	27. 03.	31. 03.
3	Огар 1 Ogar 1	31. 03.	04. 04.
4	Прхово 2 Prhovo 2	04. 04.	07. 04.
5	Попинци Popinci	07. 04.	11. 04.
6	Карловчић 1 Karlovčić 1	11. 04.	16. 04.
7	Деч 1 Deč 1	16. 04.	19. 04.
8	Бечмен 1 Bečmen 1	19. 04.	23. 04.
9	Петровчић 1 Petrovčić 1	23. 04.	25. 04.
10	Огар 2 Ogar 2	25. 04.	29. 04.
11	Петровчић 2 Petrovčić 2	29. 04.	30. 04.
12	Карловчић 2 Karlovčić 2	30. 04.	02. 05.
13	Дечки виногради Dečki vinogradi	02. 05.	03. 05.
14	Михаљевци Mihaljevci	03. 05.	10. 05.
15	Карловчић 3 Karlovčić 3	10. 05.	12. 05.
16	Соко салаш Soko Salaš	12. 05.	16. 05.
17	Бечмен 2 Bečmen 2	16. 05.	20. 05.
18	Ашања Ašanja	20. 05.	25. 05.
19	Карловчић 4 Karlovčić 4	25. 05.	31. 05.
20	Бољевци Boljevci	31. 05.	06. 06.
21	Деч 2 Deč 2	06. 06.	08. 06.
22	Сибач Sibač	08. 06.	од 04. 07.
23	Јаково касарна Jakovo kasarna	04. 07.	од 04. 07.

3. Ракетни дивизион
3. Зенитный ракетный дивизион
3. Rocket division

datum, дата, date

Аутори карте, Авторы карты, Authors of the map:
потпуковник Ђорђе Анчић, подполковник Джордже Анчич,
lieutenant colonel Đorđe Ančić,
др Борис Вакањац, др Борис Ваканяц, Dr Boris Vakanjac;
Растерска основа, Растровая основа, Raster basis:
SAS.Planet.Release.151111-OpenStreetMap contributors CC-BY-SA
rendering OpenTopoMap.org, Map OSM Boundary (mapsurfer.net)
Рецензенти: др Саша Милановић и др Владица Ристић
Рецензенты: др Саша Миланович и др Владица Ристич
Reviewers: Dr Saša Milanović and Dr Vladica Ristić
Грб, Герб; Немања Јованов, Вук Миљуш
Coat of arms: Nemanja Jovanov, Vuk Miljuš
-2016-

километара
kilometers

The past is not to be forgotten...it is the path into the future

Facing the past can be emotive and raise personal as well as cultural questions. Our relationship to the past, especially in the Balkans, is one of the benchmarks of the social development of our society. This year is the 20th anniversary of the beginning of the NATO air campaign in the Federal Republic of Yugoslavia. On 24 March 1999 at 19:45 the air raid sirens sounded for the first time since the Second World War. For the next seventy-eight days and nights bombs rained down on Yugoslavia in a military intervention, unauthorized by the UN Security Council, known as Operation Allied Force. The bombing of Yugoslavia ended on 10 June with UN Security Council Resolution 1244 under which Serbia kept sovereignty over Kosovo and Metohija, although they became international protectorates of UNMIK and KFOR.

What stood between NATO bombers and civilians were the Yugoslav armed forces. One of the units which fought this cruel war was 3rd Missile Battalion from 250th Air Defence Missile Brigade. This battalion was the one which shot down the pride of the US Air Force, the formidable Nighthawk F-117A. The greatness of this achievement is that it used an old, almost obsolete, Soviet SA-3/S-125 missile system which is considered little more than a 'slingshot' in military circles.

Yugoslav air defence is officially the only air defence force in the world, at the time of writing, which was able to bring down the stealth airplane, but it will definitely not be the last. This shootout in the sky over Serbia was an event which secured a place in history books. The myth of invincibility and invisibility was crushed on the night of 27 March when at 20:42 the missile hit its mark. A missile system without people to manage it is just a pile of steel. These people, members of the combat shift, are the unsung heroes of this event and they rightfully deserve their place in history.

This book is an exciting story about the Soviet-made air defence missile system SA-3/S-125 Neva, as well as stealth technology. It also covers the people behind these systems. The importance of this book is that it covers a subject which is little known about and prone to endless speculation. Its historic value is that it covers the whole event without prejudice. It will, without doubt, become the foundation for future reference and research.

Both authors are experienced technical and military professionals and speak with the full authority of their rich knowledge. Lieutenant Colonel (retired) Djordje Anicic is one of the heroes of the combat shift which engaged and downed the Stealth, one of the combat crew commanders and the man who developed the tactics and procedures which radically improved air defence. Mr Mihajlo (Michael as he is known in Canada) Mihajlovic is a professional engineer with a vast knowledge of the engineering aspects of missile systems, radars and stealth technology as well as military experience in the Yugoslav and Canadian armed forces.

This book represents an enormous contribution to the history and the culture of remembrances and I am recommending it with the great pleasure.

Belgrade, 11 February 2019

Vladica Tosic, historian, politicologist and specialist in international affairs.

Organization of this Book

This book covers four main topics:

- Radars
- Low-observables and low probability of intercept (LO and LPI) radars often called STEALTH
- The air defence missile system
- Personal accounts of the clash between the air defence missile system and the stealth airplane.

In some sections, all of these topics are covered, as they often interact.

Chapter One provides an introduction and history of radars – RF/microwave LPI/LO techniques and some basic LPI/LO equations. It also includes a basic explanation of electronic warfare (EW).

Chapter Two covers stealth technology.

Chapter Three covers missile guidance for the most common system

Chapter Four surveys the development of surface to air missile system SA-3/S-125 Neva and its derivatives.

Chapter Five addresses anti-radiation missiles and their use.

Chapter Six covers SA-3/S-125 missile system combat history.

Chapter Seven describes the F-117 stealth programme development.

Chapter Eight covers war and combat engagement between the F-117 and the Yugoslav (Serbian) SAM during the NATO attack on Yugoslavia with the personal details of SAM crews, the stealth pilot, other aircraft pilots, and combat search and rescue teams (CSAR). It also covers the downing of F-16CG.

Chapter Nine deals with the aftermath of the war and consequences for stealth and air defence developments.

The Appendix covers the NATO codification system and contains a detailed glossary of potentially unfamiliar terms and abbreviations.

About the Authors

Djordje (Sava) Anicic was born in 1958 in the village of Jazak, municipality of Irig, in the foothills of the Serbian mountain of Fruska Gora in the northern Serbian province of Vojvodina. He finished elementary school in Vrdnik and high school (mathematical department) in Aleksinac and Ruma. After high school he enrolled into the Air Force technical academy, air defence branch. After graduation, he started his first commission as a Sub-Lieutenant in Skopje (now in Macedonia) and later in Belgrade, serving in SA-3 air defence missile units. During his service he passed through all the duties in the missile battalion from platoon commander to battalion XO. On a few occasions he went to the former USSR for combat and live missile launching.

At the beginning of the NATO air campaign he was 3rd Battalion XO with the rank of Lieutenant Colonel. He was one of the two commanders of the combat crew which downed F-117A on 27 March 1999. He holds the record for the officer with the most combat hours in the entire Yugoslav air defence.

After the war, during the reorganization of the Yugoslav military and the dismantling of the 3rd Battalion, he was demoted, despite being decorated by the president personally. His criticisms of the military establishment were drastically sanctioned after the war.

After spending less than a year in the lower rank, he was sent to the military academy to teach 'missile unit tactics'. He was retired on his own request in 2002 after a bitter struggle with the military establishment. After retiring he decided to publish the missile battalion diary which he kept day-by-day during the entire war in the form of book with the title *Smena* (The Shift). In it he disclosed all aspects of the combat both positive and negative, military organization, function and command structure. He contributes to the few Internet portals and often participates in TV documentaries and shows. He is also a member of the 3rd Battalion defence veteran's organization slobodnonebo.org.rs.

Mihajlo (Michael) (Slobodan) Mihajlovic was born in 1966 in the town of Zrenjanin in the northern Serbian province of Vojvodina. He finished elementary school in the village of Velike Livade and Zrenjanin as well as high school (physics and natural sciences). After enrolment to the University of Novi Sad he was drafted into compulsory military service. He served in artillery and air-defence units in the Yugoslav republic, Bosnia, Herzegovina and Croatia. After graduation from the Faculty of Technical Sciences, Mechanical Engineering, Automation and Computer Science branches, he worked as a teacher and lecturer at the technical college, teaching engineering subjects as well as defence industry. He was also engaged in military intelligence.

Since 2002 he has lived and worked in Toronto, Canada. Besides his degree in engineering, he has professional certifications which include a Canadian Professional Engineering licence. His engineering experience is in engineering design and technology for the defence industry where he designed light armoured vehicles, weapon platforms, passive and active decoys, camouflage systems and ballistic protection. Other expertise includes engineering in the civilian corporate and government sector such as commercial, industrial, institutional, residential and government buildings, military bases, mining and metallurgy plants and smelters, project development, commissioning, technology development and technical courses and lecturing. He is also a lifelong historian interested particularly in military history and technology. He is the author of *Specijalne Snage Sveta* (World Special Forces) and *Podmornice* (Submarines) published in Serbian. He also writes scientific and technical articles on both military and non-military subjects.

He served in the Canadian forces reserve as an officer in RCEME (Royal Canadian Electrical and Mechanical Engineers).

His job provided him the opportunity to work all over the world, including tours with Canadian forces in Afghanistan (Kabul and Kandahar).

Chapter One

Early History of Radar

With man's desire to camouflage and hide things, it was also his desire to uncover things – measure always to be met with countermeasure. To detect objects in the air, a device named RADAR[2] has been invented. Radar is an electromagnetic system that uses radio waves for detection and location of reflecting objects such as aircraft, ships, spacecraft, vehicles, people, and the natural environment.

Radar uses the principle of sending a radar wave, which is a form of electromagnetic radiation, in a desired direction with a transmitter, and then collecting the reflected signals from a target with a receiver. Once reflected, the signals are received and the range to a target can be calculated by evaluating the interval of the radar signal's travel; half the time of the total interval gives the distance of the target. Neither a single nation nor a single person is able to say that he/she (or they) is the inventor of the radar method. One must look at 'Radar' as an accumulation of many earlier developments and improvements which scientists of several nations share. There are nevertheless some milestones in the process.

The Scottish physicist James Clerk Maxwell developed his electro-magnetic light theory (Description of the electro-magnetic waves and their propagation) in 1865. In 1886, German physicist Heinrich Hertz showed that radio waves could be reflected from solid objects and proved Maxwell's theory. In 1895, Alexander Popov, a physics instructor at the Imperial Russian Navy school in Kronstadt, developed an apparatus using a coherer tube for detecting distant lightning strikes. The next year he added a spark-gap transmitter. In 1897, while testing this equipment for communicating between two ships in the Baltic Sea, he took note of an interference beat caused by the passage of a third vessel. In his report, Popov wrote that this phenomenon might be used for detecting objects, but he did nothing more with this observation.

---

2. The word **RADAR** came from using the capitalized letters of the phrase **RA**dio **D**etection **A**nd **R**anging. The widespread military use of it during the Second World War changed the focus of the war from the Battle of Britain to the Pacific. It later became an indispensable navigation and traffic control system for civilian purposes.

SHOOTING DOWN THE STEALTH FIGHTER

In 1904 the German high frequency engineer Christian Hülsmeyer invented the 'Telemobiloskop' for traffic supervision on the water. He measured the running time of electromagnetic waves to a metal object (ship) and back. A calculation of the distance was thus possible. This is the first practical radar test. Hülsmeyer patented his invention in Germany and in the UK. It operated on a 50 cm wavelength and the pulsed radar signal was created via a spark-gap. His system already used the classic antenna setup of horn antenna with parabolic reflector. It was presented to German military officials in practical tests in Cologne and Rotterdam harbour but was rejected.

In 1915, Robert Watson-Watt used radio technology to provide advance warning to airmen.

In 1917 the French engineer Lucien Lévy invented the super-heterodyne receiver. He first used the denomination 'Intermediate Frequency', and avoided the possibility of double heterodyning.

At the same time, Serbian-American scientist and inventor Nikola Tesla proposed that radio waves be used to detect and 'follow' objects on the surface of the sea. By measuring the signal, distance and direction could be determined.

During the 1920s Robert Watson-Watt went on to lead the UK research establishment to make many advances using radio techniques, including the probing of the ionosphere and the detection of lightning at long distances. Through his lightning experiments, Watson-Watt became an expert on the use of radio direction finding before turning his attention to shortwave transmission. Requiring a suitable receiver, he told the 'newbie' Arnold Frederic Wilkins to conduct an extensive review of available shortwave units. Wilkins would select a General Post Office model after noting its manual's description of a 'fading' effect (the common term for interference at the time) when aircraft flew overhead.

In 1921 American physicist Albert Wallace Hull invented the 'Magnetron' as an efficient transmitting tube.

In 1922 the American electrical engineers Albert H. Taylor and Leo C. Young of the Naval Research Laboratory showed that a wooden ship passing through the beam path caused the received signal to fade in and out. Taylor submitted a report, suggesting that this phenomenon might be used to detect the presence of ships in low visibility, but the navy did not continue the work.

Eight years later, Lawrence A. Hyland at the Naval Research Laboratory (NRL) observed similar fading effects from passing aircraft; this revelation led to a patent application as well as a proposal for further intensive research on radio-echo signals from moving targets to take place at NRL, where Taylor and Young were based at the time.

In 1930 Lawrence A. Hyland (also of the Naval Research Laboratory) located an aircraft for the first time.

In 1931 a ship was equipped with radar. Antennae used parabolic dishes with horn radiators.

The development of the 'Klystron' in 1936 by the technicians George F. Metcalf and William Hahn, both from General Electric, would prove to be an important component in radar units as an amplifier or an oscillator tube.

Before the Second World War, researchers in the UK, France, Germany, Italy, Japan, the Netherlands, the Soviet Union and the USA, independently and in secret, developed technologies that led to the modern version of radar. Australia, Canada, New Zealand, and South Africa followed pre-war Great Britain's radar development, and Hungary developed its radar technology during the war.

In France in 1934, following studies on the Split Anode Magnetron, the research branch of the Compagnie Générale de Télégraphie Sans Fil (CSF) headed by Maurice Ponte with Henri Gutton, Sylvain Berline and M. Hugon, began developing an obstacle-locating radio apparatus, aspects of which were installed on the ocean liner *Normandie* in 1935.

During the same period, Soviet military engineer P.K. Oshchepkov, in collaboration with Leningrad Electrophysical Institute, produced an experimental apparatus, RAPID, capable of detecting an aircraft within 3 km of a receiver. The Soviets produced their first mass production radars RUS-1 and RUS-2 Redut in 1939 but further development was slowed following the arrest of Oshchepkov and his subsequent gulag sentence during the purges. Only 607 Redut stations were produced during the war. The first Russian airborne radar, Gneiss-2, entered service in June 1943 on Pe-2 fighters. More than 230 Gneiss-2 stations were produced by the end of 1944. The French and Soviet systems, however, featured continuous-wave operation that did not provide the full performance ultimately synonymous with modern radar systems.

Full radar evolved as a pulsed system, and the first such elementary apparatus was demonstrated in December 1934 by the American Robert M. Page, working at the Naval Research Laboratory. The following year, the US Army successfully tested very basic surface-to-surface radar to aim coastal battery searchlights at night. This design was followed by a pulsed system demonstrated in May 1935 by Rudolf Kühnhold and the firm GEMA in Germany and then another in June 1935 by an Air Ministry team led by Watson-Watt in Great Britain (**Figure 1-1**).

In 1935, Watson-Watt was asked to judge recent reports of a German radio-based death ray and turned the request over to Wilkins. Wilkins returned a set of calculations demonstrating that the system was basically impossible. When Watson-Watt then asked what such a system might do, Wilkins recalled the

Figure 1-1: Sir Robert Watson-Watt. (sciencemuseum.org)

earlier report about aircraft causing radio interference. This revelation led to the Daventry experiment of 26 February 1935, using a powerful BBC shortwave transmitter as the source and their GPO receiver setup in a field while a bomber flew around the site. When the plane was clearly detected, Hugh Dowding, the Air Member for Supply and Research, was impressed with the system's potential and funds were immediately provided for further operational development. Watson-Watt's team patented the device numbered GB593017.

Development of radar greatly expanded on 1 September 1936 when Watson-Watt became superintendent of a new establishment under the British Air Ministry, Bawdsey Research Station, located in Bawdsey Manor, near Felixstowe, Suffolk. Work there resulted in the design and installation of aircraft detection and tracking stations called 'Chain Home' along the east and south coasts of England in time for the outbreak of war in 1939. This system provided the vital advance information that helped the Royal Air Force win the Battle of Britain; without it, significant numbers of fighter aircraft would always need to be in the air to respond quickly enough if enemy aircraft detection relied solely on the observations of ground-based individuals. Also vital was the 'Dowding system' of reporting and coordination to make best use of the radar information during tests of early deployment of radar in 1936 and 1937.

Given all required funding and development support, the team produced working radar systems in 1935 and began deployment. By 1936 the first five Chain Home (CH) systems were operational and by 1940 they stretched across the entire UK including Northern Ireland. Even by standards of the era, CH was crude; instead of broadcasting and receiving from an aimed antenna, CH broadcast a signal floodlighting the entire area in front of it, and then used one of Watson-Watt's radio direction finders to determine the direction of the returned echoes. This meant that CH transmitters had to be much more powerful and have better antennas than competing systems, but it did allow its rapid introduction using existing technologies.

During the war, a key development was the cavity magnetron in the UK, which allowed the creation of relatively small systems with sub-metre resolution. Britain shared the technology with the US during the 1940 'Tizard' mission.

In April 1940, *Popular Science* showed an example of a radar unit using the Watson-Watt patent in an article on air defence. In late 1941 *Popular Mechanics* had an article in which a US scientist speculated about the British early warning system on the English east coast and came close to what it was and how it worked. Watson-Watt was sent to the US in 1941 to advise on air defence after Japan's attack on Pearl Harbor. Alfred Lee Loomis organized the Radiation Laboratory at Cambridge, Massachusetts, which developed the technology in the years 1941-45. In 1943, Page greatly improved radar with the monopulse technique that was used for many years in most radar applications.

Radar Fundamentals

Radar, as previously described, is an acronym for radio detection and ranging, which tends to suggest that it is a piece of equipment that can be used to detect and locate a target. Modern radar does much more than just detection and ranging. It is used to determine the velocity of moving targets and also find out many more characteristics about the target such as its size, shape and other physical features including, for example, the type and number of engines used on an aircraft. Radar is extensively used in many civilian and military applications. Radar has been and will continue to be an essential capability for militaries worldwide. This chapter gives a comprehensive treatment to the radar fundamentals covering a wide cross section of topics including basic radar functions, related performance parameters, radar range equation, radar waveforms, radar transmitters, receivers and displays, radar antennas and types of radar.

Radar System and Radar Range

Throughout this book, minimal use of equations and formulas will be used, but in some instances they are helpful and are included.

The radar equation describes the performance of radar for a given set of operational, environmental, and target parameters.

Radar is a stand-alone active system with its own transmitter and receiver. It is primarily used for detecting the presence of and finding the exact location of a far-off target. It does so by transmitting electromagnetic energy in the form of short bursts in most cases, and then detecting the echo signal returned by the target.

The radio waves used by radar are produced by a piece of equipment called a 'magnetron'. Radio waves are similar to light waves: they travel at the same speed, but their wavelengths are much longer and have much lower frequencies (**Figure 1-2**). Light waves have wavelengths of about 500 nanometres (500 billionths of a metre, which is about 100-200 times thinner than a human hair), whereas the radio waves used by radar typically range from a few centimetres to a metre; roughly a million times longer than light waves. Both light and radio

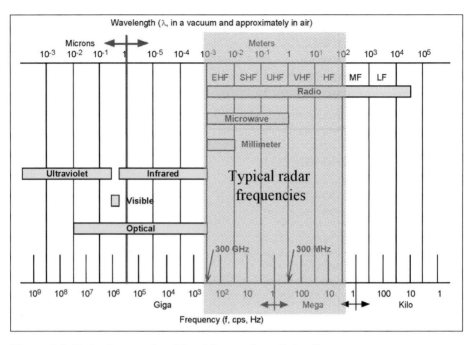

Figure 1-2: Radar frequencies. (Naval Postgraduate School)

waves are part of the electromagnetic spectrum, which means they are made up of fluctuating patterns of electrical and magnetic energy zapping through the air. The waves a magnetron produces are actually microwaves, similar to the ones generated by a microwave oven. The difference is that the magnetron in radar has to send the waves many miles, instead of just a few inches, so it is much larger and more powerful (**Figure 1-3**).

The range of the intended target is computed from the time that elapses between the transmission of energy and the reception of its echo. The location of the target can be determined from the angle/direction of the arrival of the echo signal by using a scanning antenna, preferably transmitting a very narrow width beam. As mentioned earlier, radar today does much more than just detect a target and find its location. Radar can be used to determine the velocity of a moving target, track a moving target and even determine some of the physical features of the target. No single radar type can be used to perform all the functions. There are different types which are best suited to different applications. In addition, radar is a principal source of navigational aid to aircraft and ships. It forms a vital part of an overall weapon guidance or fire-control system. Behind most radar functions lies its capability to detect a target and find its range and velocity.

6

The basic components of a radar system are shown in the block-schematic arrangement in **Figure 1-4**.

The radar signal waveform as generated by the waveform generator modulates a high-frequency carrier and the modulated signal is raised to the desired power level in the transmitter portion. The transmitter could be a power amplifier

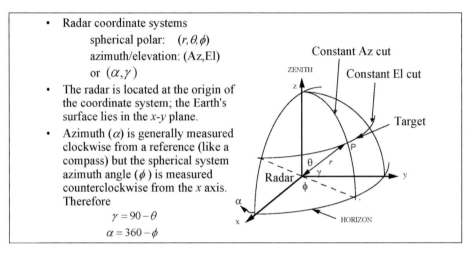

- Radar coordinate systems
  spherical polar: (r, θ, ϕ)
  azimuth/elevation: (Az,El)
  or (α, γ)
- The radar is located at the origin of the coordinate system; the Earth's surface lies in the x-y plane.
- Azimuth (α) is generally measured clockwise from a reference (like a compass) but the spherical system azimuth angle (ϕ) is measured counterclockwise from the x axis. Therefore
  $$\gamma = 90 - \theta$$
  $$\alpha = 360 - \phi$$

Figure 1-3: Radar coordinate system. (Naval Postgraduate School)

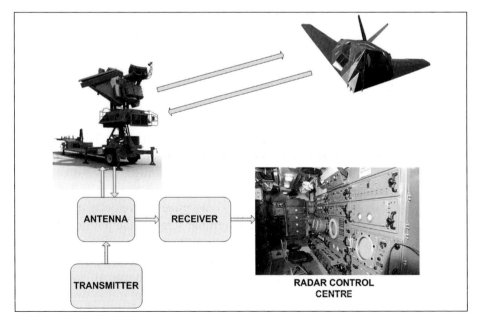

Figure 1-4: Radar system – basic components. (Authors)

employing any of the microwave tube amplifiers such as Klystron, Travelling Wave Tube (TWT), Crossed Field Amplifier (CFA) or even a solid state device. The radar waveform is generated at a low power level, which makes it far easier to generate different types of waveforms required for different radars. The average output power requirement of radar could be as small as a few tens of milliwatts for very short-range radars to several megawatts for Over-The-Horizon-Radar (OTHR).

The duplexer allows the same antenna to be used for both transmission as well as reception. It acts as a switch disconnecting the receiver from the antenna during the time the relatively much higher power transmitter is ON to protect the receiver from getting damaged. On reception, the weak received signal is routed to the receiver by the duplexer. The duplexer usually makes use of gas-filled transmit/receive tubes that are basically sections of transmission line filled with a low breakdown voltage gas. These tubes get fired due to the presence of high power to direct the transmitter output to antenna. After the transmitter signal is radiated, these tubes de-ionize or recover quickly to direct any received signal to the receiver input. A circulator is sometimes used to provide further isolation between transmitter and receiver. A circulator as a component can also be used as a duplexer. The circulator duplexer contains a high-power RF circulator comprising signal couplers and phase shifters such that a signal entering one port has a low attenuation path only to the next port in a particular direction. All other paths are high attenuation paths (**Figure 1-5**).

The antenna acts as an interface between the radar transmitter output and free space. Mechanically steered parabolic reflector antennas and electronically steered antenna arrays are commonly used. The echo signal received by the antenna is directed to the receiver input. The receiver is usually of the super heterodyne type. The receiver filters out-of-band interference. It also amplifies the desired signal to a level adequate for operating subsequent circuits (**Figure 1-6, Figure 1-7**).

The purpose of signal processing is to reject the undesired signals such as clutter and enhance the desired signals due to the targets. It is done before the section that makes the decision as to whether the target is present and in case of a target being present, extracts the information such as range, Doppler, and so on. Data processing refers to the processing done after the detection decision has been made.

Radar clutter is nothing but unwanted echoes. These undesired echoes could originate from a number of sources such as objects on land or sea surfaces, insects, animals or birds, weather conditions like rain or atmospheric turbulences, objects deployed as countermeasures like chaff and decoys, and so on. The term 'clutter' to an extent is application specific. Clutter in one application may be a genuine target in another. For example, for radar tracking a land target such

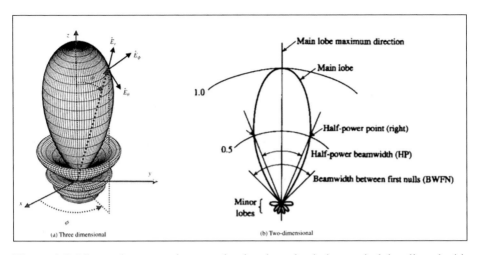

Figure 1-5: Most radar energy is transmitted and received via a main lobe aligned with the antenna's boresight, but smaller amounts enter through sidelobes that point in almost all directions. (Naval Postgraduate School)

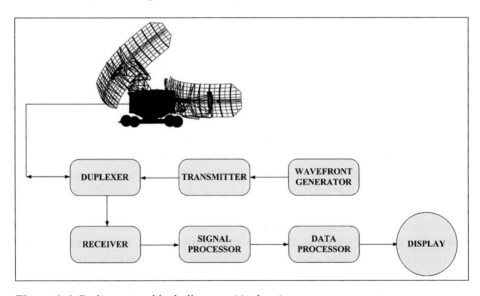

Figure 1-6: Radar system block diagram. (Authors)

as tank a to guide a missile to hit the target, scattering from vegetation on land surface or from weather conditions such as rain would be clutter. On the other hand, for airborne remote sensing radar, reflection of radar energy from natural vegetation is the primary target. Also, backscattering from atmospheric particles and turbulences would be a genuine signal for weather radar.

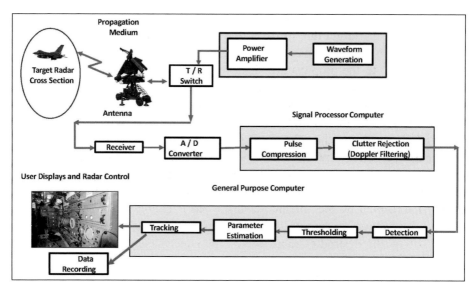

Figure 1-7: RCS processing. (Authors)

Surface clutter includes both ground clutter and sea clutter. The magnitude of clutter, that is, the magnitude of undesired radar signal backscattered in the direction of radar, depends upon the nature of material composition, surface roughness and the angle the radar beam makes with the surface in azimuth and elevation directions. The backscattered radar energy is also a function of radar signal wavelength and polarization. The reflected signal is the phasor sum of reflections from a large number of individual scatterers. These individual sources of scatter may be static, such as in the case of buildings, tree trunks and so on, or moving as in the case of rain drops, leaves or ripples on the sea surface. Individual sources of clutter vary spatially and temporally.

Functions like automatic tracking and target recognition are examples of data processing in a radar system. The display puts the processed information in a form usable by radar operators and others wanting to use the information such as air traffic controllers, weapon system operators, and so on. The operation of radar and the sequence of events that take place from start to finish can be summarized in the case of typical pulsed radar as follows:

The transmitter generates a repetitive pulse train with each pulse having a burst of RF signal. The pulse parameters, of course, vary with the type of radar and the mode in which it is operating. The duplexer routes the pulsed electromagnetic energy to the transmitting antenna which concentrates the energy fed to its input into a narrow beam in the direction of the intended target. At the same time, a time base is initiated coinciding with the transmission time instant of the pulse.

The electromagnetic wave propagates through the atmosphere. This wave gets reflected from the target due to the difference in the impedance characteristics of the targets. The impedance offered by the atmosphere (or more precisely, the free space) to the propagating electromagnetic wave is 377 Ω (Ohms) and any discontinuity encountered causes the wave to get reflected. The amount of reflection depends on the characteristics of the target. The target reflects the wave in all directions and the portion of the reflected energy travelling in the direction of the radar constitutes the echo or the backscatter.

Backscatter energy travels back to the radar and a portion of it along with a portion of the clutter is intercepted by the radar's receiving antenna, which in the present case is same as the transmitting antenna. The amount of backscatter energy intercepted by the antenna depends on the capture area of the antenna. The received signal is routed to the receiver by the duplexer. The signal that contains both the desired echo as well as the interfering signals and noise gets processed in the receiver.

The processed information is then subjected to the detection threshold comparison and if the signal is larger than the detection threshold, detection is said to occur. If the detection is caused by the desired target, a target is said to be present and if the same occurs due to interfering signals, detection is a false alarm. The detection threshold is chosen to minimize the probability of false alarm.

Another detection error occurs when the radar fails to detect an existent target due to the target echo signal being weak and not being able to cross the detection threshold. When detection occurs, that is, when the processed signal crosses the detection threshold, the time base initiated at the start is strobed and the round-trip propagation time measured to determine the target range. The antenna's position encoders are also strobed to determine the angle-of-arrival of the echo at the time of detection. If the target is a mobile one, its radial velocity information is contained in the Doppler shift, which can be used to determine the target velocity.

Radar Range Equation

The radar range equation relates the radar's detection range to various radar and target parameters (**Figure 1-8**). These parameters include the transmitted power, transmit antenna gain, radar cross section of the target, receive antenna aperture, minimum detectable power at the receiver input, and various loss factors. The range equation has been derived from first principles step-by-step in the following paragraphs. A brief description of different parameters entering the range equation has also been given, along with different steps of derivation of the equation, in particular emphasizing the significance of these parameters vis-à-vis the maximum detection range of the radar.

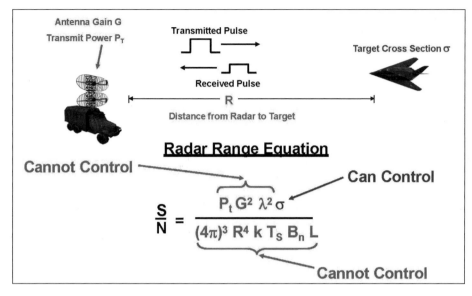

Figure 1-8: Radar range equation. (IEEE AES Society, modified by authors)

One form of the basic radar range equation is:

$$SNR = \frac{P_s}{P_N} = \frac{P_T G_T G_R \lambda^2 \sigma}{(4\pi)^3 R^4 k T_0 B F_n L}$$

Where:

SNR signal-to-noise ratio in watts.

P_S the signal power at some point in the radar receiver – usually at the output of the matched filter or the signal processor – watts.

P_N noise power at the point specified – watts.

P_T peak transmit power, and is the average power when the radar is transmitting a signal. P_T can be specified at the output of the transmitter or at some other point like the output of the antenna feed – watts.

G_T the directive gain of the transmit antenna, in watts.

G_R the directive gain of the receive antenna, in watts. Usually, $G_R = G_T$ for monostatic radars.

λ radar wavelength in watts.

σ the target radar cross-section or RCS – m².

R range from the radar to the target – metres.

k Boltzman's constant: 1.38x 10-23 w/(Hz 0K).

T_0 denotes a reference temperature in degrees Kelvin. We take and usually use the approximation kT0= 4 x 10-21 w/Hz.

B the effective noise bandwidth of the radar. Units: Hz.

Fn   is the radar noise figure and is dimensionless, or has units of watts.

L   is a term included to account for all losses that must be considered when using the radar range equation. It accounts for losses that apply to the signal and not the noise. L has units of watts. It accounts for a multitude of factors that degrade radar performance.

When radar transmitter and receiver are in the same place, then it is referred to as monostatic radar. In some cases the radar transmitter and receiver can be in different places when viewed from the target, and this is referred to as bistatic radar. The third classification is when the two antennas are located at the same site but just slightly separated. This is referred to as quasi-static. For a monostatic system a single antenna is generally used to transmit and receive the signal.

$$P_t = \frac{P_r \, G_t}{4\pi r^2} \sigma \frac{A_{eff}}{4\pi x r^2}$$

P_t power transmitted by the radar (watts)

G_t gain of the radar transmit antenna (dimensionless)

r distance from the radar to the target (metres)

σ radar cross section of the target (metres squared) – RCS

A_{eff} effective area of the radar receiving antenna (metres squared)

P_r power received back from the target by the radar (watts)

In practice, the radar receiver will sense a non-zero signal even when there is no target present. Other sources can come as a clutter, interference or noise.

Clutter is reflections from the ground, foliage, or other objects in the environment to the radar receiver. Interference is signals from other electronic systems that when radiated will be received. They might be intentional to distract the radar (i.e., a jammer) or they may be unintentional interference occupying the same frequency band (e.g., radio stations, other radars, etc). Noise is the thermal motion of electrons which gives rise to random voltages and currents. Surprisingly, for a well-designed radar operating at microwave frequencies, thermal noise generated in the radar's receive channel can be the limiting factor in detecting a barely observable target.

Detection Range

One of the important uses of the radar range equation is in the determination of detection range, or the maximum range at which a target has a given probability of being detected by the radar. The criterion for detecting a target is that the SNR be above some threshold value. If we consider the above radar range equations, we note that SNR varies inversely with the fourth power of range. This means that if the SNR is a certain value at a given range, it will be greater than that value at shorter ranges. The upshot of this discussion is that we define the detection range as the range at which we achieve a certain SNR. To find detection range, we need to solve the radar range equation for

$$R = \left(\frac{P_T G_T G_R \lambda^2 \sigma}{(4\pi)^3 (SNR) k T_0 BF_n L} \right)^{1/4} \text{ m}$$

The Antenna

The purpose of the radar antenna is to concentrate, or focus, the radiated power in a small angular sector of space. In this fashion, the radar antenna works much as the reflector in a flashlight. As with a flashlight, a radar antenna doesn't perfectly focus the beam. As the electromagnetic wave from the target passes the radar, the radar antenna captures part of it and sends it to the radar receiver.

The guided electromagnetic waves look more appropriate when the feeder connecting the output of the transmitter and the antenna or the input of the receiver and the antenna is a waveguide, which is generally true when we talk about microwave frequencies and microwave antennas. In case of other antennas, such as those at high frequency (HF) and very high frequency (VHF), the term 'guided electromagnetic waves' mentioned previously would be interpreted as a guided electromagnetic signal in the form of current and voltage. Sometimes an antenna is considered a system that comprises everything connected between the transmitter output or the receiver input and free space. This includes, in addition to the component that radiates other components such as the feeder line, balancing transformers and so on. An antenna is a reciprocal device, that is, its directional pattern as receiving antenna is identical to its directional pattern when it is used as a transmitting antenna, provided, of course, it does not employ unilateral and nonlinear devices such as some ferrites. Also, reciprocity applies, provided the transmission medium is isotropic and the antennas remain in place with only transmit and receive functions interchanged. Antenna reciprocity also does not imply that antenna current distribution is the same on transmission as it is on reception.

When a radio frequency (RF) signal is applied to the antenna input, there is current and voltage distribution on the antenna that lead to the existence of an electric and a magnetic field. The electric field reaches its maximum coincident with the peak value of the voltage waveform. If the frequency of the applied RF input is very high, the electric field does not collapse to zero as the voltage goes to zero. A large electric field is still present. During the next cycle, when the electric field builds up again, the previously sustained electric field gets repelled from the newly developed field. This phenomenon is repeated again and again and we get a series of detached electric fields moving outwards from the antenna. According to laws of electromagnetic induction, a changing electric field produces a magnetic field and a changing magnetic field produces an electric field. It can be noticed that when the electric field is at its maximum, its rate of change is zero and when the electric field is zero, its rate of change is maximum. This implies that the magnetic field's maximum and zero points correspond to the electric field's zero and maximum points, respectively. That is, the electric and magnetic fields are at right angles to each other and so are the detached electric and magnetic fields. The two fields add vectorially to give one field that travels in a direction perpendicular to the plane carrying mutually perpendicular electric and magnetic signals back to the radar receiver.

The common types of antenna radiation patterns include (1) the omnidirectional (azimuth plane) beam, (2) the pencil beam, (3) the fan beam and (4) the shaped beam. The omnidirectional beam is commonly used in communication and broadcast applications for obvious reasons. The azimuth plane pattern is circular, and the elevation pattern has some directivity to increase the gain in horizontal directions. A pencil beam is a highly directive pattern whose main lobe is confined to within a cone of a small solid angle; it is circularly symmetrical about the direction of maximum intensity. This is mainly used in engagement, guiding and target tracking radars (fire control radars). A fan beam is narrow in one direction and wide in the other. A typical application of such a pattern would be in search or surveillance radars in which the wider dimension would be vertical and the beam is scanned in azimuth. The last application would be in height-finding radar where the wider dimension is in the horizontal plane and the beam is scanned in elevation. There are applications that impose beam-shaping requirements on the antenna. One such requirement, for instance, is to have a narrow beam in azimuth and a shaped beam in elevation such as in the case of air search radar (**Figure 1-9**).

The typical antenna in the older surface-to-air missile systems is curved so it focuses the waves into a precise, narrow beam, but radar antennas also typically rotate so they can detect movements over a large area. The radio waves travel outwards from the antenna at the speed of light and keep going until they hit something. Then some of them bounce back towards the antenna in a beam of reflected radio waves also travelling at the speed of light. The speed of the waves is crucially important. If a target is approaching at, for example, 3,000 km/h, the radar beam needs to travel much faster than this to reach the plane, return to the transmitter, and trigger the alarm in time. If for example the target is 160 km away, a radar beam can travel that distance and back in less than a thousandth of a second.

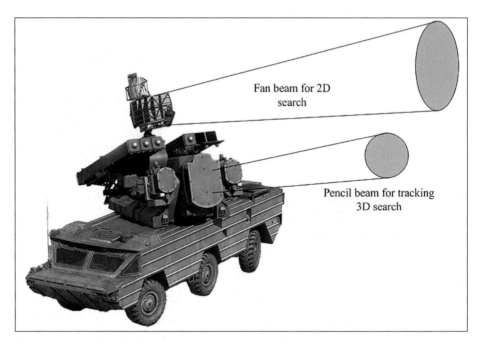

Figure 1-9: Radar beams. (Authors)

As the antenna is the emitter of electromagnetic waves, it is the primary target for anti-radiation missiles such as HARM, which are guided to the electromagnetic source. More of this can be found in Chapter Five describing anti-radiation missiles.

Radar Displays

Some of the more commonly used radar displays in military radars include the A-Scope or A-Scan, B-Scope, F-Scope and Plan Position Indicator (PPI). Each of these is briefly described in the following paragraphs. Of particular interest are the last two because most of the Soviet-made radar systems in air defence applications have them.

Plan Position Indicator (PPI)
This is an intensity-modulated map-like circular display that gives target locations in polar coordinates. The radar location is in the centre of the display. The target range is represented by the radial distance from the centre, and the target's azimuth angle is given by the angle from the top of the display, usually north, clockwise. In some types of PPI display, called 'Offset or Sector' PPI, the radar location is offset from the centre of the display. This is commonly used in search radars (**Figure 1-10 and 1-11**).

Figure 1-10: Plain position indicators from Fan Son radar (right) and SA-6 KUB (below). (SAM simulator, Wikipedia)

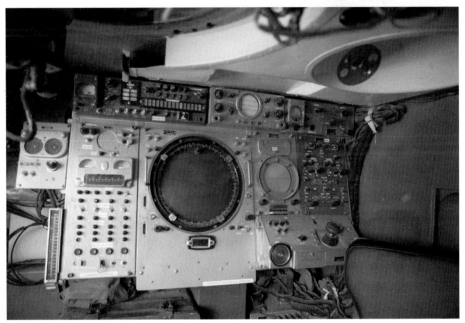

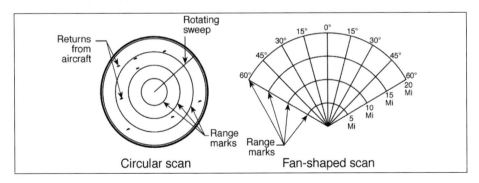

Figure 1-11: Plain position indicators. Circular scan (left), fan-shaped scan (right). (Naval Postgraduate School)

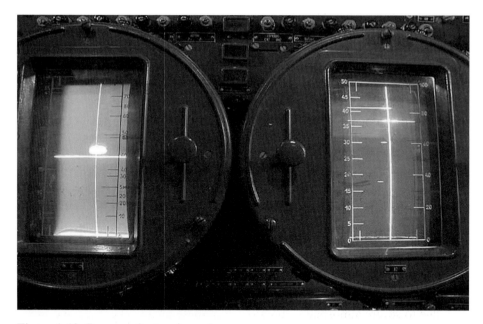

Figure 1-12: F scopes. (tertraedar.org)

F-Scope
Horizontal and vertical axes of an F-scope display represent azimuth and elevation track error, respectively. Often it is marked as 'Fi' from the Greek letter Φ. The centre of the display indicates the antenna's beam axis location. The blip's displacement from the centre indicates the target's position with respect to the antenna beam axis (**Figure 1-12**).

Radar Classification

Radars can be classified on the basis of:

1. Operational frequency band
2. Transmit wave shape and spectrum
3. PRF (Pulse Repetition Frequency) class
4. Intended mission and mode

Operational Frequency Band
Radars typically operate in a frequency range of a few tens of MHz to a few tens of GHz.

Radars operating up to about 30 MHz make use of ionospheric reflection to detect targets lying beyond the radar horizon. Over-The-Horizon-Radar (OTHR) belongs in this category. Very-long-range early warning radars are found in the VHF and UHF bands (30 MHz to 1 GHz).

- L band (D Band in the new designation) radars operating in the 1–2 GHz frequency band are usually long-range military radars and air traffic control radars.
- S band (E/F band in the new designation) radars operating in the 2–4 GHz band are usually the medium-range ground-based and shipboard search radars and air traffic control radars.
- C band (G Band in the new designation) radars operating in the 4–8 GHz frequency band are usually search and fire-control radars of moderate range, weather detection radars and metric instrumentation radars.
- X band (I/J band in the new designation) radars operating in the 8–12.5 GHz frequency band are mostly airborne multimode radars.
- Ku, K and Ka bands (J, K and L bands in the new designation) operating in the 12.5–18 GHz frequency band (Ku), 18–26.5 GHz frequency band (K) and 26.5–40 GHz frequency band (Ka) are used for short-range applications due to severe atmospheric attenuation in these bands. These include short-range terrain avoidance and terrain following radars and space based radars.
- Radars operating in the infrared and visible bands (laser radars) are mainly used as range finders and designators.

Transmit Wave Shape and Spectrum
Based on the transmit wave shape and spectrum, radars are classified as unmodulated CW (continuous wave) radar capable of finding target velocity only, modulated CW radar capable of finding both range and velocity, gated CW pulsed radar and modulated pulsed radar. FM-CW (Frequency Modulated-Continuous-Wave) radars belong to the class of modulated CW radars. Pulse Doppler radar is a popular type belonging to the category of gated CW pulse radars. Pulse compression radar falls in the category of modulated pulse radar.

PRF Class
Based on PRF class, we have Low PRF (Pulse Repetition Frequency) radars including Moving Target Indicator (MTI) and Moving Target Detector (MTD), and High PRF radars such as Pulse Doppler radar and Medium PRF radars.

Intended Mission and Mode
Radars with surface-to-surface mission are usually short-range radars that do not use Doppler. There are many functions and types of radar. Radars with surface-to-air missions include surveillance radar, early warning radar, weather radar,

fire-control radar, metric instrumentation radar, OTHR and so on. Radars with air-to-surface mission include terrain following and avoidance radars, synthetic aperture radars (SAR), ground mapping radars, radar altimeter and so on.

Basic Radar Functions

The basic functions that radar can perform include target detection, identifying target location in range and angular position, and determining target velocity. The radar performs these tasks provided that the target echo signals after signal processing are sufficiently stronger than the interfering signals like: noise generated in the receiver; unwanted clutter echo due to reflections from land, sea, clouds and so on; a jamming signal; electromagnetic interference (EMI), which is an accidental interference from friendly sources such as communication systems, other radars and spillover, due to leakage from transmitter into receiver occurring mainly in CW radars. Not all radars are capable of measuring all of these listed parameters.

Target Detection

Detection is the process of determining whether or not a target is present. There are four possible conditions of detection: If a target is present and is detected, the result is considered correct; if there is no target and the radar display also shows no detection condition, the result is again correct; if the target is present and radar fails to show it on the display, an error is said to have occurred; but if the target is absent and radar shows detection, it is referred to as a false alarm. The last two are error conditions; the false alarm is usually considered far more serious and undesirable. Such a tricky situation usually occurs because the target echo and interference signals have more or less the same shape after they have been processed in the receiver and the only way to discriminate between the two is by amplitude comparison. The radar can often confuse a weak target with a strong interference residue. For this reason, detection can only be described by probabilities; the probability of detection and the probability of false alarm.

Target Location

The target location is expressed in terms of its range, azimuth angle and elevation angle. Range is the shortest distance of the target from the radar regardless of direction. Azimuth angle is the angle between the antenna beam's projection on the local horizontal and some reference. The azimuth reference in case of land-based radars is usually true north. Ship-borne radars usually reference the ship's head, which is a line parallel to the ship's roll axis. Airborne radars reference the roll axis on the local horizontal plane. Elevation angle is the angle between radar antenna's beam axis and the local horizontal. The local horizontal in the case of land-based radars is the plane passing through the antenna's centre of radiation and perpendicular to the earth's radius passing through the same point. For airborne radars, it is also the plane containing the vehicle's pitch and roll axes.

Military Applications of Radar Systems

Though radar systems are extensively used in a wide range of civilian applications in the areas of science, meteorology and air traffic control, use of radars by law enforcement agencies and military applications outnumber all other radar applications. Major radar systems in use by the armed forces and law enforcement agencies include police radar used for detecting traffic rule violations, surveillance-based radar systems including battlefield surveillance radar, ground penetration radar, air surveillance radar and tracking-based applications such as air defence radar, weapon locating radar and ballistic missile defence radar. Military radars are also used for navigation, weather forecasting and Identification Friend or Foe (IFF). This chapter will discuss only the application of the radars used in air defence.

Surveillance-Based Applications
Surveillance radar sensors are used to monitor activity surrounding critical and/or strategic assets such as military installations, border crossings, airports, ports and harbours, nuclear research and nuclear power generation facilities, missile and satellite launch stations, oil refineries, ammunition storage depots, and so on. Surveillance functions may include intended targets below ground level, at ground level or in the air space surrounding the critical asset. There are primary radars and secondary surveillance radars. While primary radar systems measure only the range and bearing of intended targets by detecting the transmitted radio frequency signal reflected off the target, secondary surveillance radar (SSR) relies on targets equipped with a radar transponder that replies to each interrogation signal by transmitting a response containing encoded data. Air traffic control (ATC) radar is an example of a secondary surveillance radar system. ATC radar not only measures the range and bearing of the aircraft, it also requests additional information from the aircraft itself such as its identity and altitude. The IFF system is another example of an SSR system. Common surveillance-based military radar systems include ground (or area) surveillance radar, air surveillance radar and ground penetration radar (GPR).

State-of-the-art ground (or area) surveillance radar scans track movements of targets such as an individual walking or crawling towards a facility with precision, speed and reliability. Such radars typically have ranges of several hundred metres to over 10 km. Battlefield surveillance radar is the most commonly used application of ground surveillance. These radars are generally suitcase-sized tripod-mounted portable systems. Those with longer ranges are mounted on a vehicular platform. There are hundreds of other ground surveillance radars with similar or enhanced features available from major international manufacturers of defence and security equipment.

Military application of air surveillance radar primarily involves monitoring the airspace to detect hostile aircraft and directing defensive measures against them. Conventional air surveillance radar called two-dimensional (2D) radar measures the location of a target in two dimensions including range and azimuth. Air surveillance radar capable of determining the elevation angle in addition to the target range and azimuth angle is known as three-dimensional (3D) radar. The elevation angle allows computation of target height. 3D air surveillance radar measures range in a conventional manner but has an antenna that is mechanically or electronically rotated about a vertical axis to obtain a target's azimuth angle and has either fixed multiple beams in elevation or a scanned pencil beam to measure its elevation angle. There are other types of radar such as the electronically scanned phased arrays and tracking radars that measure the target location in three dimensions. It is essential for air surveillance radar to be able to look 'around the corners' to provide better coverage and capability to detect ground-hugging airborne targets. Over-the-horizon-radar (OTHR) exploits certain features of Earth's atmosphere enabling it detect low-flying aircraft over ranges of thousands of kilometres. Air surveillance radars are generally located on elevated platforms to maximize coverage area. Coverage area and capability to detect ground-hugging aircraft can be further enhanced by mounting radar on an airborne platform. The Airborne Warning and Control System (AWACS) is one such example. State-of-the-art air surveillance radars are designed to detect, locate, track and classify a wide range of targets including traditional fixed and rotary-wing aircraft, non-traditional targets like ultralights, paragliders, Unmanned Aerial Vehicles (UAVs) also referred to as drones, ballistic missiles, and even birds, thereby providing early warning, situational awareness and tactical ballistic missile surveillance and defence. Radars used by air traffic controllers for both approach phase surveillance and on-route surveillance are also examples of air surveillance radars.

Tracking Radar-based Applications
Tracking radar detects and follows intended targets so as to determine their trajectory, a function that is put to use in a wide range of civilian and military applications. One such widely used application of tracking radar is for air traffic control. Air traffic controllers rely on systems installed both at airports and at strategic spots on the ground beneath air traffic lanes for effective control extending to hundreds of kilometres. Tracking radars installed at airports are generally short-range radars intended to track airplanes, vehicles and even individuals on the

surface in and around the airport. There is a large number of military applications that rely for their functioning on tracking radars. Armed forces use tracking radars to keep track of friendly and enemy platforms, which include land-based vehicles such as tanks, airborne targets such as aircraft, unmanned aerial vehicles, missiles, rockets and ships. Radar is used to monitor enemy targets to determine if they represent an immediate threat. In case of an imminent threat, radar may track the target and then use the track information to employ suitable defensive or offensive countermeasures such as guided missiles or aircraft to intercept the target. Another important application of tracking radars is in removal of space debris. Space debris comprises used rocket stages and leftovers from completed missions, fragmented and inactive satellites and asteroids. Tracking radar may be used to track space debris to determine if it poses any threat to space assets such as space stations. The spacecraft may be manoeuvred out of the way in case of any possibility of collision. Common military radars employing tracking radar concept or a combination of tracking and surveillance concepts include fire-control radar, weapon-locating radar also called counter-battery radar or shell tracking radar.

Engagement and fire-control radar is a 'tracking radar' specifically designed for integration with air-defence weapon systems. The radar component of the platform measures the coordinates of the intended target or targets in terms of their azimuth, elevation, height, range and velocity, which may be used to determine the target trajectory and to predict its future position. These radars provide continuous position data on single or multiple targets enabling the associated guns or guided weapons to be directed and locked on to targets.

Radar Cross Section (RCS)

The RCS of a target, denoted by 'σ' (sigma), is measured as a ratio of the transmitted radar signal power backscattered from the target per unit solid angle (in the International System of Units (SI), a solid angle is expressed in a dimensionless unit called a steradian (symbol: sr)) in the direction of the radar to the radar signal power intercepted by the target. Conceptually, RCS is measured by comparing the strength of the reflected signal from the target to the reflected signal from a perfectly smooth conducting metal sphere with a frontal or projected area of 1 m². RCS is measured in m² and is therefore the projected area of an isotropically radiating perfectly conducting sphere that would reflect the same power in the direction of radar as the one that is actually reflected by the target for a given incident power. RCS is also measured in dBsm (or dBm²), which is decibels relative to 1 m². RCS in dBsm, or dBm², is expressed as 10 log σ where σ is RCS in m² (**Figure 1-13**).

A sphere is used for comparison while computing RCS because a sphere projects the same area irrespective of its orientation. Also, the RCS of a sphere is independent

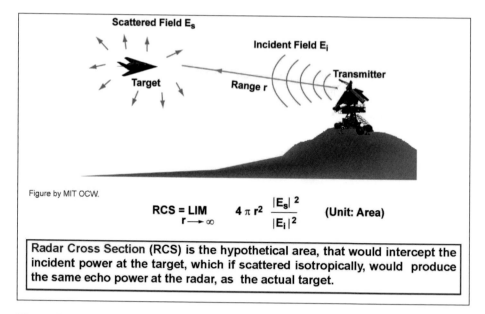

Figure by MIT OCW.

$$RCS = \lim_{r \to \infty} 4\pi r^2 \frac{|E_s|^2}{|E_i|^2} \quad \text{(Unit: Area)}$$

Radar Cross Section (RCS) is the hypothetical area, that would intercept the incident power at the target, which if scattered isotropically, would produce the same echo power at the radar, as the actual target.

Figure 1-13: Radar cross sections. (IEEE AES Society modified by author)

of frequency provided that the operating wavelength is much smaller than both the range as well as the radius of the sphere. Most structures including a sphere exhibit different RCS dependence on operating frequency. Radar cross section of target is influenced by both radar signal parameters such as operating wavelength and polarization as well as target characteristics such as size, shape, orientation and so on. Important factors that influence radar cross section include the following:

- Target size and shape and surface roughness
- Target material composition with reference to its electromagnetic properties
- Relative size of target in relation to operating wavelength, and
- Target orientation

Target Size and Shape
RCS is directly proportional to target size. The larger the target, the greater is its RCS value. In addition to the absolute size of the target, its shape also influences the RCS. Different shapes present different incident angles to the radar signal. Radar waves that make large angles of incidence are reflected away from the direction of the radar and therefore contribute to reducing the RCS. Very large incidence angles produce equally large angles of reflection leading to forward scattering. This makes the target stealthier. For example, the F-117A Nighthawk fighter aircraft by Lockheed-Martin is designed to have flat and large angled

surfaces, which significantly contributes to its having a low RCS. The RCS of the F-117A stealth fighter is estimated to be between 10 and 100 cm². Similarly, air frame shaping such as alignment of planform edges and fixed-geometry S-ducts (or serpentine inlets) that prevent line-of-sight of the engine faces from any exterior view in F-22 Raptor fighter aircraft are important factors that give it an extremely low RCS of 1 cm² (**Figure 1-14, Figure 1-15**).

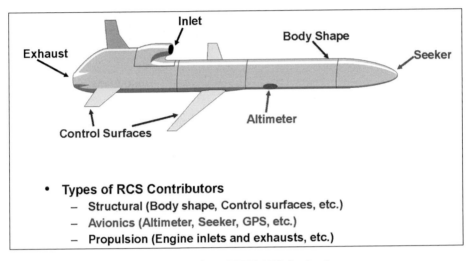

Figure 1-14: Types of RCS contribution. (IEEE AES Society)

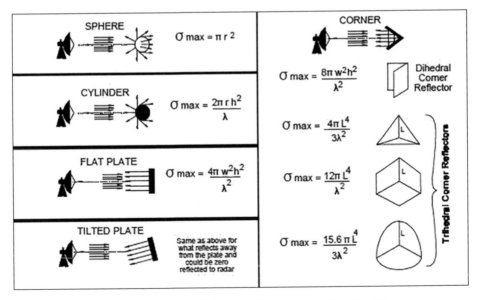

Figure 1-15: Radar cross sections of simple objects. (Radar Handbook)

Indentations present in relief in a surface such as those arising from open bomb bays, ordnance pylons, joints between constructed sections and engine intakes are potent corner reflectors contributing to increase in RCS from many orientations. It is more so as it is impractical to coat these surfaces with radar absorbent materials.

Target Material

The materials used in the construction of the target and also the materials used to coat the surfaces play a significant role in determining the RCS. There are materials such as metals that are strong reflectors of radar waves. Even a thin layer of metal coating makes the object a strong reflector of radar energy. Chaff that is often made of metallized plastic or glass is a good example. There are materials such as wood, plastic, and fibreglass that are less reflective. Use of radar absorbent materials significantly reduces the RCS. The F-117A Nighthawk stealth fighter and the B-2 bomber are well-known examples of stealth technology that minimize RCS by using both aerodynamic geometry and radar absorbent materials applied to the surface of their fuselages. Radar absorbent materials minimize the reflection of radar waves thereby reducing the RCS. There are two broad categories of radar absorbing materials: impedance matching absorbers and resonant absorbers. There are other absorbing material configurations that have features of both of the classifications.

Operating Wavelength

RCS is strong function of operating frequency or wavelength. There are three frequency regimes, namely the low frequency or Rayleigh regime, mid-frequency or 'Mie' regime and high-frequency or optical regime. RCS is a function of relative size of target with respect to operating wavelength and is approximately equal to the real area of the target when the target size is much smaller than the operating wavelength. For a target size roughly equal to the operating wavelength, the RCS may be greater or smaller than the real area depending upon operating wavelength before it approaches the real value in the optical region.

Target Orientation

Target orientation with respect to radar line-of-sight strongly influences the RCS. For example, a fighter aircraft presents a much larger area when viewed from the side than when it is viewed from the front. The fact that military targets such as fighter aircraft have many reflecting elements and shapes and also that targets move relative to radar line-of-sight, relative orientations of various reflecting elements and shapes on the target structure, make RCS dependence on target orientation a very complex phenomenon.

Estimated radar cross section for some targets.[3]

Target	Radar Cross Section (RCS) m^2
Cruiser (length 200 m)	14000
B-52 Stratofortress	100-125
C-130 Hercules	80
F-15 Eagle	10-25
Su-27 Flanker	10-15
Panavia Tornado	8
F-4 Phantom II	6-10
Tank (typical)	6-9
Truck (typical)	6-10
MiG-29 Fulcrum	3-5
Su-35	2
MiG-29K	1-1.5
MiG-35	0.3
F-16A	5
F-18 C/D Hornet	1-3
J-20 Chengdu	1-3
Mirage 2000	1-2
F-16 C (With reduced RCS)	1.2
T-38 Talon	1
B-1B Lancer	0.75-1
JAS-39 Grippen	0.5
Su-57	0.1-0.5
Tomahawk SLCM	0.5
Tomahawk ALCM	0.05
Exocet, Harpoon	0.1
Eurofighter Typhoon	0.5
F-18 E/F Super Hornet	0.1 class

---

3. Real RCS values are highly classified. The above values, most probably, refer to the frontal aspect ('head on') RCS of a 'clean' aircraft (without external loads), in the X-band (8-12 GHz). **(Figure 1-16)**.

Target	Radar Cross Section (RCS) m²
F-16 IN Super Viper	0.1 class
Rafale	0.1 – 0.2
227 mm MLRS	0.018
B-2 Spirit	0.1 or less
Mortar bomb	0.01
U-2	0.01
bird	0.01
F-117A Nighthawk	0.001-0.01 (0.003)
F-35 Lighting II	0.0015-0.005
F-22 Raptor	0.0001-0.0005
Artillery shell	0.0001
insect	0.00001
B-21	0.000001

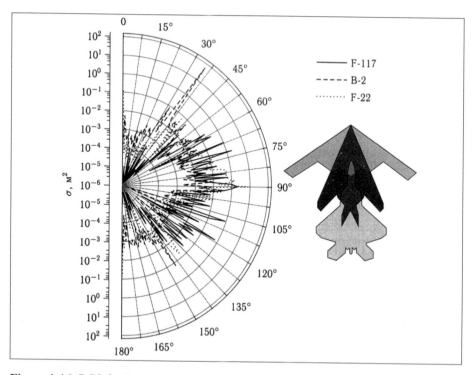

Figure 1-16: RCS for F-117, B-2 and F-22. (Harakteristiki Radiolokacionih Zametnosti Letalnih Aparatov)

Measurement of an RCS basically involves illuminating the test target with the radar signal at different viewing angles, collecting the radar signal backscattered from the target and then comparing it with radar a signal backscattered from a calibrated target. The test target and the calibrated target are mounted on a positioning platform enabling different target orientations for the purpose of measurement. The target needs to be placed far enough away so that the incident wave is an acceptably plane wave. The test setup basically comprises instrumentation radar, a positioning system for targets, test and calibrated targets, a low background environment with electromagnetic far field behaviour and a suitable data acquisition and control system (**Figure 1-17**).

Reducing RCS

The five basic methods of reducing RCS are: shaping, use of radar energy absorbing materials, passive cancellation, active cancellation and plasma.

Shaping
The most important factor affecting the RCS is the geometry or the shape of the target, not its size. To reduce the RCS, the surfaces and edges should be orientated in such way as to reflect the radar energy away from an expected radar antenna and not back to it. Considering the flat surfaces (facets) and the acute angles of the F-117, it is understood that it was designed in a way that the expected radar energy would be reflected in irrelevant directions and not back to the emitting radar. The designers tried to avoid any possible surface or edge whose normal vectors would look in a direction where possible enemy radar might be, especially for the frontal aspect (**Figure 1-18**).

Therefore, in the frame of RCS reduction, all bumps, curves etc should be avoided. In the same way, any external load (pylons, bombs, missiles, fuel tanks, pods) would considerably augment the total RCS. This is the reason why low observability aircraft carry their armament internally, in special bays. Furthermore, armament bay and landing gear bay doors should close tightly, with no gaps. Any irregularity of the surface could incur an RCS increase. Propellers are strictly forbidden, while the first stage engine blades should be carefully hidden inside the intake duct. The whole air intake construction is critical when designing a low RCS aircraft.

Other than these contributors, the angle of the incoming radar signals is also very important. This is because, as the normal of a surface to a signal changes, total reflected energy and the RCS also change. For example, an aircraft with a 25 m² head on RCS may have a 400 m² broadside RCS. The amplitude values for the pattern are relative so don't represent a real aircraft. The target is located in a plane where 0 degrees represents the nose-on position. To understand the RCS

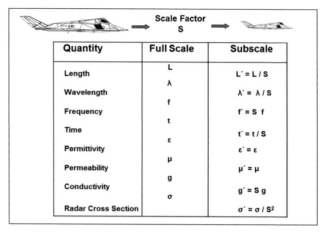

Quantity	Full Scale	Subscale
Length	L	L´ = L / S
Wavelength	λ	λ´ = λ / S
Frequency	f	f´ = S f
Time	t	t´ = t / S
Permittivity	ε	ε´ = ε
Permeability	μ	μ´ = μ
Conductivity	g	g´ = S g
Radar Cross Section	σ	σ´ = σ / S²

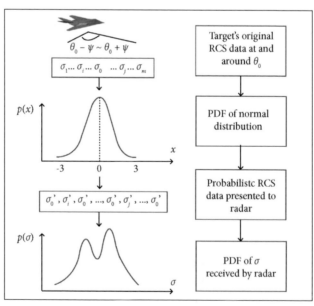

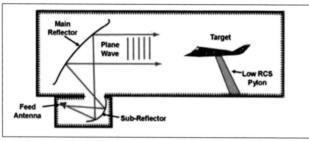

Figure 1-17: RCS scaling (top), measuring in the anechoic chamber (middle) and some of results (bottom). (IEE AES Society)

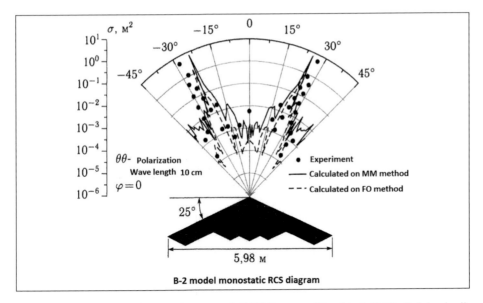

B-2 model monostatic RCS diagram

Figure 1-18: B-2 model shape and monostatic RCS diagram. (Harakteristiki Radiolokacionih Zametnosti Letalnih Aparatov)

value variation of an aircraft, in level flight, against radars at the same altitude but at different angles, the target is rotated in the yaw axis. Such patterns are used to analyze the ability of an aircraft to penetrate air defences.

The RCS of the airframe can be reduced by geometrically controlling the incoming signals' reflection (directionally) and scattering. The first way to accomplish this is to use flat surfaces and rectilinear surfaces all around the aircraft fuselage which are oblique to the radar signals. The F-117 Nighthawk is a very good example of this kind of RCS reduction technique with shaping. It uses careful faceting techniques to reduce RCS by scattering the incoming signals in nearly every direction (**Figure 1-19**).

Some features of an airframe design present dramatically large RCS values. A flat panel which is a good reflector and normal to the radar beam is one of these. If this surface is rotated, this will result in reflecting the incoming beams to other angles and will create a smaller RCS for a monostatic receiver. Bill Sweetman, a former editor for *Jane's* and a well-known Stealth advocate, quotes a stealth designer: 'A flat panel is the brightest target, and also the dimmest. If the panel is at right angles to an incoming beam, it is a perfect reflecting target. Rotate it along one axis and most of the energy is deflected away from the radar. Rotate it along two axes and the RCS becomes infinitesimal.'

Conventional vertical stabilizers are one of these flat reflector panels. Canting them inwards or outwards, with high angles, can prevent incoming radiation

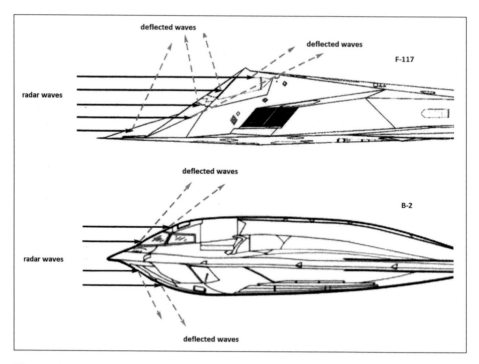

Figure 1-19: F-117 and B-2 radar beam deflection. (Harakteristiki Radiolokacionih Zametnosti Letalnih Aparatov)

from returning to the radar; and also when a rudder-elevator combination is used, the retro reflector of a dihedral should be avoided. Here, a retro reflector dihedral is two surfaces that are positioned at 90° from one another and these surfaces reflect the radar wave front back along a vector that is parallel to but opposite in direction to the angle of incidence. Thus this double-bounce manoeuvre will result in increasing the RCS.

Rather than leaving them as external parts or hung on pylons, hiding the engine(s) and ordnance inside the fuselage/wings of the aircraft or making them blended components within the whole body or wings will reduce the RCS. Moreover, internal storage gives better aerodynamic performance, as drag reduces. However, available space inside the body for ordnance is usually limited, which decreases the operational performance of the asset.

Compressor blades are another large signal reflector. Along with increasing the RCS of a target, some identification systems, such as radars using non-cooperative target recognition (NCTR) techniques, or one of the measurement and signature intelligence systems (MASINT) technologies, can be used to collect and process the strong radar returns from the engine compressor movements or periodic rotation of the blades of a turbine to discriminate between enemy and friendly assets. Thus an aircraft engine (with all possible components) should be kept out of reach of radar signals for low-observable designs.

Using wire mesh (as in the F-117 and RPV Q-2C), specially curved air inlet nacelles that prevent the direct reach of RF signals to compressor blades (such as the B-1B), and carefully chosen engine (inlet) locations will also help to reduce RCS. However, placing engines at their most optimum location to reduce RCS raises another important problem: determining the direction of expected RF signals. For example, if a radar threat is expected from below, putting the engine inlets at the top of the wing or airframe would be an effective measure. This is the more likely situation for high-altitude bombers, reconnaissance and maritime patrol aircraft. B-2 and F-117 bomber aircraft are good examples of this kind of design (see Chapter Seven for more details). However, for an air-superiority fighter, estimating the threat direction is more complex and there is no satisfying solution to this problem. So, the use of serpentine ducts and inlet wire meshes are more effective solutions to conceal engines from radar signals.

Cockpits and their interior instruments, such as pilot's helmet, seat, control components and displays, reflect RF signals and increase the RCS, as canopies and windshields are normally transparent to radar beams. Some special absorbent (or reflecting) layers and coatings are used on the canopies of stealth aircraft to decrease the RCS of the cockpit as well as their unique external shapes. Along with stealth aircraft, some other fighters and EW assets such as the F-16 Fighting Falcon and EA-6B Prowler also use such coatings either to reduce RCS or to shield the powerful signal emitted by the jammers from reaching the cockpit and crew. Controlled cockpit canopy shape, with a transparent conductor thin film (vapor-deposited gold or indium tin oxide) on it, block incoming radar signals from reaching inner components and diminish the amount of reflected radar waves back to the radar.

Other RCS reduction methods concerned with shaping include avoiding gaps and holes in the design and using covert gun ports to hinder discontinuities on the airframe surface. Performing high precision maintenance also helps to obtain and sustain these low RCS levels. In one case, a single screw not tightened as required was discovered to be the reason for an unexpected RCS increase in the F-117 prototype.

The biggest effort in reducing the RCS is given to the forward aspects of the aircraft. However, there are greater returns to be had for other aspects, or at least for some angles. These trade-offs promise some advantages over well-designed bistatic radar networks. Secondly, though shaping is the first principle in reducing RCS and must be carefully considered in the design of low-observables, long wavelengths are less affected by the shape of the airframe and its details.

The RCS of the airframe can be reduced by geometrically controlling the incoming signals' reflection (directionally) and scattering. The first way to accomplish this is to use flat surfaces and rectilinear surfaces all around the aircraft fuselage, which are oblique to the radar signals. The F-117 Nighthawk is a very good example of this kind of RCS reduction technique with shaping. It uses careful faceting techniques to reduce RCS by scattering the incoming signals in nearly every direction (**Figure 1-19**).

The second reduction method is similar and involves reflecting the incoming signals in a limited number of directions rather than scattering them in all directions. So a monostatic receiver never gets the transmitted signal back unless the radar signal reflects with two 90 degree angles from a surface, which is improbable when extreme look-down angles are not present. If a bistatic system is considered, its receiver can only get the radiated beam when the spatial geometry

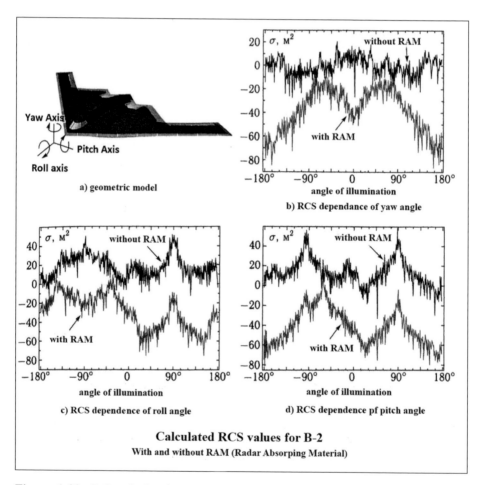

Calculated RCS values for B-2
With and without RAM (Radar Absorping Material)

Figure 1-20: B-2 calculated RCS values with and without RAM. (Harakteristiki Radiolokacionih Zametnosti Letalnih Aparatov)

is perfect. In this technique, every straight line on the entire airframe should be designed carefully; the shape of the aircraft, from main aircraft components such as wings, vertical and horizontal stabilizers, engine inlets, rudders, to all other moving parts such as rudders, elevators, ailerons, weapon bays, landing gear doors, canopy fasteners, etc, should be aligned in the direction of the few selected spikes (to reflect the incoming signal in only these specific directions). Using serrated (sawtooth shape) parts on surfaces may also help achieve the desired results.

The third method is modelling the aircraft with a compact, smoothly blended external geometry which has changing curves. These curves do not have regular reflection characteristics and they usually diminish the radar signal's energy by capturing them inside the curvature. The B-2 Spirit, especially its engine nacelles, was made with this kind of RCS technology. However, this method requires very precise calculations, thus only the latest (after 1980s) low-observable aircraft have had the chance to use it in their computer based designs (**Figure 1-19, Figure 1-20**).

As mentioned, the main purpose of shaping is reducing or, ideally, eliminating the major RCS contributors. However, shaping measures for low RCS has some trade-offs, such as poor aerodynamic performance, increased costs, more maintenance requirements or less ordnance capacity. Despite these drawbacks, which will be discussed in the following sections, the gains in RCS reduction compensate for the diminished qualities for the purpose of improving aircraft survivability during operations.

Radar Absorbing Materials (RAM)

Special shaping is the most important low observability method and is responsible for the greater part of RCS reduction. The second technique is the use of special Radar Absorbent Materials (RAM) which absorb (part of) the received radar energy and convert it to heat, thereby reducing the reflected energy. RAMs neither absorb all received radar energy nor are they efficient in all frequency bands. It is considered a supplementary approach, helping in reducing RCS when shaping techniques cannot be applied, e.g. in leading edges or engine intakes.

This approach has been followed since the Second World War, where special paints containing carbon (an imperfect conductor) have been used to reduce the radar return of the snorkels of German submarines. Even though carbon is still being used for such purposes, today magnetic absorbers, based on compounds of iron, are preferred for operational systems. Iron ball paint is a common RAM type and has been used in various low-observability aircraft.

Modern aircraft are generally made of composites, which consist of two or more different materials that have dissimilar physical, chemical or electromagnetic properties. Generally, composites are not metal and their RF signal reflection properties are very poor, thus non-metallic airframes are considered to not show up on radar. However, the non-reflected RF signals penetrate the non-metallic airframe and this time the reflection occurs from inside which results from the radar images of engines, fuel pumps, electrical wiring and all other components. Coating or painting the surfaces of airframes with special metallic finishing is the preferred way to prevent the penetration of RF signals through composites. On the other hand, composites are still important. Forms of composites, which consist of some poor conductors of electricity, such as carbon products, and insulators, such as epoxy resin, are used in the airframes to cancel the forms of creeping and travelling waves, by resisting electrical and magnetic currents which reradiate.

Though RAM's performance to decrease the RCS has been enhanced by a factor of ten since the mid-1980s, an expert still indicates 'shape, shape, shape and materials' as the most important factor in designing a stealth aircraft. It is clear that RAM is not an alternative for the airframe design, and it cannot transform a conventional aircraft into a stealthy one, however, for better RCS values, some parts of the asset, especially edge reflections and cavities (such as inlets), should be healed using RAM, where no other solution is likely.

One special RAM coating is made of reinforced carbon-carbon (RCC). For the most part, RAMs, such as RCC, reduce RCS by absorbing (an amount of) the incoming signal and converting RF energy into heat, or by destructive interference. With their appropriate dielectric or magnetic properties, different RAMs are used to get desired RCS results over the maximum possible frequency range. RAM technology is based on the idea of establishing desirable impedance which poses good matching and absorbing qualities so that the RAM can accept and then attenuate the incident wave. The dielectric qualities of RAM can also be explained as naturally-occurring electromagnetic waves of radar bouncing from conductive objects. However, the molecular structure of glossy materials causes RF energy to expend its energy by producing heat. The heat is then transferred to the aircraft and dissipated while the residual RF energy loses its effectiveness, basically with the help of friction and inertia or molecular oscillations. Finally, this results in less reflection back to the radar receiver.

Together with absorption, another method of RCS reduction, by using RAM, is destructive interference. However, there is an important distinction between the phenomenon of absorption and destructive interference. As mentioned above, the absorption process, which covers ohmic loss (based on the motion of free charges in an imperfect conductor), dielectric loss (based on permittivity), and magnetic loss (based on permeability), is possible by transferring the incident RF wave's energy to the airframe material as it passes through. On the other hand, the destructive interference principle (also known as 'resonant RAM' or 'impedance loading') is based on coatings, or the 'Salisbury Screen' method, which are used to reduce RCS by cancellation of multiple reflections. This method is considered both a RAM and a passive cancellation method. This study will discuss destructive interference in the passive cancellation technique section.

RAM includes many types of materials. Six of the most common RAM examples are: low dielectric foam (epoxy); lightweight lossy foam (urethane); thermoplastic foam (polytherimide); sprayable lightweight foam (urethane); thin MAGRAM silicone resin sheet; and resistive card (R-card) made of metalized Kapton. Another example, a ferrite-based paint, which is called 'iron ball', was used on the U-2 and SR-71 to reduce the RCS.

RAM has some limitations. Although the use of RAM is strengthening for low observability, it never gives perfect results and can never be expected to decrease an aircraft's RCS values to a large extent. It can absorb a portion of the incident energy, with the rest being reflected. Moreover, certain kinds of RAM can give satisfactory results only for certain frequencies and angles of the incident radar wave. Using different kinds of RAM to broaden the RF spectral coverage, along with thicker and heavier amounts, increases effectiveness. However, the optimum RAM weight and depth should be evaluated while considering the impact of the application of bulky coatings, which may compromise other characteristics of the asset. Weather conditions, such as rain, may also decrease the performance of most RAMs. Furthermore, aircraft shelters should be constructed with RAM protection in mind. This is why early B-2 planes were not deployed at US bases abroad where these kinds of special shelters were not available.

Because thick and solid RAM coatings or paintings, which are heavy and bulky, are required but not feasible to get desired RCS reduction over wider bandwidths, an alternative method of using such materials at the inner skin of the airframe is preferred. Radar absorbing structures (RAS) involve building special materials in special ways, such as honeycomb to attenuate radar waves into load-bearing structure.

Honeycomb structures have important advantages. First of all, their hexagonal passages, which are bonded together, are physically strong, flexible and light. From an RCS perspective, their depth, which is not heavy, is used to form many surfaces to reflect, absorb and attenuate the radar signal. One kind of honeycomb is made up of an outer skin of kevlar/epoxy composite, which is transparent to radar, and an inner skin of reflective graphite/epoxy. The nomex core, between them, has absorbent properties, and its increasing density, front to rear of the honeycomb, improves effectiveness. The small amount of front-face reflection of the incident radar wave is followed by the radar wave to reach the thinly spread absorber on the outer edges of the core where another small part of the energy is absorbed and the remainder is bounced. So the travelling wave meets more densely-loaded core material as it goes on. Each time, some amount of energy is either absorbed or reflected, and finally the outermost layer of the absorber once again attenuates it and the radar wave, which is checked into the structure, never checks out to free space again.[4]

Another RAS form is used on the leading and trailing edges of low-observables, such as the wings and fuselage skin strakes of the SR-71 Blackbird. In this method, gradually increasing absorption is applied to trap the energy, similar to the honeycomb structure. However, in this case, the physical shape of the structure is a saw-tooth pattern. The external surface is coated with a high frequency ferrite absorber. The interior begins with a low-absorption layer and is followed by a more absorbent layer. So while the depth increases the absorbent properties are also augmented. The V-shaped geometry causes the radar signal to bounce towards the opposite side, while the material properties of the structure absorb some of the incoming signal. Each bounce absorbs more of the energy.

The state-of-the-art F-22 Raptor is the US modern stealth fighter. It has many low-observable material properties including RAM, RAS, and IR topcoat. RAS is used to minimize scattering from hard edges while RAM is used to reduce scattering from surface breaks. Moreover, the IR topcoat reduces the IR signature, along with ensuring the radar and infrared signatures are balanced. Early low-observable programmes made extensive use of RAM and RAS, which resulted in weight and manufacturing problems. However, modern stealth aircraft designers, with the help of analysis and design tools, combined with extensive testing, have minimized the use of RAM on assets, such as F-22, while still maintaining a low signature. So modern aircraft use less RAM and RAS materials compared to early generations of low-observable aircraft which saves significant weight and cost.

RAM may require special treatment and maintenance. For example, the B-2 Spirit requires air-conditioned hangars and costly maintenance to retain its low observability capabilities. It should be mentioned that the F-35 features a new low observability substance called fibre mat, which according to Lockheed Martin officials has been 'cured into the composite skin of the aircraft', implying that it requires no maintenance.

Passive Cancellation
Sometimes also mentioned as 'impedance loading', passive cancellation is based on the idea of creating a (passive) echo source, whose amplitude and phase would be adjusted to cancel another echo source (e.g. by drilling a cavity or port of specific dimensions and shape on the object body). This may be possible for very simple objects; however, it is prohibitively difficult for complex objects like an aircraft, while a small change of the radar parameters or the simple movement of

---

4. Once electromagnetic energy (radar wave) gets into the RAM, it stays 'captured' there. This is 'encapsulation'.

the object-target could lead to the amplification of the radar return. This approach attracted some interest in the past but now seems not so promising anymore.

Special materials used for signal cancellation purposes to reduce RCS fall into two categories: RAM RCS reduction methods (resonant RAM) and passive cancellation. The resonant RAM method was also introduced as destructive interference or impedance loading in RAM applications. So passive cancellation system refers to 'RCS reduction by introducing a secondary scatter to cancel with the reflection of the primary target.'

In this method, special coatings, which are also called 'resonant absorbers', are chosen to cancel the incoming signals by being reflected twice (sometimes more than twice is also possible for wider frequency covering), one from the front and one from the back of the layer. Theoretically, having a back-face wave that travels one half wavelength more than the one that is reflected from the first layer is essential. Having the correct thickness causes the second reflection to have a 180-degree phase difference with the round-trip (first layer) reflection, thus first and second waves will cancel each other. However, this method strictly relies on layer thickness or one quarter of the wavelength matching.

This method is also known as 'Salisbury Screen'. A resistive screen which is placed in front of the reflective back plate bounces nearly 50 per cent of the incident radar beam back to incoming direction, while the other 50 per cent passes through and reflects from that grey plate. When the distance between these two plates are one quarter of the radar signal's wavelength, red and purple waves cancel each other. Because such a thickness is only effective for specific frequencies, this cancellation is called a 'narrow-band technique'. On the other hand, from a RAM application technique's perspective, dielectric and magnetic loss mechanisms are categorized as broadband absorbers, while they can generally be deployed to cover wider frequency bands than passive cancellation coatings.

Passive cancellation was studied enthusiastically in the 1960s; however, its limited use made it unpopular and resulted in the connotation that it was not a useful RCS reduction method. Obviously it is not practical to design such a treatment to neutralize all of the echo sources while passive cancellation RCS reduction techniques cannot suppress the radar and weapon systems' relatively wide frequency extent. Moreover, there is also a risk of strengthening the reflected signal with the change of frequency, or viewing aspect.

Active Cancellation
Also called 'active loading', active cancellation is based on the same principle as passive cancellation, which is the creation of an appropriate 'destructive' echo, which would cancel the real echo of the target to the radar. Therefore the target should emit electromagnetic energy synchronized with the received radar energy with proper amplitude and phase to minimize the reflected signal.

In other words, the target should take into account the direction of arrival of the radar energy, the amplitude, the frequency, the phase, its own RCS characteristics for the specific frequency and direction, and should be adequately intelligent to create the proper waveform, emitting the right pulse at the right time in the right direction. The technical difficulties are obvious, as well as the possibility of converting the target into a 'beacon' of radar energy if wrongly implemented. This technique has been reported to have been used by the Rafale and has been implicitly confirmed by Dassault aviation, without revealing any details. Another attempt in the category of 'active stealth' is so-called 'plasma stealth' technology. There have been reports that the Russians have been conducting experiments on this idea. According to available information, this technology employs ionized gas (plasma) which is produced by a special device on board and injected in front of the aircraft, creating a protective cloud and reducing the aircraft RCS considerably. The next section will address plasma stealth.

Since the concept of stealth technology was revealed to the public in the early 1970s, the term stealth has been taken to mean invisible to radar. In fact radar is only one of several sensors that is considered in the design of a low-observable (LO) platform. Others include **infrared** (IR), **optical** (visible), and **acoustic** (sound) sensors. It is also important that a low-observable target has low emissions. For example, a stealthy platform may be undetectable to an enemy radar, but if a standard high-power search radar is operating on the platform, the search radar is likely to be detected by the enemy's electronic support measures (ESM). Stealthy targets are not completely invisible to radar, as is often implied by the popular media. To be undetectable, it is only necessary that a target's RCS be low enough for its echo return to be below the detection threshold of the radar.

Radar cross section reduction has evolved as a countermeasure against radars and, conversely, more sensitive radars have evolved to detect lower RCS targets. A point of diminishing returns is quickly reached with regard to RCS reduction however. After the strong scattering sources on a complex target are eliminated, the remaining RCS is due primarily to a large number of small scatters. Treating these scatters is much more difficult, and it eventually becomes a question of cost. The financial aspect of low observability has caused a re-examination of the 'stealth philosophy'. In the early days of stealth, heavy emphasis was placed on reducing RCS, even if it came at the expense of other operational and performance parameters. The modem view of low observability is focused more on achieving an optimum balance between whole hosts of performance measures, of which RCS is only one among equals. They include such things as IR and acoustic signatures, cost and maintainability, operational limitations, and the incorporation of electronic warfare (EW) techniques.

While in most cases every effort is made to minimize the RCS, there are some applications that require enhancement or accentuation of RCS. These include targets such as training aircraft, artificial airborne targets such as pilotless target aircraft, and aerial decoys that can be towed behind the attacking airplanes to create a false radar signal and deceive radar operators. Training aircraft need to be continuously tracked, and enhancement of RCS makes tracking more reliable. Similarly, pilotless target aircraft used for evaluation of missile systems are also tracked by radars. The radar cross section of a small pilotless drone may be augmented to give it the radar cross section of a much larger aircraft. Augmentation of RCS achieves reliable tracking. Common methods to enhance the RCS include the use of 'Luneburg lenses', 'corner reflectors' and 'transponders with amplifiers'.

The Luneburg lens is a passive RCS augmentation device. It is used to increase the radar reflectivity of a target without the use of additional energy. A Luneburg lens is usually composed of concentric dielectric shells. Radar energy incident on one of the faces of the lens is focused at a point on its rear conductive surface, which then reflects radar energy back to the source. A corner reflector like a Luneburg lens is also a passive retro-reflector that reflects the incident radar energy back in the direction of the source.

Unlike Luneburg lenses and corner reflectors, that are passive augmenters of RCS, a transponder is an active augmentation device that works on the principle of capturing a portion of the radar emission and transmitting it back. Interference is eliminated by suppressing the radar's reception for the duration of the transponder's transmission.

Plasma
Plasma is a partially ionized and electrically conductive gas which owes its existence to the fact that positive and negative charges can move somewhat independently within it. Its free electrons make plasma respond strongly to electromagnetic fields. Thus plasma has been proposed as a possible method of RCS reduction; it is sometimes considered as an active cancellation technique. The inspiration for this method emerged in the late 1950s after spacecraft with a natural plasma layer over their airframes experienced communication interruption incidents while travelling through the ionosphere. Basically, radar waves (actually all electromagnetic waves of certain frequencies) travelling through this conductive plasma cause electrons to change places, ending up with the electromagnetic waves losing their energy and transforming into other forms, such as heat. Interaction between plasma and electromagnetic radiation is strongly dependent on the physical properties and parameters of the plasma. The most dominating of these properties are the temperature and the density of the plasma. Another important issue is the frequency of the incident radar beam. Radar waves, below a specific frequency, are reflected by the plasma layer. The plasma layer's physical properties have a significant effect on this process. Long distance

communications with HF signals by means of ionosphere scattering and reflection is a good example of this phenomenon. Thus, RCS reduction plasma devices should also control and dynamically adjust the plasma properties, such as density, temperature and composition, for effective radar absorption results.

Plasma stealth technology has some drawbacks from a low-observable perspective. These include emitting own electromagnetic radiation with a visible glow, existence of a plasma trail of ionized air behind the aircraft before dissipation by the atmosphere, and difficulty in producing a radar-absorbent plasma around an entire aircraft travelling at high speed. However, some Russian scientists have claimed to achieve a hundredfold RCS reduction with plasma technology and this result (if real) is sufficient reason for further research.

Another application of plasma technology is to deploy antenna surfaces to generate low observability characteristics. While metal antenna poles are reflective, a hollow glass tube filled with low pressure plasma can provide an entirely radar-transparent surface when not in use.

Although there are some problems in the operational processes associated with plasma, such as the high energy requirement in long-interval applications and the necessity of holes in the plasma field for aircraft on board radar activation,[5] Russian plasma stealth research teams have announced the development of a plasma generator which weighs 100 kg and is thus feasible for a tactical air platform. This critical technology may be available on Su-27 versions (such as Su-34 and Su-35), MiG-35 fighters and also the MiG 1.44 experimental prototype, according to recent claims by Russian officials.

Acoustic Stealth (Reducing Aural Signature)

Because the probability of detection of radar occurs at greater distances than other signal detection methods, it demands the highest priority in the development of aircraft low-observable technology. Radar signature is the most prominent aspect of stealth, then infrared (IR), then visual, then sound. Practically speaking, acoustic detectors are unable to meet the demands of today's sensor technologies in the aviation world, due to the very low propagation speed of sound waves. However, a comprehensive stealth design includes measures to diminish the ability of acoustic sensors to locate an aircraft, and this may change in the future. Acoustic detection devices may be preferable in some other mediums, such as seawater for submarine warfare, but it is not the subject of this study.

Aircraft acoustic signature reduction focuses on the engines, which produce a significant amount of noise. The slipstream of the aircraft also produces noise, but it is inconsequential when compared to the roaring of the engines. There

---

5. Plasma is an 'impenetrable shield' for electromagnetic waves in and out. To use an aircraft's onboard equipment, such as an airborne radar, that shield must be circumvented.

are several ways to prevent the sound of engines from being detected. Flying at high altitudes reduces the detection risk; however, mission requirements may sometimes compel low-level flight. Cruising around at the speed of sound may be another solution, but this cannot conceal the asset when it flies away from the detection source. Additionally, most aircraft cannot fly more than 10 to 20 minutes at such high speeds and designing an aircraft which can fly for longer periods introduces a number of complexities. For example, the F-22 Raptor can almost fly an entire mission above the speed of sound using its 'super-cruise' capability, which does not require afterburner use. However, this capability has many drawbacks, including high engine cost and complex fuselage design. The most promising approach in minimizing aircraft aural signature is making assets quieter by design. More efficient engines tend to produce less noise. Aircraft engines which inhale a large volume of air but push out a small amount, such as high-bypass-ratio turbofans, are quieter than those that inhale a small volume of air but push a large amount, such as low-bypass-ratio engines. Despite this efficiency and these acoustic signal reduction advantages, most combat aircraft use low-bypass-ratio engines, which are more suited for applications that require immediate thrust, high velocity and acceleration, and agile manoeuvrability.

When quietness becomes a bigger concern, high-bypass-ratio turbofans are preferred, even though high performance and speed is reduced. The A-10 Warthog is a good example of this kind of design. Because it is deployed for close air support missions, to friendly ground forces, and its main targets are ground enemy forces, like tanks, armoured vehicles and large groups of troops, it needs to fly over these targets several times. A reduced aural signature is crucial in increasing the A-10's operational success rate because of this. Thus, noiseless engines, together with other low observability features, improve an aircraft's survivability and mission capability.

A successful example of acoustic stealth is the Lockheed YO-3A reconnaissance aircraft. This aircraft, which was used by the US Army in the Vietnam War, was deployed for tracking enemy forces that were moving at night, in large groups with equipment, in dense jungle. Conventional reconnaissance or observation aircraft were easily detected by enemy forces from their engine sounds, so several studies focusing on reducing engine noise were commissioned. One of these resulted in the Q-Star prototype, which was developed from X-26 sailplanes, using a liquid cooled engine buried in the rear fuselage for more effective silencing. After several experiments, fourteen Lockheed YO-3A aircraft were produced and used to fulfil the mission. These aircraft had a modified light plane engine with a long exhaust pipe. This exhaust pipe was attached to another long muffler fitted on the fuselage side. Moreover, the engine had a large, slow-rotating propeller, six-bladed, wooden and rubber belt driven. This propeller was later replaced with a three-bladed, constant-speed counterpart for improving silencing the YO-3A with noise cancelling mufflers on the right side of the fuselage.

The US F-117 Nighthawk and B-2 Spirit, all-aspect stealth aircraft, also incorporate design features that reduce engine noise, such as sound-absorbing linings inside their engine intakes and exhaust cowlings. Further, their engine inlets and exhausts are located on top of their wings, they have the ability to fly at relatively high altitudes, and they cruise at subsonic speeds with non-afterburning engines. Supersonic speeds generate sonic booms which are usually incompatible with stealth purposes.

IR signature and STEALTH

All substances emit electromagnetic waves, so long as their temperature is above absolute zero ($0°$ K or $-273.15°$ C). The heat content of a material produces molecular vibrations which cause electron oscillations. These oscillations provide electromagnetic coupling that produces an emission of energy. This emission is called infrared radiation (IR). IR has a wavelength spectrum of 0.7 to 14 micrometres, and the amount of radiation emitted is primarily dependent on the temperature of the associated object (proportionally). The emissivity characteristics of an object are related to the material's molecular structure and the surface conditions of the object. IR energy that comes from another body is either absorbed or reradiated by the object according to its emissivity properties.

As with visible light, IR energy travels in a straight line at the speed of light. Similarly, IR energy is either reflected or absorbed and converted to heat when it hits the surface of an object. These absorption and reflection qualities change with material specifications. For example, polished surfaces reflect more IR energy but also have a much lower emissivity than matte/matt surfaces. IR energy considerations are important to stealth designers because IR detectors, also known as infrared homing devices, such as passive missile guidance systems, can use the IR emission from a target to track it. Detector systems, especially missile guiding seekers, which detect the radiated infrared signals of their target, are often referred to as 'heat-seekers'. If unaided by IR countermeasures, aircraft are vulnerable to detection by such systems by means of the strongly radiated energy from their hot bodies. Some precautions to mitigate such detection include: reducing or suppressing an aircraft's IR signature and adding some noise; deploying decoys or flares; and jamming the sensor by emitting high power signals towards the detector. For an asset designed to remain undetected, one of the most important measures is reducing or suppressing the aircraft's IR emission. Thus, sources, surfaces or components which produce and/or conserve heat are of great concern to low-observables.

Moreover, the IR detection capability of the new IR Search and Track (IRST) systems and Electro-Optic (EO) systems deployed on the Su-27, Eurofighter Typhoon, and F-35 Lightning II, reveal the importance of IR signature reduction. These EO detectors absorb electromagnetic radiation and output an electrical signal that is useful for tracking and targeting. Another major advantage of these systems is that they are passive systems in which a target never knows that there is a threat trying to detect it. When radar detection range is minimized by RCS reduction methods, other signatures such as IR, visual and acoustic become more pronounced, especially for close range engagements.

IR signal reduction is focused on engine exhausts. When the afterburner is applied, the heat increases significantly, by nearly fifty times, since IR energy emitted from the engines is proportional to the fourth power of absolute temperature. Thus the second generation stealth F-117 Nighthawk and the third generation strategic stealth bomber B-2 Spirit have non-afterburning engines. On the other hand the fourth generation stealth F-22 Raptor has the ability to cruise at supersonic speeds without afterburner. Being dependent on high Mach numbers for operational survivability, the first generation stealth SR-71 Blackbird is also an exception, with its high-power afterburner engines.

One way to decrease the IR signature of engines is to use exhaust masking. This is accomplished by placing the engines on top of the body and the wings. This is why the F-117 A and B-2 exhausts cannot be seen from below. Over the rear conical sector of the aircraft, the hottest parts of the tailpipe can be easily detected by IR seekers. While outside this sector, sensors can only detect the hot parts of the nozzle surface. Another technique to decrease the IR signature is to use the aircraft's aft fuselage and vertical surfaces to shield the jet pipes from view over as large a part of this rear sector as possible. Another way to decrease IR signature is the shaping of exhaust geometry. Exhausts that are shaped flat and wide are more effective in this regard.

Integrated Air Defence Systems (IADS)

As we saw in previous sections, radar systems have the inherent capability to determine accurate range, azimuth, and/or velocity information on airborne targets. Radar systems can provide this information in nearly all types of weather, day or night, and at distances that far exceed the capabilities of the human eye. Military commanders have taken advantage of these capabilities by employing radar systems to provide air defence for high-value targets. The primary missions of radar systems employed for air defence are attack warning and threat engagement.

Radar systems specifically designed to provide attack warning are called Early Warning (EW) radars. These radars are characterized by high-power output, large antennas, and low frequencies. These same characteristics limit the accuracy of the target parameters available from early warning radars. The long-range detection of aircraft and the earliest possible attack warning capabilities of early warning radars provide the first line of defence for an air defence system.

Radar systems designed to provide target engagement information include **Ground Control Intercept (GCI)** radars, **Acquisition Radars (AR)**, **Target Tracking Radars (TTR)**, and **Airborne Interceptor (AI)** radars.

GCI radars are designed to provide sufficiently accurate target aircraft range, azimuth, and altitude information to vector airborne interceptor (AI) assets to intercept and destroy attacking aircraft. To provide this data, early warning radars can be deployed along with specialized height finder radars. This combination of radar systems is commonly referred to as a GCI site. Newer GCI radar systems, employing phased array antennas and Doppler processing, can provide the required 3-dimensional target information. Any radar system, or combination of radar systems, that can determine 3-dimensional target data and is equipped with the communication equipment to pass this information to AI assets, can act as a GCI site. GCI radar systems can be used to supplement early warning radar systems to provide critical attack warning. Acquisition radar systems are designed to act as GCI radars for ground-based TTRs. Acquisition radar systems generally have shorter range capability than early warning radars and operate at higher frequencies. These radar systems provide accurate target range and azimuth data to TTRs to facilitate target engagement. Acquisition radars can be a distinct radar system or be incorporated as part of the TTR.

The primary role of TTRs in support of an air defence system is to provide continuous and accurate target parameters to a fire control computer. The fire control computer uses this data to guide missiles or aim anti-aircraft artillery (AAA) to destroy attacking aircraft. TTRs employ various tracking techniques to continuously update target parameters. TTRs generally employ high frequencies, narrow beam widths, and computer signal processing to enhance the accuracy of target parameters provided to the fire control computer.

Airborne Interceptor radar systems are TTRs employed by fighter aircraft to engage and destroy airborne targets. These radar systems are characterized by high frequency, sophisticated computer processing, and accurate target tracking capability. They are designed to allow the AI asset to employ air-to-air missiles and guns/cannons. TTRs and AI radars constitute the highest radar threat associated with an air defence system.

Another growing lethal threat associated with an air defence system is infrared (IR) missiles. IR missile systems can be man-portable, mounted on vehicles, or employed by AI assets. These missile systems guide on the distinctive IR signature of aircraft. The recent proliferation and enhanced performance of IR systems has increased the contribution of these systems to air defence.

All these radar systems can be deployed to provide air defence for a particular country or geographical area. When the employment of these radar systems is integrated by a command and control (C2) structure, this constitutes an IADS. The C2 structure allows the military commander to take advantage of the threat

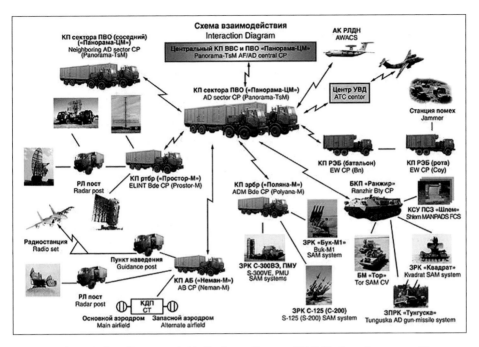

Figure 1-21: Modern Integrated Air Defence System (IADS). (ausairpower.net)

warning provided by early warning radars. Based on this threat warning, the military commander can allocate specific assets (GCI and AI assets, or acquisition radars and TTRs) to engage airborne targets. This allocation decision is based on the capabilities of these systems and the tactical situation. This allocation process enables the military commander to maximize the capabilities of his forces to engage and destroy attacking aircraft (**Figure 1-21**).

Radar systems are the cornerstones of a modern IADS. Radar and IR threat systems operate at frequencies that span most of the electromagnetic spectrum. Each system has unique capabilities and operating characteristics that enable it to accomplish assigned tasks in support of the IADS. To effectively employ offensive air power on the modern battlefield, the systems that support the IADS must be negated. A basic knowledge of how radar and IR systems operate, their capabilities, limitations, and available counter-measures is the key to defeating these systems.

The former Yugoslavia had an IADS, but far from the most sophisticated one.

Radar Jamming

Radar jamming is the intentional radiation or reradiation of radio frequency (RF) signals to interfere with the operation of radar by saturating its receiver with false targets or false target information. Radar jamming is one principal component of electronic combat (EC). Specifically, it is the electronic attack (EA) component of electronic warfare (EW). Radar jamming is designed to counter the radar systems that play a vital role in support of an enemy integrated air defence system. The primary purpose of radar jamming is to create confusion and deny critical information to negate the effectiveness of enemy radar systems.

The following sections will introduce the two typical types of radar jamming, the three radar jamming employment options, and discuss the fundamental principles that determined the effectiveness of the radar jamming used by NATO aircraft during the campaign.

There are two types of radar jamming: **noise** and **deception**.

Noise jamming is produced by modulating an RF carrier wave with noise, or random amplitude changes, and transmitting that wave at the victim's radar frequency. It relies on high power levels to saturate the radar receiver and deny range and, occasionally, azimuth and elevation information to the victim radar. Noise jamming takes advantage of the extreme sensitivity of the radar receiver and the transmission pattern of the radar antenna to deny critical information to the victim radar.

Since noise from numerous sources is always present and displayed on a radar scope, noise jamming adds to the problem of target detection. Reflected radar pulses from target aircraft are extremely weak. To detect these pulses, a radar receiver must be very sensitive and be able to amplify the weak target returns. Noise jamming takes advantage of this radar characteristic to delay or deny target detection.

Deception jamming uses complex receiving and transmitting circuits to process and retransmit jamming pulses that appear as a real target to the victim radar. A deception jammer receives the signal from the victim radar and alters the signal to provide false range, azimuth, or velocity information. The altered signal is then retransmitted. The victim radar processes this signal, which disrupts the victim radar and confuses the radar operator. To be effective, deception jamming must match not only the victim radar's operating frequency, but all the other operating characteristics, including pulse repetition frequency (PRF), pulse repetition interval (PRI), pulse width, and scan rate. However, the deception jammer does not have to replicate the power of the victim radar system. Because these systems retransmit, or repeat, a replica of the victim's radar signal, deception jammers are known as repeater jammers.

A deception jammer requires significantly less power than a noise jamming system. The deception jammer gains this advantage by using a waveform that is identical to the waveform the radar's receiver is specifically designed to process. Therefore the deception jammer can match its operating cycle to the operating cycle of the victim radar instead of using the 100 per cent duty cycle required of a noise jammer. To be effective, a deception jammer's power requirements are dictated by the average power of a radar rather than the peak power required for a noise jammer. In addition, since the jammer waveform looks identical to the radar's waveform, it is processed like a real return. The jamming signal is amplified by the victim radar receiver, which increases its effectiveness. The reduced power required for effective deception jamming is particularly significant when designing and building self-protection jamming systems for tactical aircraft that penetrate a dense threat environment. Deception jamming systems can be smaller, lighter, and can jam more than one threat simultaneously. These characteristics give deception jammers a great advantage over noise jamming systems.

Although deception jammers require less power, they are much more complex than noise jammers. Memory is the most critical element of any deception jammer. The memory element must store the signal characteristics of the victim radar and pass these parameters to the control circuitry for processing. This must be done almost instantaneously for every signal that will be jammed. Any delay in the memory loop diminishes the effectiveness of the deception technique. Using digital RF memory (DRFM) reduces the time delay and enhances deception jammer effectiveness. Deception jamming employed in a self-protection role is designed to counter lethal radar systems. To be effective, deception jamming systems must be programmed with detailed and exact signal parameters for each lethal threat.

Both noise and deception jamming effectiveness are heavily dependent on another component of EW, specifically, electronic warfare support (ES). ES assets, either airborne or ground-based, provide the threat-system-specific radar parametric data and update this critical information based on observed threat system operations. This data provides the foundation for developing noise and deception jamming techniques. Intelligence and engineering assessment of this data is used to identify specific threat system weaknesses that can be exploited with the optimum noise, deception, or combination of jamming techniques. This information is then programmed into jamming systems to counter specific threats.

There are currently two primary employment options for both noise and deception jamming techniques. These options are:

1. Support jamming, and
2. Self-protection jamming.

Support jamming can be broken down further into **standoff jamming** (SOJ), and **escort jamming**. To counter early warning, ground control intercept (GCI), and acquisition radars associated with an enemy IADS, noise and deception jamming techniques are employed by specialized support jamming aircraft. The goal of support jamming is to create confusion and delays within the command and control structure of the IADS to deny, delay or degrade the enemy's ability to engage friendly forces. Support jamming operations can be focused against a national level IADS through the use of a stand-off jamming (SOJ) profile or against a target area threat array using an escort jamming profile.

Standoff jamming: From an orbit area outside the surface-to-air missile (SAM) engagement zone, SOJ aircraft employ specialized jamming techniques to deny the enemy information about the attack package. SOJ aircraft employ specialized noise jamming techniques to generate jamming strobes on the victim radar display. This effectively denies range and azimuth information on aircraft ingressing and egressing the area covered by the noise jamming strobes. The area covered is based on the amount of jamming that can be injected into the main beam and sidelobes of the victim radar. The effectiveness of SOJ noise jamming is determined by the power the jammer can generate relative to the power the victim radar can generate. This is called the jamming-to-signal (J/S) ratio.

SOJ aircraft can also employ a deception technique to generate false targets to confuse the radar operator and mask the presence of real targets. In this specialized technique, the deception jammer must tune to the frequency, PRF, and scan rate of the victim radar. The jammer then transmits multiple jamming pulses that the victim radar receiver processes like real target returns. With enough power, the deception jammer can generate multiple false azimuth targets by injecting jamming pulses into the sidelobes of the victim radar. False moving targets and false range targets are generated by varying the time delay of the jamming pulses based on the PRF and scan rate of the victim radar.

Escort jamming is a specific tactic used by the EA-6B Prowler. The EA-6B is employed as an integral part of the attack package and is normally positioned behind and above the attack package. Using noise jamming, the EA-6B attempts to deny range and azimuth information to the victim radar by injecting high power signals into the main radar beam and sidelobes. To be effective, the EA-6B must be properly positioned in relation to the ingressing or egressing attack package (**Figure 1-22**).

Self-protection radar jamming targets the radar systems that support jamming cannot negate. Self-protection jamming systems are part of a self-protection suite that includes a self-protection jamming pod, a chaff/flare dispenser, and, on some aircraft, a towed decoy system. The overall purpose of these systems is individual aircraft survivability. These systems are designed to counter the individual SAM, AAA, and AI assets associated with the enemy IADS. They employ deception

Figure 1-22: EA-6B Prowler, electronic warfare specialized airplane, extensively used in Yugoslav SEAD missions. (USN)

jamming techniques against the target tracking radars (TTRs) associated with these threats. They are designed to break the radar track or generate sufficient tracking errors to cause the missile or bullet to miss the aircraft.

Self-protection radar jamming systems usually employ deception jamming techniques based on several factors. First, effective deception jamming techniques generally require less power than noise jamming techniques. Second, less power means less weight and space, which are very important considerations for modern tactical aircraft. Finally, deception jammers can be designed to jam multiple threats, which is a critical requirement for operations in a dense threat environment.

Despite the advantages of deception jamming techniques for self-protection jamming, there are some limitations that must be considered. First, deception jammers are complex electronic systems that must receive the victim radar's signal, memorize all its characteristics, modify the signal, and retransmit this modified signal at a high-power level. Second, to be effective, deception jammers must be programmed with all the signal parameters (frequency, PRF, PRI, pulse width, scan rate, etc) of the victim radar. Finally, because many deception techniques can be effective against specific threats, selecting optimum techniques to employ against these threats must be based on an identified threat.

A radar noise jamming system is designed to generate a disturbance in a radar receiver to delay or deny target detection. Since thermal noise is always present in the radar receiver, noise jamming attempts to mask the presence of targets by substantially adding to this noise level. Radar noise jamming can be employed by support jamming assets or as a self-protection jamming technique. Radar noise jamming usually employs high-power jamming signals tuned to the frequency of the victim radar.

The requirement for exact signal parameters increases the burden on electronic warfare support (EWS) systems to provide and update threat information on operating frequency, PRF, PRI, power pulse width, scan rate, and other unique signal characteristics. ELectronic INTelligence (ELINT) architecture is required to collect, update, and provide changes to deception jamming systems. In addition, intelligence and engineering information on exactly how a specific threat system acquires, tracks and engages a target is essential in identifying system weaknesses. Once a weakness has been identified, an effective deception jamming technique can be developed and programmed into a deception jammer. For example, if a particular radar system relies primarily on Doppler tracking, a Doppler deception technique will greatly reduce its effectiveness. Threat system exploitation is the best source of detailed information on threat system capabilities and vulnerabilities. Effective deception jamming requires much more intelligence support than does noise jamming.

Most self-protection jamming techniques employ some form of deception against a target tracking radar (TTR). The purpose of a TTR is to continuously update target range, azimuth, and velocity. Target parameters are fed to a fire control computer that computes a future impact point for a weapon based on these parameters and the characteristics of the weapon being employed. The fire control computer is constantly updating this predicted impact point based on changes in target parameters. Deception jamming is designed to take advantage of any weaknesses in either target tracking or impact point calculation to maximize the miss distance of the weapon or to prevent automatic tracking.

Decoys

A decoy is a device designed to appear to an enemy radar more like an aircraft than the actual aircraft itself. Decoys do three primary missions: they saturate the enemy's integrated air defence system (IADS), trick the enemy into exposing his forces prematurely, and defeat tracking by enemy radar.

Saturation Decoy
A saturation decoy is usually an expendable vehicle designed to emulate a penetrating aircraft. Its mission is to deceive and saturate an enemy's IADS. Employing multiple saturation decoys can force an IADS to devote critical resources to engage these

false targets. This depletes enemy assets available to engage penetrating aircraft. In addition, ground or air launched saturation decoys can be used to stimulate the IADS, to collect intelligence data, or to initiate attacks by suppression of enemy air defence (SEAD) assets. The three main characteristics of saturation decoys are their electronic signature, their flight programme, and their mission type.

Saturation decoys must present an electronic signature, or radar return, that is indistinguishable from the aircraft they are protecting. Decoys can do this by either passive or active measures or use a combination of both. A passive decoy is essentially a flying radar reflector. The size, shape, and materials used in the decoy are optimized to ensure that the proper amount of radar energy is returned to the enemy radars. Active decoys employ radar repeater systems to receive the enemy radar signal, amplify it and send back a radar return of the proper size to confuse the enemy. Reflecting or transmitting the proper size radar return is critical for both passive and active decoys. A return that is too large or too small will allow the enemy radar operator to differentiate between decoys and aircraft, causing the decoys to be ignored.

To continue deceiving an enemy IADS, a decoy must do more than provide the proper-sized radar return. Possessing flight characteristics similar to the aircraft it is protecting increases the probability that the decoy will effectively deceive an IADS for a sustained period of time. Modern decoys can either be powered with rockets, miniature engines, or simply glide for very long distances based upon the altitude and airspeed of the jet that releases them. Additionally, their flight paths can be preprogrammed into an on-board autopilot, allowing the decoy to fly an independent ground track, thus increasing their appearance as attack aircraft worth tracking. Saturation decoys carry out two of the three decoy missions. Launched in significant numbers, they can saturate or overburden an IADS. Meanwhile, their realistic electronic image and preprogrammed flight paths entice the enemy to turn on radars and show his forces.

An extremely successful example of using decoys to stimulate the IADS was carried out in the Bekaa Valley in 1982. The Israelis opened the conflict by launching saturation decoys to successfully simulate an attack. While the Syrians reloaded, Israeli fighters attacked, destroying 17 of 19 Syrian SA-6s at the beginning of the battle. With the ground threat neutralized, the Israeli Air Force went on to destroy 85 Syrian fighters in the pure air-to-air conflict that resulted (as per western media details presented in Chapter Six).

Towed Decoy

A towed decoy is a small jammer that is physically attached to the aircraft. Unlike the saturation decoys that work against the IADS, the towed decoys are for individual aircraft survival. Towed decoys are designed to defeat enemy missiles in the final stages of an engagement; therefore towed decoys, as well as other expendables, are known as endgame countermeasures.

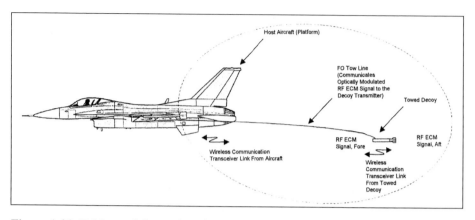

Figure 1-23: F-16 towed decoy. (ausairpower.net)

While towed decoys are primarily designed to provide sufficient miss distance between an attacking semi-active radar missile and the protected aircraft, they may also be effective against pulse Doppler radars and monopulse radars (**Figure 1-23**).

To be effective, the towed decoy must turn on within the threat radar's resolution cell after the radar is tracking the protected target. To successfully decoy the missile, the towed decoy must return radar signals with sufficient power to simulate a radar cross section (RCS) significantly larger than that of the protected target.

Expendable Active Decoys
Expendable active decoys are designed to lure the tracking gates[6] of an enemy's radar away from the aircraft. They are endgame countermeasures like towed decoys, but they differ in that expendable decoys free-fall or glide to the ground as opposed to being towed behind the aircraft.

Expendable decoys are small, active jamming systems designed to be expended by existing aircraft chaff and flare dispensers, such as the AN/ALE-40 or the AN/ALE-47. Expendable decoys can employ noise or deception jamming with noise jamming being the most common. Deception jamming techniques can be employed to enhance effectiveness against pulse Doppler radars. There are two challenges associated with expendable jammers: the amount of the time the jammer is effective and the packaging.

---

6. A tracking gate is used for target location prediction. The combination of range, bearing, course and speed at any one time is known as the target's solution. It is used to predict where the target will be at the next observation. Once a solution has been determined, the computer uses a tracking gate to predict the target's position.

Expendable decoys are designed to provide protection for the dispensing aircraft for a specific period. The dispensing altitude and rate of fall determine this period of effective coverage. Expendable decoys can employ small parachutes of aerodynamic design to slow the rate of fall and increase the time of effective coverage.

Chaff

Chaff was first used during the Second World War when the Royal Air Force, under the code name WINDOW, dropped bales of metallic foil during a night bombing raid in July 1943. The bales of foil were thrown from each bomber as it approached the target. German AAA fire control and ground control intercept (GCI) radars were rendered almost totally ineffective. Based on this early success, chaff became a standard bomber tactic for the rest of the war.

Even today, chaff is one of the most widely used and effective expendable electronic attack (EA) devices. The most important chaff characteristics are radar cross section (RCS), frequency coverage, bloom rate, Doppler content, polarization, and persistence. It is a form of volumetric radar clutter consisting of multiple metalized radar reflectors designed to interfere with and confuse radar operation. It is dispensed into the atmosphere to deny radar acquisition, generate false targets, and to deny or disrupt radar tracking. Chaff is designed to be dispensed from an aircraft and function for a limited period. Chaff screening and self-protection are the two basic chaff employment tactics. Chaff screening tactics, including area saturation and chaff corridor employment, are designed to confuse and deny acquisition information to the early warning, GCI, and acquisition radars supporting surface-to-air missile (SAM) systems. Self-protection tactics are designed to counter acquisition and target tracking radars (TTRs). When used with jamming and manoeuvres, chaff can cause TTRs to break lock or generate survivable miss distances if a SAM is fired at the aircraft.

Flares

Since their introduction in the 1950s, infrared (IR) missiles have been an increasing threat from both ground-based and airborne systems. The range, reliability, and effectiveness of IR missiles have been continuously improved by advanced detector materials and computer technology. Since IR missiles are passive, they are relatively simple and inexpensive to produce. These characteristics have contributed to the proliferation of IR missiles in the combat arena. Nearly every aircraft flying in either the air-to-air or air-to-surface role now carries an all-aspect IR missile. Additionally, every modern infantry unit down to the platoon level is equipped with shoulder-fired IR missiles.

Flares are the primary countermeasure used to defeat the IR missile. Advanced IR missiles use different techniques to overcome self-protection flares.

SHOOTING DOWN THE STEALTH FIGHTER

There are two important characteristics of infrared (IR) missiles that influence the effectiveness of self-protection flares. The first is the ability of the IR missile seeker to discriminate between the IR signature of the aircraft and the IR signature of background interference, especially clouds. The second is the flare rejection capability built into the missile seeker and the missile guidance section.

The purpose of employing a self-protection flare cartridge is to decoy the seeker head of an IR missile. This is accomplished by presenting the IR missile with a second heat source with an IR signature that exceeds the aircraft signature. The flare or IR source must appear in the field of view of the IR missile at the same time as the aircraft. As the flare separates from the aircraft, the IR missile seeker tracks the most intense IR signature, which ideally is the flare, and is decoyed away from the aircraft.

Self-protection flares were developed to counter threat systems operating in the IR spectrum. Self-protection chaff and flare dispensers, such as the ALE-40, ALE-45, or the ALE-47, are designed to allow the pilot to dispense flare cartridges when engaged by an IR threat. These flare cartridges are pyrotechnic and pyrophoric devices designed to produce an IR source that is more attractive than the IR signature of the aircraft. The most important flare characteristics that determine the ability of a flare to decoy an IR missile are IR wavelength matching, flare rise time, and flare burn time.

Through the years advances in seeker technology have resulted in significant changes to IR missile engagement tactics. This section will discuss spinning reticle, conical scan, cooled, and imaging IR seekers. First generation IR missiles, like the SA-7, use a spinning reticle as the means to track the target. Due to their relatively low cost and ease of use, IR missiles of the first generation can still be encountered. The spinning reticle is inserted in the seeker just before the IR radiation reaches the detector. The reticle is a thin plate of optical material which has a transparent and opaque pattern on it. As the reticle is rotated, the IR energy is chopped at a rate determined by the reticle pattern. This system produces error signals when the target is not exactly centred in the field of view. If the target is located in the upper half of the pattern, the IR intensity on the detector is constant as the reticle rotates. As the pie-shaped half of the disc rotates over the target, the IR energy is pulsed and the amplitude of the pulses is an indication of relative elevation angle. When the target moves to the right or left, the pulsing starts and stops at different times, indicating target azimuth. Centre spun spin-scan seekers, also called centre null reticles, are relatively insensitive when the target is in the centre of the seeker scan where there is no tracking error. This is because the point target tends to bleed energy into all the spokes at once, eliminating the pulsed signal output of the detector. Once the target falls off the centre of the reticle, the seeker generates an error signal that initiates guidance commands to re-centre the target. This is the reason early IR missiles flew an undulating path towards the target.

A significant improvement to IR seekers resulted from the cooling of the detector with an inert gas such as argon. Older IR missiles, using uncooled lead-sulphide detectors, have a peak sensitivity in the 2 micron region. This limits these missiles, the SA-7 for example, to stern attacks because the missiles can only discriminate the IR signature of the engine turbine from background IR energy. By cooling the detector with an inert gas, like argon, the detectors of newer IR missiles can track longer wavelength IR radiation associated with airframe friction. Using newer detector materials like indium antimonide (InSb) requires cooling to have increased target detection range and all-aspect tracking capability.

Imaging IR is the most recent advancement in IR seeker technology. The technology for these seekers is similar to that found in the AGM-65 Maverick missile. Imaging IR seekers are harder to decoy with flares than older seekers, and they are resistant to pulsed light jamming. Imaging detection involves creating an IR picture of the scene in one of two ways: scanning or staring. A scanning system uses one detector (or a mix of detectors and mirrors) which moves relative to the scene until the entire scene is scanned. This is an easy system to fabricate, but it can be noisy because the detector can't stay very long at each position, and it does not have a lot of time to measure the signal. A staring system uses many detectors, each of which detects a small portion of the scene. Each detector can 'dwell' on its part of the scene for the entire frame time. However, these systems, also called focal plane arrays, are difficult to fabricate in such a way that each detector has the same sensitivity. One of the prime advantages with using imaging IR seekers is that they can be programmed to track a particular IR shape or scene, significantly reducing the effectiveness of decoy flares.

Flares are the primary countermeasure used to defeat the IR missile. Advanced IR missiles use different techniques to overcome the use of self-protection flares. There are two important characteristics of infrared (IR) missiles that influence the effectiveness of self-protection flares. The first is the ability of the IR missile seeker to discriminate between the IR signature of the aircraft and the IR signature of background interference, especially clouds. The second is the flare rejection capability built into the missile seeker and the missile guidance section.

Radar Warning Receiver (RWR)

Radar surveillance and radar-directed weapons represent the biggest threat to aircraft survival on the modern battlefield. The first step in countering these threat systems is to provide the pilot or crew with timely information on the signal environment. The radar warning receiver (RWR) is designed to provide this vital information to the pilot. The RWR system is an example of an electronic warfare support (ES) system. The primary purpose of an RWR system is to provide a depiction of the electronic order of battle (EOB) that can have an immediate impact on aircraft survival. Though the RWR system is complex, the basic operations of the various components are straightforward. A step above RWR systems is threat geolocation. While an RWR provides the EOB for a single aircraft, threat geolocation systems can provide accurate threat location data for numerous aircraft over an entire region. Threat location data is used for aircraft threat avoidance and, more common today, the pre-emptive attacking of enemy radar sites.

RWRs are designed to provide accurate threat positioning information when the aircraft is flying straight and level. Most RWRs will also provide accurate threat positioning information when the aircraft is manoeuvring up to certain limits of bank angle and turn rate. If aircraft manoeuvring exceeds these limits, RWR threat positioning data becomes unreliable. The two RWR limitations associated with aggressive manoeuvring are inaccurate threat azimuth and multiple threat symbols.

The physical location of the RWR antennas on the aircraft can affect its ability to detect a radar signal. Antennas are arranged to cover a predetermined area of horizontal and vertical space around the aircraft. The antennas and their patterns play an essential part in displaying the spatial relationship of a threat radar to the aircraft. The antenna patterns are the areas, or 'footprints', that the antennas are specifically designed to cover. These footprints are directly affected by the relative position of the antennas to the threat systems. This is because the signal processor measures and compares signal strength from all the aircraft antennas to compute threat signal location relative to the aircraft. This relative location is then presented on the RWR scope display. Aircraft movement and manoeuvring shifts these relative positions during flight and can distort the true threat position on the RWR scope. Precise position determination is not possible with most current RWRs.

The sensitivity of an RWR antenna directly affects its ability to detect a radar signal. The more sensitive the antenna, the further it can detect a signal. The sensitivity of a system and its ability to intercept a radar signal is usually expressed in decibels relative to milliwatts or dBm units. A 10 dBm change in sensitivity can result in a 25 nm range difference in target detection. In general, sensitivity levels of -50 to -60 dBms are required to detect signals at long ranges.

The signal processor is the heart of the radar warning receiver. It is also known as the digital processor or analysis processor in different RWR systems. Its primary functions are to process numerous complex radar signals and identify, among the thousands of similar signals, those generated by lethal threat systems. The signal processor accomplishes this task continuously over the duration of the mission and displays the identified threat system to the aircrew almost instantly.

The signal processor classifies each received signal and corresponding track file by its unique radar signal characteristics. Identifying characteristics used by a signal processor can include radio frequency, pulse width, pulse repetition frequency, EP techniques, and more. Characteristics of one signal may be identical to characteristics from different signals, while certain other characteristics can be as unique as a human fingerprint. The signal processor uses these primary characteristics to identify specific signals. When the primary characteristics of two or more signals are similar, the signal processor uses additional signal characteristics to resolve any confusion between two or more signals.

The signal characteristics in each track file are filled with processed data and are constantly updated based on the time of arrival and location of the received signals. In addition, the track files are constantly compared to the emitter identification data (EID) table installed in the signal processor's computer memory. The EID table is a predefined table of radar characteristics associated with known radar systems. It is created from information gathered from electronic warfare support (ES) assets and intelligence sources. This table can be changed and updated as necessary to reflect the most current radar characteristics available for the anticipated threats in the planned theatre of conflict. Each RWR system has unique procedures to reprogramme the signal processor and update the EID tables. Emergency reprogramming actions, such as would be taken if a new threat appears that is not part of the current EID, are called Pacer Ware.

The signal processor continually compares signal characteristics in the track files with the data in the EID tables. Once the signal processor has determined that enough of the signal characteristics match the information in the EID tables, it generates and positions a video symbol on the RWR scope. The video symbol represents a specific threat, and each threat system has its own unique symbol. In addition, an audio tone is generated to alert the pilot. The signal processor also generates symbols and audio associated with specific threat system actions, including search, track, and missile launch. The position of the threat symbol on the RWR scope always represents the relative position of the threat in relation to the aircraft which is the centre of the RWR scope. The signal processor compares the received signal strength in the different antennas to determine the proper location of the threat symbol. In addition to generating threat symbols for each identified threat, the signal processor also generates threat audio. Threat audio first alerts the aircrew to the detection of a threat system. This RWR audio is generally referred to as 'new guy' alert audio. The signal processor can also present constant audio from a selected threat.

Electronic Warfare (EW)

This section will discuss some of the most widely employed electronic protection (EP) techniques designed to counter radar jamming. The capabilities of the individual radar operator will not be discussed under this heading. However, the radar operator is as important as the EP techniques designed for the radar system. How the missile system operators work is elaborated in Chapter Eight.

Many of the most effective EP techniques are designed to ease operator interpretation of the radar display. In Electronic Warfare (EW), the capabilities of individual radar operators can be as important as the sophisticated EP techniques in determining the final outcome.

Electronic warfare is defined as military action involving the use of electromagnetic and directed energy to control the electromagnetic spectrum or to attack the enemy. Nearly every military action, from command and control of an entire integrated air defence system to precision guidance of an individual weapon, depends on effective use of the electromagnetic spectrum. Radar systems have become a vital element of nearly every military operation. Since these systems operate across the entire electromagnetic spectrum, much of the EW effort is concerned with countering radar systems. All of the jamming techniques discussed in the previous headings are specifically designed to counter radar systems. These actions are classified as electronic attack (EA), which is a part of EW (**Figure 1-24**, **Figure 1-25**).

Electronic warfare is somewhat like a chess game – a series of moves and counter-moves within the electromagnetic spectrum. As one side develops jamming techniques to counter radar systems, the others develop counter-countermeasures to negate them. In response, the one develops newer techniques and their adversaries respond with newer modifications to their radar systems. This series of moves and counter-moves can continue for decades. The development and application of radar counter-countermeasures are classified as electronic protection, also a part of EW.

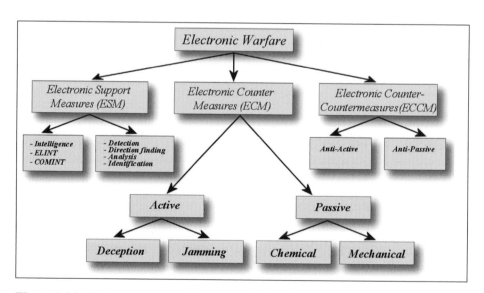

Figure 1-24: Electronic warfare. (Electronic Warfare Handbook)

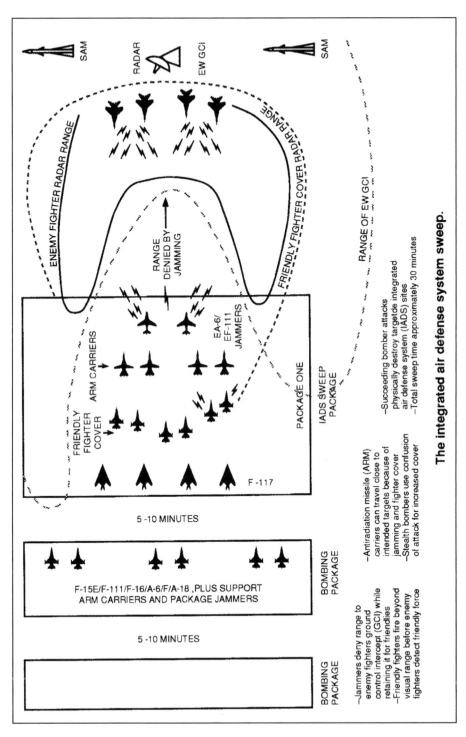

Figure 1-25: SEAD electronic attack (EA) and integrated air defence swap. (Setting the contest – Suppression of enemy air defence in an uncertain world)

SHOOTING DOWN THE STEALTH FIGHTER

The continuing battle to control the electromagnetic spectrum for unrestricted radar employment has resulted in over 150 radar EP techniques. These techniques are designed to negate the effectiveness of electronic jamming and chaff on radar systems. These radar EP techniques can be incorporated into the design of a radar system or added to an existing radar system in response to a jamming technique. It is beyond the scope of this text to discuss all the radar EP techniques in use today. This section will discuss the most common EP techniques. They have been organized by function of the technique within the radar. These functions include: radar receiver protection, jamming avoidance, jamming signal exploitation, overpowering the jamming signal, pulse duration discrimination, angle discrimination, bandwidth discrimination, Doppler discrimination, and time discrimination.

The following are some of the most common radar counter-countermeasures designed to prevent receiver overload or saturation.

- Sensitivity time control (STC) is used to counter close-in chaff or close-in clutter.
- Automatic gain control (AGC) is used to counter chaff, clutter, and most types of transmitted jamming. AGC senses the signal level of a receiver's output and develops a back-bias, producing a constant output level.
- Fast automatic gain control (FAGC) is also employed against chaff, clutter, and most types of transmitted jamming. FAGC works by sensing the signal level of receiver output and develops a back-bias, tending to hold output constant. Response time is within milliseconds, permitting fast response and recovery as the antenna traverses the jammer's bearing.
- Instantaneous automatic gain control (IAGC) is another technique to counter chaff, clutter, and most types of transmitted jamming. IAGC senses the signal level of each echo or jamming pulse and develops a back-bias that holds the stage output constant.
- Automatic noise levelling (ANL) counters noise jamming and modulated or unmodulated constant wave jamming. ANL samples receiver noise content at the end of each PRF and sets the gain accordingly for the next pulse interval.
- The logarithmic receiver (LOG) counters most types of transmitted jamming by amplifying and demodulating large dynamic-range signals in logarithmic amplifiers. This produces 'amplitude compression' of the strong signals.
- The logarithmic receiver with fast time constant (LOG-FTC) counters narrowband jamming, chaff, and clutter. This technique amplifies and demodulates large dynamic-range signals in logarithmic amplifiers, producing 'amplitude compression' of the strong signals.
- Dicke-Fix (DF) counters wideband and fast-swept jamming and is similar in employment to wideband limiting (WBL). DF amplifies without ringing,

clips down all pulses to a common level, then amplifies the narrowband echo signal more than the wideband jamming.

- WBL is used to counter wideband jamming and fast-swept jamming. WBL amplifies without ringing, clips down all pulses to a common level, then amplifies the narrowband echo signal more than the wideband jamming.
- Adaptive video processing (AVP) counters chaff corridors, weather, sea clutter, and most types of transmitted jamming.

Information Warfare

One of the very important parts of the 'war in the waves' is information warfare. The information warfare (IW) objective is to help friendly forces keep information superiority. Within this mission, a military force, by attacking or defending information, conducts information warfare. Therefore, an information system can be both a weapon (i.e. our information system) and a target (i.e. the enemy information system) (**Figure 1-26**).

Information warfare includes all the actions designed to worsen the enemy information system and all the actions designed to protect one's own information system. It often starts before the outbreak of hostilities and continues for a long time afterwards.

All references in this chapter are in 'Further Reading and Bibliography' at the end of the book.

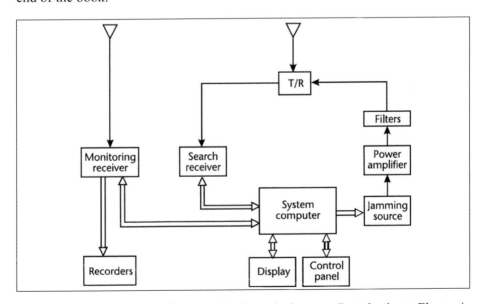

Figure 1-26: Block diagram of communication noise jammer. (Introduction to Electronic Defense Systems)

Chapter Two

Stealth

The Second World War sped up the development of radars and in parallel the first countermeasures whose main intention was to confuse and jam enemy radar. Sometime around the middle of the war the idea of the stealth airplane occurred to British engineers.

In August 1941, British researchers submitted a round of proposals for modifications to aircraft to render them 'undetectable by normal radio detecting frequencies (RDF)' or radar. Their plan was to adjust an aircraft's radiation to match the background level of radiation from the air around it. Increasing the resistivity of the aircraft's skin might short-circuit the radio wave, and instead of reflecting back, the wave could be shunted into a gap where the wavelength would be impeded. If material with the right intrinsic impedance was found, a modified matching system could prevent reflection, but only at certain frequencies.

Although they never took the idea beyond a few theoretical papers, these British engineers had hit upon a concept that would become much more compelling by the 1960s. If an aircraft could perhaps be shaped to make the return signal less powerful, the net effect would be to make the aircraft appear on the radar operator's scope later than expected, or perhaps not at all, thereby giving the aircraft an added measure of surprise.

Historically, the first attempt at the construction of an aircraft with 'low observability' characteristics is considered to be the German Horten (Ho-229, also designated the Go-229) built shortly before the end of the war. That aircraft, which never saw operational action, incorporated special graphite paint which absorbed radar waves. In addition to the aircraft's 'flying wing' shape, most of the Ho-229's wooden skin was bonded together using carbon-impregnated plywood resins intended to absorb radar waves. Designer Reimar Horten claimed that he wanted to add charcoal to the adhesive layers of the plywood skin of the production model to render it invisible to radar, because the charcoal 'should diffuse radar beams, and make the aircraft invisible on radar'. This statement was published in his 1983 co-authored book *Nurflügel* ('Only the Wing').

While this refers to the never-made production model, it seems possible that the experimental charcoal addition could have been used on the Horten Ho-229 V3 prototype. The mere mention of early stealth technology sparked the imagination of aircraft enthusiasts across the world and spurred vibrant debate within the aviation community (**Figure 2-1**).

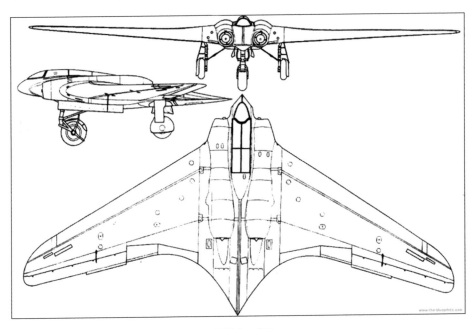

Figure 2-1: Horten Ho-229 (Go-229). (Wikipedia)

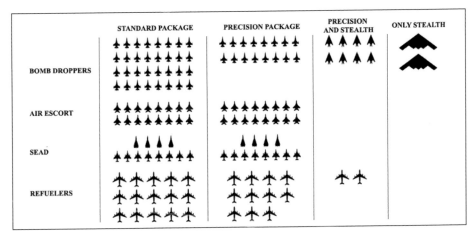

Figure 2-2: The value of STEALTH. Two STEALTH bombers can fulfill the task of multiple bombers, fighter escorts, SEAD and support airplanes.

In early flight tests, the Horten attained a level speed of 800 km/h but the prototype crashed on landing and was destroyed. Gotha still had production prototypes in progress when US troops captured the Friedrichroda plant in late April 1945. At that time one Go-229 prototype was being prepared for flight testing and several others were in various stages of production. Had the aircraft gone into service, its estimated maximum speed would have been a formidable 977 km/h (607 mph), maximum ceiling 52,000 feet, and range 1899 km.

Reducing radar return was not forgotten after the war. In March 1953, when the US Air Force drew up specifications for a new reconnaissance aircraft, it was stipulated that 'consideration will be given in the design of the vehicle to minimizing the detectability to enemy radar'. Within a decade, designers would take the first steps towards a low-observable aircraft.

Stealth technology in an aircraft is not just to avoid missiles being fired at it but also to give deniability to covert operations. See **Figure 2-2**.

The Stealth Challenge

- Survive and prosper in the future environment of improved sensors, dense counter-measures, anti-radiation weapons, and emitter locators.
- Become invulnerable or invisible.

In simple terms, stealth technology allows an aircraft to be partially invisible to radar or any other means of detection, but still there are many threats (**Figure 2-3**). Stealth technology cannot make an aircraft completely invisible to radar. All it can do is to reduce the detection range of an aircraft. In this way it is similar to camouflage used by soldiers in jungle warfare. Stealth technology applies to aircraft, ships and missiles. Thus the need to develop visual, infrared, acoustic and radar stealth. Many countries have announced that they have developed counter-stealth techniques that allow them to negate stealth.

The Stealth Approach

- Force threats to use active sensors sparingly by employing anti-radiation missiles and electronic countermeasures.
- Decrease predictability and increase 'randomness' to force threats to increase complexity and increase the cost of intercept receivers, surveillance, fire control, and missiles.
- Make weapon systems less visible.
- Use tactics that combine with the order of battle as well as the natural and man-made environment to enhance the effect of the reduced observables.
- Use prior knowledge and off-board sensor cueing to minimize on-board active and passive exposure.

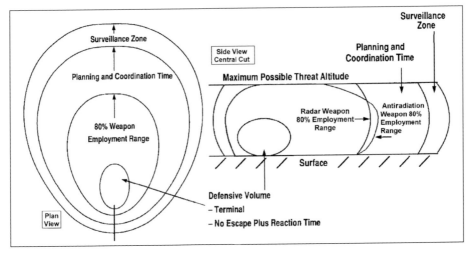

Figure 2-3: Each threat system has a characteristic engagement balloon. The balloons will not be the same shape, in general, but in a modern stealth system they should be close, as depicted in the figure. This means, for example, that the intercept range for a threat anti-radiation missile should be roughly comparable to the range at which a threat radar guided missile would be effective against the platform radar cross section. Each signature should be balanced to the corresponding threat—UV, visible, IR, radar, RF, acoustic, magnetic, and so on. (RF Stealth)

Stealth is not only one thing, but rather an assemblage of techniques which makes a system harder to find and attack. Stealth radar and data-link design can reduce active and passive signatures.

Active signature is defined as all the observable emissions from a stealth platform: acoustic, chemical (soot and contrails), communications, radar, IFF, IR, laser, and UV. Passive signature is defined as all the observables on a stealth platform that require external illumination: magnetic and gravitational anomalies; reflection of sunlight and cold; reflection of acoustic, radar, and laser illumination; and reflection of ambient RF (sometimes called splash track – **Figure 2-4**).

Active radar and data-link signature reduction requires the use of techniques that minimize radiated power density at possible intercept receiver locations. Active signature reduction also depends on the implementation of tactics that reduce exposure time during emission. Active signature reduction methods are commonly called low probability of intercept (LPI) techniques. Passive signature reduction techniques are often called low-observables. They require the development of radome, antenna cavity, and antenna designs as interactive elements of a common subsystem that yields low in-band and out-of-band radar cross section (RCS). Additionally, passive radar signatures are reduced in-band by employing special antenna design techniques that minimize retro-reflective echoes. Low probability of intercept system (LPIS) design is an engineering problem.

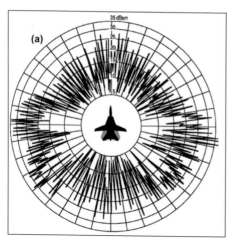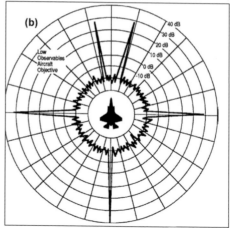

Figure 2-4: The difference between conventional (a) and stealth (b) RCS signatures. (Introduction to RF Stealth)

Stealth Principles

Stealth technology is not a single technology. It is a combination of technologies that attempt to greatly reduce the distance at which a vehicle can be detected. Stealth technologies aim at minimizing signatures and signals, and prevent/delay detection and identification, thus increasing the efficiency of a vehicle's own countermeasures and sensors.

The concept behind stealth technology is very simple. As a matter of fact, it is totally the principle of reflection and absorption that makes aircraft more or less 'stealthy'. Deflecting or absorbing incoming radar waves to reduce the number of waves which return to the radar does this. The level of stealth an aircraft can achieve depends on its design and the materials from which it is made.

Another motive for incorporating stealth technology in an aircraft is not just to avoid missiles being fired at is but also to give deniability to covert operations. This is especially useful when striking targets which are difficult to access. One objective of a stealth aircraft pilot is not to let others know that he was ever there.

Scientific Theory behind the Stealth

At the start of the twentieth century, a new division of mathematical physics appeared: diffraction. Using it, rigorous solutions to the problem of diffraction by a wedge, sphere, and infinite cylinder were obtained. Subsequently, other solutions were added; however, the total number of solutions was relatively small. For relatively short waves (in comparison with the dimensions of the body or other characteristic distances) these solutions, as a rule, are ineffective and direct numerical methods are unsuitable. Hence an interest arose in approximation (asymptotic) methods allowing the investigation of the diffraction of shorter waves by various bodies leading to more reliable results than geometric or physical optics. In the 'geometric theory of diffraction' proposed by Keller, the results obtained in the mathematical theory of diffraction of short waves were exactly the ones which were used and generalized. Here the concept of diffraction rays came to the fore. This concept was expressed rather as a physical hypothesis and was not suitable for representing the field in all of space: it was not usable where the formation of the diffraction field takes place (at the caustic, at the boundary of light and shadow, etc). Here it is impossible to talk about rays, and one must use a wave interpretation.

There is one name that stands out from the many researchers in the field post-war: Pyotr Ufimtsev (**Figure 2-5**). Ufimtsev was born into a peasant family in the village of Ust-Charysh Pristan, in the Altai region of the former USSR. At the age of 3 his father was repressed by the regime and later died in a forced labour camp. In 1949 Ufimtsev finished school and entered the physics-mathematics department at Almaty State University (now in Kazakhstan). Because of advancing nearsightedness he had to move in 1952 from Almaty to a specialized clinic located in Odessa where he continued his studies at Odessa State University. After graduating in 1954 he was selected to work at Scientific

Research Institute No. 108 (later renamed the Central Research Radio Engineering Institute).

How to make airplanes fly more discreetly was studied in a secret Russian radar institute known as 'Institute 108'. The institute was and still is located in Moscow and conducts research in radio-physics, radio-technics, physical and quantum electronics, and informatics. It was established in 1953 as an institute of the USSR Academy of Sciences. In 1957 by a decision of the Central Committee of the CPSU and the Council of Ministers the institute was assigned the task of establishing stations that would receive the signals of Sputnik 1. There were very few professional stations in the USSR at the

Figure 2-5: Pyotr Ufimtsev, 'father of stealth technology'.

time, and the institute cooperated with radio amateurs throughout the country and provided necessary equipment to thirty selected large DOSAAF amateur radio clubs from the Baltic Sea to the Pacific Ocean.

In 1954 Dr Ufimtsev started work on the problem of physical diffraction which directly lead to the development of stealth. He began developing a high-frequency asymptotic theory for predicting the scattering of electromagnetic waves from two-dimensional and three-dimensional objects. Among such objects were the finite size bodies of revolution (disk, finite cylinder with flat bases, finite cone, finite paraboloid, spherical segment, finite thin wire). This theory is now well known as the 'Physical Theory of Diffraction (PTD)'. Experiments showed theoretical possibilities for large objects, such as military aircraft, to reduce radar cross section. As we saw in Chapter One, RCS is the hypothetical area required to intercept the transmitted power density at the target such that if the total intercepted power were re-radiated isotropically, the power density actually observed at the receiver is produced.

Traditional methods could not satisfy this purpose, so scientists needed to look for a more unorthodox approach. Six years later, a book was published in which algorithms explained methods of radar deflection. Using this theory, a unique aircraft shape could be created. It turned out that the shape proposed by Ufimtsev was completely out of line with that of aircraft of that time. It was a step into the unknown.

In theory it was possible to make an airplane invisible to radar, but it had to be made from as many flat surfaces as possible, which, by all aerodynamics principles of the day, was not feasible. The shape had to be changed completely. At that time, it was the goal of every aeronautical engineer and designer to create an aerodynamically perfect aircraft. The new form was so unorthodox that it was not taken seriously. The general opinion was that an airplane of that aerodynamic form would not be able to fly at all.

The Soviets could not understand the new concept and Ufimtsev was not allowed to continue his work in this direction. Interest in his ideas faded, the theoretical department's role diminished, and then it was disbanded. The Soviet government did not realize the value of what Ufimtsev discovered. The authorities of the time would evaluate the researches of scientists and only if they decided that they had no military or economic value would they give permission for them to be published. Ufimtsev accordingly received permission to publish his research results internationally.

Pyotr Ufimtsev received his PhD in Electrical Engineering from the Central Research Radio Engineering Institute of the Defence Ministry in 1959. He received his next PhD in Theoretical and Mathematical Physics from St. Petersburg University in 1970.

The first results of PTD were collected in *Method of Edge Waves in the Physical Theory of Diffraction*, published by Soviet Radio in Moscow, 1962.

In 1971 it was translated into English with the same title by US Air Force, Foreign Technology Division (National Air Intelligence Center), Wright-Patterson AFB, OH, 1971. In a few years this translation became the 'Rosetta Stone' for the stealth programme. PTD became an 'industrial strength' theory in comparison with the 'university academic' approaches. A stealth engineer at Lockheed – Denys Overholser – read the publication and realized that Ufimtsev had created the mathematical theory and tools to do finite analysis of radar reflection. This discovery paved the way for the design of the first true stealth airplane, the Lockheed F-117. More details can be found in Chapter Seven.

The Physical Theory of Diffraction (PTD) that Professor Ufimtsev introduced in the 1950s – a methodology for approximate evaluation at high enough frequency of the scattering from a body, especially a body of complicated shape – has proved to be a truly great idea. Like many good theories, PTD is much easier to apply than to explain. For that reason, in this book just the very basic principles of PTD are explained (**Figure 2-6**).

First of all, PTD is based on two important principles which it will be convenient to refer to here as the physical principle and the geometrical principle. The physical principle shows how the scattered field at a point outside a scattering body can be determined from an integral of appropriate field quantities over the surface of the body. In acoustics these quantities are the pressure at a hard surface, the normal velocity at a soft surface, both at an impedance boundary or the surface of a penetrable body. In electromagnetics they are the tangential magnetic and electric fields at an impedance boundary or the surface of a penetrable body (**Figure 2-7**).

The geometrical principle states that at high enough frequency, when the wavelength is small enough compared to the critical dimensions of the scattering body, the surface integrals can be evaluated asymptotically to yield a description of the total field outside the body in terms of geometrical rays, including diffracted rays. The change in field amplitude along a ray can be calculated geometrically by tracing the divergence and convergence of ray

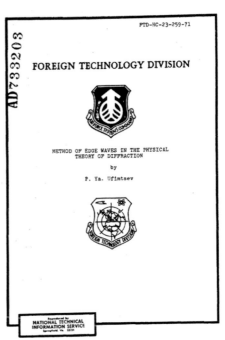

Figure 2-6: Translated book cover page. (DTIC)

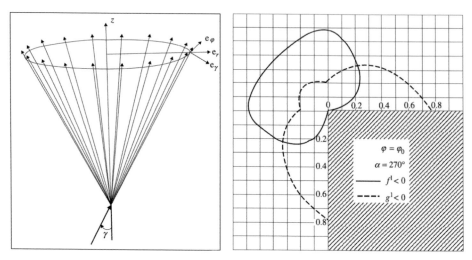

Figure 2-7: Diffraction cone (left) and directivity patterns edge (right). (P. Ufimtsev – Fundamentals of the physical theory of diffraction)

bundles except in the regions surrounding **(a)** a geometrical shadow boundary, for which ray tracing predicts a field discontinuity across the boundary, and **(b)** a caustic, that is, a locus where adjacent geometrical rays meet or cross (such as, in the simplest case, a focal point), at which ray tracing predicts an infinite field. The correct value for the field in these regions, which shrink as frequency increases, can be found by using uniform asymptotic techniques to evaluate the surface integrals.

One of the important features of PTD is this ability to calculate the field accurately in shadow boundary and caustic regions. It is especially important in low-observables design because we are often interested in far-field scattering of a plane wave from a body with straight or slightly curved edges, a configuration for which parts of the far-field region lie in caustic regions (**Figure 2-8**).

The other major advantages of PTD arise from the way the surface fields are handled. There is a uniform part which is defined everywhere on the surface and a non-uniform part that serves as a correction term. For electromagnetics the uniform part is usually, though not always, given by the physical optics (PO) approximation, namely that the surface fields at a point are the same as if the point lay on an infinite plane surface tangent to the actual body at the point and with the same boundary conditions as at the point. For acoustics the uniform part is usually given by the analogous approximation (**Figure 2-9**).

The basic idea of PTD is that the diffracted field is considered as the radiation generated by the scattering sources (currents) induced on the objects. The so-called uniform and non-uniform scattering sources are introduced in PTD.

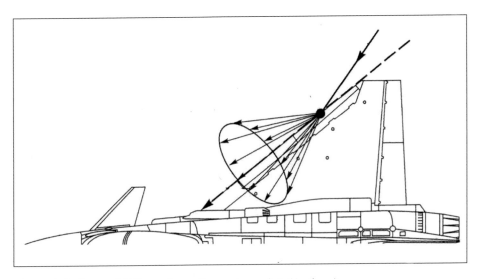

Figure 2-8: Cone of diffracted rays from edge point. (Authors)

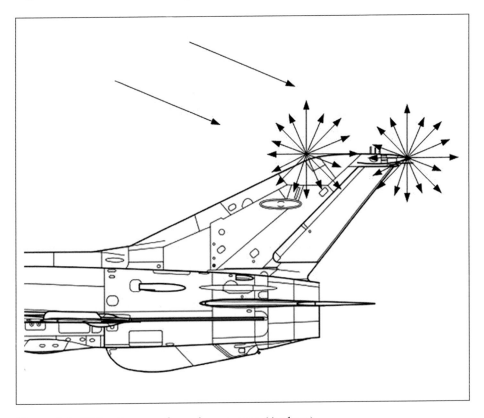

Figure 2-9: Diffraction rays from sharp corner. (Authors)

Uniform sources are defined as sources induced on the infinite plane tangent to the object at a source point. Non-uniform sources are caused by any deviation of the scattering surface from the tangent plane. For large convex objects with sharp edges, the basic contributions to the scattered field are produced by the uniform sources and by those non-uniform sources that concentrate near edges (often called fringe sources (**Figure 2-10**)).

The integration of uniform sources leads to the physical optics (PO) approximation for the scattered field. The PTD is the natural extension of the PO approximation, taking into account the additional field created by the non-uniform/fringe sources.

Firstly, PTD can accurately find the reflection and diffraction from a body of complicated shape without having to match the entire body to canonical formulae, just the regions that give rise to diffraction. Secondly, PTD minimizes the difficulty of reconciling the geometries of the body and of the canonical formulae. Thirdly, and most importantly, in low-observable work the PTD yields

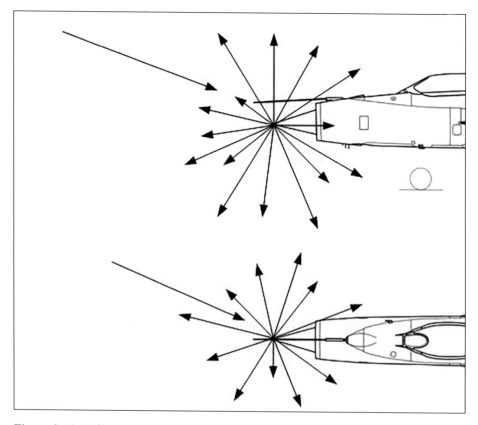

Figure 2-10: Diffraction rays from conical point. (Authors)

diffracted rays in all directions from each element of a linear diffracting feature, not just in the direction of the diffraction cone. Off-cone rays can sometimes yield the strongest fields in a region.

As his research was not directly related to military programmes, Dr Ufimtsev was allowed to participate in international conferences. In 1989 he participated at the conference in Stockholm, where he met a group of US scientists who introduced themselves as Dr Ufimtsev's 'students'. It was surprising for Dr Ufimtsev because he didn't have students, especially not Americans. They were the scientists involved in the STEALTH programme. Dr Ufimtsev got an offer to move to the US to work as a visiting professor at the California University, Los Angeles. He accepted and moved there in 1990.

Ufimtsev was affiliated with several research and academic institutions, including the Institute of Radio Engineering and Electronics of the Academy of Sciences (Moscow); the Moscow Aviation Institute; Northrop-Grumman Corp (California); and the University of California at Los Angeles and Irvine. As a guest professor, he taught courses on diffraction theory at Singapore National University; the Air Force Institute of Technology; Moscow State University; Sienna University in Italy; and Dogus University in Istanbul.

In his two books, *Theory of Edge Diffraction in Electro-magnetics* and *Fundamentals of the Physical Theory of Diffraction*, Ufimtsev presented the further development and application of PTD and its validation by the exact mathematical theory. A new version of PTD, based on the concept of elementary edge waves, is presented in his *Fundamentals of the Physical Theory of Diffraction*.

PTD is not only related to STEALTH but is universal and, with appropriate modifications, modern PTD can be used to solve many problems, among them the design of microwave antennas, mobile radio communication, construction of acoustic barriers to decrease a noise level, and evaluation of radar cross sections for large objects such as tanks, ships, missiles and so on.

Disadvantages of Stealth

During the Cold War, US forces focused on defeating the Warsaw Pact military in their homeland. This required an air force that could maintain air superiority over all battlefields in the Soviet Union. However, the leadership of the Warsaw Pact preferred to defeat their opponents with long range strategic missiles protected by heavy air defences formed with surface-to-air missiles (SAMs). This exposed penetrating US reconnaissance and bombing aircraft to heavy defences. The US force structure compelled Russia to focus on detection and tracking technologies to counter US Air Force asset penetration into its airspace. These strategic approaches resulted in the expansion of US interest in low-observables and Soviet Russia's efforts to form a strong air defence by means of more powerful acquisition systems and SAM launchers.

SHOOTING DOWN THE STEALTH FIGHTER

These challenges reveal that stealth technology is an indispensable requirement for today's modern forces to dominate the battlefield. Its many advantages give the user tactical combat superiority and an overwhelming dominance over an opponent. However, designing, manufacturing, operating and maintaining stealth assets presents challenges. These challenges must be balanced by designers and users.

The first is the poor aerodynamic properties of stealth air-frames. Rather than aerodynamic perfection, stealth aircraft are designed according to the requirements of RCS reduction, and in general this results in handling difficulties. Most modern aircraft are made unstable at one axis for greater manoeuvrability however, stealth aircraft are usually unstable in all axes. Unlike other modern fighters, stealth assets require redundant fly-by-wire systems for flight safety, which increases the cost and adds extra weight to the airframe. During training and experimental flights, there have been many failures of these flight control systems, some of which resulted in crashes: one known B-2 crash, one of seven F-117 crashes, and both F22 crashes were related to flight control unit malfunctions. Also, most stealth aircraft do not have engines with afterburners, thus they do not have high speed performance and are not suitable for dogfighting. The F-22 Raptor and F-35 Lighting are exceptions and may be a future solution to this problem.

The second disadvantage of stealth aircraft is the requirement to either restrict electromagnetic emissions completely or emit them very carefully, such as via LPI radars. Fully autonomous systems and applications using different systems other than radar reduce this risk; however, these systems have many constraints that limit the operational capability of an aircraft. LPI is a potential remedy and is a property of radar that, because of its low power, wide bandwidth, frequency variability, or other design attributes, makes it difficult for it to be detected by means of a passive intercept receiver. So, radars and radio and data connection methods, based on the same principle, are realistic solutions for retaining stealth. LPI technology is more necessary to low-observables than any other asset. LPI can be used to support systems such as altimeters, tactical airborne targeting, surveillance and navigation, while it also matches with other stealthy attributes. However, such sophisticated LPI systems, which require continuous development to counter new receiver designs, result in high costs and deployment of complex electronical instrumentation and software.

Another drawback is the high maintenance cost associated with stealth. To remain low-observable, an aircraft's surfaces must be faultless. Surfaces must be examined very carefully; even an improperly tightened screw might degrade the stealthiness of an aircraft. All RAM coated parts and special paintings must be treated before each mission. Moreover, this kind of maintenance requires special shelters, such as the B-2's climate-controlled hangars. After each sortie, the B-2 Spirit has to be maintained for nearly 120 hours by experienced staff and high-tech automated devices. It is preferable to deploy these aircraft on missions from their home bases only where they can be prepared for flight. The issue is that long-range sorties conducted from the homeland against overseas targets still places a serious economic burden on stealth aircraft operators.

The fourth disadvantage is that stealth aircraft are limited by the amount of ordnance they can carry. This is because in full stealth mode, aircraft are required to carry all of their ordnance internally, at least until stealth weapons become operational. Thus, pre-operational intelligence is critical and the judicious use of ordnance is important, as re-attack of targets is limited by inventory. Furthermore, when weapon bays are opened, even for just a few seconds, the RCS increases and raises the chances of detection.

Another drawback of stealth aircraft is their visual signature. Although decreased by painting, night missions (dependency on nights and weather conditions is another drawback) and other camouflage tactics, stealth aircraft are still visible to the naked eye. Currently, experiments are being conducted to develop approaches for the total cancellation of visual illumination; however, there are no known applications of such a system on operational stealth aircraft at this time.

The sixth disadvantage is the negative reaction of the public to aircraft failures. Based on mission experience during various wars, stealth aircraft have proved to be extremely successful. However, there are several known failures that have had a negative influence on public opinion. Incidents include the shooting down of an F-117 (and there are indications that more than one F-117 took severe, beyond-repair, damage from enemy fire) on 27 March 1999 during the bombing of Serbia. Other losses include shoot-downs of U-2 Dragon Ladies and several low-observable UAVs during the Cold War. Normally such small numbers of shoot-down incidents over battlefields and other losses of military aircraft during training are neglected. But the loss of such expensive military assets, which are thought to be impervious to enemy defences, receives significant public interest. In addition to the shoot-down of the F-117 over Serbian airspace, several F-117s, two F-22A Raptors and one B-2A Spirit have been lost during training flights. There are also speculations that one B-2 was lost during a combat mission. This will be discussed in detail in Chapter Eight.

The final and the most important disadvantage of stealth technology is the cost. Cost is affected by three factors.

The first factor is the cost of the development of the technology itself.

The second cost factor is the development of other technologies, such as complex fly-by-wire systems, high-tech computer and control units, special super cruise engines, LPI radars, navigation, precision targeting systems, and stealth armaments. These costs for the three currently operational stealth aircraft are extremely high. Moreover, it is difficult to recover development costs through sales to other nations, a common practice for non-stealth weapon systems. Stealth assets are protected from foreign military sales due to security concerns. The US Congress has banned their sales by declaring them critical technology.

The third cost factor concerns operational and maintenance expenses. For example, while the B-2 Spirit can be deployed from a US base to a mission anywhere in the world within twelve hours, its permanent relocation to most foreign US bases is limited by its special maintenance requirements. Despite all the challenges in producing stealth assets, stealth technology has fulfilled air force requirements for battlefield survivability, and many assets have been developed and deployed.

Radars operate across a wide range of wavelengths, from the HF band at tens of metres up to the Ka-Band in millimetres. Devising stealthy shapes that are effective from all directions against all wavelengths is simply impossible; at best a design can aim to make a vehicle stealthy against radars in some bands from some directions.

By far the best performer to date is the Northrop B-2A Spirit heavy bomber. Its superlative shaping is effective from the metric VHF band up to the sub-centimetric Ku/K/Ka bands, and effective from all azimuths, providing a genuine 'all aspect' stealth capability.

Fighters have generally been optimized by shaping to perform best between the decimetre S-Band and sub-centimetre Ku-band, since these are the bands in which most surveillance radars, acquisition radars, surface to air missile engagement radars, fighter-borne air intercept radars, and missile radar seekers operate.

Optimization of stealth shaping by aspect varies widely in fighter designs, with the F-22A Raptor remaining by far the best design to date, with excellent stealth performance in the nose and tail sectors, and very good performance from the sides. Computer modelling of later designs such as the F-35, Russian PAK-FA/Su-57 and Chinese J-20, shows significantly worse stealth performance from behind and, in most instances, from the sides. This is not open to argument, as sufficient high-quality images are available to construct accurate shaping models and perform simulations using accurate software models.

A curious aspect of these poor designs in stealth shaping is that not all were necessary and appear to reflect a lack of discipline in design offices where other criteria were put first. In the F-35 the choices were driven by the STOVL variant configuration and a marketing requirement for 2,000-lb internally-carried bombs; in the PAK-FA/T-50/Su-57 manoeuvrability was of prime importance; and in the J-20 it was supersonic drag.

The major design issue over coming decades will be the proliferation of counter-stealth sensors, built to exploit weaknesses in existing stealth designs. But shaping is fixed in the basic design of an aircraft, so there are no meaningful upgrades that can be made to an aircraft's shape once a design is established and in production.

Chapter Three

Missile Guidance

The design of a guided missile is a substantial undertaking requiring the effort of many engineers with expertise in aerodynamics, flight control, structures, and propulsion, to mention but a few aspects. The different design groups must work together to produce the most efficient weapon at the lowest possible cost.

This chapter presents an overview of missile guidance and control laws applicable to surface-to-air missiles (SAMs) as well as the basic equations that are used in intercepting a target.

The table on the next page illustrates basic guidance concepts in surface-to-air missiles, of which two are most common:

    a. The homing guidance system, which guides the interceptor missile to the target by means of a target seeker and an onboard computer; homing guidance can be modelled;

    b. Command guidance, which relies on missile guidance commands calculated at the ground launching (controlling) site and transmitted to the missile.

Guided missile (also known as guided munitions) systems (**Figure 3-1**) contain a guidance package that attempts to keep the missile on a course that will eventually lead to an intercept with the target. Most guidance SAMs or air defence systems employ either homing or command guidance to intercept the target. At this point it is appropriate to note that short-range, shoulder-fired SAMs using IR guidance have been developed by various nations.

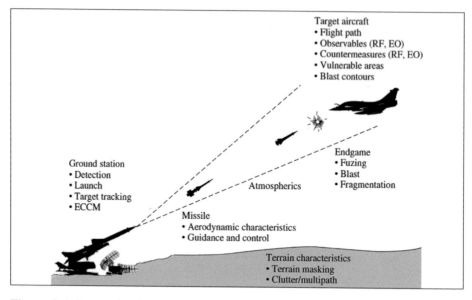

Figure 3-1: Interaction between an airborne target and a SAM air defence system. (Missile Guidance and Control Systems, modified by authors)

Types of guidance systems[7]

Type	Methods of Navigation	Sensing Devices	Characteristics
Active homing	Proportional Navigation Pure Pursuit Deviated Pursuit	Radar Infrared Imaging Infrared Laser TV	Ground system not committed to single target.
Semi-active homing	Proportional Navigation Pure Pursuit Deviated Pursuit	Radar Infrared Imaging Infrared TV Laser	Ground system committed to single target. Until intercept takes place
Passive homing	Proportional Navigation Pure Pursuit Deviated Pursuit	Infrared Visible Light Electromagnetic Energy	Ground system not committed to single target. All sensing devices have limited capability compared with radar.

7. From: Missile Guidance and Control Systems.

Type	Methods of Navigation	Sensing Devices	Characteristics
Command guidance	Any Method	Radar Infrared Visible Light	Ground system committed to single target. Missile dynamically linked to ground system. Ground computer required for programmed flight. Low-cost missile.
Beam Rider (or CLOS)	Line-of-Sight Programmed	Radar Infrared Visible Light	Ground system committed to single target. Missile dynamically linked to ground system. Ground computer required for programmed flight. Low-cost missile.

Electromagnetic radiation is the most popular form of energy detected by homing systems. Radar can be the primary sensor for any of the three classes of homing guidance systems, but it is best suited for semi-active and active homing. Currently the use of electromagnetic radiation via radar in a target seeker is foremost in effectiveness. Radar is little restricted by weather or visibility but is susceptible to enemy jamming. Heat (infrared radiation) is best used with a passive seeker. It is difficult to mislead or decoy heat-seeking systems when they are used against aerial targets because the heat emitted by engines and rockets of the aerial targets is difficult to shield. With a sufficiently sensitive detector, the infrared system is very effective. Light is also useful in a passive seeker system. However, both weather and visibility restrict its use. Such a system is quite susceptible to countermeasure techniques.

Various flight paths or trajectories may be deployed with respect to fixed targets, but for moving targets special requirements must be met. In homing systems, sensing elements must be sharply directional to perceive small angular displacements between a missile and its target. Surface to air missile systems typically use command and other type of guidance.

Surface to air missile guidance is generally divided into three distinct phases:

1. Boost or launch
2. Midcourse
3. Terminal

The boost phase lasts from the time the missile leaves the launcher until the booster burns all of its fuel. The missile may or may not be actively guided during this phase. The midcourse phase, when it has a distinct existence, is usually the longest in terms of both distance and time. During this phase, guidance may or may not be explicitly required to bring the missile onto the desired course and to make certain it stays on course until it enters a zone (in parametric space) from which terminal guidance can successfully take over. The terminal phase is the last phase of guidance and must have high accuracy and fast reactions to ensure an intercept with the target. In this phase, the guidance seeker (if one is used) is locked onto the target, permitting the missile to be guided all the way to the target. Therefore, proper functioning of the guidance system during the terminal phase, when the missile is approaching its target, is of critical importance. Much work has been done to develop extremely accurate equipment for use in terminal-phase guidance.

There are several guided systems that fall into this category. The most common ones are the short-range homing systems and some types of inertial system. These terminal systems may also be the only guidance systems used in short-range missiles. Pre-launch aiming errors must be minimized because these errors tend to translate directly into miss distance. Subsequent to launch, the missile has certain requirements. First, the missile needs a target signal. For example, in the case of a semi-active guided missile, the target signal is the result of energy reflected from the target. The source of this energy is the interceptor, which in turn receives energy from the illuminator. Thus, subsequent to launch, the missile requires that the target be continuously illuminated. Target illumination by itself does not require that the interceptor track the target, although this may occur.

In addition, the missile requires the presence of certain modulations on the target return, which are conveniently impressed on the illuminating signal itself. Typically this is an 85 Hz FM ranging signal, which the missile uses to select the target from clutter or noise.

Guidance techniques, as well as other command/homing methods which are part of the post-launch phase, can be affected in a number of ways, the more prominent of which are listed below:

Command Guidance: Command guided missiles are missiles whose guidance instructions or commands come from sources outside the missile. In this type of guidance, a tracking system that is separated from the missile is used to track both the missile and the target. Therefore a missile seeker is not required in command guidance. The tracking system may consist of two separate tracking units, one for the missile and one for the target aircraft, or it may consist of one tracking unit that tracks both vehicles. Tracking can be accomplished using radar, optical, laser, or infrared systems. A radar beacon or infrared flare on the tail of the missile can be used to provide information to the tracking system on the location of the missile.

The target and missile ranges, elevations, and bearings are fed to a computer. Consequently, using the position and position rate information (i.e. range and range rate), the computer determines the flight path the interceptor missile should take that will result in a collision with the target. The computer at the launch point determines whether the interceptor missile is on the proper trajectory to intercept the target. If it is not, steering commands are generated by the ground computer and transmitted to the in-flight missile. Furthermore, the computer compares this computed flight path with the predicted flight path of the missile based on current tracking information and determines the correction signals required to move the missile control surfaces to change the current flight path to the new one. These signals are the command guidance and are sent to the missile receiver via either the missile tracking system or a separate command link, such as radio. In addition to the steering instructions, the command link may be required to transfer other instructions to the missile, such as fuse arming, receiver gain setting, and warhead detonation. Finally, in command guidance, the launch point commands the missile.

Command guidance all the way to the target is used mostly with short-range missile systems because of the relatively large tracking errors that occur at long range. A disadvantage of command guidance is that the external energy source must illuminate the target often enough (i.e. high data rate) to make guidance effective. The target may thus get alerted of the illuminating radar's presence and operation, and may resort to evasive action (**Figure 3-2**, **Figure 3-3**).

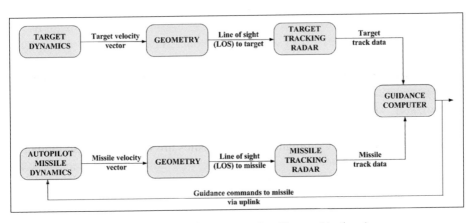

Figure 3-2: System block diagram for command guidance. (Authors)

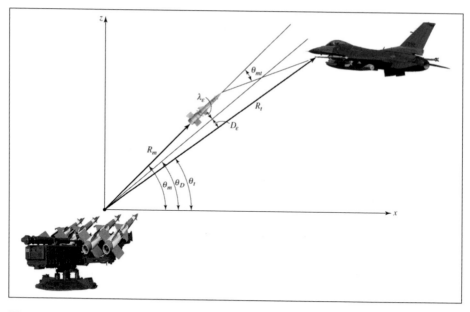

Figure 3-3: Command guidance geometry. (Missile Guidance and Control Systems modified by authors)

Where:

D_e displacement from the site to the target
λ_e lateral displacement from the missile to the desired course
R_m missile range
R_t target range
q_D depression angle
q_m missile depression angle
θ_t target depression angle

Beam Rider: Beam riding is another form of command guidance. Specifically, in this type of guidance the aircraft (target) is tracked by means of an electromagnetic beam, which may be transmitted by a ground (or ship or airborne) radar or a laser tracking system (e.g. a LADAR (LAser Detection And Ranging or laser radar)). To follow or 'ride the beam', the interceptor missile's onboard guidance equipment includes a rear-facing antenna which senses the target-tracking beam. By using the modulation properties of the beam, steering signals that are a function of the position of the missile with respect to the centre (or the scanning axis) of the target-tracking beam are computed on board and sent to the control surfaces. These correction signals produce control surface movements intended to keep the missile as nearly as possible in the centre of the target-tracking beam (or scanning axis) (**Figure 3-4**).

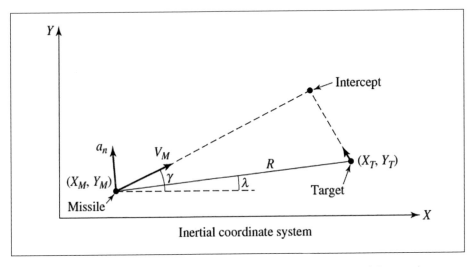

Figure 3-4: Target intercept geometry. (Missile Guidance and Control Systems)

Where:
V_M missile velocity
λ line of sight angle
R missile-target range
γ missile flight path (or heading) angle

For this reason, the interceptor missile is said to ride the beam. Either the beam that the missile rides can track the target directly or a computer can be used to predict the direction the missile beam should be pointing to effect an eventual collision of the interceptor missile with the target. In this case, a separate tracker is required to track the target. Some ground-tracking systems use a V-shaped beam to track the target. In such a case, the interceptor missile rides in the bottom of the V. If the missile moves out of the V bottom, sensing circuits in the missile cause the missile to return to the bottom of the V. As long as the launch point continues to track the target, and the missile continues to ride the radar beam, the missile will intercept the target. As in any system, there are advantages and disadvantages in using one method versus another. The advantage of the beam-riding guidance technique is that it permits the launching of a large number of missiles into the same control or target-tracking beam, since all of the guidance equipment is carried in the missile. A disadvantage of this guidance technique is that the tracking beam must be reasonably narrow to ensure intercept, thus increasing the chance of the interceptor missile losing track of the target, particularly if the target undergoes evasive manoeuvres. The problem of large tracking error for long-range targets usually restricts the use of this guidance technique to short ranges (**Figure 3-5, Figure 3-6**).

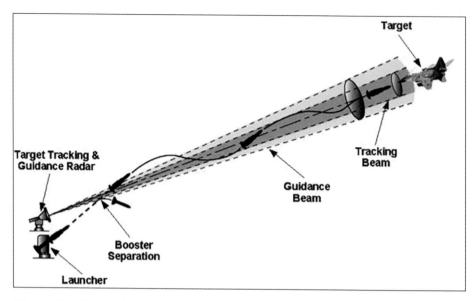

Figure 3-5: Beam riding geometry. (US Naval Training Command Gunner's Mate Manual NAVTRA)

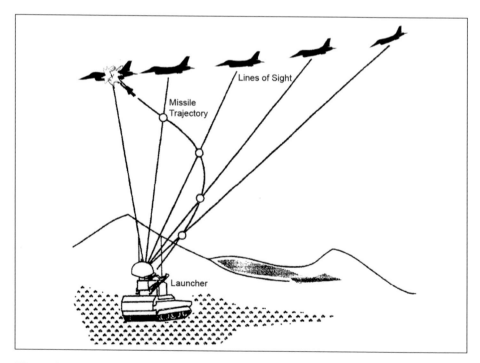

Figure 3-6: Beam riding geometry. (MIL-HDBK-1211 modified by authors)

Command to Line of Sight (CLOS) (Figure 3-7): A particular type of command guidance and navigation where the missile is always to be commanded in the line of sight (LOS) between the tracking unit and the aircraft is known as 'command to line of sight' (CLOS) or three-point guidance. The missile is controlled to stay as close as possible on the LOS to the target after missile capture. In CLOS guidance an up-link is used to transmit guidance signals from a ground controller to the missile. More specifically, if the beam acceleration is taken into account and added to the nominal acceleration generated by the beam-rider equations, then CLOS guidance results. Thus the beam rider acceleration command is modified to include an extra term. The beam-riding performance described above can thus be significantly improved by taking the beam motion into account. CLOS guidance is used mostly in short range air defence and anti-tank systems.

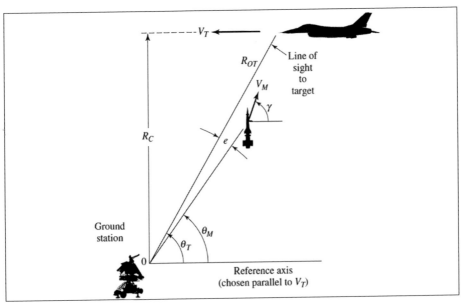

Figure 3-7: Geometric relationship for line of sight (LOS) command system. (Missile Guidance and Control Systems modified by authors)

Where:

V_t target velocity

R_{OT} distance from missile to ground station

V_M missile velocity

q_M angle of sight line from ground station to the missile

q_T actual pitch heading

γ missile velocity vector angle with respect to the reference axis

e missile R_{OT} angle

The following target intercept rules are possible within command/homing guidance strategies:

Pursuit: (**Figure 3-8**) In the pursuit trajectory, the interceptor missile flies directly towards the target at all times. Thus the heading of the missile is maintained essentially along the LOS between the missile and the target by the guidance system. The missile is constantly turning during an attack.

Missiles flying a pursuit course usually end up in a tail-chase situation, similar to a dog chasing a rabbit. Pursuit guidance is considered impractical as a homing guidance law against moving targets because of the difficult manoeuvres that are required to end the attack in a tail chase. That is, the manoeuvres required of the missile become increasingly difficult during the last, critical, stages of the flight. Another disadvantage of this guidance method is that the missile speed must be considerably greater than that of the target. The sharpest curvature of the missile flight path usually occurs at the end of the flight, so that at this time the missile must overtake the target. If the target attempts to evade, the last-minute angular acceleration requirements placed on the missile could exceed the aerodynamic capability, thereby causing a large miss distance. Furthermore, near the end

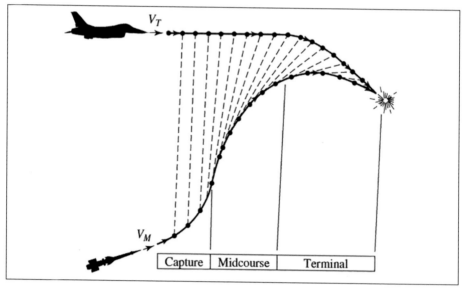

Figure 3-8: General pursuit guidance course. (Missile Guidance and Control Systems modified by authors)

Where:

V_T target velocity
V_M missile velocity

of the flight the missile is usually coasting because the booster (and sustainer) motor thrusts last for only a short part of the flight. The result is that more energy is required on the part of the missile to make short-radius, high-speed turns at a time when the missile is losing speed and has the least turning capability. The most favourable application of the pursuit course guidance law is against slow-moving aircraft, or head-on towards an incoming aircraft.

Deviated Pursuit: (**Figure 3-9**) The interceptor missile tracks the target and produces guidance commands. This guidance law is similar to pure pursuit, except that the missile heading leads the LOS by a fixed angle. When the fixed lead angle is zero, deviated pursuit becomes pure pursuit. No missile is designed to fly deviated pursuit; however, random errors and unwanted bias lines often result in a deviated pursuit course.

Lead Pursuit: A lead pursuit course is flown by an interceptor (i.e. a missile) directing its velocity vector at an angle from the target so that projectiles launched from any point on the course will impact on the target if it is within the range of the weapon. Note that the interceptor in conjunction with the missile trajectory flies lead pursuit.

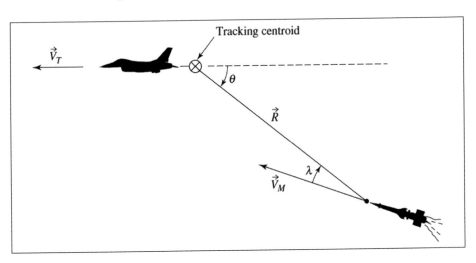

Figure 3-9: Deviated pursuit geometry.

Where:
V_T target
V_M missile
λ line of sight angle
R missile-target range
θ pitch angle

Lead Collision: Lead collision is a straight-line course flown by an interceptor such that the interceptor will achieve a single given firing position. Specifically, in lead collision homing, if the target speed and heading remain constant, a constant-speed missile will fly a straight-line path to the target–missile collision. The target and missile flight paths form a single triangle with the missile to the target. An obvious advantage of collision homing is that the missile is subjected to a minimum of manoeuvres since the flight path approximates a straight line. The time of flight of the weapon is a constant.

Pure Collision: (**Figure 3-10**) Pure collision is a straight-line course flown by an interceptor or weapon such that it will collide with the target.

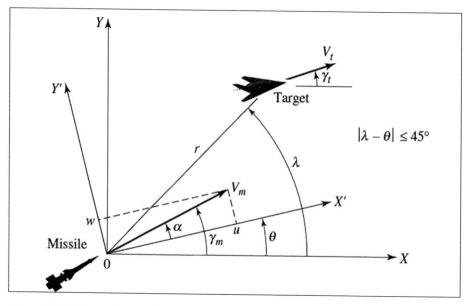

Figure 3-10: Target interception manoeuvre capability and geometry. (Missile Guidance and Control Systems modified by authors)

Where

V_t target

V_m missile velocity

λ line of sight angle

r missile-target range

θ aspect angle

γ_m missile flight path (or heading) angle, that is, angle between the missile vector and inertial reference

γ_t target path angle

Constant Load Factor: A constant load factor course is flown by an interceptor or missile so that a constant g-load factor load on the interceptor will result in collision with the target. No missiles presently fly constant load factors. Normal acceleration is constant in this course.

Proportional Navigation: (**Figure 3-11, Figure 3-12, Figure 3-13**) The conceptual idea behind proportional navigation is that the missile should keep a constant bearing to the target at all time.

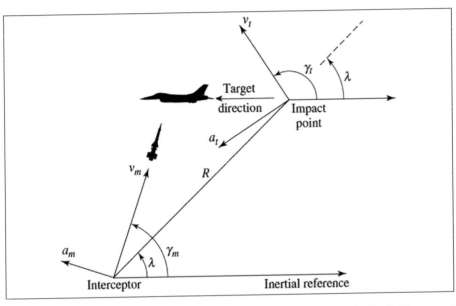

Figure 3-11: Geometry for derivation of proportional navigation. (Missile Guidance and Control Systems modified by authors)

Where:

v_t	target velocity
v_m	interceptor missile velocity
λ	line of sight angle
R	range between missile and target
θ	aspect angle
γ_m	missile flight path (or heading)
γ_t	target path angle

As most seamen know, this strategy will result in an eventual impact. Proportional navigation (also referred to as collision homing) is flown in such a manner as to change the lead angle at a rate proportional to the angular rate of the line of

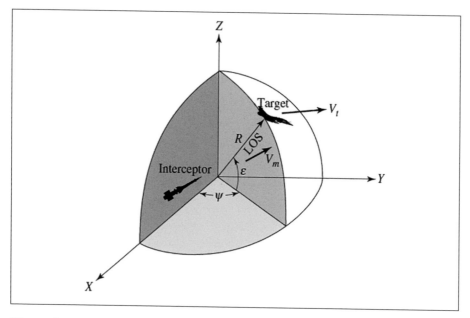

Figure 3-12: Three-dimensional pursuit-evasion geometry. (Missile Guidance and Control Systems modified by authors)

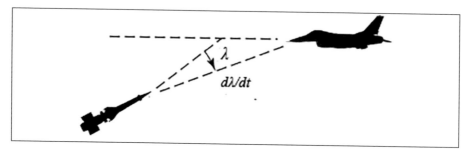

Figure 3-13: Proportional navigation. (Missile Guidance and Control Systems)

sight to the target. The missile measures the rotation of the LOS and turns at a rate proportional to it. Specifically, classical proportional navigation guidance law tries to null the heading error for intercepting the target. The constant of proportionality between the turn rate and the line-of-sight rate is called the navigation constant (N). In essence, the trajectory flown by the missile is heavily influenced by its navigation constant. This constant is maintained between the missile lateral acceleration (a_n) and the product of the line-of-sight rate ($d\lambda/dt$) and closing velocity Vc. Mathematically, proportional navigation can be expressed as:

$$(a_n = NVc(d\lambda/dt)$$

a the commanded normal (or lateral) acceleration (m/sec^2) or (ft/sec^2)
N the navigation constant (also known as navigation ratio, effective navigation ratio, and navigation gain), a positive real number (dimensionless)
Vc the closing velocity (ft/sec) or (m/sec)
$d\lambda/dt$ the LOS rate measured by the missile seeker (rad/sec)

Three-Point: (**Figure 3-14**, **Figure 3-15**) In three-point guidance, the missile is constantly being steered to lie between the target tracker and target. This type of trajectory is typically used only in short-range missile systems employing command-to-line-of-sight (CLOS) or beam-rider guidance. Thus three-point guidance refers to the ground tracker, missile, and target. Three-point guidance is also known in the literature as constant bearing guidance. Constant bearing guidance is a specialized case of proportional navigation; that is, constant-bearing guidance is obtained in the limit as N'→∞.

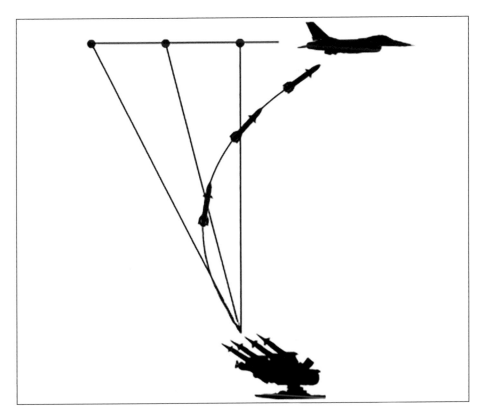

Figure 3-14: Three-point guidance method. (Missile Guidance and Control Systems modified by authors)

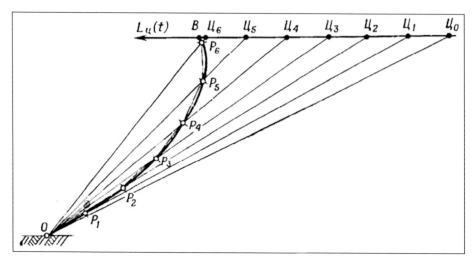

Figure 3-15: Three-point guidance method – from the Soviet S-125 manual. This method was used in shooting down the Stealth aircraft.

Hyperbolic Guidance: The guidance or control of a guided missile or the like in which the difference in the time of delay of radio signals transmitted simultaneously from two ground stations, arriving at the missile at different time intervals, controls the position of the missile. This system is based on the geometric theorem that the locus of all points of fixed difference in distance from two base points is a hyperbola.

In conclusion of this chapter, it should be noted that no one type of guidance is best suited for all applications. Consequently, many missile systems use more than one type of guidance, with each one operating during a certain phase of the interceptor missile's trajectory. For example, a system may use beam-rider guidance or semi-active homing from launch until midcourse, at which time the guidance mode switches to active or passive homing for more accurate tracking and guidance during the terminal phase. An advantage of this technique is that this combination allows the launching aircraft to break away from the engagement earlier than otherwise possible. Such systems are commonly referred to as composite guidance systems. Several types of guidance may be used simultaneously to avoid countermeasures employed by the aircraft, such as a decoy flare to draw an infrared homing missile off the radiation from the aircraft. However, if an active homing system is used in conjunction with a passive one, the missile may reject the flare and continue on towards the target aircraft.

Of particular significance, from the point of view of defensive weapons, is the surface-to-air missile. A surface-to-air missile is launched from the ground or from the surface of the sea against an airborne target. It is generally a defensive weapon, since its function is to intercept an enemy aircraft or an incoming missile that is approaching the point or area to be defended. In synthesizing a surface-to-air air defence missile system the designer must make two basic decisions:

1. The method of guiding the missile, and
2. The type of path over which it travels to the target. The homing, beam-rider (or CLOS), and command types of guidance are all applicable to surface-to-air missile.

Before a surface-to-air missile system can go into action against any hostile airborne target, the system radar must detect the target. Detection must take place at a range long enough to take advantage of the range of the missile for the following reasons:

1. It may be necessary to launch a number of missiles to destroy all the targets in a group detected one at a time
2. It is obviously desirable to destroy the target before it comes close to the point being defended
3. With many types of missile guidance, excessive accelerations are required of the missile to engage the target at close ranges.

The system radar must also be capable of acquiring and tracking a target of the specified radar cross section (RCS) and may be required to do this at low altitudes in the presence of ground or sea clutter return. Finally, there must be a high probability that a target will be detected if and only if a target exists. Closely associated with the early detection requirement is the system reaction time, defined as the time elapsing between detection of a target and the launching of a missile towards it. If this time is long, then the target would need to be detected correspondingly early during its approach.

A final comment on pursuit guidance is in order. For pursuit against a non-manoeuvring target, the collision course exhibits a constant bearing property, whereby the LOS maintains a fixed direction in space; that is, the LOS moves parallel to itself in space during the engagement. Consequently the pursuer will appear to be coming in straight at the target, though pointed off by the lead angle. If a constant bearing guidance law is adopted against a manoeuvring target, the resulting pursuer trajectory no longer remains a straight line; however, it still has the desirable property that the demanded pursuer lateral acceleration is at most equal to that of the target. From a theoretical point of view, a constant-bearing guidance law would be a desirable one against both manoeuvring and non-manoeuvring targets. However, a constant-bearing law is difficult to implement, especially for the general case of manoeuvring targets, since it requires the pursuer to be able to detect the component of target motion perpendicular to the LOS, and to adjust its own motion instantaneously, in such a way that its velocity component perpendicular to the LOS equals that of the target.

Chapter Four

Missile Complex S-125 'Neva'/SA-3 Goa

The S-125 Neva/Pechora/SA-3 Goa Surface to Air Missile system was developed to supplement the proven S-75 Dvina/SA-2 Guideline in Soviet and Warsaw Pact service. The S-75 Dvina/SA-2 Guideline was designed to provide medium-to-high altitude air defence coverage primarily against bomber aircraft. As such, it was not well suited to the engagement of low flying targets, especially fighter aircraft and cruise missiles. The design aim of the S-125 Neva/Pechora/SA-3 Goa was to produce a system with a low-to-medium-altitude engagement envelope, providing protected airspace overlapping air defence coverage for all altitudes. Specifically, targets travelling at speeds of up to 1,500 km/h, at altitudes of 100 to 5,000 metres, at ranges of up to 12 km were to be engaged and destroyed. Such performance is today characteristic of a point defence weapon, but during the 1950s it was more typical of area defence weapons.

The Soviets sought to build on the experience gained with the S-75 Dvina/ SA-2 Guideline using command link guidance and a proximity fused warhead, but recognized from the outset that a fundamentally new engagement radar design was required with much better clutter rejection performance than the workhorse RSNA/SNR-75/Fan Song series. The requirement for narrower antenna mainlobes drove the designers into the 9 GHz frequency band, well above the ~6 GHz operating range of the earlier RSNA/SNR-75/Fan Song series.

Development was initiated in 1956. The resulting weapon was more compact than the previous S-75 Dvina/SA-2 Guideline, permitting two rail launchers and use of a solid propellant sustainer, the first in air defence missile design. Canard controls were also employed. Like its predecessor, the missile used a solid rocket first-stage booster. Numerous development problems were encountered throughout the system, especially with the performance of the radio proximity fuse and command link guidance at very low altitudes. Trials of the V-600P missile and a new radar demonstrated the capability to engage targets at speeds of up to 2,000 km/h, at altitudes between 200 and 10,000 m, with the target pulling up to 4G at 5,000 to 7,000 m and up to 9 G below 1,000 m at transonic speeds. Estimated single shot hit probability was 0.82-0.99 per cent, deteriorating to 0.49-0.88 per cent if chaff was deployed.

While the new system met the needs of the air defence branch, its stow and deploy times were similar to those of the SA-2 Guideline and thus too great for the army air defence units, who rejected the design, resulting in the development of the high mobility 2K12 Kub/SA-6 Gainful system. The S-125 Neva/SA-3A Goa achieved military acceptance in 1961 and was first deployed as part of the Moscow region SAM belt.

Complex SA-3 is a single-channel by target and two-channel by missile air defence missile system. The composition of its equipment allows engaging the targets in conditions of the enemy's extensive passive and active countermeasures. The complex is designed to engage strategic, tactical and naval aircraft, as well as air-based missiles in a wide range of conditions and use.

As in the previous SA-2, in the complexes of the SA-3 family, several types of target tracking methods are used:

1. 'manual' by all coordinates
2. 'automatic' by angular coordinates and hand-by-range
3. 'automatic' by all coordinates

In the case of electronic countermeasures and jamming, the 'manual' mode by angular coordinates applies (with the guiding to the 'centre' of the source) with the setting of a distance mark on the far edge of the affected area. The missile radar guidance is conducted by signal of onboard radio transmitter only in automatic mode on all coordinates.

All equipment is mounted on trailers, semi-trailers and on towed wheeled chassis, which made it possible to deploy to full combat readiness in virtually any conditions. A typical deployment area for battalion level might be 200 x 200 m^2 with low-rise protection berms around.

The basic tactical unit is a battalion; in the Soviet classification, 'divizion'. Missile components are assigned to the 'battery'. Typical battery composition is a single SNR-125 Low Blow series engagement radar, four dual rail 5P71 or four dual rail 5P73 launchers, and multiple PR-14 series dual round transporter/loader trucks carrying reserve missiles. Most SA-3 operators deploy the system at fixed sites, with revetments using concreted pads and bays, and/or earthwork berms, for protection. The basic SA-3 Goa qualifies as a semi-mobile system, requiring several hours to deploy. A prepared peacetime position for the SNR-125 missile guidance station (Stanitsa Navedenya Raket) is a semi-buried reinforced concrete structure or fully underground bunker with an additional dirt cover. This type of building provides additional facilities for the battalion command post, as well as a room for on-duty combat crew, and a classroom which can also be used as a shelter for communication and power supply unit staff. The premises is equipped with a filter and ventilation system. Protection against chemical attack and gas is provided too.

Missile launchers at the prepared positions are located in semi-ring embankments, usually with the concrete slabs facing the battalion's designated responsibility sector. The launchers may be covered with camouflage nets. Field conditions require solid ground beneath the launchers and gravel is often used (**Figure 4-1**).

Reinforced concrete structures were built to store 8-16 missiles, which included working space for the personnel of the preparation unit. On the structure roof, a visual observation post (PVN as per Russian abbreviation) was usually built, where anti-aircraft machine guns or shoulder launched missile systems were located. In special conditions, for example in the absence of building materials or suitable sites, it was allowed to store a set of missiles in packs in an open position.

UNK (fire control centre) equipment is installed in the cabin, mounted on the semi-trailer OAZAZ-828 equipped with a filtration unit. To ensure acceptable conditions for combat operations and carrying out combat duty on an unprepared position, a van may be equipped with an air conditioning unit and electric space heaters.

Figure 4-1: Typical SA-3 site deployment. (ausairpower.com via peters-ada.de)

Figure 4-2: SNR-125M, with UNV and UNK van. (Miroslav Gyurosi)

It is important to say that the potential opponent in most cases is aware of the prepared position and in war these prepared positions are the first to be attacked (**Figure 4-2**).

SNR-125 'Low Blow' Fire Control and Engagement Radar

The main purpose of the S-125 air defence system – engagement of low and medium altitude targets – determined the construction requirements of the radar antenna system and the configuration of the antenna post UNV (**Figure 4-3**).

UV-10 antenna is used to search and illuminate the targets. During target acquisition, pencil radar beams (3 cm wavelength narrow radar beam) scan the space in the sector 1-1.5 degrees by azimuth and 10 degrees by angle vertically. The antenna emits a bundle of probing electromagnetic pulses from the transmitter, and reflected signals from the aerial target are received for processing. The transmitter/receiver switch provides protection for the receiver

Figure 4-3: SNR-125 antennas CAD model. (Authors)

from the powerful signal of the transmitter during its operation. The antenna is controlled from the UNK cabin and can scan by azimuth without restriction and by elevation from -5 to +79 degrees. It is possible to search for targets in almost the entire upper hemisphere.

When conducting autonomous combat operations, automatic aerial target searching mode is provided:

- Radial survey (Krugovoi Obzor) – rotation of the antenna post 360 degrees in 20 seconds
- Small sector search (Malii Sektornii Poisk) – scan sector 5-7degrees by azimuth with change in manual mode, position of antennas in elevation angle
- large sector search (Bolshoi Sektornii Poisk) – scan sector 20 degrees by azimuth with the possibility of adjusting the amplitude of the azimuth change to the small sector search mode.

When working at brigade level (directed by the brigade command and control post), target search is performed in the designated sectors. Depending on the complexity of the aerial situation, tracking is in automatic or manual mode. When the target is detected, UV-10 antenna scanning stops; the mechanical scanner stops, and the antenna is used only to determine the range to the target (the transmission is formed not by a bundle of probing signals but by a continuous series of pulses). UV-11 wide beam receiver antenna with 3 cm wavelength is mounted in angled configuration and receives the signals on two different angles designated as F1 and F2. Illumination of UV-11 receiver antennas in two angled planes with 1 x 10 degrees for missile to lock and be guided into the target.

A UV-12 decimetre wavelength missile command transmitter antenna with a wide beam is used to transmit control commands to the missile (**Figure 4-4**).

The base for the UNV antenna post is the artillery platform KZU-16K. When deployed to the combat position the complete post rests on the hydraulic jacks. The total height of the antenna post in the combat position is around 6.5 metres (**Figure 4-3**, **Figure 4-5**).

For antenna post transportation, trailer 2-PN-6M is used. In transit the complete antenna assembly is folded. The spare parts for both the UNK and UNV are located in a mobile repair shop.

Other Equipment
The transportable launcher 5P71 (SM-78A-1) on earlier versions is a two-beam missile launcher, later modified and modernized as a four-beam missile launcher (PU – Puskovoia Ustanovka) with a variable start angle. It is equipped with a

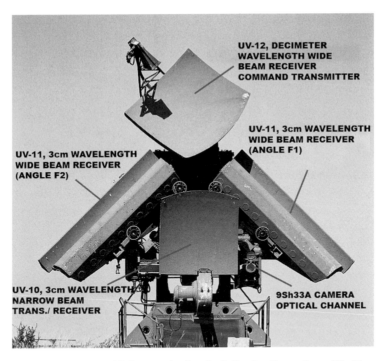

Figure 4-4: SNR-125 antennas with frequencies bands. (Miroslav Gyurosi, modified by author)

Figure 4-5: SNR-125 and 5P71 launcher. (Wikipedia)

synchronous-servo electric drive for positioning by the azimuth and elevation in any given direction. The mass of missiles placed on the launcher could reach 945 kg. When deployed at the starting position with an allowable site slope of 2 degrees, the horizontal alignment of the launcher is made with the help of screw jacks.

5V24 and 5V27 Surface-to-Air Guided Missiles

The 5V24 (V-600P) missile is a two-stage solid fuel guided rocket (**Figure 4-6** top). The first stage of the rocket is a booster with a solid propellant engine, PRD-36 (military designation 5S45), developed in KB-2 of plant N81 under the leadership of II. Kartukov. The PRD-36 is equipped with fourteen single-channel cylindrical gunpowder pens, type NMF-3K, with a diameter of 134 mm and a length of 1,180 mm. The total mass of the engine charge, which received the index 5B84, is 280-281 kg. The maximum operating time for the booster is four seconds. The booster is equipped with an igniter 5B94. The nozzle of the starting engine is equipped with a 'pear', which enables regulating the critical section depending on the ambient temperature. Each console of the rectangular fin stabilizer is fixed with a hinge on the front frame of the tail section. During ground operation, the longer side of the stabilizer adjoins the cylindrical surface of the starting motor housing.

During blast off the screed which secures the stabilizer arms is cut with a special knife under the action of inertial forces and the fins turn more than 90 degrees, joining the outer surface of the tail section of the booster in the form of a cone. The slowdown of the stabilizer's console before contact with the surface of the tail section is provided by the use of a brake piston device, as well as a

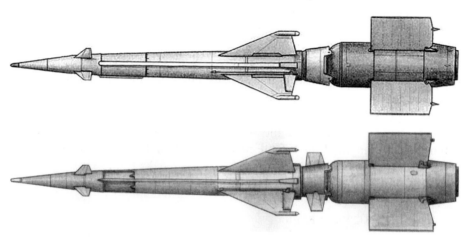

Figure 4-6: 5V24 missile. (top) and 5V27 (bottom). (SAM simulator)

collapsible pin fixed to the stabilizer console. The extreme rear flight position of the consoles provided a high degree of static stability of the spent launch vehicle after separation from the marching stage, which led to an undesirable expansion of the danger zone of the fall of the starting stage. In subsequent versions of the missile, measures were taken to eliminate this shortcoming.

The 5V24 surface-to-air missile was adopted for service in 1962. It was designed primarily to engage different air targets, mainly strategic and tactical aircraft, used in a wide range of operational environments. It was the first Soviet missile to be equipped with only solid-propellant rocket motors. This missile incorporates a range of unique design and technological solutions, such as stabilizing fins which unfold after the missile is fired (the stabilizing fins are fitted on the booster) and the spring mechanisms of steering devices providing for the required efficiency of aerodynamic control surfaces at a wide range of altitudes and speeds.

In the 1960s and 1970s a few derivatives of the 5V24 SAM were developed, including the 5V27, 5V270, etc, which were much more effective than the basic version. The 5V24 and 5V27 SAMs are two-stage rockets featuring canard configuration. The missile is fired from an inclined position. Its launcher is aimed in azimuth and elevation. In flight, the missile is controlled and guided towards the target via radio commands sent by a ground-based (shipborne) guidance station. The warhead is activated at a certain distance from the target by a command generated by the electronic fuse or sent by the ground-based guidance station. The first stage of the 5V24 SAM is essentially a solid-fuel booster fitted with four stabilizing fins which unfold after the missile is launched, and two braking surfaces (fitted to later models) designed to shorten the booster flight path after separation. The sustainer stages of the 5V24 and 5V27 SAMs consist of compartments containing the electronic fuse, control surface actuators, an HE fragmentation warhead, airborne equipment, a solid-propellant rocket motor and the control command receivers (**Figure 4-6** bottom, **Figure 4-7**).

The SAM's flight control system elements include four aerodynamic control surfaces located in the tail section of the sustainers and the ailerons fitted to the sustainers' wings. The ailerons are used in the launch phase.

The response time of the missile self-destruction device is set to 26 seconds after the launch, after which the missile is destroyed if it has not already detonated. The length of the V-600P missile is 6.09 m, the starting mass 912 kg. The diameter of the hull of the flight stage is 0.375 m, the diameter of the booster is 0.55 m.

The S-125 surveillance radar stations P-12 (P-12NM) or P-15 Trail (Flat Face according to NATO codification) are equipped with autonomous diesel power stations for the installation of antennas on the automobile chassis. To increase the range of target detection at low altitudes the P-15 station is equipped with an

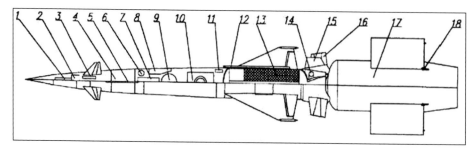

Figure 4-7: 5V27 (V60P) Goa Missile Cutaway. (Vestnik-PVO/Aviatsiya i Kosmonavtika)

1. Proximity fuse transmit antenna
2. 5E18 radio proximity fuse
3. Canard controls
4. 5P18 72 kg fragmentation warhead (4,500 fragments)
5. Receive antenna
6. Transducer
7. Splitter/converter box
8. Battery
9. 5A22/APS-600 autopilot
10. 5U42/UR-20A Command link control module
11. Aileron control
12. Aileron drive
13. Sustainer powerplant with 151 kg of 301-K solid propellant providing twenty seconds of burn
14. Compressed air tank
15. Initiator for sustainer powerplant
16. Adaptor destabilizing fins
17. 5S45/PRD-36 boost powerplant with 2-4 seconds burn duration/14 tubes of NMF-3K propellant
18. Stabilizing pivot

additional antenna on the mast device 'Unzha' (P-15 with antenna placement on the mast device (Squat Eye)) (**Figure 4-8**).

The complex uses ground-based radio friend/foe checker 'Silicon-2M' and 'Password-1'. Usually in combat positions at the prepared locations, the hardware vans and diesel-electric power stations of the surveillance radar stations are located in concrete engineered structures.

For the purposes of training the operators, as well as the guidance officers, combat simulator 'Akkord' is assigned to the S-75 and S-125 systems, typically one set for four battalions. The combat simulator is placed in the semi-trailer OdAZ-828.

Figure 4-8: P-15 radar. (Wikipedia)

In the course of serial production, the equipment has been constantly improved, the production process developed, new materials introduced, and technologies developed to ensure the reliability of the components.

During the tests of the S-125 system, a number of shortcomings of the 5E15 radio detonator appeared. In addition, the zone of damage already seemed clearly insufficient for a two-stage SAM with a mass of almost a ton. This was evident in comparison with the new missile system developed for the army, 3M9 'Kub', which development started in 1958.

ZRK S-125M 'Neva-M'

On 31 March 1961, before the full adoption of the S-125 system into the service, a decision had been made by the military-industrial complex to modernize the missile and hardware of the SNR-125 (**Figure 4-9**). It was based on the proposals for the modification of a missile that would increase the range and the upper limit of the target destruction zone, with an average speed increased to 630 m/s. It was suggested that the launcher be thoroughly altered, ensuring that four missiles were placed on it. According to one of the versions, the last task was put personally by D.F. Ustinov, soviet defence minister at that time.

The work on the new B-601P (5V27) missile was officially launched in June 1961. The main directions of work were the development of a new radio-detonator 5E18 and a propulsion engine on a fundamentally new blended fuel. The high specific impulse and increased density of this fuel, while maintaining the dimensions of the rocket, had to increase the motor's power characteristics (**Figure 4-6** (bottom), **Figure 4-10**).

During the B-601P factory tests, conducted from August 1962, a total of twenty-eight launches were carried out, including six missiles in simulated combat configuration, with which two MiG-17 targets were shot down. At the end of 1962, joint tests began, the course of which was delayed somewhat due to the unreliability of the motor at the lower temperatures. At lower temperatures the motor was systematically destroyed (one in five at -30° C and five of seventeen at -40° C).

The main difference between the new missile and the previously-created V-600P missile was the new more advanced propulsion motor, new 5E18 fuse,

S-125M Battery Components			
System	Qty	Function/Composition	Vehicle
SNR-125 UNV Cabin / Low Blow	1	Radar head van	Towed
SNR-125 UNK Cabin	1	Radar operator van (OdAZ-828 semitrailer)	Towed
5E96 Cabin	1	Power generator van	Towed
5P71 / 5P73	4	Launcher, Two/Four Rail	Towed
PR-14A/AM	8	Transporter/transloader	ZIL-131
AKKORD	1	Training Emulator (OdAZ-828 semitrailer)	Towed
P-15M Squat Eye	1	UHF-Band Low Level Acquisition Radar	Ural-375
P-15/19 Flat Face	1	UHF-Band Acquisition Radar	Ural-375
1L22 Parol 4 / 75E6 Parol 3	1	IFF Interrogator	KrAZ-255
PRV-10 Konus / PRV-11 Vershina / Side Net	1	Heightfinding Radars	Towed
5F20/5Ya61/62/63 Tsikloida	1	Radio relay van (OdAZ-828 semitrailer)	Towed

S-125 Optional Battery Components			
RD-75 Amazonka	1	Rangefinding radar	Towed
P-12M/P-18 Spoon Rest	1	VHF-Band Acquisition Radar	Ural-375
AT-S	N	Tow Tractor	-

Figure 4-9: S-125 battery components. (ausairpower.com)

Affix
stamp
here

Pen and Sword Books
c/o Casemate Publishers
1950 Lawrence Road
Havertown, PA 19083

HISTORY BROUGHT BACK TO LIFE WITH PEN & SWORD BOOKS

Pen & Sword Books have over 6000 books currently available and we cover all periods of history on land, sea and air.

If you would like to hear more about our other titles sign up now and receive 30% off your next purchase. www.penandswordbooks.com/newsletter/

By signing up to our free discounts, reviews on new releases, previews of forthcoming titles and upcoming competitions, so you will never miss out!

Not online? Return this card to us with your contact details and we will put you on our catalog mailing list.

Mr/Mrs/Ms ....

Address...

Zip Code.......................... Email address...

Website: www.penandswordbooks.com
Email: Uspen-and-sword@casematepublishers.com · Telephone: (610) 853-9131
Stay in touch: facebook.com/penandswordbooks or follow us on Twitter @penswordbooks

We hope you enjoyed this book!

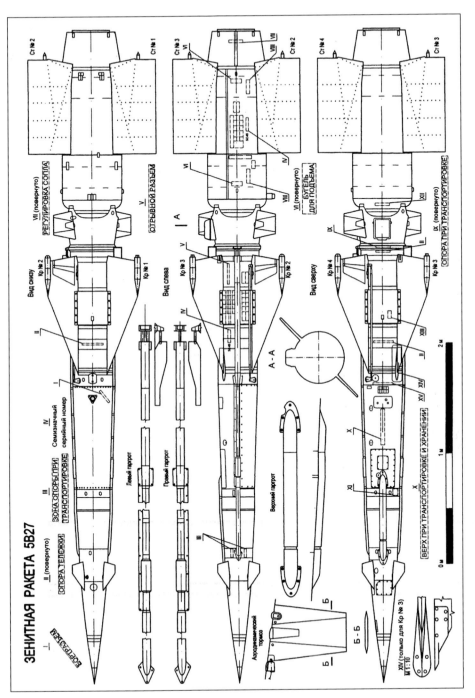

Figure 4-10: 5V27 missile. (S-125M1 manual)

new 5B79 safety-action mechanism and a 72 kg fragmentation 5B18 warhead with 4,500 fragments with a mass of 4.72-4.79 g.

Externally, the V-601P missiles were easily identified by two aerodynamic surfaces that were installed on the transitional connecting compartment behind the upper right and lower left consoles to reduce the range of the launch vehicle after its separation. After separating the stages, these surfaces unfolded, which led to an intensive rotation and braking of the accelerator with the destruction of all or several stabilizer arms and, as a result, to its erratic fall at a relatively small distance from the launcher.

The operating time of the booster is 2 to 4 seconds and the propulsion motor up to 20 seconds. To expand the zone of damage, the missile was also guided on the passive part of the trajectory, while the self-destruct time was increased to 49 seconds. It could manoeuvre with overloads of up to 6 g (six times the force of gravity). It was designed to operate at between -40 and +50 degrees C. Simultaneous with the adoption of the V-601P missile, the government requested enhancement of the combat capabilities of the complex, in particular to engage aerial targets flying at speeds of 2,500 km/h and altitudes of 18 km, and to increase protection against electronic countermeasures. The necessary measures were carried out quite quickly, but officially it took three years.

The V-601 missiles of all modifications were manufactured by Kirov plant N32. It was supposed to organize the production of missiles at the Leningrad plant N272, but this enterprise was switched to missile production for the S-200 complex.

The transportable four-beam launcher 5P73 (designated SM-106 by TsKB-34) (**Figure 4-11**) was designed under the supervision of the chief designer B.S. Korobov. Without gas reflectors and running gear, it was transported by a YAAZ-214 truck. To prevent the missile from touching the ground or ground-based objects while 'settling' in the initial uncontrolled stage of the flight when shooting at low altitude targets, the minimum angle of the missile's collision prevention was set at 9 degrees. To prevent erosion of soil during rocket launches around the platform, a special rubber-metal multi-section circular coating was applied.

The charging of the launcher with its missiles was carried out in succession by two TZMs missile transporters which approached the right or left pair of beams (**Figure 4-12**). It could load the launcher simultaneously with the V-600P and V-601P missiles of early modifications. To provide the guides to the PR-14M (PR-14MA) transport vehicles, access routes were installed to the fixed position of the TZM relative to the left or right pair of PU beams (**Figure 4-13**).

The launcher was produced by several plants, including the plant in Yurga (since 1977). When the battalion was located at the prepared position, the necessary electric power was provided from a mobile transformer substation (TPS) mounted on the body of an axial trailer.

Figure 4-11: 5V27 missile on 5P73 launcher. (Author's archive)

Figure 4-12: 5PR-14A/AM transporter. (S-125M1 manual)

For target designation during combat operations without ACS, the S-125 battalion was assigned surveillance radar: a metre range type P-12 (P-18) and a decimetre range P-15. The surveillance radar stations P-12NM (P-18) (**Figure 4-14**) and P-15 were equipped with their own autonomous power supplies AD-10-T/230MAB-8-O/230M and AB-4-T/230M. To improve the detection capabilities of low-altitude targets, SRC P-15 was attached to a jack-up antenna-mast device 'Unzha' to lift the antenna to a height of up to 50 metres. Determination of 'friend-or-foe' was made by the ground-based radar interrogators (NRZ) 'Password-3P' (75E6)) or 'Password-4P' (1L22).

The S-125M complex was adopted on 27 September 1970.

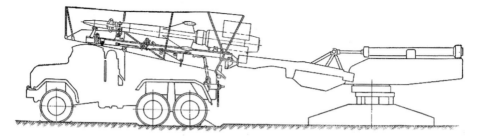

Figure 4-13: PR-14A/AM transporter and 5P73 launcher. (S-125M1 manual)

Figure 4-14: Modernized P-18 surveillance radar. (Wikipedia)

CHAPTER FOUR

Missile System S-125M1 (S-125M1A) 'Neva-M1'

In the early 1970s the S-125M complex was upgraded by improving the electronic countermeasure equipment and missile control channels. With the introduction of television-optical sighting equipment (TOV) and the Karat-2 target (9S33A) it was possible, under good visual conditions, to visually observe the target and engage it without the engagement of the fire control radar. The target electronic countermeasures under visual observation conditions were greatly reduced. However, the optical sighting lost its effectiveness in bad weather and cloud, as well as when the television screens were unreadable when pointing in the direction of the sun or at the pulsed light source sent by the attacking aircraft. In addition, the television-optical sight did not provide information about the range to the target, which limited the choice of guidance methods and significantly reduced the efficiency of firing at high-speed targets.

In the second half of 1970s, new equipment was introduced to improve the engaging of targets at low altitude and on the surface. In addition, a new modification of the 5V27D missile with increased flight speed was introduced, which allowed the engagement of targets both in approach and in chase. The length of the missile was increased, its starting mass was increased to 980 kg, and the mass of the booster increased to 407 kg. For the heavier 5V27D it was possible to load only three missiles on the 5P73 launcher when placed on beams.

The S-125M1 SAM with the 5V27D missile was adopted in May 1978. Since the early 1980s and the increased use of anti-radiation missiles, SA-3/S-125 systems of all modifications were upgraded with equipment to 'attract' and 'lure' anti-radar missiles. The new equipment, designated 'Dubler', was installed with one or two remote simulators of the fire control radar emission (imitator) and located beside the battalion firing position. The export version of the SA-3/S-125 Neva was designated the 'Pechora'. It was supplied to many countries and used in a number of armed conflicts and local wars. The system and guidance diagrams are shown in **Figure 4-15** and **Figure 4-16**. The complex in the 'tropical' version was painted with a special termite-repellent coating.

The 'Pechora'

The export version of S-125 'Neva' designated 'Pechora', which according to experts is one of the world's best air defence weapon systems, was delivered to thirty-five countries. S-125 complexes are in service in Algeria, Angola, Afghanistan, Bulgaria, Bosnia, Hungary, Vietnam, Egypt, India, Iran, Iraq, Yemen, DPRK, Cuba, Libya, Mali, Mozambique, Mongolia, Peru, Poland, Syria, Tanzania, Finland, the Czech Republic, Ethiopia, Serbia and almost all CIS countries. In twenty years, approximately 523 complexes were delivered, most of which, after several decades in service, are still operational today.

SHOOTING DOWN THE STEALTH FIGHTER

New technological developments mean that with upgrades the combat effectiveness of the system can be brought up to date at significantly lower cost than the purchase of a new system with comparable characteristics. In recent years, several options for upgrading the complex have been proposed, including the Pechora-M, M1A, and 2A, which have been deployed in several countries.

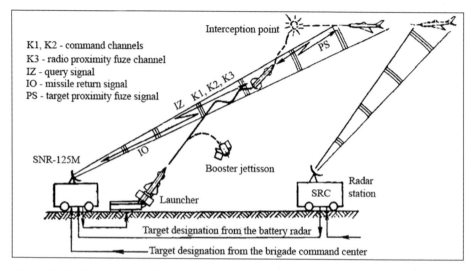

Figure 4-15: S-125 system diagram. (S-125M1 manual, modified by authors)

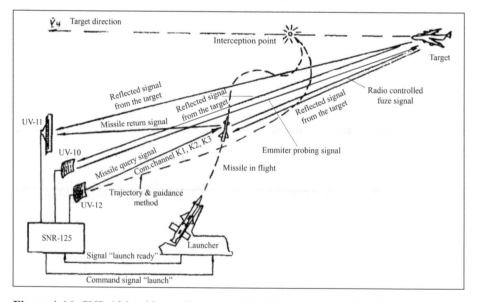

Figure 4-16: SNR-125 guidance diagram. (S-125M1 manual, modified by authors)

Pechora-2A Upgraded Surface-to-Air Missile System

The purpose of the Pechora-2A upgraded surface-to-air missile system is to defend vital administrative, industrial and military installations against air attack weapons with radar cross section (RCS) more than $0.2m^2$ and speed up to 700 m/s. In 1998-2001 the Almaz Research and Production Association (R&PA) developed a new modernization package for the Pechora-2A SAM system which is offered to foreign users. The specific objectives of this modernization package includes (**Figure 4-17**):

- extension of system service life by replacing the analogue signal processors, target and missile coordinates measuring devices, guidance control command generator devices, crew training equipment, etc, with up-to-date digital equipment;
- enhancement of tactical and technical characteristics by introducing digital algorithms in information processing and misguidance and control elements;
- improvement of system operation and maintenance procedures.

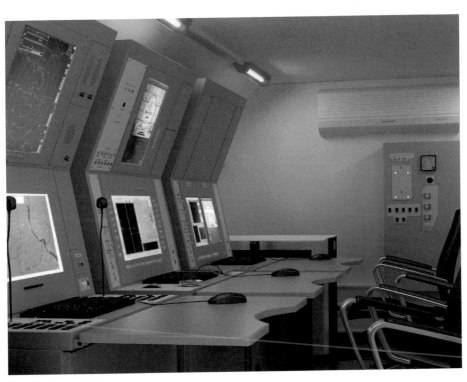

Figure 4-17: Pechora 2M digitalized workstation in fire control centre. (Author's archive)

The Pechora-2A SAM system comprises:

- upgraded missile guidance station SNR-125M-2A;
- upgraded command and control equipment van UNK-M2A;
- antenna station UNV;
- maintenance vehicle PRM;
- missile battery, including up to four launchers 5P7 and eight reload vehicles PR-14AM;
- power generating system;
- maintenance facilities, and
- surface-to-air guide missiles 5V27D.

Surveillance and target designation radars P-12 and P-15 can additionally be attached to the SAM system. The operation of the SAM system is controlled from the equipment van. The air situation data supplied by either of the above radars are displayed on a remote indicator.

After the target has been selected, the station is turned in azimuth towards it and its azimuth and elevation are measured again. Then tracking of the acquired target in azimuth, elevation and altitude is assumed. The operator tracks the target either automatically or manually. A combined tracking mode is also available. If the target tracking channel is affected by passive noise or clutter, a moving target indication (MTI) mode is switched on. In the event of active noise, a coherent pulse accumulation mode is engaged. In addition, a TV channel is used, which enables the operator to track the target in its angular coordinates manually or automatically. The Pechora-2A SAM system has one target channel and two missile channels. Two missiles can attack the target simultaneously. When fired, the missiles are located on their launcher in the inclined position. The launcher is coupled with the missile guidance radar via synchronous power drives. In flight, the missile is controlled and guided towards the target by radio commands coming from the missile guidance radar. The missile's warhead is detonated either by a command generated by an electronic fuse when the distance to the target permits its activation, or by a command generated by the guidance radar when air targets flying below 50 metres are being attacked.

All equipment of the Pechora-2A is carried on trailers and semi-trailers. Power is supplied from mobile diesel-driven generators or from industrial power lines. Maintenance time in the upgraded system is reduced by at least half.

Pechora-2M and ML Upgraded Missile System

Compared with the original version, the upgraded Pechora-M missile system had expanded range, better resistance to jamming and better mobility. Analogue equipment was partially replaced by digital equipment and an automated rocket launching process and an indication of the guaranteed zone of destruction of airborne air defence systems was introduced. Missile launchers were mounted on the chassis of off-road vehicles, such as ZIL-131. Time to combat deployment was about 100 minutes (**Figure 4-20, Figure 4-21, Figure 4-22**).

The SAM system upgrade included a new teleoptical system for target acquisition and automatic tracking in passive mode by day and night via a laser rangefinder, counter-counter-measure devices and a digital moving target indication (MTI) system.

It included automated workstations for the commander, guidance operator and launch operator; a guidance and control computer; information exchange devices; parameter recording devices; a trainer, etc.

Figure 4-20: Venezuelan Pechora 2M. (Wikipedia)

Figure 4-21: Egyptian Pechora launcher. (Egyptian TV)

115

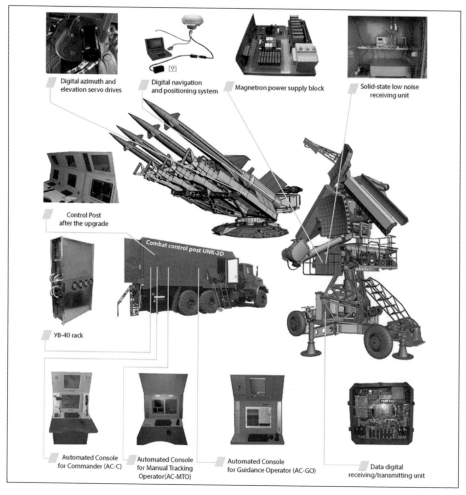

Digital azimuth and elevation servo drives

Digital navigation and positioning system

Magnetron power supply block

Solid-state low noise receiving unit

Control Post after the upgrade

Combat control post UNK-2D

УВ-40 rack

Automated Console for Commander (AC-C)

Automated Console for Manual Tracking Operator(AC-MTO)

Automated Console for Guidance Operator (AC-GO)

Data digital receiving/transmitting unit

Figure 4-22: Ukrainian AAMC S-125 (SA-3 GOA) upgrade to S-125-2D Pechora-2D. (UkrObornEksport)

Modernization of the launcher involved the introduction of a new monitoring system, launch control system, drive control system, information exchange (with equipment van UNK-2) system, a satellite navigation system and an automatic leveling system. The launcher was reloaded with missiles from an upgraded reloading vehicle.

Modernization of surface-to-air missile 5V27D (**Figure 4-18**, **Figure 4-19**) involved upgrades to the first-stage rocket motor, warhead and electronic fuse to increase the slant range of the missile's target engagement envelope to 32 km and to raise target hit probability. The total weight of bomblets was 1.6 times and the number splinters is 3.7 times those of the previous warhead model.

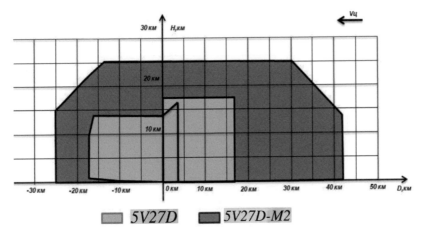

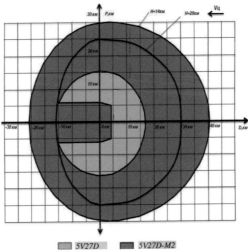

Figure 4-18: 5V27D and 5V27D-M2 envelope comparison (top and right).

Pechora 2T (below) destruction envelope for the modernized system. (ausairpower.com)

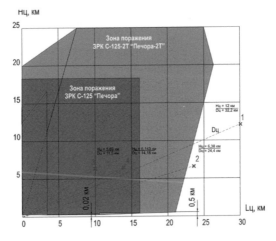

Figure 4-19: 5V27D Launching sequences. (Author's archive)

Chapter Five

Anti-Radiation Missile (ARM) Against the Radar

Since the middle of the twentieth century radars have been destroyed by specialized weapons designated as anti-radiation missiles (ARM) homing in on the electromagnetic radiation of the radars. Over the decades the radars have been modified and modernized. New ones have been constructed and different exploitation techniques have been developed. The technical progress of these devices is a never-ending competition.

The anti-radiation missiles destroy radars which are elements of the opponent's air defence system. This allows for the free operation of friendly aircraft in the enemy's airspace. Aircraft carrying these missiles attempt to fulfill the task without entering the striking distance of the ground elements of the enemy's air defence system (rockets and barrel artillery). Such operations demand proper evaluation of the space striking abilities of the system and to ensure the system is equipped with weapons of the proper strike range needed for destroying the defence system elements. Air defence system elements are attacked while crossing the border of their strike range. Also, the weapons systems protecting important objects within the opponent's territory are eliminated.

While estimating the influence of the anti-radiation missiles' strike range one cannot neglect the inseparable parameter of the missile flight speed. These two parameters determine the time in which the missile reaches the target after being launched from the plane. Anti-radiation missiles can be divided roughly according to their range into short-range (maximum 100 km), mid-range (maximum 200 km) and long-range (over 200 km).

Another important parameter of anti-radiation missiles is the efficiency of target damage done by the warhead exploding; this is significant for the radar's survival on the battlefield. In the 1950s the low accuracy of anti-radiation missiles was compensated by using warheads of high explosive power, large enough for strategic aircraft to carry them. During the 1960s three new weight categories of warheads appeared (approximately 150 kg, 86-90 kg and 66 kg); these are mostly still in use. Accuracy was improved and the distance (altitude) of the fuse from the target was optimized.

SHOOTING DOWN THE STEALTH FIGHTER

At the beginning of the 1990s the British ALARM missile appeared, which could attack a radar within one metre of accuracy (without GPS). The AGM-45 Shrike missile (with a 66 kg warhead) was striking radars within 15 metres of accuracy. Its 'A' version was equipped with high explosives containing 20,000 cubic piercing fragments. The Ch-58USzE missile (with a 150 kg warhead) could hit radars within twenty metres. The target accuracy of the Ch-15P and Ch-58USzE missiles is 5 to 8 metres, of the Ch-31P missile up to 7 metres, and of the AGM-88 A/B HARM missile target accuracy is estimated between 7.3 and 9 metres. For the Ch-58USzE the target hitting probability within 20 metres is 0.8. The AGM-88C HARM warhead is equipped with 12,845 tungsten cubes of 5 mm able to perforate a ½ inch soft metal sheet or a ¼ inch armoured plate from a distance of 6 metres. The German ARMIGER missile has quite a small warhead, only 20 kg, but its target accuracy is less than 1 metre. Probably the accuracy of the American AGM-88E AARGM missile is on a similar level to that of the ARMIGER since both are based on the same construction (AGM-88D HARM) and both represent the same technological advancement level.

To deploy the missile within efficient strike range it must be equipped with a proper guidance system. Missiles produced in the 1950s and 1960s were homed to the electro-magnetic radiation of the radars with the support of the inertial guidance system only. The whole process was controlled by a technologically simple autopilot. In the 1970s the dynamic development of miniature transistor-circuit systems began, and they were employed by the constructors of the anti-radiation missiles homing systems. The following two decades were characterised by the improvement of the existing electronics of the missiles, the aim being the possibility of constructing devices equipped with programmable databases. They allowed for the comparison of the parameters of detected radars and thus the ability to choose those most dangerous or those predefined to a specific combat task.

A conventional anti-radiation missile is homed primarily to the radar's mainlobe emission, but also to the emission of its horizontal sidelobes and backlobes emission – depending on the distance between the radar and the missile. However, in the case of the older radars the primary target is their high horizontal sidelobe and backlobe emissions, which radiate continually. This allows the missile to have uninterrupted tracking of the radar and the passive anti-radiation homing receiver does not become saturated. Modern radars with very low horizontal sidelobe and backlobe emissions are a 'blinking' target for a missile, the 'blinking' being the result of the intervals in receiving the radar mainlobe emission during the turn of its antenna. In such a situation, the onboard systems of missiles without GPS are forced to estimate the radar's position on the basis of an intermittently received emission. When the turn speed of the antenna is low (long intervals in receiving the emission), the guidance system of the missile is supported by its inertial system, especially during the final phase of flight, which often results in a bigger margin of error (a few metres) in detecting the position of the radar than was assumed beforehand. The error is usually increased to such an extent that at the moment of hitting the target the warhead is not set off by a contact fuse but by a proximity fuse. To maintain the attack efficiency, the warhead must be equipped with a much stronger explosive.

In 1973, during the Yom Kippur War, conventional anti-radiation missiles of the 1950s' generation were used. At that time, Egyptian Tu-16 bombers fired thirteen KSR-2 and twelve KSR-11 (KSR-2P) missiles from above the Mediterranean towards the targets located on the coast and inside Israeli territory. Most of the missiles (about twenty) were intercepted and destroyed by either the air force or HAWK surface-to-air missiles. Five of them penetrated the Israeli air defence system and reached their targets. Three radars and one logistic point on the Sinai Peninsula were eliminated.

Missiles of the 1970s' generation were used during the Iran-Iraq war (1980-88) by Iraqi aircraft targeting Ch-28 missiles towards the radars of the Iranian HAWK systems. The effects of these attacks have not been revealed, unlike the results of the Ch-22MP BURJA missiles which were launched from the Iraqi Tu-22K bombers. Despite numerous launchings towards the HAWK radars, only one missile hit its target. The reason was the poor training of the Iraqi bomber crews, the low efficiency of the guiding system (on the missiles and the deck systems of the bombers), as well as difficulties in efficiently detecting the radars' position from a long distance. Therefore, later launchings took place at a distance of 60 km or less and the missiles were carried by the Tu-16 bombers. The targets attacked were near Teheran oil refineries and some other places protected by anti-aircraft systems.

Missiles of the 1980s' generation were used for the first time on 15 April 1986 during the US bombing of Libya (Tripoli and Benghazi), Operation El Dorado Canyon. AGM-88A Harm anti-radiation missiles were homed, very efficiently eliminating the radars of Libyan air defence system rocket launchers SA-2 Guideline (S-75), SA-3 Goa (S-125 Pechora) and SA-5 Gammon (S-200 ANGARA) around the Gulf of Sidra.

In the 1990s the British ALARM missile introduced some changes in the context of fighting radars. ALARM can be used in the same way as conventional missiles, but in addition it is able to detect and destroy radars independently. It climbs to an altitude of 12,000-21,000 metres within the task zone. There its motor is turned off, the parachute opens, and the missile starts diving slowly while its passive anti-radiation homing receiver searches for the target radar. When detected, the parachute detaches itself and the missile, directed by the guidance system, falls towards the radar. The ALARM missile was created before GPS started to be used in such constructions and its operating method has its reasons. The so-called vertical attack of this missile is the result of an assumption made before the ALARM project appeared. Its passive anti-radiation homing receiver independently homes itself towards the radar emission radiating vertically up, i.e. towards the vertical sidelobes. Since most radars had become able to locate the air objects with high accuracy, the emission level of the horizontal sidelobes and backlobes had lowered in comparison to the high emission level of the vertical sidelobes. Regardless of the direction of the mainlobe emission of the radar, the ALARM passive anti-radiation homing receiver is able to continuously track the fluctuating microwave emission leaking upwards from the radar's antenna.

Guiding to the vertical sidelobes (vertical attack at an angle of 90 degrees) has an additional aspect, namely reducing the influence of emission coming from radiation reflected by ground objects, which in case of attack at an angle of 20-40 degrees normally widens the margin of error. Taking advantage of it, the ALARM missile is able to attack the target with high accuracy. The accuracy is 1 metre, so the explosion should be initiated 1 metre from the radar antenna for maximum explosive power. The programmable warhead of this missile can have a data base containing information on the general construction of every type of radar, which shows, among other details, where the antenna is located. This enables the missile to initiate a precise explosion destroying the antenna system or the main electronic systems located in the main blocks of the radar's board (depending on what task has been programmed before). This is of special importance when eliminating radars whose antennas are raised high, for detecting air objects flying at low altitude. The warhead of an anti-radiation missile equipped with a smaller explosive exploding close to the antenna will result in the same destructive level as a warhead with a bigger explosive exploding at a greater distance.

ALARM missiles were used for the first time during the First Gulf War (1990–91). British Tornado aircraft launched 121 missiles in 24 missions aimed only at destroying the Iraqi air defence system and 52 SEAD missions (Suppression of Enemy Air Defences) operating in enemy airspace. In a few cases the launching of the ALARMs of the first experimental series was unsuccessful. To eliminate the Iraqi air defence system, coalition forces used also HARM anti-radiation missiles. During Operation Desert Storm about 2,000 were launched at Iraqi radars. A question might be asked as to whether Iraq really had so many air defence radars. One can conclude that these missiles were often used only as a precaution. Some sources prove that the initiators of such launchings were mainly the pilots of the US Navy (F/A-18 planes), who were using an imprecise warning system – the first version of ALR-67 RWR – while the crews of aircraft designed especially for the SEAD missions carried out well planned target selection, had more time for destroying their targets (it was their main task); and they were better trained and equipped, with much better electronics (**Figure 5-1**, **Figure 5-2**).

During the First Gulf War ALARM missiles, climbing vertically, were a novelty for many allied pilots. Quite often the missiles speeding upwards (aiming at

Figure 5-1: Attacking the SAM site. (Setting the contest: SEAD and joint war fighting)

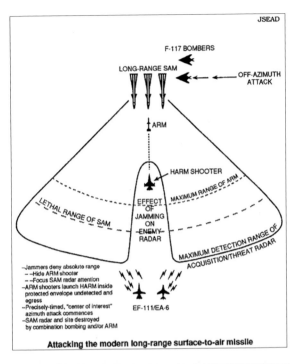

Attacking the modern long-range surface-to-air missile

Figure 5-2: US Navy F/A-18 Hornet during the first Gulf War armed with HARM. (ausairpower.com)

reaching maximum speed and starting the parachute dive) were mistaken for Iraqi air defence system rockets, which would alarm the battle group unnecessarily, with accounts of such events becoming transformed into various anecdotes.

The analysis of the conflict of the 1990s and experiences resulting from it led to the upgrading of some of the missiles by equipping their guidance systems with additional elements.

HARM

One of the most important experiences came from the period of NATO operating over the Balkan Peninsula. During NATO Operation Deliberate Force of 1995, American first-version AGM-88 HARM missiles were used (**Figure 5-2**). The American F-16 aircraft were equipped with the Harm Targeting System (HTS), which was used then for the first time in combat. During 1999, ALARM, AGM-88B HARM and AGM-88C HARM missiles were launched all over Serbia, but they were not able to do serious damage to the extremely mobile Yugoslavian air defence forces. The damage was symbolic and resulted from the too low accuracy of the inertial guiding systems homing the missiles. This provided a strong impulse for the use of GPS in the guidance systems (**Figure 5-2**).

NATO planes launched 743 HARM missiles, six ALARMs and eight ARMATs at the radars of the Yugoslavian air defence forces. About 115-130 ground targets emitting electromagnetic radiation were attacked. Yugoslav air defence limited the time of radar radiation emission to ten seconds, constantly changed the position of anti-aircraft weapons, and used many different methods of field camouflage. The NATO official reports state that the efficiency of the HARM missiles was 3 to 6.6 per cent, depending on the operation's phase. The high efficiency of the Yugoslavian forces was proved by the fact that during the operations the Americans decided to deploy to Italy their experimental Tiger Team from China Lake Weapons Division (USA), an institution testing new weapons. During thirty-six days its pilots tested 400 HARM missiles and worked on developing new tactics. According to the US Navy more targets were then destroyed; however this is not confirmed.

This confirms that NATO used this campaign to test and develop new systems, in effect using Yugoslavia was the laboratory. After the war when one of the authors moved to North America he had a chance to speak with people from different branches and development centres in the USA and several confirmed that during the bombing they were stationed in Italy and performed on site evaluation and testing of their equipment.

HARM can be launch from F/A-18, F-16, Tornado, EA-6B. Attacking aircraft used them on a daily basis. The missile has a range of 150 km but is usually launched much closer to the target. It can fly at over 2,200 km/h, so the crew at the fire control station doesn't have much time to react before they are hit. From

30 km, just outside SAM effective engagement zone, the crew in the fire control station has about 49 seconds to impact. If the airplane is flying at supersonic speed towards the target and within the range of the missile, than the crew will have a maximum of 25 seconds to turn on the target guidance radar, acquire the target, lock on, and launch. Those few seconds were just enough time to turn off the radar before HARM hit it (**Figure 5-3**).

The blast-fragmentation type warhead in HARM is designed to destroy enemy radars and vehicles such as command modules. When the missile carrying the warhead reaches a position close to an enemy missile control radar or other target, a pre-scored or pre-made band of metal on the warhead is detonated and pieces of metal are accelerated with high velocity and strike the target. Approximately 30 per cent of the energy released by the explosive detonation is used to fragment the case and impart kinetic energy to the fragments. The balance of available energy creates a shock front and blast effects. The fragments overtake and pass through the shock wave after a short distance. The rate at which the velocity of the shock front decreases is generally much greater than the decrease in the velocity of the fragments. The radius of effective fragment damage, although target dependent, thus considerably exceeds the radius of effective blast damage in an air burst. The radar, the guidance station and everything on the way is showered with fragments.

The missile consists of four sections: guidance, warhead, control and rocket motor. The AGM-88A missile is powered by a Thikol SR113-TC-1 dual-thrust (boost/sustain) low-smoke solid-fuel rocket motor and has a 66 kg (146 lb) WDU-21/B blast-fragmentation warhead (25,000 steel fragments) in a WAU-7/B warhead section. The warhead is triggered by an FMU-111/B laser proximity

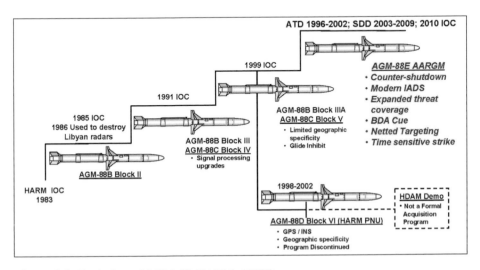

Figure 5-3: Evolution of AGM-88 HARM. (ATK)

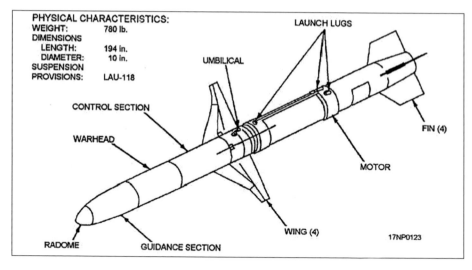

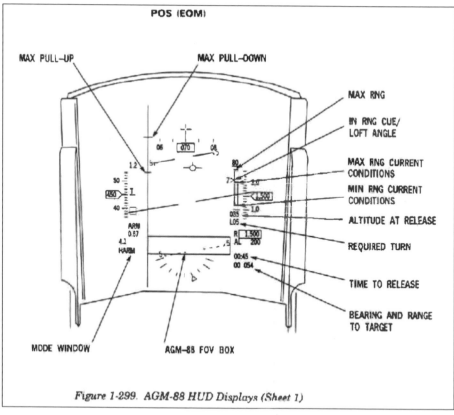

Figure 1-299. AGM-88 HUD Displays (Sheet 1)

Figure 5-3: AGM-8 HARM (top) and HUD (Head-Up) display for AGM-88 firing mode on F-16CJ HARM shooter (bottom). (T.O.GR1F-16CJ-34-1-1)

fuse. The seeker of the WGU-2/B guidance section has to be pre-tuned to likely threats at depot-level maintenance, so every base or ship has to store a selection of differently tuned HARM seeker heads. In flight, the AGM-88 is controlled by the WCU-2/B control section using four movable BSU-59/B mid-body fins and stabilized by fixed BSU-60/B tailfins.

The HARM can be used in three different operational modes, known as Pre-Briefed (PB), Target-of-Opportunity (TOO), and Self-Protect (SP). In PB mode, the long range (up to 150 km) of the AGM-88 is used to launch the missile on a lofted trajectory towards a known threat. When the HARM reaches lock-on range, and detects the radar emission, it can home in on the target. If the target radar is switched off before a lock can be acquired, the missile destroys itself to avoid possible friendly casualties by the now unguided missile. In SP mode, the aircraft's radar warning receiver is used to detect enemy emissions. The CP-1001B/AWG HARM Command Launch Computer (CLC) then decides which target to attack, transmits the data to the missile, and launches the AGM-88. TOO mode means that the seeker of the AGM-88 itself has detected a target, and the missile can be fired manually if the radar emission is identified as a threat. In SP and TOO modes, the AGM-88 can even be fired at targets behind the launching aircraft, although this of course significantly reduces the missile's range. The AGM-88 missile has an inbuilt inertial system, so that whenever it has acquired a lock once, it will continue towards the target even if the emitter is shut down (although the CEP is larger in this case) (**Figure 5-4**).

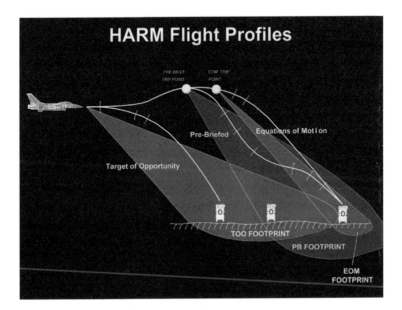

Figure 5-4: AGM-88 HARM flight profiles. (ausairpower.net)

The basic protection from HARM attacks is relatively simple. Most missile units applied tactics of short radar emissions which worked very well. One of the very useful field measures was to use wooden logs to protect the crews in the fire control centre (UNK) and power generation van (**Figure 5-5**, **Figure 5-6**). Lieutenant Colonel Djordje Anicic applied that for the first time in the 3rd missile battalion. High velocity fragments can cause damage to radar antennas, fire control station and cause crew casualties. The combat crews also started to use helmets and ballistic vests. The military developed radar emission imitators (anti-radiation missile decoy) which greatly contributed to protection from HARM's attacks, but they were never available in large enough numbers for all air defence units (**Figure 5-7**).

HARM has a proportional guidance system that homes in on enemy radar emissions through a fixed antenna and seeker head in the missile nose. To confuse HARM's guidance system, reflectors were raised 5-6 m above the ground (as high as possible) to try to activate the proximity fuses in the warhead before impact. Reflectors placed around the firing position can reflect the signals and create a saturated picture which may initiate the explosion. There were some articles in the press and on the internet mentioning the use of ordinary kitchen microwaves to confuse HARM's sensors and that Yugoslavs used them extensively. That was never applied in practice. Theoretically it is possible, but the microwaves need a power supply. Hundreds of metres of power cables

Figure 5-5: Field log protection against HARM. (Author's archive)

Figure 5-6: Fire control and command van field log protection – extensively used against HARM during the war. (Author's archive)

Figure 5-7: Fire control radar imitator – Anti-radiation missile decoy system. A very effective way to 'confuse' the anti-radiation missile guidance system. (mycitymilitary.com)

would have been needed. Air defence units struggled to find enough cables to power the equipment they had.

Large numbers of radar reflectors, log protection and camouflage and false firing control radar emitters were the optimal solution against HARM. And of course, short cycle radar emissions. Another solution is decoys. The aim of using decoys is to lure a HARM to detonate where it does not cause harm to the radar, and, if possible, to the decoys either. The decoy itself is a transmitter that repeats the same wave-form as the protected radar. The passive seeker of the HARM cannot distinguish between the transmissions of the decoys and those of the radar based on modulation, pulse width, carrier frequency etc. A desirable feature of the decoys is that the radar can continue transmitting in order to provide surveillance information. Another feature is that in the case of successful deceiving, the same decoys can be reused against a new HARM.

The effectiveness of decoys depends on their transmission power and location. If the transmission power is set too low compared to the side lobe level of the antenna of the radar, the decoys fail to lure the HARM. Setting the power too high makes the decoys vulnerable to the HARM. Similarly, regarding the locations, decoys that are too far from the flight path of the HARM may not lure it, whereas being too close makes the decoys vulnerable. Although it is better to sacrifice a single decoy instead of the radar, the best outcome is that both survive. In studies, the locations of the decoys are usually assumed to be known or there are few possible locations, but the decoys are not assigned to the locations optimally. As the locations may considerably affect the outcome of survival, there is a need for an approach for determining the best possible locations. In reality, such planning is also affected by the geographical area which limits where the decoys can be placed.

What was more dangerous than HARM missiles was NATO laser-guided bombs or even ordinary gravity bombs.

How this works: a laser is kept pointed at the target and the laser radiation bounces off it and is scattered in all directions. The missile, bomb, etc, is launched or dropped somewhere near the target. When it is close enough for some of the reflected laser energy from the target to reach it, a laser seeker detects which direction this energy is coming from and adjusts the projectile trajectory towards the source. While the projectile is in the general area and the laser is kept aimed at the target, the projectile should be guided accurately to the target. However, this does not work against targets that do not reflect much laser energy, including those coated in special paint which absorbs laser energy. Countermeasures to laser guidance are laser detection systems, smokescreen and anti-laser active protection systems. Some of the missile battalions were hit in this way and the equipment obliterated, and in some cases the people got killed. The attack could be avoided if the laser locked the weapon onto the decoy. That is where camouflage plays a crucial role (**Figure 5-8**, **Figure 5-9**).

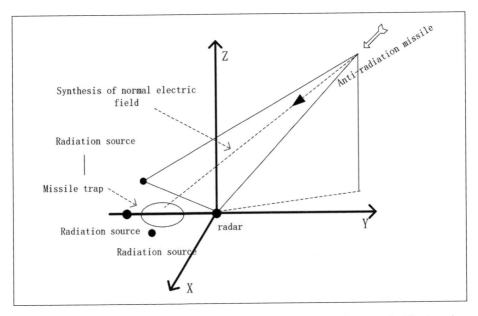

Figure 5-8: Schematic diagram of active decoy system. (Advances in Engineering Research, volume 118)

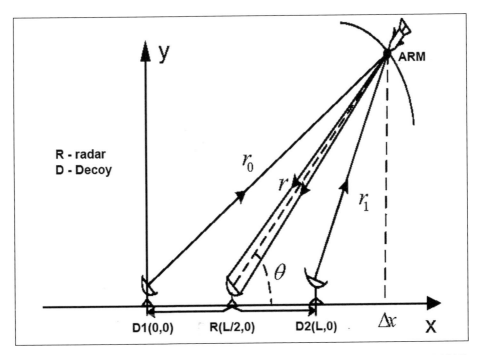

Figure 5-9: Dual frequencies coherent decoys (D1 and D2) jamming ARM. (IEEE 2013)

New Century

The best-known military conflict of the first decade of the twenty-first century, during which anti-radiation missiles were used, was the Second Gulf War of 2003. The elements of the Iraqi air defence system were then destroyed by, among others, HARM missiles – over 400 were launched at all kinds of Iraqi radars. Taking into account the economic situation of Iraq and its low possibilities of recreating its air defence system after the war of 1990-91 and various subsequent air operations (e.g. Desert Fox), the number of launched anti-radiation missiles might seem too large, especially given that they were better developed technologically and also that AGM-88C HARM missiles were readily accessible. At that time, American planes were equipped with an instrument for launching the anti-radiation missiles for self-protection, and probably this function was used often by the crews.

The most recent military conflict (as of the end of 2019) during which anti-radiation missiles were used, was the war in Southern Ossetia of 2008 (Georgia's forces vs. combined forces of Southern Ossetia, Abkhazia and Russia). At that time, Georgian radar forces had only a few ST-68U (36D6-M) radars of Soviet production which were quite difficult to manoeuvre. In a short time, the Russian air force managed to eliminate all the Georgian radars.

All the above-mentioned experiences triggered further development. The first decade of the twenty-first century was a period of intensified development of the guidance systems homing the anti-radiation missiles towards the radars. The following systems became equipped with GPS: American AGM-88D HARM, AGM-88E AARGM, German ARMIGER, and Israeli STAR-1 missiles. ARMIGER was also equipped with an infrared sensor, providing a picture processed by a special system. Probably this was caused by the fact that earlier the German Tornado ECR, equipped with such sensors, was able to lower the electromagnetic emission of the plane's board. But it was the configuration of the AGM-88E AARGM missile that was subject to the greatest modification. This missile does not have an infrared sensor but it is equipped with active millimetre-wave radar with an extremely precise Doppler modulator (active radar seeker) which increased the possibilities of fighting both stationary and mobile targets (e.g. a radar changing position after being turned off). This missile also contains a system for information exchange via radio (used for updating the data on the radar for the missile as a part of targeting and to transfer information about the radar being fought, recorded just before the moment of explosion). The systems built into the AGM-88E AARGM missile allow its own millimetre-wave radar to fully cooperate with the digital passive receiver of electromagnetic waves. This makes the radar operator unable to stop the missile's attack on the radar by turning it off, changing its position, or turning on a decoy. The head of the millimetre-wave radar is meant to track the location of the attacked radar in a way which allows the missile to hit the real radar and not the false source of emission (decoy), even if the radar starts to move.

It is also worth mentioning a slightly different type of anti-radiation missile, namely the American AGM-136 TACIT RAINBOW and Israeli STAR-1. They are in fact cruise missiles, in which the warhead is built into the vehicle and which after being launched travel in front of the air strike force following a pre-programmed flight path. Their task is to destroy the anti-aircraft radars located in the plane's flight path (**Figure 5-10**).

The second decade of the twenty-first century brought only scant promises for the construction of new missiles, regardless of the fact that the scientists of many states must have been working on new technical solutions. In 2012 it was announced that new Russian anti-radiation missiles would have the same characteristics as their existing Western counterparts. The code of the Ch-31PD missile (probably produced in 2003) reveals only that they will exploit satellite guiding systems. Because of the expected export market, the Russians will not use the Russian Glonass satellite system exclusively, and they also will produce a missile using the western GPS system.

In sum, one could single out a few main ways of fighting radars:

- direct attack – a missile launched usually at a middle- or long-distance climbs to a great altitude (e.g. for Ch-32P, 22,000 metres), then accelerates, achieving its maximum speed in the final phase of the flight, denying the radar crew a chance to react.
- shallow dive trajectory attack – the missile is launched from a short distance (usually), and flies at a low altitude.
- delayed attack – the missile may be launched at any height, it reaches its maximum height, then its engine turns off and it starts diving with a parachute, which detaches after detecting the radar; then the missile free falls, homing towards the target.
- manoeuvring attack – a cruise anti-radiation missile built like a plane. It can manoeuvre in a defined area while waiting for a radar to be turned on. Its main task is destroying anti-aircraft radars located in the planes' flight path.

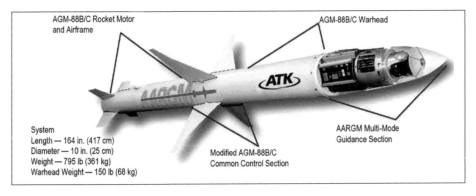

Figure 5-10: AARGM. (ATK)

Chapter Six

SA-3/S-125 Combat Engagements

The most vivid period in the history of anti-aircraft missile systems was during the Vietnam War. To a large extent they determined the nature and outcome of the fighting. In the mid-1960s, SA-3/S-125 complexes were secret technology, so at a time of strained relations with China the Soviet leadership didn't want to use it or deliver to the North Vietnamese in case Chinese experts got their hands on it.

The golden hour of the SA-3/S-125 came in the spring of 1970 when a large group of missileers and pilots were sent by Russia to Egypt for Operation Caucasus to provide air defence against Israeli aviation during the so-called 'War of Attrition' of 1968-70. The fighting was conducted mainly in the zone of the Suez Canal, the east bank of which the Israelis fortified after winning the Six-Day War of 1967.

Early in February 1970, American and Israeli intelligence detected large new Soviet air and sea shipments of equipment to Egypt, but the first really disquieting news was not received until 25 February when in a secret briefing in the White House Israeli diplomats were told that a large number of Soviet aircraft and cargo ships carrying SAM-3s batteries, radars and Soviet military crews had begun to arrive in Egypt. A complete air defence system, including SAM-3s missiles and some eighty fighters (MiG-21 and MiG-23) were to be deployed. The delivery was masquerading as agricultural equipment.

The SA-3/S-125 battalions with Soviet personnel were to strengthen Egyptian air defence forces equipped with the older SA-2/S-75 air defence system. The main advantage of the Soviet missile system, apart from the higher level of proficiency of its crews, was that the SA-3/S-125 complex operated on a different frequency range than the already well-known SA-2/S-75. Therefore, at first, Israeli aircraft were not equipped to counter it.

Because of the flat nature of the terrain, Israeli pilots, as a rule, operated at extremely low altitudes inaccessible to the SA-2/S-75, performing a slide run and diving into the 'funnel' of the non-shooting zone above the SAM.

CHAPTER SIX

War of Attrition and Yom Kippur War

The Soviet short-range anti-aircraft systems provided more protection to the SAMs. In particular, for self-defence of the SAM positions, each battalion was assigned three or four self-propelled anti-aircraft ZSU-23-4 'Shilka' vehicles and SA-7/Strela-2 portable shoulder-launched anti-aircraft missile systems. Later in Egypt, 'Shilka' was located 200-300 metres from the SAM, and the Strela-2 operators were put forward about 5-7 km in the probable direction of enemy aircraft. SA-7/Strela 2 early versions could engage enemy aircraft only from the back, meaning that the aircraft would fly over the shoulder-launched system and then approach the SAM positions. Visual observers were put on the perimeters. The connection between all the posts and the battalion command post was carried out by wired phone lines. DShK 12.7 mm heavy machine guns were also used for site defence.

The new air defence system from the Soviet Union needed special installations which had to be constructed under continuous pressure from enemy air raids, day and night. The Egyptians began large-scale construction works along their second defence line, some 15 to 30 kilometres west of the Canal. From the beginning of March, the Israelis concentrated all the power of their air force on preventing the Egyptians from preparing these positions. Egyptian engineers prepared the positions, building reinforced concrete structures covered with sand 4 to 5 metres thick, providing reliable protection against bombs up to 500 kg. The missile launchers were protected with embankments. The tactic was to create the primary position, a few reserve positions, and some decoy positions as well.

The operation exacted tremendous cost in lives, both military and civilian, and was accomplished under the worst imaginable conditions. Setting up the installations for the air defences became a national symbol, a test of will and self-sacrifice. The enormous engineering works were completed in forty days.

The first SA-3/S-125 engagement was bloody. On the night of 14/15 March 1970, a Soviet missile crew made its 'debut' by shooting down an Egyptian Il-28 which entered the zone of destruction of the SA-3/S-125 air defence system at an altitude of 200 metres. The 'Friend-or-Foe' transmitter on the Il-38 was out so the missile crew had no chance to check the origins of the plane. Alongside the Soviet officers at the guiding station there were also Egyptian officers who were there as a liaison. They assured the Soviet missile crew that there was no friendly aircraft in the zone of fire. The combat crew engaged the target and launched the two missiles that struck the plane.

Three days later a second incident happened when one of the shoulder-launched Strela-2 operators fired upon an Egyptian airplane, this time an Antonov An-24. Fortunately the passenger plane managed to land safely despite missing an engine. The incident was first reported as an 'inglorious end of the Israeli aggressor', but it was obvious that coordination between the Soviet crews and the Egyptian liaison was not working properly.

In a few weeks came an engagement with the real enemy. At first they were unsuccessful. Israeli pilots were briefed on the main location of the missile batteries and they tried to bypass the zones of destruction of the SAMs deployed in their defensive structures. Israeli pilots fired on enemy aircraft on the far edge of the launch zone, and then turned around and escaped.

It was clearly necessary to correct and adjust the SAM tactics. The missile system complexes were withdrawn from the permanent areas well known to the Israeli pilots, to 'ambush' positions on unprepared locations which were hard to detect. Because of the desert terrain however, it was just a matter of time until Israeli reconnaissance airplanes pinpointed the new locations. Missile launches were carried out at target ranges up to 15 km – not from the furthest range, so that the target did not have time to counter the missile.

As a result, on 30 June 1970, Captain V.P. Malauki's battalion managed to bring down the first Phantom, and five days later the battalion of S.K. Zaversnitsky shot down the second F-4E.

This was followed by retaliatory attacks by the Israelis and in the course of a fierce battle on 18 July eight men from V.M. Tolokonnikov's battalion were killed. The Israelis lost four Phantoms.

Three more Israeli planes were shot down by the battalion of Kutyntsev on 3 August, and a few days later an agreement was reached to cease hostilities in the Suez Canal zone.

The above is based on the memories of participants in the events published in the 2001 collections 'Then in Egypt' and 'Internationalists'. According to the commander of the Soviet air defence battalion, Lieutenant General A.G. Smirnov, the effectiveness of the SA-3/S-125 air defence system from June to August 1970 is shown by the nine shot down and three damaged enemy aircraft. According to some estimates the SAMs achieved twenty-one victories. The Israelis however confirmed the loss of only five of their F-4E aircraft shot down by the SA-3/S-125 systems. Casualties on the Soviet side were never published, but western estimates are that several battalions were hit with equipment and material losses. The SA-3/S-125 systems were instrumental in forcing Israel to accept a UN ceasefire. (**Figure 6-1**).

Before the Yom Kippur War in October 1973, the Egyptian commander, Field Marshal Ismail Ali, ordered his commanders and staff to study the lessons of past combat experiences, especially the use of air defence against the powerful Israeli Air Force. Ismail Ali recognized that the Israeli Air Force had achieved air superiority. The Israelis were using the F-4 Phantom and the A-4 Skyhawk, provided by the US. These aircraft were equipped with a dazzling array of sophisticated weaponry and electronics which defended them against surface-to-air missiles. They carried television guided bombs and thermal guided rockets. They also had state-of-the-art radar jamming equipment, SAM evasion electronics and electronic counter-measures with which to defeat SAMs. Ismail Ali determined that Egypt would have to establish a sophisticated, modernized air defence umbrella using SAMs and anti-aircraft guns.

Figure 6-1: Egyptian SA-3 on the firing position. (Egyptian War Museum)

The Egyptians installed an interlocking SAM system over the Suez Canal to protect their rear areas and airfields. They learned their lessons well from the 1967 war. They updated their system from the SA-2 to the SA-3, SA-6 and SA-7, all supplied by the Soviet Union. These were state-of-the-art SAM systems in use by the Soviets. Additionally, SAM batteries were moved in echelon from Cairo to the Suez Canal, which would be the line of departure for the Arab assault forces. Slowly moving the batteries forward enabled the Egyptians to build up their umbrella without the Israelis realizing it. By June 1970 there were four echelons of SAM batteries between the Egyptian capital and the Suez Canal.

The Egyptians planned to launch their offensive on a very broad front across the Suez, attempting to deny the Israelis the opportunity of using interior lines and preventing them from concentrating their firepower against a flank. The Egyptian high command ordered their troops to attack on a 170-kilometre front across the Suez. They planned to send unsupported infantry across the Canal and have them establish a bridgehead with a depth of ten to fifteen kilometres. Once bridges were built across the Suez, armour support would come across, reinforce the infantry, and allow the drive to continue into the Sinai. The Egyptians planned on using forward deployed air defence assets to protect exposed infantry from Israeli air attacks.

Massed formations of Egyptian armour and infantry, backed by artillery and air strikes, assaulted across the Suez Canal in the afternoon of 6 October. Simultaneously, Syrian forces – later supported by Iraqi and limited Jordanian detachments – attacked Israeli positions on the Golan Heights. The Israeli Air Force scrambled aircraft to support embattled ground forces; however, Egypt and Syria had received huge shipments of Soviet air defence equipment since the end of the War of Attrition and dense SAM 'umbrellas' shielded Arab forces from Israeli Air Force attacks on both fronts. By 8 October, Arab forces had made consolidated gains in both the Golan and the Sinai.

SHOOTING DOWN THE STEALTH FIGHTER

The Israelis' greatest mistake before the 1973 war was that they underestimated the Egyptians. They had been proclaiming to the world for years that the Egyptian army was inefficient, unimaginative, and lacking in the will to fight. The problem began when the Israelis believed their own propaganda. They relied on the Suez Canal to protect them from invasion, as well as a series of fortresses on the Sinai Peninsula thought to be invulnerable. On 6 October 1973 the myth of Israeli invincibility was shattered. The Israeli Air Force flew 446 daytime sorties and 262 night missions. Because of the efficiency of the Egyptian air defence umbrella, all the missions failed to reach their targets. The accuracy and deadly effect of the air defence system devastated the Israeli Air Force.

The first days of the air campaign were therefore traumatic for the Israeli Air Force. In the southern sector, the Israelis lost fourteen strike aircraft in the first three hours of the war alone. The Israelis launched an operation against Egyptian air defences on 7 October, Operation Tagar, but this was compromised by the coincident need to attack Egyptian ground formations. Moreover, only the first phase of Tagar, focused on the suppression of Egyptian airfields and some AAA sites, could be completed before the air force was diverted to support operations in the north. Egyptian SAM sites were therefore left untouched. For many senior Israeli Air Force officers the incomplete execution of Tagar was the most critical mistake of the war.

Early failure was equally stark in the northern sector. One hundred and twenty-nine sorties were flown against ground targets in the first thirty hours of fighting and Israeli aircraft losses were high. The potency of Syrian SAM defences in these early hours of the war was evident in the fate of a close air support mission attempted at dawn on 7 October. An entire four-ship of A-4 Skyhawks called in by infantry commander Lieutenant Colonel Oded Erez was shot down by Syrian missiles. A second flight of Skyhawks lost two of its number to further missiles as appalled Israeli ground troops watched. Given such losses, Erez quietly 'declined to call for any more air support'. The Israeli Air Force attempted to prosecute a preplanned operation against the northern Syrian defences later on 7 October, Operation Dugman. As in the south, the operation was a failure. The Israelis lacked updated positions for mobile SA-6 systems, and electronic warfare helicopters had been transferred to the Egyptian sector and could not be repositioned in time. Desperate calls for close air support by ground forces engaged on the Golan Heights further compromised Israeli Air Force efforts to focus on the counter-SAM mission. As a result, the Dugman attacks against Syrian missile sites resulted in the destruction of only a single SAM battery – and the loss of six Phantoms, with another ten heavily damaged. Israeli Air Force confidence was shaken, and the air force remained committed to close air support missions without having achieved control of the air. By the end of 7 October, the Israeli Air Force had lost 14 aircraft in 272 strike sorties in the Golan.

In the south, the Israeli Air Force achieved freedom from ground threats only when Egyptian forces attacked beyond the coverage of their SAM 'umbrella' on 14 October. The results were decisive: the Egyptians lost 260 tanks to Israeli ground and air attack in the largest tank battle since the Battle of Kursk in 1943. This Egyptian reverse was followed by an Israeli armoured raid across the Suez Canal on 16 October during which Israeli forces destroyed a number of SAM positions.

The partial collapse of the Egyptian SAM 'umbrella' allowed the Israeli Air Force to provide effective close air support to Israeli troops in the canal zone. Attrition rates fell. The air force lost only four aircraft in 2,261 strike sorties in the Sinai zone between the canal crossing on 16 October and the end of the war on 24 October.

Syrian air defences were never truly degraded in the northern zone. Echoing the experience in the south, the Israeli Air Force enjoyed freedom of action only when the ground battle moved beyond the range of Syrian SAMs. The Israelis were here assisted by the deployment of the Syrian air defence system well to the east and the reluctance of Syrian commanders to redeploy SA-6 systems to support early gains. Arab formations that manoeuvred beyond the extent of their air defence coverage were decimated by Israeli ground and air forces, just as in the south. However, a combination of the persistent air defence 'shield' and heavily fortified rear positions ultimately created a stalemate in the Golan.

Overall, Israeli Air Force support to ground forces had been compromised by dense Arab air defences, especially in the early part of the war. However, the Israeli Air Force was not totally ineffective and it achieved significant successes in other roles. The Israelis still maintained clear dominance in air-to-air combat.

It was the difficulties experienced by the Israeli Air Force, and especially their struggles against Soviet-supplied Arab air defences, that attracted most analysis in the war's aftermath. The Israeli Air Force lost approximately 100 aircraft in less than three weeks of fighting and struggled to impose itself on the ground battle. As the war ended, it appeared that the future of tactical air power was in doubt. It seemed that the 'missile bent the aircraft's wing'. For the US Air Force, the uncomfortable view was of Soviet missiles bending American and French-supplied wings (**Figure 6-2**).

The Israelis also learned a hard lesson in radio security. During the opening phase of the war, the Israeli air commander broadcast an attack order to his pilots over a radio channel that was monitored by the Egyptians. As a result, the SAM batteries were waiting for the Israelis.

According to the Soviets, Syrian defences shot down 43 Israeli airplanes using SA-3/S-125, losing 5 of its own battalions. According to Israeli estimates, six of their planes were shot down by the Arab SA-3/S-125 air defence system during the October 1973 war (**Figure 6-3**).

Figure 6-2: Wreck of the downed Israeli Mirage III/Nesher. (Egyptian War Museum)

Figure 6-3: Wing of downed Israeli A-4 Skyhawk. (Egyptian War Museum)

CHAPTER SIX

'Small Wars'
The Osirak Raid

After 1973 the SA-3/S-125 complexes were used by both Iraqis and Iranians in the 1980-88 war but there are not many documents available. The use of Air Forces on both sides was primarily on the front line with sporadic attack deep into enemy territory such as the Iranian Air Force's attempt to bomb the Osirak nuclear reactor near Baghdad. To protect the reactor, Iraqis deployed SA-3/S-125 missile battalions and anti-aircraft artillery. The reactor attack was performed by the Israelis because of the fear that Iraqi dictator Saddam Hussein would use nuclear weapons.

The Israeli Air Force launched one of the most daring attacks in the history of air warfare. The attack squadron consisted of eight F-16As, each with two unguided Mark-84 2,000lb delayed-action bombs. A flight of six F-15As was assigned to the operation for fighter support.

On 7 June 1981 at 15:55 the operation was initiated. The Israeli planes left Etzion Airbase, flying unchallenged in Jordanian and Saudi airspace. According to some not officially confirmed stories, to avoid detection the Israeli pilots conversed in Saudi-accented Arabic while in Jordanian airspace and told Jordanian air controllers that they were a Saudi patrol that had gone off course. This is highly unlikely because in these kinds of operations radio silence is paramount. The Israeli planes were so heavily loaded that the external fuel tanks that had been mounted on the planes were exhausted in-flight. The tanks were jettisoned over the Saudi desert.

On route to the target, the Israeli planes crossed the Gulf of Aqaba. Unknowingly, the squadron flew directly over the yacht of King Hussein of Jordan, who was vacationing in the Gulf at the time. Hussein witnessed the planes overfly his yacht and noticed their Israeli markings. Taking into account the location, heading, and armament of the jets, Hussein quickly deduced the Iraqi reactor to be the most probable target. He immediately contacted his government and ordered a warning to be sent to the Iraqis. However, due to a communication failure the message was never received and the Israeli planes entered Iraqi airspace undetected.

On reaching Iraqi airspace the squadron split up, with two of the F-15s forming close escort to the F-16 squadron and the rest dispersing into Iraqi airspace as a diversion and ready back-up. The attack squadron descended to 30 metres over the Iraqi desert, attempting to fly under the radar of the Iraqi defences.

At 18:35, 20 km from the Osirak reactor complex, the F-16 formation climbed to 2,100 m and went into a 35-degree dive at 1,100 km/h, aimed at the reactor complex. At 1,100 metres they began releasing their Mark 84 bombs in pairs at 5-second intervals. At least eight of the sixteen bombs struck the containment dome of the reactor.

The crucial role in attack was the intelligence. Israel meticulously studied the protection around the reactor and found the patterns in the air defence system which was used to plan the attack. It was later revealed that half an hour before the Israeli planes arrived, a group of Iraqi soldiers manning the surveillance radars had left their posts for an afternoon meal, turning off their radars. The Israeli planes were still intercepted by Iraqi defences but managed to evade the remaining anti-aircraft fire. The squadron then climbed to high altitude and started their return to Israel. The attack lasted less than two minutes.

Bekaa Valley

One of the greatest air defence suppression engagements after the Yom Kippur War was the Bekaa valley battle (Operation Mole Cricket 19), fought on 9 June 1982 between Syrian air defence and the Israeli Air Force. In this battle SA-3/S-125 systems were not deployed however. The more modern and mobile KUB (SA-6) system was engaged and this battle cemented the future of air suppression and air defence tactics for the wars to come. This is also the first engagement in which remotely piloted vehicles (RPV) were used, later known as unmanned aerial vehicles or drones.

The IDF (Israeli Defense Forces) attack against nineteen Syrian SA-6 sites was the execution of a highly orchestrated, combined arms plan that involved planning, intelligence, training, surprise, command, control, communications, and countless elements of electronic combat in a three-phased attack.

The plan for the suppression of enemy air defences was designed to take advantage of two Syrian air defence mistakes. The most fundamental mistake was the lack of movement by the missile batteries. The SA-6 was designed as a mobile SAM system, yet the Syrians had had their SA-6 batteries dug in for over a year in the Bekaa clearly visible to Israeli air reconnaissance. The second mistake was the lack of radar emission control by the Syrian SAM operators. The Syrians turned their radars on frequently and often used more radars than required when practising engagements. This allowed the Israelis to fingerprint or identify the exact frequencies used by the Syrians. The fingerprinting allowed for jamming operations and the targeting of anti-radiation missiles. Most of this information was the direct result of the Israeli prewar intelligence effort. For an extended period of time before the Lebanon invasion, Israeli drones overflew the area defended by the Syrian SAMs and collected intelligence for the attack plan. The two workhorses of this effort were the UAVs Mastiff and the Scout. The Mastiffs contained a gyro-stabilized television and a high-resolution panoramic camera which proved extremely effective in photo-reconnaissance. The Scouts were configured for electronic intelligence and picked up the radar emissions which enabled the fingerprinting of the SAM radars. Both RPVs were capable of relaying their information to ground and airborne command posts for immediate analysis. But good intelligence and a good plan must be followed by training.

The Israeli Defense Forces conducted extensive northern border training exercises which were actually rehearsals for the upcoming invasion. These exercises, which took place over thirteen months, included rehearsal sorties against simulated SA-6 sites in the Negev desert. Countless rehearsals eliminated many of the problem areas that planners do not always foresee in coordinating an integrated plan. They also achieved a planned desensitization of the PLO and Syrians. Fearing that a real invasion was underway, the PLO and Syrians reacted to the first five northern border exercises, but to the rest, little or nothing, nor to the real thing.

Israel was able to achieve real surprise in their invasion because of Palestinian 'alert fatigue' or 'cry wolf' syndrome.

A second reason for their surprise was that the PLO assumed they had a real deterrent to invasion. They incorrectly assumed their threatened massive rocket attacks against northern Israeli settlements and the threat of Syrian military reaction would deter.

And finally, with the devastating success of the SA-6 against Israeli aircraft in the 1973 war, Syrians concluded the Israelis would consider an attack against the SAM sites too risky. With the element of surprise in hand, along with a good plan, precise intelligence, and with extensive training completed, Israel now looked to her military commanders to conduct the fight.

They actually invaded on their ninth exercise and found no real resistance.

Israeli commanders proved that an effective command, control, and communications (C3) system is the essential ingredient to a successful combined arms effort, and denial of C3 to the enemy. C3 is the nerve system of a modern military force and the tactical commander is the brain. In the Israeli SEAD effort, the tactical commander received most of his information through an Israeli version of the Boeing 707 and from E-2C aircraft. The 707 served primarily as an electronic support measures (ESM) and electronic countermeasures (ECM) platform. ESM involves the gathering of communication and electronic intelligence. ECM primarily involves the jamming and deception of enemy communications. The E-2C served primarily as an airborne command post. With the facilities aboard these aircraft, the tactical commander was able to process real time intelligence, develop a picture of the tactical situation, coordinate his offensive assets with the proper timing, monitor the attack in progress, and then immediately assess the effectiveness of the attack. Furthermore, the tactical commander was also able to coordinate the jamming and deception that so effectively disrupted Syrian defences. On the afternoon of 9 June 1982, the commanders commenced their attack.

The first phase, deception, involved the stimulation of the Syrian radar systems. The initial drones over the target were probably a combination of

Mastiffs and Scouts. These drones verified the locations of the SAM sites and their radar frequencies, and also served to stimulate the radars into activity. The slow speed of the Mastiffs and Scouts probably did not generate any more than the usual amount of disinterest shown over the previous year. The large force of air-launched Samsons and ground-launched Delilahs, though, did receive their full attention. These decoy drones more closely resemble the speed and appearance of attacking aircraft when viewed on a radar screen. The direction of the attack placed the afternoon sun directly behind the incoming drones, degrading Syrian optical guidance systems on the SAMs. This forced greater reliance on their radar and increased vulnerability to anti-radiation missiles. The Syrians took the bait as expected. They showed poor target discrimination and firing discipline. They launched most of their available SAMs against the incoming drones. When the Boeing 707's ESM sensors confirmed the Syrian radars were fully activated and the SAM batteries were in their first reload cycle, the next phase of the attack was initiated. During this phase, Syrian missiles destroyed a number of drones.

The second phase of the attack integrated many activities into an extremely effective harassment and suppression effort. The 707 now used its ECM capabilities and began to jam Syrian radar frequencies, blinding their missiles. The 707 was augmented with ground-based jammers and with other airborne jammers located on CH-53 helicopters and on the attacking aircraft. Artillery fire, with their aim adjusted by the TV pictures from the Mastiff, now harassed the SAM operators. The sites were shelled with 155 mm howitzer rounds and with Ze'ev missiles carrying terminally guided cluster munitions. Chaff-dispensing rockets further obscured the radar picture for the Syrian radar operators. With radar screens blinded by jamming and chaff, and operators harassed by artillery fire, the Israeli Air Force went to work. F-4s launched their Shrike and Standard anti-radiation missiles which homed in on the radar signals emitted by the SAM radars, destroying the radar antennas. After this attack, the tactical commander was able to determine how many and exactly which SAM sites remained effective. Armed with the information fed to him via RPV television pictures and the ESM assets aboard the 707, he then commenced the final phase of the attack.

The final phase destroyed the remaining pieces of the Syrian SAM sites in the Bekaa valley. The E-2C airborne warning and control aircraft now guided Israeli Air Force F-16s, A-4s, and Kfir C-2s. The E-2C vectored them through the undefended areas for the follow-on attacks against the surviving radar vans and SA-6 missile launchers. Using standoff munitions, cluster bomb units, and general-purpose bombs, the Israeli aircraft simultaneously attacked from multiple directions after a low-level ingress. The Syrians continued to launch missiles from the now radarless sites in a futile effort to defend themselves. Lacking acquisition and target tracking capability without their radars, the missiles were ineffective against the manoeuvring aircraft. The Syrians tried to obscure the

SAM sites with smoke to prevent the use of laser guided weapons by the Israelis, but the fires were started too late to create enough smoke. In fact this tactic only made target acquisition easier. Finally, the Syrian operators turned the remaining radars off to avoid destruction, the ultimate act of futility.

Losing the battle on the ground, the Syrians launched about a hundred MiG-21 and MiG-23 aircraft to repel Israeli aircraft. Selective airborne communications jamming disrupted the airwaves for the MiG-21s and MiG-23s and cut them off from ground control, making them vulnerable to AWACS-directed attacks from the Israeli F-15s and F-16s.

The IAF positioned RPVs over three major airfields in Syria to report when and how many Syrian aircraft were taking off. The data was transmitted to the E-2Cs. The IAF took advantage of the fact that the MiGs had only nose and tail alert radar systems and no side warnings or look-up and look-down systems, by jamming the GCI communications net. E-2Cs guided the Israeli aircraft into positions that enabled them to attack the Syrian aircraft from the side, where the latter would have no warning. Because of the jamming, the Syrians GCI controllers could not direct their pilots towards the incoming Israeli aircraft. Sparrow missiles attacked at speeds of Mach 3.5 at ranges of 22 to 40 km, outside the Syrians' radar range. The Sidewinders' 'head-on' capabilities at close range gave the Israelis a further firepower advantage. At nearly 16:00, with fourteen SAM batteries destroyed and an hour left until dark, the Israelis decided to call off the operation, assuming the optimal result had been achieved.

Angolan Border Wars

During the South African border war with Angola there were numerous engagements of South African air forces attacking Angolan and Cuban positions. The Angolan forces with the help of Soviet instructors developed an extensive anti-aircraft system over time, which included guns and a full range of surface-to-air missiles. The latter included the SA-7, SA-14 and SA-16 shoulder-launched missiles; SA-9 and SA-13 infra-red homing missiles mounted on armoured vehicles; the self-propelled SA-8 medium-range system (the first used outside the major Warsaw Pact forces); and the longer-ranged transportable SA-6 and static SA-3. The weapons were backed up by a comprehensive radar system. All in all the Angolan air defence system in the second half of the 1980s was very similar to that encountered by the allied forces in Iraq in 1991. The SAAF was, however, generally able to continue to operate effectively, bypassing the air defences or conducting air defence suppression strikes. Several aircraft were lost to SAMs. Most of the SAAF's aircraft losses, however, were suffered by helicopters and Impalas (light trainer and attack aircraft) flying low, and most of them were lost to light anti-aircraft guns.

During the fifteen years of bush war between 1979 and 1989, the SAAF lost a total of twenty-two aircraft to enemy action. Also many aircraft were struck by enemy fire but landed safely. Most of these were hit by either SA-3, SA-7 or SA-9, some by small arms. A pilot, Arthur Piercy, suffered a hit by an AA-8 (R-60) missile launched from a MiG-23.

Operation Desert Storm

At the start of the Persian Gulf War, US and allied aircraft rained tons of bombs and missiles on Iraq in an attempt to render its air defence system inoperative.

A USAF F-16 (serial 87-257) was shot down on 19 January 1991. It was struck by an SA-3 just south of Baghdad. The pilot, Major Jeffrey Scott Tice, ejected safely but became a PoW. It was the eighth combat loss and the first daylight raid over Baghdad (**Figure 6-4**).

On the opening night of Desert Storm, on 17 January 1991, a B-52G was damaged by a missile. Different versions of this engagement are told. It could have been a SA-3/S-125 or a 2K12 Kub, while other versions report a MiG-29 allegedly fired a Vympel R-27R missile and damaged the B-52G. The US Air Force disputes these claims, stating the bomber was hit by friendly fire, an AGM-88 HARM that homed on the fire-control radar of the B-52's tail gun; the jet was subsequently renamed 'In HARM's Way'. Shortly after this incident, General George Lee Butler announced that the gunner position on B-52s would be eliminated and the gun turrets permanently deactivated.

Despite the intensive bombing, Saddam Hussein's extensive network against air attack was never really obliterated during the Gulf War. A substantial portion of it survived the pummeling by allied aircraft, which had been intent on shutting the system down. Saddam's main air defence command centres, located deep underground in hardened bunkers, escaped elimination. And numerous above-ground antennas and radar facilities that were struck were repaired from large stocks of spare parts that Iraq had on hand before the war. But the Iraqi system suffered from a reliance on outdated Soviet-era technology, a lack of airborne monitoring equipment and a lack of foreign technical assistance.

Iraq's air defence network was modelled on the Soviet system and built by the French. Centred in Baghdad, the network branched into several regional operations centres, which in turn control tracking centres, aircraft interceptors, surface-to-air missile batteries and anti-aircraft guns. The Iraqi system contained considerable redundancy, with one centre able to pass control to another if damaged, and hundreds of mobile anti-aircraft missile launchers could shift locations at will to set traps for enemy aircraft.

Figure 6-4:
Tail section of
downed USAF
F-16 during
Operation
Desert Storm.
(Wikipedia)

The Iraqis stopped operating their air defences after the first few days of fighting in 1991 to spare what they could, so they emerged with a large part of their system intact. But in 2003 Iraqi air defence was finally obliterated during the US and British invasion.

Syrian Civil War

At approximately 04:25 on 18 February 2019 an Iranian drone from Syria entered Israeli territory from Jordan and was shot down by an Apache helicopter near the northern Israeli city of Beit Shean.

In response, the Israeli Air Force conducted a series of reprisal strikes in Syria. During the raids, Israeli planes faced a massive barrage of Syrian anti-aircraft fire, which reportedly included at least four different types of Russian-made air defence systems, specifically the SA-5, SA-17, SA-6 and SA-3, as determined through the radar emissions.

One Israeli jet was hit either by an SA-3 or an SA-5. At one point, Syria's aerial defence system fired an unusually large number of missiles, more than twenty, at a number of Israeli planes. The lead plane managed to spot the missiles and dive to evade them. The crew that was hit did not.

An F-16 was hit during the raid. Its two pilots bailed out of the plane, which crashed into a field in the Jezreel Valley in northern Israel. One of the airmen was severely injured, the second lightly. In response, the Israeli military conducted another round of strikes, specifically targeting Syrian air defence systems.

Chapter Seven

The First Stealth Programme

The air war over North Vietnam and the Yom Kippur War 1973, in which US and Israeli Air Forces suffered heavy losses inflicted by Soviet-made anti-aircraft missile systems, initiated studies into developing a manned aircraft with a sufficiently low RCS to defeat modern air defence systems. In 1974 the Tactical Technology Office (TTO) at the Defence Advanced Research Projects Agency (DARPA) requested submissions from the leading defence contractors – Northrop, McDonnell Douglas, General Dynamics, Fairchild, and Grumman – under the code name 'Project Harvey' (derived from an old movie featuring an invisible rabbit named Harvey), addressing two considerations:

> What were the signature thresholds that an aircraft would need to achieve to become essentially undetectable at an operationally useful range?
> Did the relevant companies possess the capabilities to design and produce an aircraft with the necessary low signatures?

Fairchild and Grumman declined the invitation to participate. The submissions from McDonnell Douglas and Northrop demonstrated both a grasp of the problem and a degree of technical capability for developing an aircraft with a reduced signature and both companies were awarded contracts for further studies.

Radar experts from the Hughes Aircraft Company were also involved, their role being to identify and verify appropriate RCS thresholds. Bill Elsner was the primary USAF technical expert on the programme, and by the beginning of 1975 McDonnell Douglas had identified likely RCS thresholds that could produce an operational advantage. In the spring, these were confirmed by Hughes and were established by DARPA as goals for the programme. DARPA then challenged the participants to find ways of achieving them.

Lockheed had not been one of the five original companies approached by DARPA, simply because it had not produced a fighter for nearly ten years. While networking his contacts at the Pentagon and Wright-Patterson Air Force

Base, Ed Martin, Lockheed California Company's Director for Science and Engineering, was made aware of the study. He flagged this to Ben Rich (**Figure 7-2**), who at this time was deputy to the Skunk Works legendary president Clarence L. 'Kelly' Johnson (**Figure 7-1**). The two men then briefed Johnson, who in turn obtained a letter from the Central Intelligence Agency granting the Skunk Works permission to discuss with DARPA the low-observable characteristics of their earlier A-12 and D-21 drone programme.

Rich and Martin presented this data to Ken Perko and Dr George Heilmeier, head of DARPA, and formally requested entry into the competition.

Figure 7-2: Clarence 'Kelly' Johnson. (Wikipedia)

Figure 7-1: Ben Rich. (Lockheed Martin, Wikipedia)

However, Heilmeier explained that two $100,000 contracts had already been awarded and there was no more cash available. Drawing upon his negotiating skills, Rich convinced the DARPA boss to allow Lockheed into the competition without a government contract – a move that ultimately paid a handsome dividend. The Skunk Works team was then given access to technical reports already provided to the other participants, and the first step that would culminate in a revolutionary aircraft was taken.

Hopeless Diamond and Have Blue

The F-117 was the first warplane to be specifically designed from the outset for low radar observability. The Lockheed Advanced Development Company (better known as 'Skunk Works') began working on Stealth as far back as the late 1950s. Low radar observability had played a role in the design of the A-12/YF-12/SR-71 series of Mach 3+ aircraft.

During 1975, Skunk Works engineers began working on an aircraft which would have a greatly reduced radar cross section that would make it all-but-invisible to enemy radar but would nevertheless still be able to fly and carry out its combat mission.

We saw in Chapter Two the stealth theory and the influence of the work of Soviet scientist Dr Pyotr Ufimtsev. Denys Overholser (**Figure 7-3**) was an exceptional Skunk Works mathematician and radar specialist. One day in April 1975 he visited Ben Rich in his office and presented him with, as he believed, the 'Rosetta Stone' breakthrough for stealth technology. The material that he showed to Rich would make an attack airplane so difficult to detect that it would be invulnerable against the most advanced radar systems yet invented, and survivable even against the most heavily defended targets in the world.

Overholser had learned of that material deep inside a long, dense technical paper on radar written by Dr Pyotr Ufimtsev nine years earlier. The paper had only recently been translated by the Air Force Foreign Technology Division from the original Russian. In Overholser's

Figure 7-3: Denys Overholser. (Lockheed Martin via statesmanjournal.com)

own words, the paper was so obtuse and impenetrable that only a geek of geeks would have dug through it all and found what he found. As Overholser explained to Rich, Ufimtsev had revisited a century-old set of formulas derived by Scottish physicist James Clerk Maxwell and later refined by the German electro-magnetics expert Arnold Johannes Sommerfeld. These calculations predicted the manner in which a given geometric configuration would reflect electromagnetic radiation. Ufimtsev had taken this early work a step further.

Overholser found in Ufimtsev's book how to accurately calculate radar cross sections across the surface of the wing and at the edge of the wing and put together these two calculations for an accurate total picture. Radar cross section calculations were, as Ben Rich mentioned in his autobiography, a 'branch of medieval alchemy as far as the non-initiated were concerned'. Making big objects appear tiny on a radar screen was probably the most complicated, frustrating, and difficult part of modern warplane designing. A radar beam is an electromagnetic field, and the amount of energy reflected back from the target determines its visibility on radar. For example, the RCS of USAF B-52 was the equivalent of a flying dairy barn when viewed from the side. The F-15 tactical fighter was as big as a two-story house. It was questionable whether the F-15 or the newer B-70 bomber would be able to survive the ever-improving Soviet defensive net.

The F-111 tactical fighter-bomber, using terrain-following radar to fly close to the ground and 'hide' in ground clutter, wouldn't survive either. Operating mostly at night, the plane's radar kept it from hitting mountains, but as discovered above North Vietnam, it also acted like an alarm to North Vietnamese air defences which were able to pick up the F-111 radar emission from a few hundred kilometres away. The Skunk Works desperately needed new answers, and Ufimtsev had provided them with an 'industrial-strength' theory that now made it possible to accurately calculate the lowest possible radar cross section and achieve levels of stealthiness never before imagined.

In his book, Ufimtsev presented mathematical equations which served as a base for how to create computer software to accurately calculate the radar cross section of a given configuration in two dimensions. In his own words, Overholser explained to Rich that they could break down an airplane surface into thousands of flat triangular shapes, add up their individual radar signatures, and get a precise total of the radar cross section (see Chapter Two for more details). Two dimensional flat plates were the maximum that computers of the day could handle. Three-dimensional designs, or rounded shapes, demand enormous numbers of additional calculations. The B-2 bomber or F-22 fighter, with its rounded surfaces, were designed entirely by the new generation of supercomputers, which can compute a billion bits of information in a second,

Overholser's idea was to compute the radar cross section of an airplane by dividing it into a series of flat triangles. Each triangle had three separate points and required individual calculations for each point using Ufimtsev's calculations. The result was called 'faceting' – creating a three-dimensional airplane design out of a collection of flat sheets or panels, similar to cutting a diamond into sharp-edged slices.

The Skunk Works would be the first to try to design an airplane composed entirely of flat, angular surfaces. Overholser estimated that he would need six months to create his software based on Ufimtsev's formula. Rich gave him three.

The Skunk Works RCS-prediction software was called 'Echo 1'. It was a leap ahead, in a time when most engineers used slide rules for calculations.

As tests with the programme proceeded, it became apparent that edge calculations were incorrect due to diffraction. It was necessary to solve the diffraction problem with Ufimtsev's theory. Overholser incorporated elements of Ufimtsev's work to refine the software and he and his old mentor, Bill Schroeder, who had come out of retirement in his 80s to help him after serving as Skunk Works mathematician and radar specialist for many years, delivered the first results in only five weeks.

Echo 1 allowed the team to quickly decide which of the twenty possible designs were optimal, finally settling on the faceted delta-wing design. Many in the division were sceptical, calling it the 'Hopeless Diamond' (**Figure 7-4**) because they thought it would never fly. It was Kelly Johnson who coined the name in a conversation with Ben Rich.

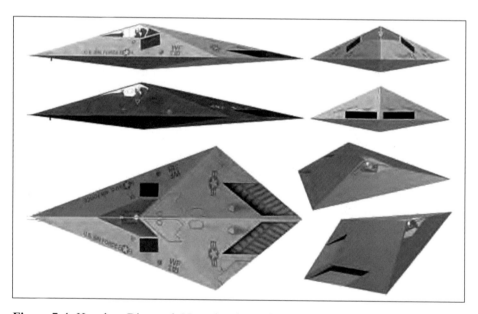

Figure 7-4: Hopeless Diamond. Note the shape that was as if a diamond had been cut to the shape of an aircraft. The technique came to be called 'faceting'. From any angle, the faceted aircraft would present a finite number of edges and flat surfaces to the radar wave; computing the total scattering pattern would still be difficult, but it would be far more attainable than attempting to predict scattering from curved surfaces. (Pinterest)

Faceting involved breaking up the ordinarily smooth surface of the airframe into a series of trapezoidal or triangular flat surfaces arranged in such a way that the vast majority of the radar incident on the aircraft from a source is scattered away from the aircraft at odd angles, leaving very little to be reflected back into the receiver. An additional reduction in radar cross section was to be obtained by covering the entire surface of the aircraft with radar absorbent material (RAM).

One of the disadvantages involved in the use of faceting on aerodynamic surfaces was that it tended to produce an inherently unstable aircraft in all three axes: pitch, roll, and yaw.

In early 1977, Lockheed received a contract from DARPA for the construction of two 60 per cent scale flyable test aircraft under a project named 'Have Blue' (**Figure 7-5**). The name 'Have Blue' seems to have no specific meaning, probably having been chosen at random from an approved list of secret project names.

Placement of these facets is critical to achieving a low radar cross section. Production tooling had to be ten times more precise than the tooling used to build conventional aircraft (**Figure 7-7**).

The entire outer skin of the F-117A is covered by radar absorbing material (RAM). The exact composition of the RAM is classified, but it is believed to

Figure 7-5: Have Blue. The twin rudders were located outboard of the exhausts and angled inwards rather than outwards like in the F-117. The trailing-edge shape was less deeply notched. There was no weapon bay, and the nose probes were absent, because the problem of designing a stealthy system for airspeed measurement had not been solved. The prototypes had a conventional pitot tube, which was retracted when they were tested against radars. (Pinterest)

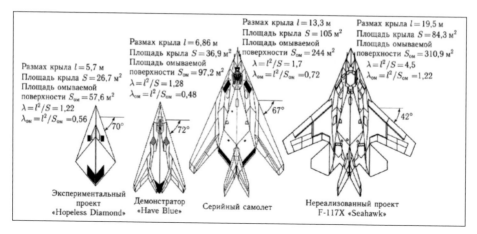

Figure 7-6: Evolution as seen by the Soviet and later Russian sources. (Harakteristiki Radiolokacionih Zametnosti Letalnih Aparatov)

Figure 7-7: Serial F-117A. (USAF)

consist of a matrix of magnetic iron particles held in place by a polymer binder. Originally, RAM came in large flexible sheets and was bonded to a wire mesh which was in turn glued to the airframe of the F-117A. Later when the aircraft entered service, the Air Force built a special facility for the application of the RAM. To provide uniform and accurate application – as well as to prevent people from coming into contact with the highly toxic solvents which make the RAM liquid – the process was completely automated. During the application of the RAM, the F-117A is supported spit-like and slowly turned as the RAM is sprayed on by computer-controlled nozzles. Minor touch-ups are made in the field using a hand-held spray gun.

The engines powering the F-117A are a pair of non-afterburning General Electric F404-GE- F1D2 turbofans, derivatives of the afterburning F404-GE-400 turbofans that power the Mc-Donnell Douglas F/A-18 Hornet. They are housed in broad nacelles attached to the sides of the angular fuselage. The General Electric turbofans are fed by a pair of air intakes, one on each side of the fuselage. Two gratings with rectangular openings cover each intake (**Figure 7-8**). The purpose of these gratings is to prevent radar waves from travelling down the intake ducts and reaching the whirling blades of the turbofans, which would tend to produce large echoes. This works because the spacing between the grids on the grating are smaller than the wavelengths of most radars. The grating is covered with RAM which helps reduce the reflections even further.

The small fraction of incident radar energy which does pass through the grating is absorbed by RAM mounted inside the duct. Unfortunately these gratings also restrict airflow to the engines, so a large blow-in door is fitted atop each engine nacelle to increase airflow during taxiing, take-off, or low-speed flight (**Figure 7-9**). Ice buildup on the intake gratings is a persistent problem which tends to clog the rectangular openings and restricts airflow even further. To clear the ice, the F-117 uses an electrical heating system. A light on either side of the fuselage illuminates the intake covers, enabling the pilot to watch the de-icing operation during night flights.

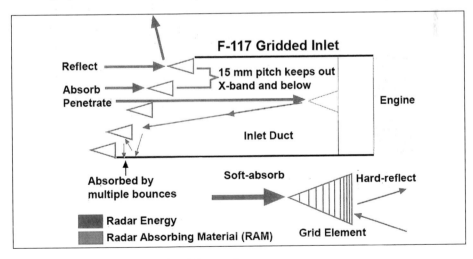

Figure 7-8: F-117 Gridded inlet. (Pinterest)

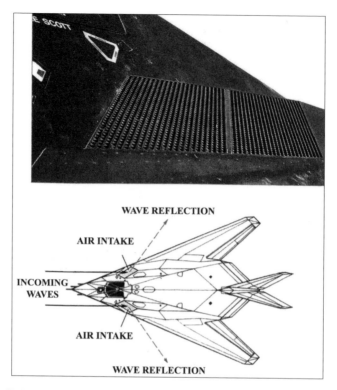

Figure 7-9: F-117 Engine inlet wave reflection. The engine inlets are covered with a RAM grid. The grid is coated with an electrically conductive paint that heats it, keeping it clear of ice. (Harakteristiki Radiolokacionih Zametnosti Letalnih Aparatov)

One of the more unusual aspects of the F-117 is its engine exhaust system. Like the air inlets, the exhaust outlets are mounted on top of the wing chord plane – one on each side of the centreline. The engine exhausts are narrow and wide and are designed to present as low an infrared signature as possible and mask the rear of the engine from radar illumination from the back. The exhaust ducts are round at the rear of the turbofans but are flattened out and become flume-like by the time that they reach the front of the narrow-slotted exhaust outlets at the rear of the fuselage. At the end of each of the narrow-slotted exhaust ducts, there are twelve grated openings, each about six inches square. These grated openings help reduce unwanted radar reflection from the rear as well as providing additional structural strength to the exhaust ducts. The exhaust gratings are shielded from the rear and from the bottom by the F-117's platypus-bill-shaped rear fuselage section.

The extreme rear edge of the aircraft behind the exhaust slot is covered with heat-reflecting tiles. These ceramic tiles help to keep the rear of the aircraft cool since they tend to reflect the infrared radiation emitted from the exhaust, rather than absorbing it as metals tend to do. The bypass air from the engine is also used to help cool down the entire metal structure of the rear of the aircraft.

The exhaust system is complex, incorporating sliding elements and quartz tiles to accommodate heat expansion without changing shape. Although the system works fairly well, Lockheed has reported that the design of this exhaust system was the single most difficult item in the entire F-117 project.

A typical fighter has a head-on RCS of about 5m^2, which is technical language for saying that it seems as large on radar as a perfectly-reflective sphere of the same cross sectional area. However, if critical flat surfaces or whirling turbine blades happen to be exposed to the radar, the RCS can be much larger. Reportedly, the combination of faceting and the application of RAM gives the F-117A an effective radar cross section of somewhere between 0.01 and 0.001 m^2 (**Figure 7-10**). That makes the F-117A appear no larger than a small bird on a radar screen, so beyond about 8-16 miles a typical radar will not be able to detect an F-117A (**Figure 7-12**).

Directional stability and control of the F-117A is provided by a pair of all-flying tails mounted on the aircraft's central spine and oriented in a V arrangement, reminiscent of the tail of the Beechcraft Bonanza. Unlike most V-tails however, they have no pitch-control function. Each vertical tail consists of a fixed stub and

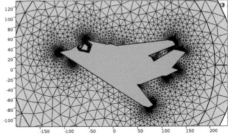

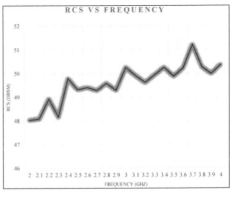

Figure 7-10: F-117 scale model preparing for RCS measurements (left) (Source Locked Marin); Mathematical mesh model (top) and RCS vs frequencies within S frequency range. (Semantic Scholar)

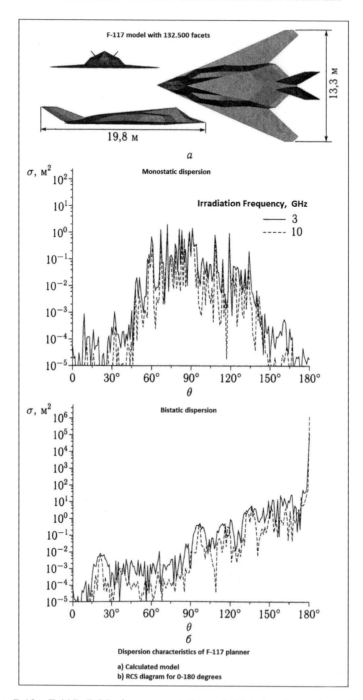

Figure 7-12: F-117 RCS for monostatic and bistatic dispersion. (Harakteristiki Radiolokacionih Zametnosti Letalnih Aparatov)

an all-flying rudder which pivots around a fixed shaft. The hinge line between stub and movable tail is Z-shaped rather than straight in accord with the stealth principle of the avoidance of any straight edges.

Both the fixed stub and the all-flying rudder are faceted to further reduce radar reflectivity. On the Have Blue test aircraft, the vertical tails were mounted further outboard on the wings and canted inwards rather than outwards. The purpose of the inward-canted vertical tails on the Have Blue was to shield the upward-facing 'platypus' exhaust nozzles from infrared detectors above the aircraft (**Figure 7-11**). In practice, however, these tails tended to act as reflectors for infrared radiation, bouncing the rays towards the ground and making the aircraft more visible from below.

Originally, the stealth design philosophy was to have the lowest observability from the bottom and from the front, with the upper hemisphere having less stringent requirements. Consequently, on the F-117A, the tails were moved back further on the fuselage so that they are no longer directly over the exhaust. In addition, the Have Blue tails were in effect mounted on twin booms which were a structurally inefficient arrangement.

The leading-edge wing sweeps on the Have Blue was 72.5 degrees, and the resulting low aspect ratio gave a rather poor payload-range performance. To improve the performance, the wing sweep was reduced to 67.5 degrees on the F-117A. The flying surfaces on the F-117A consist of four elevons on the wing

Figure 7-11: F-117 'platypus' exhaust. (USAF)

trailing edge (2 inboard and 2 outboard) and two all-flying rudders mounted in a V arrangement on the rear fuselage. The elevons and the rudder are all faceted to reduce their radar signature, and the hinge lines between the wings and the elevons are sealed with flexible RAM. The four elevons can deflect upwards or downwards by 60 degrees and the rudders can deflect 30 degrees left or right. The elevons act in the pitch and roll axes, the rudders act in the yaw axis. The angle-of-attack during landing is about 9 degrees. The elevons do not double as flaps, which makes the landing speed of the F-117A rather high.

The Have Blue cockpit canopy windshield has a centre bow reminiscent of that of the F-102/F-106 interceptor. The F-117A replaced this windshield with a centre flat panel since a heads-up display would not work very well with a centre bow blocking the view. This resulted in a change in the shape of the nose to a steep downward-sloping section for good downward visibility with a sharp pyramid-shaped nose cap for aerodynamics and stealth. This change made the F-117 slightly more observable by radar than the Have Blue.

The cockpit of the F-117 is covered by a large and heavy hood-like canopy with separate flat transparencies, one on either side and three in front (**Figure 7-13**). The visibility from the cockpit is rather limited upwards, downwards, and to the rear. The canopy opens to the rear and has serrated edges to limit the radar reflectivity of the joint between canopy and fuselage when the canopy is closed. The five flat transparent panels are specially treated to further reduce the aircraft's RCS. The windshield is coated with a special gold film to prevent the pilot's helmet from being detected by radar. This was found to be a problem during tests. The cockpit is equipped with a Heads-Up Display (HUD).

Since the aircraft cannot use any sort of radar navigation system, the fly-by-wire system relies on information about airspeed and angle-of-attack from four individual static pitot probes of diamond section with pyramid-like tips mounted in the extreme nose. Each of the 4-sided pitot heads have tiny holes on each facet and differential readings from each hole provide air speed and pitch and yaw information to the flight control system. The design of these four sensors, with the requirement that they not produce any unwanted radar reflections, was one of the more difficult engineering problems the Lockheed team had to solve.

The F-117A also differed from the Have Blue in having a weapons bay. Since external hardpoints for bombs or fuel tanks are taboo for a stealth attack aircraft, all stores must be carried internally. The weapons bay is located in the belly on the centreline. It has two wells, each covered by an inward-opening door. The outer edges of the weapons bay doors have serrated edges that are designed to reduce radar reflection from the joint with the fuselage belly.

The weapons bay can carry 5,000 lbs of ordnance (2,500 in each well). It can carry two Mark 61 nuclear weapons, although it has never yet had to.

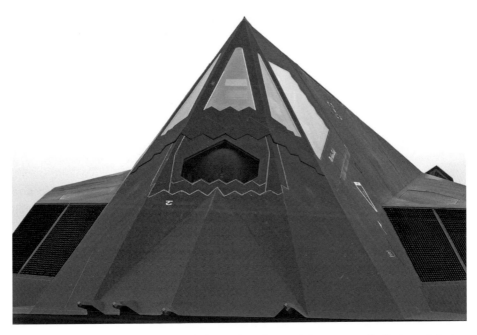

Figure 7-13: The FLIR assembly is located in front of the canopy (ball shaped device in the cavity). The back of the FLIR head is visible through the RAM-mesh screen that covers the seeker head bay. The FLIR head is shown in the stowed position. In flight, it is rotated through 80 degrees so that the infra-red sensors point forward. The edges of the FLIR housing are saw-toothed and faceted. Note that the fasteners are also covered with RAM. There are static pitot tubes at the leading edge of the nose. These pitot tubes are constructed of an electrically conductive plastic developed by Lockheed and are heated to keep them clear of ice. (USAF)

For long-range flights, fuel tanks can be installed in the weapons bays in the place of bombs. The F-117A has no air-to-air capability or at least none that has been announced to the general public. It does not carry internal cannon. The F-117A can in principle launch an infrared homer provided the missile can be dropped from an extendable rack so that its seeker could acquire the target before launch.

The F-117A has no radar, because the transmission of a radar signal would give away the location of the aircraft and hence defeat the whole purpose of stealth. For low-level navigation and weapons-aiming purposes, the F-117 aircraft is provided with forward-looking infrared (FLIR) and downward-looking infra-red (DLIR) systems. Both are built by Texas Instruments.

The FLIR is mounted in a recess just ahead of the cockpit front windshield. It is located in a steerable turret containing a dual-field-of-view sensor. When not in use, the FLIR is rotated 180 degrees to prevent debris from damaging the sensor.

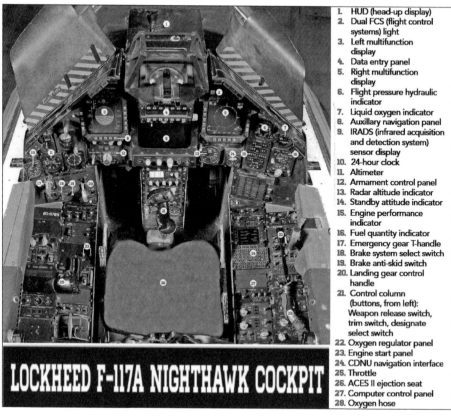

1. HUD (head-up display)
2. Dual FCS (flight control systems) light
3. Left multifunction display
4. Data entry panel
5. Right multifunction display
6. Flight pressure hydraulic indicator
7. Liquid oxygen indicator
8. Auxillary navigation panel
9. IRADS (infrared acquisition and detection system) sensor display
10. 24-hour clock
11. Altimeter
12. Armament control panel
13. Radar altitude indicator
14. Standby attitude indicator
15. Engine performance indicator
16. Fuel quantity indicator
17. Emergency gear T-handle
18. Brake system select switch
19. Brake anti-skid switch
20. Landing gear control handle
21. Control column (buttons, from left): Weapon release switch, trim switch, designate select switch
22. Oxygen regulator panel
23. Engine start panel
24. CDNU navigation interface
25. Throttle
26. ACES II ejection seat
27. Computer control panel
28. Oxygen hose

Figure 7-14: F-117 cockpit. Note there is no radar warning receiver indicator. (Pinterest)

The DLIR sensor system is located in a recess mounted underneath the forward fuselage and to the right of the nose landing gear well. Both the FLIR and the DLIR recesses are covered by a RAM mesh screen to prevent unwanted radar reflections from the active elements. The edges of the recesses are serrated, with fasteners covered with RAM putty. The DLIR is provided with a bore sighted laser for illuminating the target for attack by laser-guided weapons. Together, these systems form the infrared acquisition and designation system (IRADS).

The laser is embedded to the IRADS and is an integral part of the infrared system. The spot size of the laser on the ground is about 30-45 cm and is stabilized in position by the IRADS. A highly-accurate Inertial Navigation System (INS) backs up the sensors. This system uses an electrostatically-suspended gyro as the primary means of guidance. The INS guides the aircraft to the target area and points the FLIR's wide-angle field of view towards the general location of the target.

As the aircraft approaches the target, the pilot monitors the view presented by the FLIR on the heads-up display screen. When the specific target is identified, the pilot switches to the narrow view on the FLIR and locks the screen of the display onto the target. As the target disappears underneath the aircraft, control is handed over to the DLIR which acquires the target and continues to track it. When the pilot decides to attack, he releases a laser-guided Paveway bomb.

Approximately 7-10 seconds before bomb impact, the DLIR's laser is turned on and illuminates the target, and the bomb homes onto the infrared laser light reflected from the target. Video from the FLIR/DLIR displays that have been released to the public by the DoD have shown that the F-117A flying during a clear night can hit a target one metre in size from an altitude of 25,000 feet.

A parachute braking system is provided since the lack of flaps makes the landing speed quite high – 160 knots.

An in-flight refuelling receptacle is added behind the pilot's cockpit. A small light is mounted near it to guide the refuelling boom operator in night-time refuelling operations. Midair refuelling is one of the more difficult aspects of F-117A flight, since it is always done at night and the F-117A pilot's upward vision is blocked by the canopy so he cannot see the boom of the refuelling aircraft.

The landing gear is of the standard tricycle type with single wheels and tires that retract forward. The landing gear doors have serrated edges that help to reduce the radar cross section.

A set of retractable communications antenna are fitted to the upper fuselage just behind the pilot. These are deployed during day flights but are retracted for stealth missions at night.

Detachable radar reflectors can be mounted on the fuselage sides so that local air traffic control can track the aircraft when it is not in stealth mode. Reports of the F-117A being tracked by radar during Operation Desert Storm may have been due to the mounting of these reflectors.

During the production run of the F-117A, the two metallic all-moving tail fins were replaced with ones made of graphite thermoplastic materials. This change resulted from the loss of one fin and rudder from a F-117 in 1987 during a flight test. The aircraft landed safely despite the loss of the fin. The retrofit programme was interrupted by Persian Gulf deployment, so most of the F-117s deployed to Saudi Arabia had the original metal tail fins. The cockpit of the F-117A had been updated and improved in accordance with advances in electronics and display technology.

The original navigation system of the F-117A was the SPN/GEAS inertial navigation system. Later this was replaced by a ring laser gyro and a global positioning system receiver. To improve the pilot's situational awareness, a Honeywell color multi-function display was fitted which had the capability of integrating a Harris digital moving map. Two displays are used to call up digital maps, target photos, or target identification diagrams. A data panel allows the pilot to select from 256 avionics functions. The new cockpit equipment is designed to minimize the chance of pilot disorientation at night time, which was suspected as the primary cause of two accidents involving operational F-117s.

In the early 1990s, auto throttles were added to provide the capability for arrival at a precise predetermined time over a target. This innovation was, however, not available in time for Desert Storm.

The results of the Have Blue testing were sufficiently encouraging that William Perry, who was at that time Under-Secretary of Defense for Research and Engineering in the Carter Administration, urged the Air Force to apply the technology to an operational aircraft.

In November 1978, Lockheed was awarded a contract to begin full-scale development of the project. This was a Special Access (i.e. 'black') programme and it was codenamed 'Senior Trend'. The Senior Trend aircraft came to be defined as single-seat night strike fighters with no radar but with an electro-optic system for navigation and weapons delivery. No air-to-air capability was envisaged.

The first five Senior Trend aircraft built by Lockheed were to be pre-production full-scale development (FSD) aircraft. They had the same general configuration as the Have Blue test aircraft but were much larger and heavier. The engines were a pair of non-afterburning General Electric F404-GE-F1D2 turbofans.

In early June 1981 the first Senior Trend service test aircraft (tail number 780) was delivered to Groom Lake for testing. On 18 June 1981, Lockheed test pilot Harold C. 'Hal' Farley made a successful first flight in number 780. During mid-1981 and early 1982, the other four FSD Senior Trend aircraft joined the programme, tail numbers 781 through 784.

The first production Senior Trend (785) arrived at Groom Lake in April 1982. It differed from the pre-production Senior Trend aircraft in having a pair of enlarged fin/rudder assemblies with three facets rather than two. Aircraft 785 was ready for its first flight on 20 April, with test pilot Robert L. Ridenauer scheduled to make the first flight. Unbeknown to anyone, the fly-by-wire system had been hooked up incorrectly (pitch was yaw and vice versa). On liftoff, Ridenauer's plane immediately went out of control. Instead of the nose pitching up, it went horizontal. The aircraft went inverted and ended up travelling backwards through the air. Riedenauer had no time to eject, and the aircraft flew into the ground. He survived the crash but was severely injured and forced to retire from flying.

The aircraft was damaged beyond repair, but some of its parts could be salvaged. Since it crashed before USAF/TAC acceptance, it was not counted in the production total.

When it came time for the establishment of the first operational unit for the stealth bomber, the Air Force was faced with a problem. Groom Lake was too small to be useful as the base for an operational unit. In addition, there were security concerns because an operational unit based at Groom Lake would involve many more people who could now see things that they should not be seeing. Therefore the USAF decided to build a new secret base for the stealth bomber on the Tonopah Test Range which sits on the north-western corner of the Nellis complex. The facility is not perfect from a security standpoint since it is overlooked by public land and is kilometres from the town of Tonopah itself. However, the security surrounding the Tonopah Test Range was so effective that the new base was not publicly reported until 1985 by which time it had been operating for nearly two years.

The 4450th Tactical Group was secretly established as the initial operator of the stealth fighter. The cover for the 4450th was that it was a Nellis-based outfit flying LTVA-7Ds. Nellis did use these planes for support training. The group received its first production stealth aircraft on 2 September 1982. The 4450th moved to Tonopah in 1983, equipped with a partial squadron of stealth bombers plus a few A-7Ds. The group achieved initial operational capability on 28 October 1985, with fourteen aircraft. To avoid having the 4450th's aircraft seen by curious observers, all flying took place at night. During the day, the aircraft were always kept behind closed doors inside special hangars. The stealth bomber turned out to be quite easy to fly. It was concluded that no two-seat trainer version was required. However, there was a training simulator.

The Air Force considered using the stealth bomber in the invasion of Grenada during Operation Nickel Grass in 1983. However, the action lasted only a couple of days and the combat debut of the stealth was put off. In October 1983 the US government considered using the stealth fighter in a retaliatory attack on Hezbollah terrorist forces based in southern Lebanon in response to the destruction of the Marine barracks in Beirut. In anticipation of action, the 4450th TG at Tonopah was put on alert. Five or seven stealth bombers were armed and had their INS systems aligned for attacks on targets in Lebanon. The plan was for these planes to fly from Tonopah to Myrtle Beach, South Carolina, where they would be put in secure hangars. They would then wait for forty-eight hours for the crews to rest before being given the order to take off for a non-stop flight to Lebanon. However, Defense Secretary Casper Weinberger scrubbed the mission forty-five minutes before the aircraft were to take off for South Carolina.

On 4 April 1986 in Operation El Dorado Canyon the USA attacked Libya in retaliation for state-sponsored terrorism. During the initial planning for the raid, the use of the still-secret stealth fighter in the operation was seriously considered. However, once again, the operation was short and the stealth fighter was not used.

In spite of the extreme security, some bits and pieces of the stealth fighter story did manage to leak to the press. In October 1981 *Aviation Week* reported that an operational 'stealth fighter' was in development. Several people reported catching some fleeting glimpses of a rather odd-looking aircraft flying at night out in the Western Desert. More and more stuff leaked to the media, so that all through the 1980s it was a sort of open secret that the USAF was operating a stealth fighter invisible to conventional radar. However, questions directed to the Pentagon by the press about the stealth fighter were met either with official denials or by a curt 'no comment'. Which only served to whet peoples' curiosity even further.

The designation of the rumoured stealth fighter was assumed by just about everyone to be 'F-19', since that number had not yet been assigned to an aircraft. The novelist Tom Clancy placed the stealth bomber (named 'F-19 Ghostrider' by him) in a key role in his techno thriller novel *Red Storm Rising*, published in 1986. Testors model airplane company marketed a kit which purported to be the true configuration of the stealth fighter. In the meantime, training continued in the Nevada desert.

On 11 July 1986, Major Ross E. Mulhare flew into a mountain near Bakersfield, California, while flying production aircraft number 7 (tail number 792). Major Mulhare seems to have made no attempt to eject and was killed instantly, his aircraft disintegrating on impact. A recovery team was immediately dispatched to the crash site and the entire area was cordoned off. Every identifiable piece of the crashed plane was found and removed from the area to prevent them from falling into the wrong hands. This is standard practice for any US military stealth and/or secret programme.

The doomed aircraft had reportedly carried a flight data recorder, which is unusual for a USAF fighter. Even though not much was found that was any bigger than a beer can, the flight recorder was supposedly recovered intact. To throw scavengers, the media, and the merely curious off the track, the recovery crew took the remains of a crashed F-101A Voodoo that had been at Groom Lake for over twenty years, broke them up, and scattered them throughout the area. The cause of the crash has never been officially revealed, but fatigue and disorientation during night flying has been identified as a probable cause.

On 14 October 1987 while flying production aircraft number 30 (tail number 815), Major Michael C. Stewart crashed in the Nellis range just east of Tonopah. He too apparently made no attempt to eject and was killed instantly. Again the official cause was never revealed, but fatigue and disorientation may have played a role. There was no moon that night, and there were no lights on the Nellis range to help the pilot to distinguish the ground. Reportedly, the mission included certain requirements that were deleted from the final accident report. It is possible that Major Stewart was going supersonic when he crashed, had become disorientated during high-speed manoeuvres, and had simply flown his plane into the ground.

These two accidents, along with a need to better integrate the still-secret stealth fighter into its regular operations, forced the Air Force to consider flying the aircraft during daytime hours. This would force the Air Force to reveal the existence of the aircraft. The announcement was originally scheduled to take place in early 1988, but internal Pentagon pressure forced a ten-month delay.

On 10 November 1988 the long-rumoured existence of the 'stealth bomber' was finally officially confirmed by the Pentagon. A poor-quality photograph was released. The stealth bomber had been kept secret for over ten years, the security and deception being so effective that all descriptions leaked to the media were completely inaccurate.

On the same day, the Air Force confirmed that the official designation of the stealth bomber was F-117A, which surprised just about everyone. The official designation of the stealth fighter had long been assumed to be F-19, since that number had apparently been skipped in the new fighter designation sequence which was introduced in 1962. In addition, it had always been assumed that the designation F-111 had been the last in the old series of fighter designations which been abandoned in 1962 when the Defense Department restarted the whole sequence over again from F-1. This led to rumours and speculation about aircraft designation gaps and secret projects which continue to the present day.

If the stealth bomber was not designated F-19, then just what was F-19? If the F-117A was part of the old F-sequence, then what happened to F-112 through F-116? The answer is not yet known, but the most likely explanation is that the 117 number is NOT in the old F-sequence that ended in 1962 but instead originated from the radio call signs used by the Stealth pilots when they were flying out of Groom Lake and Tonopah – two of the 'black planes' bases. Those are the same airfields that secretly operated Soviet-bloc aircraft such as the MiG-15, 19, 21 and 23 that the US had 'acquired' by various means from such sources as Egypt, Israel, Romania, etc. While in flight, these aircraft were distinguished from each other by 3-digit radio call-signs (generally 11x). After a while, these radio call-signs came to be sort-of unofficial designations for these aircraft. Even later, F-prefixes began to be attached to these designations.

The F-112 to F-116 are often speculated to be Soviet aircraft such as Su-22, MiG-19, MiG-21, MiG-23, or MiG-25. There is even a rumour that there exists a F-116A which is a US-built version of the MiG-25 constructed to see what kind of threat the MiG-25 could be if Russia were to build it using Western techniques. There is also thought to be an F-118, which might be a MiG-29 that was purchased after the fall of the USSR.

Since the stealth bomber was operating in the same general area in Nevada, it came to be known by the radio call sign of '117'. The number '117' became so closely associated with the stealth bomber that when Lockheed printed up the first *Dash One Pilot Manual*, it had 'F-117A' on the cover. Since the Air Force didn't want to pay thousands of dollars to redo all the manuals, the aircraft became the F-117A officially. It may have even been initially designated F-19 in the early stages of the project and might well have continued to be known as the F-19 had this mistake not been made. A similar mistake was made when President Lyndon Johnson announced the existence of the Blackbird. It was supposed to have been designated RS-71, but LBJ announced it as 'SR-71' and no one had the guts to tell him he'd goofed. The designation stuck.

This still leaves the question of the missing F-19. Perhaps it is some other 'black' project yet unrevealed. Perhaps it doesn't exist at all. Shortly after the official revelation of the F-117A, an Air Force spokesman answered questions about the missing F-19 by stating that it had been deliberately skipped to avoid confusion with the Soviet MiG-19.

The 4450th Tactical Group was disbanded in October 1989 and the 37th Tactical Fighter Wing was established in its place. The 37th TFW had three squadrons – the 415th, 416th, and 417th. The 415th and 416th flew production F-117As while the 417th flew the pre-production F-117As.

Although the F-117A has been called Frisbee, Nighthawk, and Wobblin Goblin, there is no official name for it. Pilots often nickname it the Black Jet.

There is an F-117A on display at the National Museum of the USAF at Dayton, Ohio, and another in front of Skunk Works building, Palmdale (**Figure 7-15**).

Figure 7-15: F-117A on public display in front of Skunk Works, Palmdale, CA. (Wikipedia)

Figure 7-16: F-117A wing in Belgrade Aeronautical Museum depot. (Author's archive)

Figure 7-17: F-117A cockpit canopy on public display at Belgrade Aeronautical Museum. (Wikipedia)

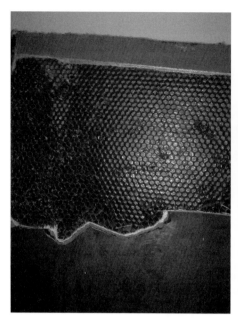 

Figure 7-19 (left): F-117A wing honeycomb structure in one of the Serbian air defence units. (Author's archive)

Figure 7-18: F-117A wing on public display at Belgrade Aeronautical Museum. (Author's archive)

The one at the National Museum was one of the five full-scale development machines. In the interests of security, the RAM covering was replaced by a layer of black paint and the narrow-slotted exhaust ports were faired over to prevent anyone peering inside to see the details of how the exhaust was constructed. Parts of other F-117As are on display at the Belgrade Aeronautical Museum (**Figure 7-16**, **Figure 7-17**, **Figure 7-18**, **Figure 7-19**), and also in Russia and China.

Maintenance Issues

F-117A is a fairly complicated airplane from the maintenance perspective. There are a lot of issues that maintenance crews need to deal with which are different from the classic 'aluminium' airplanes, often called 'aluminium chums' by the stealth pilots. Besides designated maintenance technicians which are common to all other non-stealth airplanes, the F-117A squadron has a group of technicians called MARS or known as 'Martians' by others. That group is in charge to maintain the stealthiness of all F-117A jets in the unit.

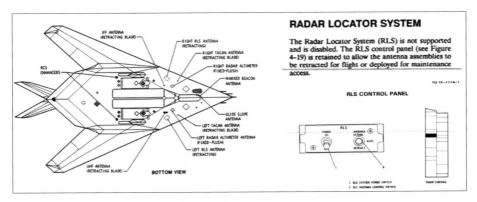

Figure 7-20: F-117A Radar Locator System. See Chapter Eight, heading The Mystery of the Radar Warning Receiver. (USAF Utility Flight Manual TO-1F-117A-1)

Most of the radar-absorbing material (RAM) comes in sections with an adhesive backing similar to masking tape. Each of the sections are joined together by a material the technicians call 'butter', a caulking compound that is applied between the old material and the new section of radar absorbing material. It is greyish and similar to the caulk used to seal the doors and windows. RAM is applied over the entire exterior of the airplane. Even screw heads on access panels along the fuselage and wings get a special coating of butter. The composition of butter and RAM are closely guarded secrets.

Overseas deployment creates additional strains. After a combat mission, a group of technicians inspects every square centimetre of the aircraft to make sure there are no cracks, bubbles or pieces of coating missing. Before any other flight, each defect must be corrected. The coating in some areas has to be constantly removed and replaced. The first combat missions over Yugoslavia created additional strain for the maintenance crews because before that the aircraft operated mostly in the desert areas where the dry air did little damage to the RAM coats.

One of the most enigmatic details of the F-117A is a component called the Radar Locating System (RLS) in the flight manual (**Figure 7-20**), also known as a Radar Warning Receiver (RWR). More information about this is addressed in Chapter Eight under the heading 'The Mystery of the Radar Warning Receiver'.

Just Cause

On 19 December 1989, thirteen months after the Pentagon disclosed the existence of the F-117A, it was used in combat for the first time. This was in Operation Just Cause, the invasion of Panama to dislodge and arrest General Noriega. At the beginning of the invasion, six F-117As flew to Panama from Tonopah. Their mission was to drop 2,000-pound bombs near the Panama Defence Forces (PDF) barracks at Rio Hato. The purpose was to stun and disorientate the PDF troops living there so that the barracks could be stormed, and the troops captured with minimal resistance and casualties.

The first combat engagement started at 14:00 hours on 19 December 1989, with eight F-117As taking off from Tonopah (two airborne spares returned following completion of the initial air refuelling). The decision to employ the F-117A was based on its bomb-delivery accuracy; Panama did not possess a radar defence network, so the aircraft's stealth features were irrelevant. It was more or less practice 'target shooting'. The 3,000-mile round trip from Tonopah to England AFB, Louisiana, required five air refuellings which were supported by KC-10 and KC-135 tankers.

Of the six aircraft in the strike package, two were airborne spares, two were tasked with attacking the Rio Hato army base, and the other two were designated to hit Noriega's residences at the Rio Hato beach house and La Escondida mountain resort. In the event, the planned attacks on the president's residences were cancelled when intelligence reports indicated that Noriega would not be present at either location. However, Major Greg Feest, flying aircraft 816, and his wingman Major Dale Hanner, dropped two 2,000 lb GBU-27s in an open field adjacent to the barracks.

The pilots were instructed to drop their bombs no closer than 50 metres from two separate PDF barracks buildings. The purpose of the target selection was to stun and confuse rather than kill the sleeping soldiers before they had an opportunity to engage US Rangers parachuting in to occupy the Rio Hato airstrip 90 seconds after the F-117 strike. However, three hours before the invasion was due to begin, the Panamanian military gained advance warning of the invasion and deployed to the Rio Hato airstrip. The bombing results were not as effective as had been planned; several Rangers were killed and a dozen or more wounded in the ensuing firefight before the airfield could be secured. As for Noriega, having initially taken refuge in a church, he was eventually extradited to Florida.

It was revealed three months later that one of the bombs missed its target by a considerable amount. It seems that there had been some miscommunication in the final stages of the mission planning, and the pilot had been given the wrong coordinates for the target. The media jumped on this and concluded that the F-117A had been a failure on its first mission. On 21 April 1990, stung perhaps by the press criticism, the Pentagon released more information on the F-117A. More photos of better quality were released, and at Nellis AFB there was a public display of two F-117As.

Thirteen months after the Panama invasion, a new war exploded on the sands of the Arabian Peninsula, which would really show what the F-117A was capable of.

CHAPTER SEVEN

Desert Storm

At 02:00 hours (Baghdad time) on 2 August 1990, Iraqi forces led by three elite Republican Guard armoured divisions invaded Kuwait. Over the next four months countless resolutions condemning Iraq were passed at the United Nations, culminating in Resolution 678 which overwhelmingly approved the use of all necessary means to drive Iraq from Kuwait. King Fahd ibn Abd al-Aziz Al Saud of Saudi Arabia invited Western troops into his country on 6 August and within two days a vast buildup of aircraft and troops began.

On 5 September, General Buster Glosson presented the air campaign plan to General Norman Schwarzkopf, who enthusiastically endorsed and approved it. Meanwhile, USAF aircraft acted as ferrets, flying to Iraqi border areas to 'stimulate' their air defences, thereby enabling communications intelligence (COMINT) and electronic intelligence (ELINT) assets to map the Iraqis' electronic air order of battle (EAOB).

The Iraqi air defence network was very sophisticated and its destruction would chronically disable their tight central control system. Over 400 observations posts could send basic heading and altitude data to a command post. This data was supplemented by 73 radar-reporting stations feeding into 17 Intercept Operations Centres (IOCs). Four Sector Operations Centres (SOCs) then controlled the IOCs, and from these three-story, reinforced-concrete buildings the defence of Iraq could be planned. Basic targeting information was then supplied to a vast number of missile and AAA batteries.

The suppression of enemy air defences – SEAD – was the top priority to establish air superiority. General Glosson's attack plan had objectives to destroy the communications network and radar warning system, disrupt communication and control nodes, force air defence units in autonomous modes, use unmanned aerial vehicles and drones for deception and employ maximum anti-radiation missiles.

Defence network command centres would be taken out by the F-117As at the outset, as would key early-warning radars and communication links. The tentacles would then be dealt with by other, non-stealthy assets. If successful, the plan would have two benefits: without the integrated defence network, SAM batteries would be forced to use their radars longer, making them more vulnerable to attack from anti-radiation missiles; and, cut-off Iraqi fighter pilots would become easy prey for allied air defence assets.

'H' hour was to be 03:00 hours Baghdad time. At 00:22 hours on the 17th, the first of three waves of F-117As climbed out of Khamis Mushait AB to deliver the opening salvos of an air campaign that would not just validate the success of the F-117A and stealth technology but would change the shape of air combat forever.

Other than at very close ranges, the F-117A was effectively invisible to the radar systems, as per USAF data. Operations over Iraq in 1991 resulted in no losses for the F-117A, only minor battle damage produced mostly by shrapnel and fragments from larger alibre anti-aircraft artillery barrages. This was not officially acknowledged by US officials.

An operation which attracted little comment was a deep penetration raid at the start of the campaign conducted by AH-64 Apache gunships and MH-53 Jolly Greens to destroy a VHF band P-18 Spoon Rest and a collocated UHF band P-15 Flat Face and P-15M Squat Eye. The reasons for this unusual raid were never disclosed, but these radars could have alerted Saddam's air defence system to the first wave of F-117As inbound to Baghdad. Those radars could detect and trace stealth aircraft like the F-117, which are designed to operate against radars operating in the C, X and Ku bands. The Apaches cleared the path for the stealth fighters to proceed to their targets deep inside Iraq undetected.

During the Gulf War in 1991, the F-117A flew approximately 1,300 sorties and scored direct hits on 1,600 high-value targets over 6,905 flight hours. The psychological effect on Iraqi troops was enormous. Leaflet drops on Iraqi forces displayed the F-117A destroying ground targets and warned 'Escape now and save yourselves'. Initial claims of its effectiveness were later found to be overstated. For instance it was claimed that the F-117A made up 2.5 per cent of Coalition tactical aircraft in Iraq and they attacked more than 40 per cent of the strategic targets; this ignored the fact that only 229 Coalition aircraft could drop and designate laser-guided bombs of which thirty-six F-117A represented 15.7 per cent, and only the USAF had the BLU-109/I-2000 bombs intended for hardened targets, so the F-117A represented 32 per cent of all coalition aircraft that could deliver such bombs. Initial reports of F-117As hitting 80 per cent of their targets were later scaled back to '41-60 per cent'. On the first night, they failed to hit 40 per cent of their assigned air defence targets, including the Air Defence Operations Centre in Baghdad, and eight such targets remained functional out of ten that could be assessed. In their Desert Storm white paper, the USAF claimed that 'the F-117A was the only airplane that the planners dared risk over downtown Baghdad' and that this area was particularly well defended. In fact most of the air defences were on the outskirts of the city and many other aircraft hit targets in the downtown area, with minimal casualties when they attacked at night like the F-117A. This meant they avoided the optically-aimed AAA and infra-red SAMs which were the biggest threat to Coalition aircraft.

The F-117A was operated in secret from Tonopah for almost a decade, but after the Gulf War it moved to Holloman in 1992 – however its integration with the USAF's non-stealth 'iron jets' occurred slowly. One senior F-117A pilot later said that because of ongoing secrecy others continued to see the aircraft as 'none of their business, a stand-alone system'. The F-117A and the men and women of the 49th Fighter Wing were deployed to South West Asia on multiple occasions. On their first deployment, with the aid of aerial refuelling, pilots flew non-stop from Holloman to Kuwait, a flight of 18.5 hours – a record for single-seat fighters that stands today.

After the Gulf War, the general public, with the help of propaganda partially fueled by the Pentagon and US media, believed that the stealth aircraft was invisible. Stealth aircraft are not invisible to either radar or infrared, and military and national security professionals have never had such illusions, but during the 1990s many grew overconfident in the capabilities offered by low-observable aircraft. The idea of stealth is that one releases weapons before the enemy is aware of you. Stealth is not a magical cloak of invisibility. The next chapter will show this.

Chapter Eight

Prelude to War

The Balkan peninsula throughout history has been known as a 'powder keg' which needs a very small spark to explode. Those sparks occurred often and the explosions occasionally ignited wars far beyond its borders.

The last decade of the last century was a time when Yugoslavia as a federal country of six republics and two provinces disintegrated in the nationalistic civil war sponsored by the 'democratic' west, which created new states in the Balkans. At that time, Serbia and Montenegro kept what was left of Yugoslavia. Brutal civil war followed.

How to summarize the whole western approach in one sentence? Maybe we can quote an analysis written by David Golpert, then vice-president of RAND and ex director of national intelligence:

> 'How to defeat Serbia?' ... for years, decades perhaps, Serbia would have to be subjected to isolation and misery, that it would have to be quarantined for as long as it takes to eradicate the virus that Serbia carries within it. Because the Serbs should be treated as lepers. The sanctions against Serbia do not have to be hermetically tight provided that they are permanent.'

The Serbian-Kosovar-Albanian conflict had its roots in the centuries before the 1999 conflict. The territory of Kosovo and Metohija has been considered the birth place of the Serbian state during medieval times. Albanian tribes came to Serbian territory as shepherds and populated mountainous regions. During the decline and disintegration of the medieval Serbian kingdom, Albanians converted to Islam and integrated themselves into the Ottoman Empire. Since then the two peoples have had problems with each other. Kosovo was liberated from Ottoman rule in the first Balkan war but at that time the Serbian population was mostly expelled from the territory as the Albanian tribes thrived. The Serbian government has never been accepted and occasional riots, sometimes paid for by foreign powers such as Austro-Hungary and Italy, arose. During the Second

176

World War the majority of the Albanian population sided with fascist Italy and even formed SS division Skanderbeg. What was left of the Serbian population in many Kosovo areas was expelled or killed in a series of pogroms. After the war, the anti-Serbian communist regime banned the return of the Serbian refugees to their homes. Some Serbian politicians objected.

The 1950s and 1960s were a period marked by policies in Kosovo under Aleksandar Ranković, a Serbian communist who later fell out with and was dismissed by Yugoslav president and communist dictator Tito. During this time nationalism for Kosovar Albanians became a conduit to alleviate the conditions of the time. In 1968 Yugoslav Serb officials warned about rising Albanian nationalism and by November unrest and demonstrations by thousands of Albanians followed calling for Kosovo to attain republic status, an independent Albanian language and an Albanian university. The ultimate goal of Kosovar Albanians is to unify with Albania forming Greater Albania, which would include some Macedonian and Greek territories.

Tito and his henchman Edvar Kardelj rewrote the Yugoslav constitution in 1974 and tried to address Albanian complaints by awarding the province of Kosovo autonomy and powers such as a veto in the federal decision making process similar to that of the republics. Kosovo functioned as a de facto republic because Kosovar Albanians attained the ability to pursue near-independent foreign relations, trade and cultural links with Albania, an independent Albanian language university and Albanology institute, an Academy of Sciences and a Writers association with the ability to fly the Albanian flag.

Military precursors to the separatist 'Kosovo Liberation Army' (KLA) began in the late 1980s with armed resistance to Serb police trying to take Albanian separatists into custody. Before the KLA, its members had been part of organizations such as the 'National Kosovo Movement' and the 'Popular Movement for Kosovo Liberation'. The founders of the later KLA were involved in the 1981 protests in Kosovo. Considerable numbers of ethnic Albanian dissidents were arrested or emigrated to European countries, such as Switzerland and Germany, where they continued subversive activities. Repression of Albanian nationalism and Albanian nationalists by authorities in Belgrade strengthened the independence movement and focused international attention on the plight of Kosovar Albanians.

From 1991 to 1992, Albanian radical nationalist Adem Jashari and about 100 other ethnic Albanians wishing to fight for the independence of Kosovo underwent military training in the municipality of Labinot-Mal in Albania. Afterwards, Jashari and other ethnic Albanians committed several acts of sabotage aimed at the Serbian administrative apparatus in Kosovo. Attempting to capture or kill him, Serbian police surrounded Jashari and his older brother, Hamëz, at their home in Prekaz village on 30 December 1991. In the ensuing siege, large numbers of Kosovo Albanians flocked to Prekaz, forcing the police to withdraw from the village. While in Albania, Jashari was arrested in 1993 by the government of Sali

Berisha and sent to jail in Tirana before being released alongside other Kosovo Albanian militants at the demand of the Albanian Army. Jashari launched several terrorist attacks over the next few years, targeting the Yugoslav Army (VJ) and Serbian police in Kosovo. In the spring of 1993, Homeland Calls meetings were held in Aarau, Switzerland, organized by Xhavit Halili, Azem Syla, Jashar Salihu and others. KLA strategist Xhavit Halili said that in 1993 the KLA 'considered and then rejected the IRA, PLO and ETA models'.

Some journalists claim that a May 1993 attack in Glogovac that left five Serbian policemen dead and two wounded was the first attack carried out by the KLA. In the early 1990s there were attacks on police forces and secret-service officials.

A Serbian policeman was killed in 1995, allegedly by the KLA. After 1995, the KLA sought to destabilize the region, hoping the USA and NATO would intervene. Serbian patrols were ambushed and policemen killed. It was only the next year that the organization of KLA officially took responsibility for attacks. In 1996-97 the KLA, originally composed out of a few hundred Kosovar Bosnian War veterans, attacked several police stations and wounded many police officers.

In 1996 the British weekly magazine *The European* carried an article by a French expert stating: 'German civil and military intelligence services have been involved in training and equipping the rebels with the aim of cementing German influence in the Balkan area... The birth of the KLA in 1996 coincided with the appointment of Hansjoerg Geiger as the new head of the BND [German Secret Service]... The BND men were in charge of selecting recruits for the KLA command structure from the 500,000 Kosovars in Albania.'

Former senior adviser to the German parliament Matthias Küntzel tried to prove later on that German secret diplomacy had been instrumental in helping the KLA since its creation.

KLA representatives met with American, British, and Swiss intelligence agencies in 1996, and possibly 'several years earlier', and according to *The Sunday Times*, American intelligence agents admitted they helped to train the Kosovo Liberation Army before NATO's bombing of Yugoslavia. Intelligence agents denied, however, that they were involved in arming the KLA.

In February 1996 the KLA undertook a series of attacks against police stations and Yugoslav government employees, saying that the Yugoslav authorities had killed Albanian civilians as part of an ethnic cleansing campaign. Serbian authorities denounced the KLA as a terrorist organization and increased the number of security forces in the region.[8] This had the counter-productive effect of boosting the credibility of the embryonic KLA among the Kosovo Albanian population. On 26 April 1996, four attacks on Serbian security personnel were carried out almost simultaneously in several parts of Kosovo.

---

8. Whether or not the KLA should be described as a terrorist organisation has been the subject of much debate: en.wikipedia.org/wiki/Kosovo_Liberation_Army#cite_note-41

CHAPTER EIGHT

In January 1997, Serbian security forces assassinated KLA commander Zahir Pajaziti and two other leaders in a highway attack between Pristina and Mitrovica and arrested more than 100 Albanian militants. Jashari was convicted of terrorism in absentia by a Yugoslav court on 11 July 1997. Human Rights Watch subsequently described the trial, in which fourteen other Kosovo Albanians were also convicted, as 'failing to conform to international standards'.

The Albanian interior conflict and collapse of security of 1997 enabled the KLA to acquire large amounts of weaponry looted from Albanian armouries. A 1997 intelligence report stated that the KLA received drug trafficking proceeds, which they used to purchase arms. They also received funds from Albanian diaspora organizations.

Some non-Albanians such as the Serbs and Romani fled Kosovo fearing revenge attacks, others were pressured by the KLA and armed gangs to leave. According to the report of the US Committee for Refugees the KLA attacks 'aimed at trying to cleanse Kosovo of its ethnic Serb population'. The Yugoslav Red Cross estimated 30,000 refugees and internally displaced persons from Kosovo, most of who were Serb. The UNHCR estimated at least 55,000 refugees had fled to Montenegro and Central Serbia, most of whom were Kosovo Serbs: 'Over 90 mixed villages in Kosovo have now been emptied of Serb inhabitants and other Serbs continue leaving, either to be displaced in other parts of Kosovo or fleeing into central Serbia.'

Pursuing Adem Jashari for the murder of a Serbian policeman, Serbian forces again attempted to assault the Jashari compound in Prekaz on 22 January 1998. With Jashari not present, thousands of Kosovo Albanians descended on Prekaz and again succeeded in pushing the government forces out of the village and its surroundings.

The next month, a small unit of the KLA was ambushed by Serbian policemen. Four Serbs were killed and two were injured in the ensuing clashes. At dawn on 5 March 1998, the KLA launched an attack against a police patrol in Prekaz, which was answered by a police operation on the Jashari compound which left fifty-eight Albanians dead, including Jashari. Four days after this, a NATO meeting was convoked, during which Madeleine Albright pushed for an anti-Serbian response. NATO now threatened Serbia with a military response. The Kosovo War ensued, with subsequent NATO intervention. A NATO-facilitated ceasefire was signed on 15 October, but both sides broke it two months later and fighting resumed.

The infamous spark which lit the powder keg happened with the killing of forty-five Kosovar Albanians in the village of Racak. The massacre – the veracity of which was disputed by the Serbs – was reported in the western media in January 1999. After OSCE mission head William Walker filed the report, NATO decided that the conflict could only be settled by introducing a military peacekeeping force. After the Rambouillet Accords broke down on 23 March with Yugoslav rejection of an external peacekeeping force, NATO prepared to install the 'peacekeepers by force'. That was the culmination of something that started much earlier and now it was time for the *coup de grâce*.

Yugoslav Order of Battle

Air Defence

1. Serbian air defence in Operation Allied Force, as the air campaign was called by NATO, represented the typical pattern of Soviet air defences from the 1960-70 period. It was representative of the effects of stagnation on modern surface-to-air missile system proliferation through much of the world that had been dependent on Soviet supplies.

2. Serbia's strategic air defence was handled by a declining number of vintage Almaz SA-2/S-75 and a small number of partly modernized Almaz SA-3/S-125 Pechora systems. Before the Yugoslav civil war, the air defence command had six battalions of SA-2/S-75s, totalling about forty single-rail launchers, of which only three battalions were still operational in 1999. There were also twelve combat battalions of SA-3/S-125s with 60 x 4-rail launchers – of which about fifty were still operational in 1999. SA-3 systems were grouped in one missile brigade (250th Missile Brigade) and one independent missile regiment (450th Missile Regiment).

250th Brigade consisted of eight battalions (1st Batajnica; 2nd Pancevo; 3rd Jakovo, 4th Zuce; 5th Jakovo, 6th Smederevo; 7th Mladenovac and 8th Obrenovac). Besides combat battalions, 250th Brigade also had two missile technical battalions whose main purpose was missile warehousing, maintenance, preparation and supplies to the combat battalions (1st Missile Technical Battalion in Sremcica and 2nd Missile Technical Battalion in Zuce). The missile defence technical school and training centre also had training equipment including one missile guidance station, one engagement and fire control radar and four launchers. There were total of eleven missile guiding stations available to the 250th Brigade whose task was defence of the capital city area. 450th Regiment with four battalions and one technical battalion covered the south-west parts of Serbia and the industrial city of Kraljevo. In total, there were fifteen missile guiding stations available for all SA-3 systems.

Air defence of the field army was handled by five independent regiments of SA-6/2K12 Kub (Soviet export version 'Kvadrat') mobile radar-directed SAMs, with one of the regiments (311th Independent Regiment) based with the Serbian forces in or near the province of Kosovo and Metohija area and two regiments (230th from Nis and 310th from Kragujevac) based not too far from the province. The 60th Regiment was based in Podgorica (Montenegro) and 240th Regiment had a base in Novi Sad. Each regiment had four batteries. The weakest point on the SAM-6 system is 1S91 (Straight Flush) radar vehicle which is needed to provide guidance for every four missile-launch vehicles. This cumbersome arrangement restricted the flexibility of the Kvadrat batteries.

Air defence at divisional level ('Trupna PVO' as per Serbian terminology) included SA-9/Strela-1 and SA-13/Strela-10 IR-guided, low altitude, vehicle-mounted SAMs. The more common of these was the older SA-9/9K31 Strela-1, with some 113 launcher vehicles delivered to Yugoslavia in the 1970s. The associated missile was manufactured in Yugoslavia under license before the war. The SA-9 system consisted of four missile launchers mounted on a wheeled BRDM-2 light armoured vehicle, and had an effective ceiling of 3,500 metres. It employed an older uncooled lead-sulphide seeker with no IR counter-countermeasure capabilities. Yugoslavia received a total of seventeen of the more modern SA-13/9K35M Strela-10 in the 1980s. This system descended from the Strela-1 but was mounted on a tracked MT-LB chassis. The SA-13/ Strela-10 had IR counter-countermeasures with later versions of the missile having a two-channel seeker. Besides these standard systems, Serbian air-force units attempted to create improvised air defence missiles for their bases using IR guided air-to-air missiles. The normal aircraft rail-launchers for AA-8 Aphid/R-60 and AA-11 Archer/R-73 were lashed to ground mountings codenamed 'Pracka' (Slingshot).

Small unit air defence was handled by anti-aircraft guns and a significant number of old SA-7/Strela-2M and new SA-16,18/9K310 Igla man-portable SAMs. The SA-7/Strela-2M was produced in Yugoslavia under the name Strela-2M2J 'Sava' and was available in large numbers. Serbia managed to purchase about seventy-five of the new SA-16/9K310 Igla-1 man-portable IR-guided SAMs from Kazakhstan and other sources in the mid-1990s. In total there were about 850 man-portable IR-guided SAMs in the Serbian armed forces in 1999. NATO took the threat posed by IR-guided SAMs the most seriously, as these had been the primary source of casualties in Operation Desert Storm. There was some confidence that the radar-directed missiles could be dealt with using traditional means of suppression of enemy air defences (SEAD) and electronic countermeasures (ECM). Unlike radar-guided SAMs, IR-guided SAMs present a serious suppression problem since the launchers rely entirely on passive sensors and are generally smaller, more mobile and easier to conceal.

The older-generation IR-guided SAMs, such as the Strela-2M (SA-7) and Strela-1 (SA-9), use seekers that are more susceptible to conventional ECM, such as flares and 'hot brick' infrared countermeasures (IRCM). The newer IR-guided systems, such as the man-portable Igla (SA-16/-18) and vehicle-mounted Strela-10/SA-13, have more robust counter-countermeasures. Rather than risk air crews to these systems, NATO planners restricted most air operations to above 10,000 ft, where these small SAMs had a very low kill probability. Furthermore, the presence of these SAMs raised concerns about operating attack helicopters such as the AH-64 Apache deep behind Serbian lines and was a significant factor in US reluctance to deploy the Apaches in combat.

The altitude limits succeeded in minimizing casualties to IR-guided SAMs. A single aircraft was hit by a shoulder-fired SAM but it failed to fuse and bounced off the aircraft. Several other aircraft were damaged, possibly by this type of weapon. The mere presence of these weapons, however, inhibited air operations to a significant extent. Weather conditions forced NATO to abandon air missions when cloud cover precluded operations below the altitude limit, and none of the air forces other than the US had munitions such as the Joint Direct Attack Munition (JDAM) that could be used in all weathers. Secondly, it contributed to collateral damage against civilian targets. Although NATO aircraft did have electro-optical sensors for surveying targets before the strike, when used from medium altitude the resolution of the image in the cockpit was often mediocre. Civilian tractors and buses could be mistaken for military vehicles (for further details see section in Chapter Nine: Deceptions).

The Yugoslav side paid close attention to the experience of both coalition and Iraqi sides during Operation Desert Storm. In the command and information department of the air defence forces numerous analyses were performed about the capabilities and tactics of allied strike forces. One of the analyses was about F-117A capabilities. The first conclusion was that the performance of the airplane such as altitude and speed were within the missile system envelopes for both SA-3 and SA-6. The issue was from how far could it be detected on the surveillance radar and were the capabilities of the existing engagement and fire control radars enough to perform target acquisition, tracking and engagement. What was not known was the radar cross section. The Yugoslav side got help from an unexpected source: the US Air Force. In one of its publications there was an article about the achieved level of stealth accompanied with appropriate graphics. The Yugoslav side conducted numerous calculations comparing the available information about the airplane and capabilities of the radars. The conclusion was that the available radars in the air defence system were able to track and provide fire control solutions and guidance to engage the stealth aircraft. One of the conditions was that all combat procedures had to be performed very precisely and accurately.

During the meeting, which was held on 10 September 1998 in the Air Defence Command centre, the analysis was presented to the Air Force and Defence commander. Shortly after, the year 4 students of the air defence academy started training how to calculate the range and altitude of stealth aircraft for all surveillance radars in air defence. With very limited equipment, the Yugoslav side had done everything possible to get ready for the imminent war.

USAF and NATO Order of Battle

In the US Forces Order of Battle, notable is the high proportion of F-16CJ defence suppression aircraft, around 40 per cent of the total fast jet strike component. Even accounting for provision of escorts to aircraft flown by other NATO nations and US heavy bombers, this is a very high proportion of the strike force committed to protection against a collection of mostly obsolescent Soviet-era SA systems (**Figure 8-1, Figure 8-2**).

Also engaged was the aircraft carrier USS *Theodore Roosevelt*'s amphibious group and support vessels. In total, more than 1,000 aircraft against the few.

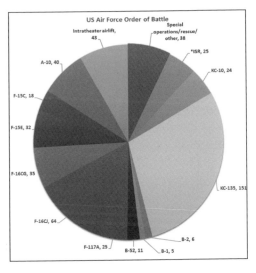

Spec. op/CSAR/other	38;
*ISR	25;
(*ISR includes RQ-1, E-3, E-8)	
KC-10	24;
KC-135	151;
B-2	6;
B-1	5;
B-52	11;
F-117A	25;
F-16CJ	64;
F-16CG	35;
F-15E	32;
F-15C	18;
A-10	40;
Intratheatre airlift	43;
RC-135, U-2 and EC-130	ABCCC
Total USAF:	app. 517
Navy:	app. 130
USMC and Army AF:	app. 83

TOTAL US forces: app. 730

Figure 8-1: US order of battle as a numerous air component (does not include US Navy aircraft). (AWOS Fact Sheet via ausairpower.org, modified by authors)

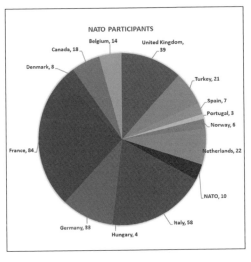

UK	39
Turkey	21
Spain	7
Portugal	3
Norway	6
Netherlands	22
NATO	10
Italy	58
Hungary	4
Germany	33
France	84
Denmark	8
Canada	18
Belgium	14
Total NATO	**327**

Figure 8-2: NATO countries order of battle (including UAV). (ausairpower.org, modified by authors)

Attack

The armed forces of Yugoslavia were able to defend the country against the combined attack of two neighbourhood counties, but to fight against the most powerful military organization in the world the chances of success were almost zero.

The first indication of imminent attack was when during the night of 23 March all international air traffic, which is very dense over Yugoslavia, was re-routed over surrounding countries. The sky was cleared. Long range surveillance radar couldn't pick up a single airplane over Yugoslav air space. The NATO air attacks started on 24 March 1999.

What NATO tried was to deliver a knock-out punch on the very first night, pretty much like the attack on Iraq. In modern war there is no chivalry – the attacker uses everything at his disposal to achieve the goal: cripple or destroy the enemy without casualties to his own side. Salvos of cruise missiles launched from NATO airplanes (B-52s), US and UK submarines and warships in the Mediterranean and Adriatic Sea, and laser guided bombs, hit radar positions, missile batteries, command centres, military airports, warehouses etc. Tomahawk missiles were timed to hit command and control centres (C2). Air-launched missiles from 2nd Louisiana Bomb Wing hit similar targets. A pair of B-2s from Whitman Missouri 509th Bomb Wing base made a 32-hour round trip to strike air defence, arms factories, airfields and weapon storage areas. Bombers were escorted by F-15C fighters, EA-6B electronic warfare aircraft, KC-135 aerial tankers and NATO E-3 Sentry airborne command and control airplanes.

Operation Allied Force total number of aircraft: approximately 1,057
The very first bombing of the 8th 'Black Sheep' F-117A squadron was performed by the squadron commander, Lieutenant Colonel Gary Woltering. The target was a 'radar installation near Belgrade'. Lieutenant Colonel Zelko also took part in the first attack (**Figure 8-3**, **Figure 8-4**, **Figure 8-5**).

> Yugoslav's had enough information through intelligence reports of NATO build-up around the borders, intensifying terrorist attacks in Kosovo by Kosovar separatists, re-routing of air traffic over surrounding countries. In the days before the attack, the air force's most modern MiG-29s were relocated in pairs in the different airports. The few that were flightworthy were simply no match for those of NATO. Pilots were basically sacrificed in the opening hours of the war. Air defence units were just starting deployment but were by no means ready for combat. What plagued Yugoslav air

Figure 8-3: Lieutenant Colonel Waltering, CO of 8th squadron during Middle East mission. (USAF)

Figure 8-4: F-117A taking off from Aviano on 24 March, night of first attack. (USAF)

defence and with them the whole military was political negligence, no investment in the new weapons systems, lack of training, lack of funding, unhappy junior officers, incompetent high ranking officers who advance through the ranks only because of their connections. With some exceptions, most of the generals in key positions were not up to the task of fighting the whole of the NATO pact, but they couldn't say 'no' to the president because that would mean automatic dismissal and loss of privileges.

The air defence of the Federal Republic of Yugoslavia was presented to the population as formidable. That was also picked up by the western press and can be seen in some documentaries. It was anything but formidable. As seen in the section 'order of battle' Yugoslav air defences were obsolete. Equipment was old and prone to breakages. There were no funds to buy the new systems or even spare parts. Routine maintenance was simply to try to make something workable, often re-using parts from the other systems which were broken.

To have a combat-motivated and effective unit, investment in people and technique is necessary. Yugoslav air defence didn't have that at all. People didn't even get regular paychecks. Even so, they did their best to do their jobs.

NATO was well aware of the capabilities of Yugoslav air defence. It was a fraction of the strength of the Iraqi's air defence which were defeated and almost destroyed in the first few weeks of fighting. All peace time locations of combat positions, radars, munition warehouses, and command centres were well known and they were first to be attacked. The question for air defence command was

Figure 8-5: Lieutenant Colonel Waltering (8th squadron CO) in the middle, after the first mission over Serbia. In his left hand is the bomb clip which was pulled from the laser guided bomb just before the bomb bay is closed. F-117A pilots, as unwritten rule, kept one of the bombs pins as a souvenir or for the good luck. (Msgt. Don Blewett, USAF)

how to survive the first blow. Since the clearing of Yugoslav air space, command had almost twenty-four hours to relocate units to alternative positions. The units waited marching orders.

3rd Battalion

The 3rd Battalion was one of eight battalions under the command of the 250th Missile Brigade. It consisted of command, command and control platoon, technical battery, missile launchers battery, and support platoons. Battalion command consisted of commander, Lieutenant Colonel Dani Zoltan; deputy commander and executive officer (XO) Lieutenant Colonel Djordje Anicic; commander's aide for logistics Major Bosko Dotlic; commander's aide for techniques and equipment, Major Boris Stoimenov; to mention a few. In total, the battalion was around 200-men strong. It had a mixed reserve and regular personnel.

Command and control platoon's main role was to provide control over the other units and link with the brigade command. Technical battery responsibility was to provide technical support to the fire control centre, radars, launchers and power supply for all equipment. Missile battery included four launchers with four missiles each, sixteen in total. The responsibility of the missile battery was to provide warehousing, transport, preparation for combat and installation on the launchers. The battery consisted of two platoons; each platoon was responsible for two launchers. Third battalion also had an automotive section with the trucks and support vehicles (**Figure 8-6**).

In the months before the NATO attack, 3rd Battalion was not in good shape. According to some of the parameters, it was the lowest ranking battalion in 250th Brigade, as of August 1998. The biggest problem was in equipment readiness. There were malfunctions in both missile channels and the target channel. The battalion was simply not combatworthy. Command structure changes were initiated, and the battalion got an infusion of 'fresh blood'. The existing commander, Lieutenant Colonel Dani, remained in his position, but new senior officers arrived. The new command initiated intensive training activities, which included extensive simulator training, combat crew coordination, procedures for different scenarios, etc, and by February 1999 the crews were brought to an acceptable state of 'war readiness'. Much of the burden of this peacetime transformation fell on the XO, who was the only senior officer trained and experienced on the SA-3 system. Besides the regulars, the reserves were also trained. Key to the training was personnel motivation.

Lieutenant Colonel Anicic knew the SA-3 system like 'the back of his hand'. The only junior officer with SA-3 training was 2nd Lieutenant Crnobrnja, who was battalion security officer during the war. The other officers did know

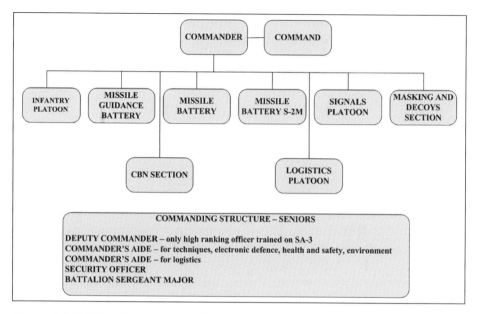

Figure 8-6: 3rd Battalion structure. (Authors)

something of the SA-3 system, but not as much as Anicic. The battalion relied on NCOs for operation and maintenance. Brigade command had SA-3 trained officers but they were not part of the battalion.

Third Battalion was in a state of readiness on 24 March when at 11:00 the order was issued to start the transition from the primary combat position (peacetime positions) to reserve combat position at Simanovci (**Figure 8-7**). The order was to deploy one vehicle at a time and at the same time to camouflage the primary position with decoys. Forward observers were deployed to the visual observation points. Deployment continued almost all afternoon. At 19:00 the last truck with the battalion commander left the primary position towing the last launcher ramp.

Base camp in the vicinity of Simanovci was at the local community farm where most of the unit was based including the transportation section and maintenance. Before the war it was used as temporary lodgings for seasonal workers. The firing position was actually reserve SA-2 position. It was built as per the older system requirements, which were not very well suited for the SA-3 system. The firing positions had all power and communication cables preinstalled and the unit need basically only to 'plug in' the equipment. In the years before the war there were an intention to modify the location to suit SA-3, including the concrete bunker, but it was never finalized. The position was well known to NATO mission planners. It was distinctive and highly visible in the flat terrain. Battalion HQ

Figure 8-7: Reserve combat position, originally developed for SA-2 system, at Simanovci. (Author's archive)

reasoned that because the position was so obvious the enemy would assume it was unmanned and not attack it, so they deployed in that position; curious logic perhaps, but that was HQ's gamble.

At 19:30 the combat readiness alarm was issued at the command of the Brigade. The primary position was in the meantime evacuated with just a few soldiers left there. 20:06 was the exact time the first missile hit the primary position. The first detonation was followed with a second one at 20:15, then the third at 20:20. The primary combat position was obliterated (**Figure 8-8**). In the meantime, all vehicles and ramps were relocated to the secondary position.

The deployment was performed by the lights of vehicle, which contrary to procedure in time of war. After the intervention of the battalion deputy commander, the lights were turned off and the equipment deployed in dark. The shoulder-launched surface-to-air missiles SA-7/Strela-2M were deployed in the surrounding area. In the meantime, the observation radars picked up the cruise missiles and the deputy commander was concerned that the position had been detected by reconnaissance airplanes and that air attack was imminent. Personnel were ordered to the shelters, despite concern that the enemy knew where they were.

By 04:00 next morning the battalion had been brought back to full combat readiness. That was almost six hours after the initial attack; it was clear that the initial confusion had taken a toll.

Fortunately the bombs had not caused any casualties at the primary position. The position, including dummies and decoys, had been obliterated, including a

Figure 8-8: 3rd Battalion peace-time position hit the first night of bombing. Stationary objects were hit but all mobile equipment was relocated before the attack. (NATO)

warehouse with 80+ missiles. People were scared but unharmed and the guard dog, Efa, was seriously shaken but otherwise unhurt. Instead of decoys, what was left was craters metres wide and smashed smoldering buildings (**Figure 8-9**).

The decoys had worked well. It seemed that the attackers could not distinguish between the decoys and the real thing. The loss of eighty combat-ready 5V27D missiles was hard and the question was asked why had they not been relocated earlier. The price of a single missile at that time was US$85,000! In October 1998, battalion command requested permission from brigade HQ to relocate all missiles to alternative locations, but permission never came. Command and organization was not working well – not for the last time in the conflict (**Figure 8-10**, **Figure 8-11**).

Now it is necessary to draw a parallel with the initial hours of Operation Desert Storm. The Yugoslavs deployed all stationary and mobile missile batteries to the reserve positions avoiding initial impact which destroyed significant numbers of Iraqis units. Stationary radar installations from Air Surveillance, Informing and Guiding Service (Sluzba Vazdusnog Osmatranja, Javljanja i Navodjenja – VOJIN), warehouses and other stationary objects were hit and destroyed. Most equipment had been relocated, but not all – due to negligence and initial disorganization. VOJIN was the first to be pounded.

The biggest issue in this beginning stage of the war was communication. Deployment to the reserve position, lack of communication equipment and radio blackout meant that the battalion could not establish a connection with brigade HQ. The solution was to use civilian phone lines from the UNK cabin. The radio link was insecure and never used during the war because of potential jamming and possibility that the enemy could located the source. The other way

Figure 8-9:
What was left of the UNV decoy – it had fully served its purpose. During the war many decoys were hit by NATO bombs. (Author's archive)

Figure 8-10: What was left of the 5V27D warehouse (Sergeant Matic is standing on the concrete block. (Author's archive)

Figure 8-11: Third Battalion men inside the missile warehouse hit by the laser bomb on the first day of the war. (Cedomir Ljubinkovic)

of communication was through field phones which were immune to electronic jamming. The battalion had only one cell phone, which was used by the commander, Lieutenant Colonel Dani Zoltan. Through the intervention of a local businessman the battalion got a civilian phone link which was extensively used and never jammed. Nevertheless, the RAF probably had better communications in the Battle of Britain than Yugoslav air defence sixty years later.

That night, battalion was visited by one of the Air force commanding generals, Colonel-General Ljubisa Velickovic. The general was angry that missile units were not downing enemy airplanes and he asked why they didn't use radars more. Clearly this top military commandant, a pilot by trade, had no idea how a missile battalion worked and what were the rules of engagement. This was the case throughout the conflict.

A typical combat shift lasts for six hours, then the crew rests. Depending on the number of operators and shift commanders available the crew had one combat shift per twenty-four hours, but it was not always so. For the first few days the crews took time to adjust to real war conditions and to get into the routine of fighting a war.

Yugoslav Air Defence (Protiv-Vazdusna Odbrana, PVO) had before the outbreak of the civil war in 1990 been considered an elite branch of the military. The education and training system were based on Soviet doctrine because most of the equipment used was Soviet-made. Training provided a solid base for effective air defence. However, years of isolation and economic sanctions had taken a toll on the cadre. Fortunately, air defence still possessed considerable manpower and technical knowledge.

What an inferior air defence *can* do against a technically far superior enemy is to improvise. Some of the tactical unit commanders improvised and achieved success, some didn't. The price 250th Brigade paid in human casualties was not small.

Improvisation, tactical manoeuvres and thinking out of the box were three key elements of survival. Everybody knew the capabilities of NATO aviation. It was likely that NATO would use the same tactics it did in the Gulf War. The leading attack would use cruise missiles, stealth bombers, fighter-bombers, supported by electronic counter-measure airplanes and fighter escort. The question was how to absorb and deflect the impact of the attack with minimal casualties.

Unit command knows well that the highest risk to the missile crew is anti-radiation missiles and laser bombs. It was well known that the attacks on the missile battery would start with anti-radiation missiles. The question was how to protect the crew. There was no a single armoured missile command vehicle for SAM-3 in the whole air defence force which could provide protection against anti-radiation missile fragments. Lieutenant Colonel Anicic, studying the effects of HARM, had the idea to improvise cabin protection with wooden logs; not just any

Figure 8-12: Improvised UNK cabin protection with wooden logs. In the distance behind there is a P-18 radar and missile launcher platform. (*Smena* (The Shift), author's archive)

kind of logs but acacia logs. About fifty unseasoned logs were collected from local farms. The ideal size, we found, was about 5 metres long by 35-45 cm thick. The reason for the length and thickness was to cover the cabin but not to interfere with the operation of the radar and the thickness is for the easier transport and the acacia log with that thickens will have enough stiffness and at the same time toughness to absorb without penetration the high velocity HARM fragments (**Figure 8-12**).

March 26

During the morning hours of 26 March a NATO reconnaissance airplane flew at approximately 500 m, almost directly above the battalion positions. It was reported as a French Mirage. Almost immediately the combat shift left the command UNK van. The troops believed that the position had been located and that an air attack that night was imminent. It was obvious that the fire position needed low level air defence. All the battalion's Strela-2M shoulder-launch systems were positioned 10-15 kilometres away, on potential cruise missile paths. It was evident that the battalion fire position was extremely vulnerable, especially during deployment from marching column to combat formation, without short-range shoulder-launch missiles.

194

Figure 8-13: Serbian Air Force MiG-29 crash site in Bosnia. (Wikimedia)

It was evident in the first few days of war that there was mistrust between the field units and brigade command on some level. In general, with the exception of few high ranking officers, most of the brigade command officers worked strictly by the book – typical soviet doctrine. This may be applicable in a clearly defined, interlocked and highly saturated space covered with the numerous mobile and stationary missile systems covering low to high altitudes and hundreds of kilometres in depth, but in these conditions that way of thinking was clearly dangerous, especially to the tactical units. During the war, tactical units which worked according to well-known templates were taken out one by one. After the initial attack, the first few days were quiet, allowing the unit to take up its position, reorganize and get reserve components mobilized.

The typical combat crew shift is six hours long. Combat readiness No. 1 means that the all equipment is 'on', operators are at their places and the battalion is ready for engagement. During the morning shift, two Yugoslav MiG-29s took off from Batajnica airbase near Belgrade and were observed on azimuth 270 flying in the direction of Tuzla, Bosnia. 250th Brigade operation centre issued a warning to the battalions not to engage and let MiGs through their sector.

Coordination between air defence fighter airplanes and missile units is crucial otherwise missile units may open fire on their own airplanes. The crew followed the MiGs on surveillance radar until they disappeared from radar over Bosnia. Shortly afterwards two MiGs were intercepted and downed on Bosnian territory.

We were most likely among the last to see those two MiGs. They flew so low that the pilots were visible in their cockpits. They then rapidly ascended and we followed them on the radar before they disappeared from the screen.

In the UNK, the crew wondered why the MiGs went to Bosnia. It is evident that at the beginning there was some mistrust between the operations unit and brigade command, something that would plague the relationship later (**Figure 8-13**).

March 27

The daily 'routine' was established. Combat shifts changes were regular – in six hours intervals. Lieutenant Colonel Anicic was on until 12:00. After returning to the resting area he was called by the courier from brigade headquarters with orders to go to the three decoy locations and perform the radar imitator emissions from 14:00 until 20:00. The idea of brigade HQ was to use the radar imitator to simulate the work of tracking and engagement radar. Brigade HQ was sure that NATO ELINT airplanes would pick up emissions and plot the locations. Moving from one location to another and emitting simulated radar emissions at twenty-minutes intervals can create an impression of more tracking radars and thus more missile batteries. If the decoys worked as planned, NATO would record all positions and plot them as SAM sites. They would then be flagged in the flight computers as potentially dangerous zones to be avoided. As the real battalion was in complete radio and radar emission silence, it would wait in ambush for an unsuspecting airplane to appear.

The plan was to use location No. 1 Subotiste and perform twenty-minute emissions on azimuth 270, then move to location No. 2 Pecinci and perform the same task on azimuth 270 for the same time, then move to location No. 3, Dobrinci and perform the emission on azimuth 230. The task would be executed by 20:00, then the radar imitator would be positioned in the vicinity of the battalion and used as a decoy. Lieutenant Colonel Anicic as deputy commander and battalion XO was scheduled to take the combat shift at 18:00, so the time frame was tight to perform all assigned tasks and get to the combat position on time to take over the shift (**Figure 8-14**).

A radar emission imitator emits electromagnetic energy at the same frequencies and wavelengths as an engagement and fire control radar used in missile guidance. There is a high probability that these false radar signals will be picked up by ELINT aircraft and fighter-bombers carrying anti-radiation missiles such as HARM. Missiles are liable to fly towards the decoy instead of towards the real radar.

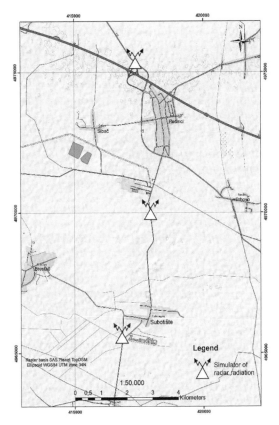

Figure 8-14: Position of radar imitator emission on March 27 afternoon (right) (Boris Vakanjac) and radar emission imitator (below left and right). (Author's archive)

SHOOTING DOWN THE STEALTH FIGHTER

The plan had the desired effect. NATO was well aware of the existence and capabilities of Yugoslav decoys. They have those kinds of devices as well. But they couldn't determine if the emissions came from real radars or imitators. If the emissions are not scheduled as a pattern of twenty minutes but random, they may appear more realistic.

Lieutenant Colonel Anicic went to find flashlights and batteries from the local territorial defence headquarter. Shortages of simple items such as flashlight batteries chronically plagued the battalion during the entire war. One role of the battalion deputy commander was to deal with these issues.

In the meantime, at 18:00 his combat crew took their evening shift and, because Lieutenant Colonel Anicic was absent, Lieutenant Colonel Dani continued his previous shift as commander until the return of Anicic. Major Boris Stoimenov took over the position of the deputy combat crew commander with the new crew. Combat readiness was No. 3 which is the lowest, usually when there is no activity in the air. The crew is on 15-minute readiness. During the previous shift, it was noted that there was a problem with P-18 radar receiver because there was no picture on the screen below 60-70 km. After a conversation with the commander, Major Stoimenov, who was also battalion technical officer, went to the radar van and together with the radar crew tried to fix the problem. There was an issue between the parameters of signal and cluster. Major Stoimenov reported to the commander that the repair might take about ninety minutes. Sergeant Ljubenkovic and Major Stoimenov worked on the equipment without turning on high voltage and radar emission. After the repair, Major Stoimenov requested from Lieutenant Colonel Dani to turn on P-18 for final adjustment and tune-up. He was back in UNK at 19:20 and reported to Dani that the radar was ready, but that the receiver needed to be adjusted. Because the probable attack had been expected from the west, the radar antenna was positioned on azimuth 90° and emission was turned on. After the final tune-up the high voltage was turned off.

The situation was quiet and nothing was on the radar screens. In the first few days the air raid alarm usually sounded around 20:00. That was the local time where NATO airplanes were approaching designated targets and were picked up by surveillance radars and visual observation pickets.

Lieutenant Colonel Dani was ordered by brigade command to put the crew into readiness No. 1 around 19:35. Missile guidance station (StVR in local terminology) and radar P-18 were turned on and the crew performed final checks. In combat readiness No. 1, the crew is ready to engage a target at any moment.

Combat procedure requires that the crew is in constant communication with the brigade command centre. The commander is in front of the P-18 screen (VIKO) (see the schematics for precise combat positions in the UNK van in **Figure 8-15**). Beside him sits the deputy commander and both can see the radar

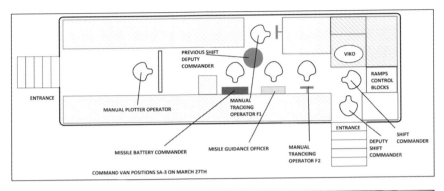

COMMAND VAN POSITIONS SA-3 ON MARCH 27TH

Figure 8-15: UNK (StRV) layout with the individual combat crew member positions on the evening of 27 March during the stealth engagement (top) and combat stations (above) viewed from the position of the manual plot operator. Commander and deputy shift commander positions viewed from the side entrance (right). (Authors)

Commander Lieutenant Colonel Dani (front) and XO Lieutenant Colonel Anicic (behind). A posed photo taken after the engagement (during the engagement places were opposite). (Author's archive)

screen. Every turn on the radar screen showed that there were airplanes in the air…but they were far away.

The UNK of S-125M is cramped; the comfort of the crew was the last thing the designers worried about. The chairs are anything but comfortable; the humming noise from electrical equipment is rather loud; the air-conditioning is barely sufficient to move the stale air, the smell of uniforms, muddy boots and unwashed bodies… all in all, not a pleasant working environment. In that space, six officers, NCOs and enlisted men performed their tasks.

23 Seconds

A missile battalion combat crew is a team. Every member plays his part, and all roles are critical. If anyone doesn't do his duty, the whole team will fail… and in war that can be fatal.

The life of a combat crew during an engagement is measured in seconds. That is how much time is available to fulfill the mission or die trying. In ordinary life seconds do not mean much, but for missile operators that is the difference between bringing down their target or being shredded to pieces by an anti-radiation missile or laser bomb.

On the evening of 27 March the crew arrived at 20:30. It consisted of Lieutenant Colonel Dani Zoltan, commander, responsible for all in the UNK; Lieutenant Colonel Djordje Anicic, battalion deputy commander and XO and assigned shift commander, responsible for all activities out of the UNK such as power supply, radar, communication, signals etc.; Major Boris Stoimenov, until the arrival of Lieutenant Colonel Anicic deputy crew commander; Captain I Class, Senad Muminovic, fire control officer; Sub Lieutenant Darko Nikolic, battery commander; Senior Sergeant Dragan Matic, manual tracking operator on F2; Sergeant Dejan Tiosavljevic, manual tracking operator on F1; private Davor Blozic, clerk and manual plotting board operator. Besides the combat crew in UNK, the detached truck with power source pack unit (Sen. Sergeant Djordje Maletic and Private Sead Ljajic) and P-18 early warning and surveillance radar station (Sergeant Vladimir Ljubenkovic and Private Vladimir Radovanovic) also played a critical role (**Figure 8-16**).

What was unusual that evening was that in the moment of engagement there were two commanders in the UNK. Combat rules allow only one commander, but in war circumstances it may be different. Lieutenant Colonel Anicic returned to his post at 20:30. At that moment there was no combat engagement, but the missiles were at Readiness No. 1 on the ramps ready for launch, but there was no combat readiness in the station which is very unusual (why we'll see in the next section). The night was clear. Moon light reflected on the stand-by missiles and their launchers.

When Anicic entered the UNK, Dani was leaning on the electronic control blocks by VIKO, apparently having a rest. Major Stoimenov got up and moved

Figure 8-16: The crew which downed the Stealth:

Standing left to right: Sergeant Dejan Tiosavljevic, Sergeant Dragan Matic, Lt. Col. Zoltan Dani, Lt. Col. Djordje Anicic, Major Boris Stoimenov.

Kneeling left to right: Sub-Lieutenant Darko Nikolic, Sergeant Djordje Maletic, Captain Senad Muminovic, Sergeant Vladimir Ljubenkovic. (*Smena* (The Shift), author's archive)

behind the fire control officer so that Anicic could take the seat (as senior officer and his shift commander). Anicic took over the headset with the microphone which is used to contact brigade operation centre. Technically, as Lieutenant Colonel Anicic entered the UNK, he was shift commander, taking over the position with his previous shift. As Lieutenant Colonel Dani was about to leave they exchanged thoughts and information of the day, reflecting on activities in the battalion and the individual tasks (as shown on **Figure 8-15**). Lieutenant Colonel Dani was sitting in the shift commander's place until formal duty handover and Lieutenant Colonel Anicic sat in the deputy commander's chair. When Dani left a few minutes later, Major Stoimenov would take the position of the deputy commander. It was routine procedure that the previous and new shift commanders exchanged information in the duty handover. There was no formal military reporting to each other, rather it was a conversation.

While the two officers talked about the afternoon situation and performed tasks, Lieutenant Colonel Anicic faced the P-18 screen and saw clearly what was happening on the radar screen. Lieutenant Colonel Dani was turned sideways and not facing the screen this time. The P-18 radar screen on VIKO showed that there were airplanes in the air, but out of range and on different azimuths, somewhere in vicinity of Belgrade. The radar imitator that Anicic brought back from the field was not yet connected (see illustration presenting UNK layout with the exact position of every crew member, **Figure 8-15**).

While exchanging thoughts of the day, suddenly the surveillance radar showed three blips at azimuth 195, distance 23 km. Anicic followed three more sweeps when he saw that one target was 17-18 km from the radar. He then informed Dani about the blip on the radar screen (**Figure 8-18**).

'Dani, this guy is coming towards us.'

Dani quickly looked at the screen. The next sweep showed that the blip was 14-15 km away, approaching. After two more radar sweeps Lieutenant Colonel Dani ordered: 'Azimuth 210!... Search!'

Sub-Lieutenant Nikolic, the battery commander, started to turn the control wheels on his UK-31 plan position indicator and the start zone (part of UK60 station) in an attempt to guide the missile guidance officer by azimuth and elevation: 'To the left...to the left stop!...right...up...up...up, stop! Antenna!'

At this moment the fire control radar is turned on. The cat and mouse game starts...Whoever is faster and more agile – wins!

The battery commander guided the fire control officer to the target. Captain Muminovic, fire control officer on his UK-32 station, frantically turned three wheels at the same time trying to find a target on his two screens (**Figure 8-31**) His first attempt was not successful. He couldn't mark up the target (bring the blip into the crosshair on his two screens) and handed over to the manual tracking operators. The target had high angular velocity and was manoeuvring, which might have been why the operators were not able to start tracking. The fire control radar emission seemed too long. What the battery commander thought was that the target had most likely got a warning signal in his cockpit that he was illuminated by the engagement and fire control radar.

The time since the target was detected, fire solution acquired, firing command issued, missile launched and target intercepted could not be more than 27 seconds. Any longer and the station would be hit by an anti-radiation missile. That was the time an AGM-88 HARM needed to fly from the launching airplane to the radar. Tension was in the air...

As the fire-control radar emission was ten seconds long, Lieutenant Colonel Anicic ordered: 'Stop searching! Equivalent!'

Sub-Lieutenant Nikolic didn't hear that command or he might have been confused with two combat shift commanders issuing orders. Lieutenant Colonel Anicic ordered much louder: 'Get – the – High – down!!!' and Nikolic immediately turned it off and reported: 'High – off!'

A few seconds later – the next attempt. Lieutenant Colonel Dani ordered: 'Azimuth 230!... Search!'

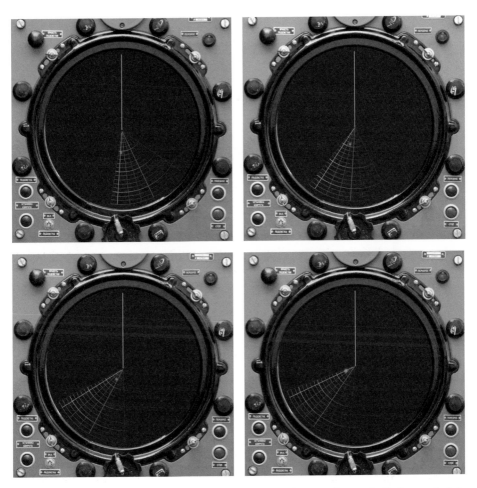

Figure 8-18: P-18 radar illustrations (left to right and top to bottom): Left top: Anicic observes the approaching target; Right top: target at azimuth 195; Bottom left: target at azimuth 210 first search; Bottom right: target at azimuth 230 second search. (Authors)

The guiding station was saturated with humming noises from the electrical equipment, the clicking of switches and wheels, and loud commands and crew responses. This time the guiding officer was able to see the target on both screens. Metal wheels clicked… Captain Muminovic pushed the wheels hard forward to get the target into the crosshairs of his two markers, but after few attempts he was not able to. When the target is in the crosshairs of both markers he can transfer to the manual tracking operators on F1 and F2. The second attempt was when the target was approximately 14 km away.

Again the radar emission was way too long and Anicic commanded: 'Stop searching! Equivalent!!!'

Figure 8-17: Sergeant Matic at his combat position on F2. (Author's archive)

Nikolic responded promptly: 'Equivalent!'

A few seconds later, Dani ordered: 'Azimuth 240! Search!'

The third attempt was when it was 12 km away.

A couple of seconds later, the guidance officer found the target and it was clear that the target was manoeuvring. More clicking of wheels and the target was escaping. Radar emission was 5-6 seconds long and Lieutenant Colonel Anicic said to his commander: 'Dani, be careful, we don't want them to screw us.'

The reason for this concern was that airplanes may use decoys, in some case towed decoys which represent a large reflective surface that can confuse radar operators and mask the real target.

It happened during the first Gulf War that Iraqi crews had the decoy target on their radar screens and locked their firing parameters, only to be hit by an anti-radiation missile fired from the side by one of the fighter-bombers equipped with HARMs.

Lieutenant Colonel Anicic was about to issue an order to stop searching again, because the search time was too long, when the operator for manual tracking on F2, Senior Sergeant Matic (**Figure 8-17**), vigorously turning his wheels in attempt to get the target in the centre of the crosshairs on his screen, yelled: 'Give it to me! Give it to me!...I have him!!!'

At that moment Muminovic pushed his wheel forwards and handed over the target to the manual tracking operators: 'Track manually!'

Sergeant Matic locked the target on F2 crosshairs on his UK-33 screen… and that was it… he got him!

The second operator on manual tracking on F1, Sergeant Tiosavljevic, got the target on his screen markers as well. The screen reflection was very big. The target was 'caught' and both manual tracking operators had it on their screens.

Captain Muminovic reported that the station had stable tracking, the target was in approaching path… distance to target 13 km. Both F1 and F2 operators reported that they had stabile target tracking. All parameters for firing were achieved.

'Station tracking target… target in approach… distance 13 km!'

The operators reported: 'F1 manual tracking on!… F2 manual tracking on!'

The battery commander didn't reported target engagement probability but Lieutenant Colonel Dani still commanded: 'Destroy the target! Three point method!… 'Launch!!!'

Muminovic pushed the start button and the first missile engine started and blasted off from the launcher.

'First missile launched! First missile tracking!' (both F1 and F2 operators manually guided the first missile).

After five seconds the second missile blasted too. The noise of launching was so loud that everybody in the surrounding area including base camp heard it. Gravel beneath the launchers was blown with the rocket engine blast and hit the UNK van like shrapnel.

'Second missile launched – second missile not tracking!!!'

As both F1 and F2 operators reported stable manual guiding for the first missile the second missile didn't acquire the target and the tracking was lost. The first missile was 5-6 seconds in flight and 10 more seconds to the interception point. The F1 operator reported that the target had large RCS.

Lieutenant Colonel Anicic rose from his seat and looked over the manual tracking operator's shoulder: 'How come it didn't catch the target?!! Why?!!'

The first missile was on a stable trajectory to the target but the second lost contact with the station and continued on its ballistic trajectory away from the target. Something went wrong with the guidance channel. The crew looked at the last few kilometres before the missile reach the target…then the large flash blips on the missile guiding officer's screen. The missile reached the target at 20:42… target destroyed… the interception was at 8,000 metres altitude. The target was acquired at 6,000 metres. Obviously the pilot saw the launch or had been warned that he was illuminated by the fire control radar and tried to perform anti-missile manoeuvres, but once locked there was no chance he could avoid being hit. The whole operation lasted about 23 seconds (**Figure 8-19**, **Figure 8-20**, **Figure 8-21**, **Figure 8-22**, **Figure 8-23**).

On impact with the ground, the wreckage caught fire and the fuselage was destroyed (**Figure 8-24**) but the left wing stayed almost intact (**Figure 8-25**).

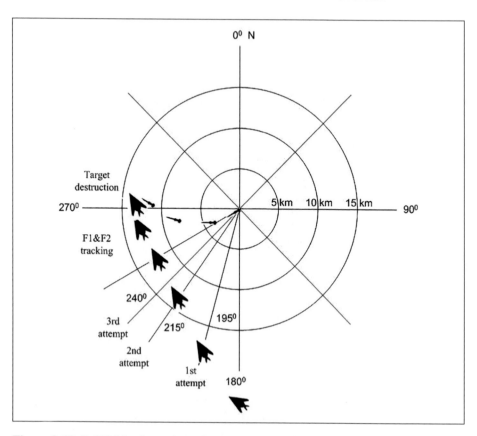

Figure 8-19: F-117A horizontal combat engagement diagram. (Authors)

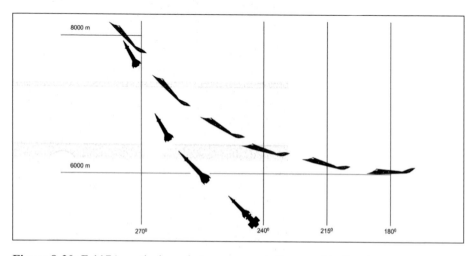

Figure 8-20: F-117A vertical combat engagement diagram. (Authors)

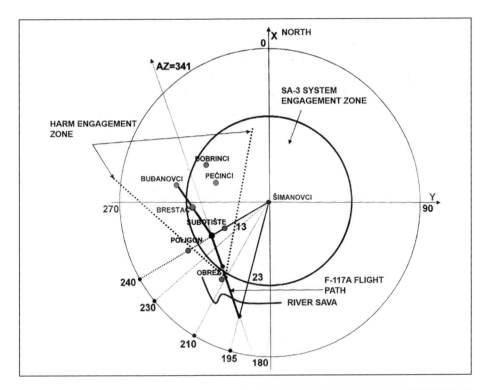

Figure 8-21: Parametric analysis of the F-117A engagement. (V. Neskovic)

Figure 8-22: Artist's impression of the F-117A immediately after the first (and only) missile hit the left wing. (Authors)

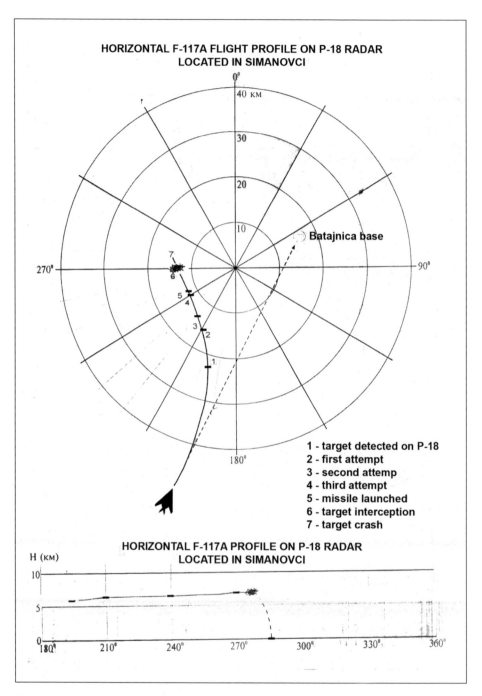

Figure 8-23: Horizontal and vertical flight profiles on P-18 radar located in Simanovci. (V. Neskovic)

Figure 8-24: F-117A fuselage wreckage near the village Budjanovci. (RTS)

Figure 8-25: F-117A wing. (RTS)

How Missile Battalion Works

Roles and duties in an SA-3 missile battalion are defined and regulated through the operation and service manuals issued by the Ministry of Defence and Air Defence branch of the armed forces. It is essentially based on Soviet military doctrine with some minor local modifications. The subjects of these manuals are not much different from those of their western counterparts: combat service, organization, system equipment, communication, safety, etc.

To have a fully trained and functional missile system combat crew, years of training and exercising are necessary. For example, for an officer direct from military academy, to be fully familiar with every component of the system, a minimum of five years on the designated system is necessary. For a commander, ten years work on the system is a necessary minimum. As we saw previously, only Lieutenant Colonel Anicic had such experience. Other officers were trained for other systems but still had some experience on SA-3, thanks to intensive pre-war training and exercises on the AKKORD simulation and training system (**Figure 8-26**).

In peacetime conditions, in the missile battalions classified as 'A formations', there are always two combat crews fully trained in the following:

- AKKORD – specially designed realistic combat simulator cabin (an identical copy of a UNK station) for simulation of different combat scenarios);

Figure 8-26: AKKORD combat simulation training system at Belgrade fair. (Authors)

210

- Training with own air force during tactical exercises and combined tactical training, and
- Unit deployment from primary to reserve fire positions.

Typically the first combat crew includes the most experienced and trained staff. They consist of four officers, two NCOs and two enlisted servicemen. The peacetime formation of the combat crew consists of: shift commander – unit commander as a shift commander; the deputy commander (XO) who is the deputy shift commander; the missile battery commander (on the missile preparation station); missile guidance officer; manual tracking NCO on F1; and manual tracking NCO on F2. The two enlisted servicemen manned the manual plotting table and fire control plan as well as the shift register. The roles of each member of the crew will be explained in detail later.

In some peacetime exercises, depending on the location of the P-18 surveillance radar, and to reduce the number of people engaged, it was possible to consolidate the duty of the shift commander and the deputy commander in one role. In war conditions this was not acceptable, nor did SA-3 combat procedures allow it. Some of the missile battalions acted in this way with a reduced combat crew consisting of three officers, two NCOs and no enlisted men. One reason why this happened was that there were some 'older cadres' trained on SA-2 systems in which the manuals and rules of engagement did not consider the position of a deputy shift commander. We will solve this dilemma when we come to the consideration of the duties of the shift commander and the deputy shift commander. The designers of the SA-3 system established the formation position and role for the deputy shift commander to achieve the optimal number of combat crew. The typical missile battalion schematic with equipment positions is shown in **Figure 8-27**.

War conditions require a completely different arrangement. NATO aviation was active around the clock, which required continuous standby and rotation of people and equipment in combat readiness Nos. 1 and 2. Equipment was sometimes ON twenty-two hours a day. This required two shifts who, rotated every six or eight hours, were under enormous psychological and physical strain.

The first combat crew was commanded by Lieutenant Colonel Dani, the second crew was commanded by Battalion XO Lieutenant Colonel Anicic.

To save one life in the event of a missile strike on the station, one of the enlisted serviceman positions – fire control plan and register – was eliminated. That position was taken by a serviceman who controlled the manual plotting board. The manual plotting board was used only in the initial period of the war until NATO degraded the airborne surveillance and guidance system (VOJIN). The data about the situation in the air received from them had a few minutes delay which meant that it was basically useless by the time it was received in

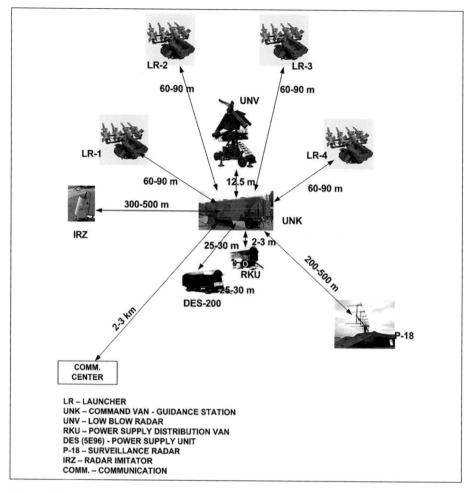

Figure 8-27: Typical 3rd Battalion combat position. Under Soviet procedures, the UNV can be located up to 75 m from the UNK. Only 12.5 m was possible in 3rd Battalion owing to lack of cables. Often the UNV was positioned right beside the UNK. (Authors)

the battalion command centre. In those few minutes, the situation could change drastically. The brigade commander insisted at the beginning of the war that the station and all its subordinate units must be manned continually and to report what they saw to the plotting board. This mistrust irritated the combat service. Very soon after the battalions got hit by the HARM missiles or laser guided bombs from the SEAD groups, this practice was terminated. Soon after that the other enlisted positions in the power generation station and P-18 radar were eliminated too. Since then, up to the end of the war, the fire control station was manned by only four officers and two NCOs. The power supply station and P-18 radar were not manned during combat engagement, but the operators were very close in case their presence in the station was necessary. This reorganization and reduction of people exposed to enemy fire reduced casualties in some battalions.

The 3rd Battalion has an impressive war record: during the 78 days of combat, the unit changed combat position 22 times. Its engineering section built eleven new combat positions. It was targeted by 23 anti-radiation missiles, remains of which were found. It is possible that it was targeted more but missile fragments were not found. Not a single missile ever hit any object and not a single battalion member was killed or injured. It is the only unit in the 250th Brigade with this record. It made two confirmed kills: one F-117A and one F-16CG which crashed in Serbian territory. During the night of 19/20 May a very large aerial target was hit, and although there is no material evidence that it crashed in Serbian territory, there is much to indicate that it was a large aircraft. At the time, the only three large aircraft used in the bombing of Yugoslavia were B-2, B-1B and B-52. This will be analyzed in the next section.

Applying the rules and manuals of engagement, with some field innovations and modifications at the insistence of the battalion XO, the combat roles of every crew member were clearly defined and not a single time did the battalion lose the connection with brigade command, properly informing them about the situation in the designated area. They never unnecessarily exposed themselves to the enemy and also were always aware of the positions of their own airplanes in the designated airspace and in the vicinity of Batajnica military airport and Surcin civilian airport.

As we have seen, the battalion has three stages of readiness.

Readiness No. 1 means that all equipment is powered and at least two missiles are in position ready for launch. The missile station and other equipment is tested for functionality. The shift commander then reports that the battalion is at full readiness with two guidance channels and in combat readiness with two, six, eight or more missiles. All communication goes through landlines.

Missiles in firing positions can be held in the following positions:

- Transport position on PR-14 vehicles
- Loading position
- Duty position – on the 5P-73 launching ramp
- Combat position on the launching ramp

In the combat position to transfer the missile from 'stand by' to readiness for launch an interval of at least 30 seconds is necessary. Command transfer is executed from the UNK with the button switch. In this regime, the maximum duration for the missile to be ready for launch is 25 minutes, after which the system automatically turns it off. There is an embedded system restriction that the missile must be 20 minutes in 'off' mode before it can be transferred again to the 30 second regime. One cycle of missile preparation includes 25 minutes in 'ready for launch' position and 20 min in 'off' position. After that the cycle starts again. There is the possibility that in case of emergency the missile can be turned on in the launch position; that is regulated in the manuals (**Figure 8-27**).

Readiness No.2 means that the crew are in combat positions; the equipment is powered but the manual switches are in the 'off' position; the temperature of the oil and coolant must be kept higher than 37°C.

Readiness No. 3 means that the crew is in base camp with 15 minutes readiness. That means that the crew must be ready to get into position, test equipment functionality and report that it is in readiness for combat within 15 minutes.

'Ready for launch' is when the brigade assigns the target to the battalion or, in the case of the sudden appearance of a target in the assigned sector, that missiles are ready for launch. It is basically the same as readiness No. 1 except that in this case at least four missiles are ready for immediate launch on two different launchers. Missiles are turned onto readiness No. 1 at 3-5 seconds intervals about thirty seconds before the functionality checking of the station is finished.

'Rapid readiness for launch' from readiness No. 2 is executed in the same way as readiness No. 1 with the exception that the functionality of the station is performed until the fire control radar is turned 'on' at high voltage which then turns 'off' the functionality check. The fire control radar then immediately starts to search for the target.

Because there is a timeframe restriction for how long missiles can be in 'ready to launch' mode, it is crucial for the commander to determine when and how missile readiness is distributed. The last thing that the commander wants is to have a target inside the engagement envelope but no ready missiles on the launchers. The 'golden rule' is not to put the missile into launching readiness unless the target is within the engagement zone.

Combat Crew – The Shift

The role of every member of the combat crew is crucial and every member has a predetermined role. The positions are as follows:

- Combat shift commander
- Deputy combat shift commander
- Battery commander
- Missile guidance officer
- Manual tracking operator on F1
- Manual tracking operator on F2
- Manual plotting board operator
- Fire control plotting board operator and shift clerk

Figure 8-15 shows the layout of the cabin. Every workplace has a determined role and not all positions are engaged at the same time. Commands and reports overlap and for a well-trained and synchronized crew that is not a problem. The goal is that within 25-27 seconds the aerial target must be engaged and downed.

On the night of March 27, the situation in the UNK was the following:

Combat Shift Commander
The working position of the shift commander is in front of the detached P-18 radar screen (VIKO) which is on his right-hand side (**Figure 8-28**). His workplace is about 32 cm higher than the other crew members' work stations. This allows the shift commander to have an unobstructed view to the rest of the cabin, excluding the position of the manual tracking operator on F1. Behind the commanders back there are electronic blocks that control the missile launchers. The commander's position is intentionally designed this way so that the deputy shift commander also has an clear view of the detached P-18 radar screen. The rules direct that at least the battalion commander, battalion deputy commander (XO) and missile battery commander must be fully trained on the SA-3 system. The 3rd Battalion had two trained crew commanders – the battalion commander and the XO. The missile battery commander was not fully trained as a crew commander. As the battalion commander was often absent because of other obligations, the battalion logistics officer was trained for the duties of the shift commander. He was not checked by the brigade command, but he was fully trained and with a lot of experience on SA-2. He was partially familiar with SA-3.

Figure 8-28: VIKO radar screen in the UNK station. View form the deputy shift commander's position. (Authors)

The combat shift commander must command as per the directives of the combat procedures manuals and fire control manuals which includes:

- Control of airspace through the detached surveillance radar (VIKO) screen from the P-18 radar
- Issues orders for target search, starts and stops the search in the designated sector taking into consideration time durations critical for operation
- Issues orders for tracking the designated target; issues order to launch missiles; determines missile guidance methods, numbers of missiles, launch methods, warhead activations
- Keeps communication link with upper command

Combat Shift Deputy Commander

His work place is beside the shift commander on his left-hand side, right at the side entrance, directly facing the VIKO screen. He has an unobstructed clear and ergonomic view of the screen. Some of his defined roles include:

- Together with the crew commander controls the airspace through the VIKO screen; marks the potential target and assigns priorities using charts and nomograms (diagram representing relations between three or more variable quantities by means of a number of scales)
- Determines the primary target
- Commands the interior battalions' units – communications, guards, P-18 surveillance radar, power supply, radar emission imitator etc.

Battery Commander

The battery commander sits at the missile preparation station. The distance from this position to the shift commander's place is about 2 metres towards the middle of the command van and is the furthest officer position from the commander and deputy commander. In the first combat shift, that duty was performed by the battery commander and in the second shift it was the first missile battery platoon commander (**Figure 8-29**). His duties include:

- Follows orders issued by the commander or deputy commander
- Turns on and off high voltage at the fire control radar transmitter
- Turns on and off the fire control radar ('antenna-equivalent' switch),
- Commands/instructs the missile guidance officer to the assigned azimuth and angle to get target acquisition radar beam at the same point the surveillance radar detected the target. Commands may include left, right, up or down. Under his instruction the missile guidance officer, turning his azimuth and angle wheels, can scan the designated aerial sector on two levels.

Figure 8-29: Battery commander station. The middle set of buttons right of screen (top picture) are missile readiness indicators. (Authors)

- Determines possibilities for target engagement based on the circular indicator PKO (**Figure 8-30**)
- Determines which missile launcher will be used
- Prepares launchers
- Commands the missile section

The deputy commander and the missile battery commander are two different functions. They do not have the same duties.

When the command 'Azimuth 210, search!' is issued, the battery commander, looking at his UK-31 screen, starts to guide the missile guidance officer to turn the UNV antennas to the commanded azimuth (in this case azimuth 210). The commands may be right, left, up or down depending on which azimuth he directed his fire control radar. The exact position of the UNV the battery commander can determine based on the instrument scale located beneath the UK-31 screen or by the reading directly from the screen in front of him. If the position was azimuth 180 and he needed to direct to azimuth 210, the command is 'RIGHT, RIGHT!' As the missile guiding officer moves his wheels to the right, on the battery commander's UK-31 screen the line which starts from the middle of the screen (zero radiation emission line, in other words, emitter, missile battery) and ending at the periphery, shows movement from 180 to 210. When the antenna movement

217

Figure 8-30: Battery commander screen (top) and command table (left). (Authors)

reaches 5-10 degrees before azimuth 210, the battery commander turns the switch 'ANTENNA-EQUIVALENT' to 'ANTENNA' and at that moment high frequency energy is radiated into space. He then reports to the shift commander: 'ANTENNA!'

With this action, the fire control radar is emitting into space and starts illuminating the area where the target is.

The battery commander continues to guide the missile guiding officer 'RIGHT, RIGHT' searching for the target up to azimuth 220. If the target is not acquired, he commands 'STOP, LEFT' until azimuth 200 is reached. That mean plus or minus 10 degrees left and right from the azimuth ordered by the shift commander.

If by any chance the target is not acquired in one sweep, he then commands the guidance officer 'UP!' which means sweeping the space at the same azimuth but at a different altitude. An experienced missile guiding officer will know how to sweep the area with 3-5 wheel turns even without commands in the shortest possible high frequency emission time. Every time the battery commander sees on his screen the line pass over the target and there is a blip he must warn the guidance officer with: 'YOU HAVE TARGET!' An experienced battery commander will do that routinely. Sub-Lieutenant Nikolic, fresh from the academy, was not experienced.

The 'Antenna-Equivalent' switch for antenna to start emission into the designated space or to switch to equivalent which means that high frequency energy is turned off and is not emitted while the radar is still on.

If high frequency radiation is emitted for too long there is a real danger that the position of the radar may be detected and an anti-radiation missile launched.

Missile Guiding (Guidance) Officer
The missile guidance officer is positioned on the left-hand side of the battery commander. His duties include:

- During combat engagement acts as per commands issued by the shift commander and battery commander
- In passive regime performs the controls of the designated sector
- Transfers the UNK station into the combat regime
- Acts as ordered by the battery commander searching for the target turning the two wheels on azimuth and angle (elevation) 3-5 clicks left-right or up-down,
- Reports to the shift commander on the detected and acquired target
- Tracks the target distance
- Commands the manual operators on F1 and F2 in manual tracking mode.
- Performs the missile launch. Reports target acquisition, guidance and hit or miss
- Assesses the results

In the first combat shift this duty was performed by the assigned missile guidance officer. In the second shift this position was assigned to the commander of the transmission platoon from the missile guidance battery.

Behind the missile guidance officer there is an empty space where it is only possible to stand during the combat engagement. This space during peacetime training was often used by the senior officers of the brigade or military control bodies during assessments and evaluations.

The missile guidance officer acts as ordered by the battery commander and his main task is to 'overlap' the target on his two UK-32 screens. The goal is to get the target into the cross of the horizontal and vertical markers. Experience and practice play a great role and can save vital seconds. The crew commander must stop the search if it is taking too long. If the commander doesn't do it then the deputy commander must issue that order. In short, time management is essential for survival.

The SA-3 system requires simultaneous manipulation of the three metal wheels (**Figure 8-31**). Hand coordination and speed are key. Captain Muminovic was not experienced at working with the three wheels at the same time: azimuth, elevation and distance – and it took him longer to acquire the target. We saw that he had acquired the target by the third attempt and at that time he was able to track it.

By the clicking of the wheels, the commander may determine the situation. Manual tracking operators on their screens also see the target. When the guiding officer pushes the wheels for himself and commands 'TRACK MANUALLY!' he transfers the tracking to the manual tracking operators who then track the target. Although the operator on F2 can acquire the target on his screen, the guidance officer can transfer tracking if he has it.

Figure 8-31: Missile guidance officer station (left) and lunch button (top). Turning wheels (at the bottom of the left picture) he can search for the target as per orders from the battery commander. Once when the target is acquired, he can transfer it to the manual tracking stations (operators on F1 and F2) and launch the missiles pressing the launch button (top picture). (Authors)

Figure 8-32: Indication of
the target position on the
missile guidance position.
(SAM simulator – authors'
modification)

On the block UK-62 in front of the guiding officer the lights 'RS F1' and 'RS F2' are illuminated (**Figure 8-31**, **Figure 8-32**).

Manual Tracking Operator F1
This NCO position is right behind the missile guidance operator. It is located in a 'cavity' off the central passage in a very tight space. In the first shift it was the system operator who was also tracking operator from the missile guidance battery. In the second shift it was the system operator (**Figure 8-33**). His duties include:

- Manually tracking the target as ordered by the missile guidance officer
- Reports to the missile guidance officer on tracking conditions

Figure 8-33: Manual tracking on
F1 screen (top). (Authors)

Manual Tracking Operator F2

This position is located beside the shift and deputy shift commander. On his right-hand side is the missile guidance officer. With a half turn he can see the VIKO screen.

His duties include:

- Assess the optical visibility on the television optical system (VPU-44)
- Manually track the target as ordered by the missile guidance officer
- Report to the missile guidance officer on tracking conditions.

When the missile guiding officer switch the tracking to the manual operators, on their stations the switch "Peredacha na RS", which is original Russian designation

Figure 8-34: Manual tracking operator on F2 station. At the top of the picture is a TV screen for visual tracking in passive mode. (Authors)

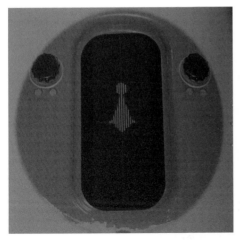

Figure 8-35: F2 screen (left) – the target is the dot at the top and the missile approaching the target is the blip below the target a few seconds before impact. F-117's characteristic shape on F2 screen (right) An experienced operator can recognize the target type from the size and shape of the blip (RCS). (Authors)

and mean "Manual tracking transfer" is illuminated on the blocks UK-68. Both F1 and F2 operators must push the button "VKL RS" to activate the manual tracking (**Figure 8-34, Figure 8-35**).

Turning their wheels their vertical markers must be positioned over the target centre. With this, they established the conditions for the missiles launch.

Manual Plotting Board Operator

This is an enlisted position. He is positioned a few metres from the shift commander, behind the 1.5 x 1.5 m transparent Plexiglas plotting board. His working position takes almost the whole width of the station. His main duty includes:

- Plot the aerial situation as per information received from the VO-JIN service or as per information received from the battalion's own surveillance radar (P-18). Information is plotted in mirror so that the shift commander can see it in normal view.

A challenge of this position is that the enlisted man must be capable of writing numbers in mirror writing. When the shift commander sees the board and the target is within the engagement zone he may order the target to be engaged. By modern standards, this manual plotting board is obsolete and no modern air defence missile system now uses it.

Fighting Sequences

Once the surveillance radar from the brigade detects the target and assigns it to the battalion or the battalion detects the target with their own surveillance and tracking radar, either under direction from the brigade post or independently, the shift commander issues the order to the battery commander to search with the engagement and fire control radar in the direction of the target and its estimated height. That is the meaning of command 'Azimuth (such and such)…Search.' At that moment, the engagement and fire control radar is turned on and high frequency energy emits into the space in the direction of the target. The target is illuminated with that energy. At the same time as the energy illuminates the target, the receiver at the target may detect that it is 'caught', and typically the audio signal accompanied with a flashing light informs the pilot that he is 'in the radar sight'. Energy can also be detected by other airplanes in the vicinity.

Typical Soviet-style combat engagement rules and manuals require that the engagement of the target shall be at the furthest zone of destruction. The disadvantage of this is that the whole procedure extends, the target has a greater chance of knowing it is being tracked, and it can then perform counter-missile manoeuvres thus lowering the chance of a hit. Also, if the target is equipped with anti-radiation missiles such as HARM it can shoot at the radar. The speed of an anti-radiation missile may be higher than the speed of the SAM missile, so there is probability that the radar will be hit before the guided missile reaches the aircraft.

Because of this, it was a wise tactical decision of the crew to let the target get deeper into the destruction zone. For example, if the effective range of NEVA is 25 km, the optimal distance for probable destruction is half that, 12-13 km. The high frequency energy emission of the engagement and fire control radar is for only a limited period of time, 5-6 seconds, which reduces the time for an anti-radiation missile to acquire and hit the radar. The Low Blow is designed to acquire targets using only bearing and range inputs from an external 2D acquisition radar, such as a P-12/18 Spoon Rest or P-15M Squat Eye. Third Battalion has only P-18 radar. When acquiring an aerial target, the Low Blow radar head is rotated to the target bearing and the UV-10 antenna scanning feed engages to produce a pencil beam 1° wide swept in elevation (**Figure 8-37**).

During target acquisition, the pencil beam of the UV-10 antenna scans a 10° sector vertically. The maximum range for target detection is 80 km. During target tracking, the pencil beam of the UV-10 antenna illuminates the target and measures its range. The two wide-beam UV-11 antennas receive the target, and angle of missiles (F1, F2). The maximum range for target tracking is 50 km. Two main range modes can be selected: 80 km and 40 km. In 80 km mode, only half of the electromagnetic impulses are sent, as they have to travel twice the range compared to 40 km mode.

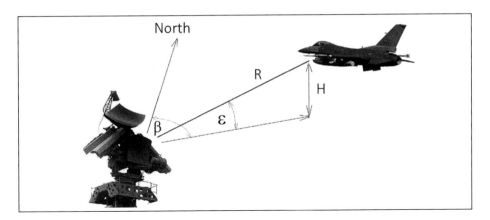

Figure 8-37: Parametric coordinate system. (SAM simulator, author's modification)

Where:
R   Target range
H   target altitude
ε   Elevation (antenna up/down)
β   Azimuth (antenna left/right)

Once the target is acquired the Low Blow is switched into tracking mode, using the UV-10 antenna to transmit, the UV-12 to receive for ranging, and the scanning UV-11 chevron receiver antennas for angle tracking. The radar head is mechanically steered in azimuth and elevation to maintain track (**Figure 8-38**).

Russian doctrine in the presence of heavy jamming was often to cease emitting and use the scanning receiver to effect angle tracking of the jammer, acquire the target with the TV telescope, and perform a range unknown missile shot against the jammer in CLOS mode.

Due to the addition of a clutter canceler and analogue MTI circuits, the Low Blow has significantly better clutter rejection performance than the earlier Fan Song radar used in SA-2. Low altitude capability is cited as low as 20 metres.

The command 'Equivalent' is to turn off the high frequency energy emission, but not to turn off the radar. This means the system keeps the equivalent load but the energy is redirected and effectively 'encapsulated' into the system and turned into heat. The heat generated means that there is still some energy emission which could be detected by an anti-radiation missile. The command 'Get the high down' means that the high voltage is turned off but the emitter is still working in normal mode but there is no high energy emission. It is the role of battery commander to work on this on his UV-61 station.

Manual operators on F1 and F2 guide the missile on F1 and F2 levels. In search and guiding regime there are two standard levels – azimuth and elevation.

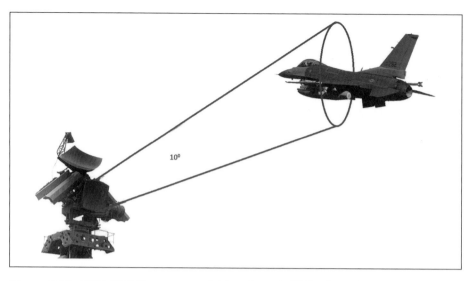

Figure 8-38: SNR-125M1 target acquisition through UNV (UV-10). (SAM simulator, author's modification)

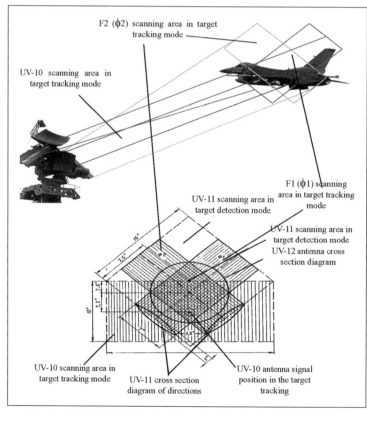

Figure 8-39: UNV antenna emissions zones (top) (SAM simulator modified by authors) and zone interlocking diagram (right). (Soviet S-125M manual, modified by authors)

226

When the command to start manual tracking is issued, this is done on levels F1 and F2. They are positioned at 90° relative to each other and 45° related to the surface (**Figure 8-39**).

The radar imitator starts emitting a few seconds before the fire control radar, on the same frequencies, and continues to do so during the entire fire sequence. It is turned off few seconds after the fire control radar is turned off or in the 'equivalent' mode. This provides additional protection for the UNK because an anti-radiation missile may pick up the emission from the imitator and divert from the UNK.

The disadvantage at that time was that the radar imitator crew needed to manually turn the imitator to the designated azimuth as per order from the UNK. It would be way better if the movement of the imitator was synchronized with the movements of the radar antenna. At that time the battalion had to make the best of what was available.

What is of the crucial importance for any missile unit is the power supply. All is useless without power. The SA-3 system is supplied with 200 kW from two diesel generators. During combat, both generators are connected in parallel providing dual supply as fail-safe.

Immediately After...

Immediately after the crew observed the hit and disintegration of the aircraft, the engagement and fire control radar was turned off. Standard procedure calls for immediate evacuation of the existing position and relocation to the previously chosen alternative. There is speculation that the crew knew that they were tracking an F-117A, but that is nonsense. UNV S-125 engagement and fire control radar and tracking surveillance P-18 radar does not have any ability to recognize what kind of airplane is in the air. It is just a blip on a radar screen and for the missile crew it is a target. No exact shape can be determined, no type, just the size because of the reflection. For the crew, that was the target that was tracked, engaged and destroyed according to the rules of combat engagement.

Lieutenant Colonel Anicic, as per the rules of engagement, reported to the brigade HQ about the engagement. That report consisted of the crew, the guidance method, launching sequences, missile usage, warhead activation method, and, as per information from the missile guidance officer, Captain Muminovic, the basic parameters of the target engagement. The shift clerk also wrote the facts into the battalion combat logbook. Anicic also, as the battalion XO, organized the march to the new location. The hard work soon took its toll on the men.

Every missile crew celebrates after a successful hit, and that is what 3rd Battalion did. This was the first target downed on Serbian territory. However, time was crucial, and the battalion needed to be relocated as soon as possible

Figure 8-40: F-117A canopy with pilot's name. The actual pilot was Dale Zelko (RTS)

Above left: **Figure 8-41**: Lieutenant Colonel Anicic (left) and Lieutenant Colonel Dani (right). (Author's archive)

Above right: **Figure 8-42**: Lieutenant Colonel Anicic (left) and Captain Muminovic (right). (Author's archive)

because there was real danger that the position had been compromised and air strikes might follow. At 21:15 Brigade command ordered the unit to relocate to the new position and it did so in about 2 hours.

At 22:00 TV station Studio B said, 'F-117A, pride of the US Air Force, has been downed into the "Srem mud".' It created shockwaves throughout the media and in military and aviation circles. Jubilant soldiers and civilians from the neighborhood of the crash site poured in to see the wreck. Hardly any media in the world didn't report it. Ken Dwelle was the name on the F-117A canopy. Most reported that name as the pilot of the airplane, which was actually wrong (**Figure 8-40**).

What happened afterwards in the battalion, how it affected the course of the war, and all speculations will be explained in the following sections (**Figure 8-41**, **Figure 8-42**).

Vega Three-One

Vega-Three-One, or Lieutenant Colonel Dale Zelko (**Figure 8-42**), was one of the most experienced combat pilots, with Operation Desert Storm under his belt. He was a member of the 8th Squadron deployed during the third week of February 1999 from Holloman AFB New Mexico to Aviano Air Base in north-eastern Italy in a demanding nonstop 14 hour and 45 minute flight. It was the longest flight he had ever flown. The most challenging part of that deployment for him and most other pilots, including the squadron commander, Lieutenant Colonel Waltering, was night-time flying over the Atlantic. It was pitch black and hard to find a horizon line. Zelko had never fought so hard against spatial disorientation before. And the F-117A's cockpit is especially conducive to spatial disorientation; it is a constant challenge not to get sucked into it. It was mentally and physically exhausting.

This chapter quotes Lieutenant Colonel Zelko's own words from his interview with Brazilian National Air Force Magazine journalist Carlos Lorch, with our inputs and comments.

For US pilots, Operation Allied Force was a different story than Operation Desert Storm. The dynamics of the politics involved created many constraints, which prevented pilots from employing optimum tactics. Zelko felt that at the beginning of Allied Force there was an element of complacency.

Figure 8-43: Lieutenant Colonel Dale Zelko. (USAF)

During the month or so that 8th Squadron were in Aviano getting ready for operations, the pilots were worried. The scenario was confusing, as there were many operations going on directed by a variety of different entities, such as NATO and the UN, and when they first started flying combat missions they still hadn't developed appropriate special instructions, having to rely on those being used by what were essentially peace-keeping forces.

On those first few nights of the war, the pilots were briefed and told that if they went down and were captured they were to claim that they were not enemy combatants! The authors didn't confirm this in conversation with the pilots, but knowing how military bureaucracy works, it would not be surprising. This, of course, was ridiculous.

All of that changed dramatically immediately after the Vega-31 episode. The F-117A AF 82-0806 downing and Combat Search and Rescue (CSAR) was a wake-up call. In Yugoslavia, pilots did not go in and pound Serbian Air Defence. They essentially left it untouched. There's a large difference, even for a low-observable platform, if one is going in against crippled air defences compared to a fully functioning system. The threat from the SAM systems over Yugoslavia, combined with the factors hindering pilots from operating optimally, all came together, opening the way for the shoot down.

The theatre of operation over Yugoslavia has been divided into a northern and southern sector (44th parallel). In the north of the country, airplanes would fly out of Aviano across Slovenia, rendezvous with refuelling tankers over Hungary, wait for push time, stealth up, drop their tanks and proceed onto their strike missions; one or two targets depending on the target and the weapons required. If the targets were in the south, airplanes would fly down the Adriatic, refuel off the tankers maybe two-thirds of the way down, push through Montenegro, and go in that way (**Figure 8-44**).

Zelko flew on the first wave on 24 March, the first night of Allied Force. He flew again on the third night and the fourth. The main objective on the night of 27 March was a critical, heavily defended target in the vicinity of Belgrade: the Strazevica underground command centre (**Figure 8-45**). According to his statement, he knew what he was up against. In most US articles, the opinion of Serbian air defence was that 'Serbia was defended by a superior IADS encompassing state of the art Russian equipment and manned by highly trained, skilled and extremely motivated operators.'

The last part, about the people, is true, but 'state-of-the-art Russian equipment' is far from the reality. Serbia was defended by outdated systems. But still, if applied correctly, it could be effective. One high-ranking US commander compared the Serbian air defence with an old car: a lot of mileage, but still running well, even if it needs a major overhaul.

The Vega-31 target for the night had been on the planning board, and flown against before, unsuccessfully. So there was another attempt on the fourth night, to neutralize the centre. Some missions for the night of 27 March were cancelled because of the weather conditions. It was decided that the attacks would be spearheaded with F-117As and B-2s. The first wave consisted of eight F-117As, four F-16CGs, two F-15Cs and eight F-16CJs for the SEAD mission. They were supported with one British E-3 Sentry (code name Magic 86), one EC-130E flying over Bosnian airspace, four EA-6B for radar and communication jamming and a group of KC-135 fuel tankers. The second wave consisted of 4 F-117As and reduced support aircraft. The third wave, three to four hours later, with B-2 bombers flying directly from the US base.

Figure 8-44: F-117A night refuelling. (USAF)

Figure 8-45: Strazevica Command Centre, located in Rakovica – hit many times, including Zelko's hit, but never damaged. (NATO)

The weather was very challenging that night and all other Allied Force strike packages had been cancelled. Only eight F-117s went out after targets in the northern part of the country.

During the early stages of ingress, Zelko was monitoring a primary strike frequency, listening to other events unfolding that were part of the strike mission. Even before stepping into the aircraft from his squadron life support storage shop[9], he had a feeling that if he was going to get shot down on any night, then this was the one. He was well aware of his vulnerabilities, and the dangers of the mission that night. As he later said:

> The information coming over the radio during ingress simply increased my gut feeling that something bad was very likely to happen that night. So when it happened it didn't surprise me at all. As a matter of fact, I watched it happen!

What is surprising is that neither Zelko nor any other pilot spoke about the Radar Warning Receiver (RWR) tone which is a common feature in all airplanes. To the question 'did he ever hear it' his answer was:

> That gets into the capabilities of the F-117. But I will tell you that I visually watched the surface to air missile engagement, and that even in its early stages there was no doubt in my mind that they had me. I did everything I could to prevent it but it was just unavoidable. And remember, I had a front row seat throughout the entire engagement. So was it pilot related? No. Was it maintenance related? No. Was it a good shot? Yes, it was a good shot. I can't get into details about exactly how they were able to put a surface to air missile warhead into the same airspace as an F-117 low-observable aircraft because that's very sensitive, even today. But I can kind of give you a sense. You know it's not invisible technology. We have never said it was invisible technology, we've always said it was low-observable technology. The F-117 relies a great deal on its low-observable characteristics to survive.
>
> So, just like anything, there are limitations and vulnerabilities. And if you give an adversary the opportunity to exploit them, they will. The Serbs are great fighters and they certainly saw the opportunity. So essentially, we gave them the opportunity because of the way we were operating. They saw the opening, they took

---

9. US pilots call a unit support warehouse a 'shop'.

advantage of it, and it was just a good shot. Was it preventable by us if we had changed things? Yes, absolutely.

However, in the book *Stealth Down* by Ross Simpson, there is a paragraph on page 102 which says: 'He was in the process of clearing the target when heard a sound that sent a cold chill up his spine. A warbling sound from the radar warning receiver told Sugar D (Zelko's flight name) he was being targeted by a surface-to-air missile, most likely Soviet built SA-3. Moments later, the SAM left its launcher in a blinding flash and headed towards him at more than twice speed of sound.'

It is obvious that there are two different stories. To support Ross Simpson's story, Serbian missile operators recorded that when they started tracking the target with the fire control radar the target started to manoeuvre. That was in the second attempt, before the missiles were launched. More information about the RWR on F-117A can be found in the following section 'The Mystery of the Radar Warning Receiver'.

Now back to Zelko. In his own words, he saw two missiles; however, he was not sure if there weren't others. He started tracking them visually right after launch. During this he started to climb rapidly from 6,000 m. This manoeuvre is not typical SAM evasion tactics. The usual defence is to employ a hard breaking and turning manoeuvre while deploying flares and chaff. The goal of the hard brake and turn is to get outside the cone in front of the missile in which it can obtain and keep a lock, and flares and chaff insert 'dirt or other confusing heat or radar signature between the plane and the missile'. A fighter airplane will dive towards the missile then suddenly change direction, imposing a high-g manoeuvre on his airplane in the hope that the missile will lose contact. The F-117A is not a manoeuvrable airplane; once 'locked' there is a very small chance that it can evade the missile.

> I thought to myself, matter-of-factly: 'You know what? This is bad. I don't think I'm going to skinny through this one.' I had been shot at many times before, but that was the first time I'd ever felt so strongly that I wouldn't make it due to SAM technology.
>
> The first missile went right over the top of me. So close, actually, that I was surprised it didn't proximity fuse on me. I could feel the shock wave of it buffeting the aircraft. As soon as it went over I quickly re-acquired the second missile visually and when I did, I thought: 'It's going to run right into me.' And it sure felt like it did.

The proximity fuse activated the warhead close to the F-117A's left wing. The impact was very violent and slammed the airplane into a left roll with negative 'G'. The impact was visible from the refuelling KC-135 tanker over Bosnia.

SHOOTING DOWN THE STEALTH FIGHTER

There is a discrepancy how many missiles the pilot saw. The battalion fired two missiles and the second one lost the target tracking channel K2 right after the launch and continued flying on the ballistic trajectory far from the airplane. Only the first one acquired the target. The pilot claims that one just missed him and the other hit him. There is no other unit which fired on him. Is it possible that in the heat of battle he is simply exaggerating? Probably.

The pilot of an F-117A sits in an ACES II ejection seat. Pulling the ejection handles retracts the shoulder harness and lock the inertia reel, fires initiators for canopy jettison, and ignites the rocket that removes the canopy. After the canopy separated from the cockpit, lanyards fired two seat ejection initiators which ignited a rocket that catapulted the pilot out of the cockpit. The ejection sequence takes only 1.4 seconds from the moment the rocket motors beneath the seat fire until the pilot separates from the ejection seat.

> Even though I strap in extremely tight, because of the way the G forces were acting on the plane and ejection seat, my body was sliding out from underneath the lap belt. Normally I like to sit with the ejection seat all the way up in order to better look outside the cockpit, so the clearance between the top of my helmet and the canopy is pretty small to start with. So I was pinned to the top of the shoulder straps, with my butt way out of the seat and my torso doubled over in the worst possible position for an ejection.
>
> I was immobilized in this awkward position by the 7 negative G force of the tumbling plane, trying to get my hands down to the side ejection handles. Despite the violence of the event, mentally and emotionally it was all very calm for me. I figured the only thing I could do was to push isometrically with my head against the top of the canopy which would perhaps straighten my spine somewhat once the canopy blew, and before the seat went up the rails. And I tried that move, almost like a wrestler who's pinned down on his back trying the bridge manoeuvre. I don't know if it had any effect. It was amazing to many that I survived at all.
>
> I remember every fragment of the entire strike mission; shoot down, ejection, and CSAR. All, that is, except one. There's just one slice of this entire affair that to this day I just can't get a hold of. I can't recall it as if it never happened. And that's actually reaching the ejection handles and pulling. I may have been unconscious which makes me know even more strongly that I had some help from Heaven getting to those handles and pulling. And in that body position I probably barely got a fingertip in those handles. The next thing I remember is I'm in the seat out of the aircraft. I can

see the cockpit falling away from me and I don't recall the 18g kick in the butt. I don't recall going up the ejection seat rails, none of that. As I was tumbling through the air, myriad thoughts went through my mind, all in a casual, light humorous sort of way. I even remember seeing a mental image of myself kicking the dirt with one foot saying: 'Nuts, isn't this inconvenient. My mom's not going to be happy with me and I might not be able to call my daughter tomorrow on her birthday', who would be turning ten. The good news is that I was able to call her.

Another thought that came to my mind had me imagining standing next to the Serbian SAM operator, enjoying a light conversation and congratulating him[10]. 'Real nice shot!' Then I remember saying to him, 'But you're not going to get me!' Not in an arrogant or cocky way, but with a surge of determination flooding my mind. I realized immediately how important it was to deny the adversary the exploitation and propaganda potential of having a captured senior officer F-117 pilot. This remained a powerful source of determination for me. I estimate I was between 8 and 9 thousand feet when I first got under canopy. It was 19:40 Zulu, 20:40 local time[11]. From pulling the handles to a fully inflated parachute it takes 1.4 seconds. To me it seemed like hours. I instantly went from this extreme violence and chaos to absolute calm when the canopy inflated. All I could hear was a gentle swishing sound of the seat kit and life raft hanging below me on its 25-foot lanyard as the canopy went through its normal oscillation. So I looked down and quickly started getting oriented. Looking north, the first thing I could see was Belgrade off to my right.

And then underneath me, slightly south/southwest, I could see two little fires burning and I figured that was the aircraft. I looked down and saw the seat kit and life raft; I didn't even think to specifically check for injuries. The first time I realized I had an injury was about an hour and a half after ejection at my hole up site on the ground. The next thing I did was check my equipment. I still had my mask on so I disconnected it and tossed it away. My helmet was still on but the visor was gone. Then I looked up and

---

10. The second meeting between the pilot and missile battalion commander happened twelve years later when Col. Zelko visited Serbia and finally met in person the man who was one of the crew commanders that shot him down.
11. The reader will notice that there is a two-minute difference between the battalion timing and the time the pilot remembered.

checked the canopy, which I could see clearly in the nearly full moon night: 'Perfect, no Mae West, no lineovers[12], no blown panels, no streamer...' and it was then that I noticed it. 'You have got to be kidding me,' I remember thinking to myself, still in a light humorous way, 'an orange and white panel parachute!' It was glowing like a Chinese lantern. I patted one of my survival vest pockets with the signal flares and jokingly considered lighting one up to help the Serbians spot me even more easily! Of course that's not what I did. In fact, I knew that despite the presence of a large number of air breathing and non-air breathing NATO assets out there, there could still be a chance that nobody was aware of what just happened. I felt it vitally important to make good two way contact with a friendly as fast as possible. I reached into my g-suit pocket and took out my personal mini-maglite flashlight, which was fitted with a red lens cap. I was familiar with the settings on the top of the survival radio but I wanted to be absolutely sure I had the correct one selected when I started transmitting. I had SAR frequencies, or I could go to 243.0, which was the guard frequency. I could also activate the emergency locator beacon. I knew where all the settings were but I wanted no uncertainty. Funny, I was already transitioning my thinking and frame of reference from 'pilot-in-cozy-cockpit', to the attitude and actions of a high-speed special operations, special tactics covert and low-profile guy on the ground. So in order to prevent anyone seeing the tiny light from my flashlight, floating thousands of feet above the ground, I tucked my body around the light as best I could while I did a quick visual confirmation of the radio settings.

According to procedures, when a pilot is forced to eject he should do nothing but take basic care of himself right after the ejection, i.e. not try to establish radio contact. Once on the ground, he should find an initial hole-up site and treat himself for shock and injuries, and only then try to initiate radio contact. Zelko had different reasoning as he felt great physically and mentally and had a high state of situational awareness. As a life-long fitness fanatic, he was physically very well prepared, maybe the best in the squadron.

He knew his radio was basic with no secure voice and no over-the-horizon capability. He knew that the best chance to get two-way contact was at altitude.

---

12. Lineovers are almost always induced during packing by allowing a brake line to come off the top of the line stack and end up on the wrong side of the nose, often during the 'cigarette rolling', or compacting of the canopy before placing it in the deployment bag. This causes the canopy to inflate with the brake line over the top of the fabric.

He also knew it was very likely that he would be captured soon after hitting the ground with no chance to get on the radio. What he wanted was to deny Yugoslavia the gift of a live and well F-117A pilot, and he wanted rescue forces to know his status. Overall, he sensed how crucial it was to get things going – to get the CSAR energized as fast as possible. So he started making mayday calls, maintaining best possible radio discipline. He know how important it was not to let the enemy fix his position. He assumed the Serbs were listening to everything, and he assumed they knew where every player was and what they were doing. After some time, he raised Frank 36, a KC-135 tanker refuelling F-16 over Bosnia.

The information Zelko passed to KC-135 was that his last known position in the aircraft was his point after target. So that gave them a rough idea of where he might be. Once he was satisfied he had made good two-way contact, he tucked the radio away and got busy with other things. All the while he was on the radio he tried to orient himself. He was coming down through layers of cloud. When he was out of the clouds he could see pieces of ground. As a backup he checked the magnetic compass which was in his survival vest pocket.

He broke through the bottom layer of cloud somewhere around 2,000 feet, giving him roughly two minutes remaining under canopy to better orient himself. As soon as he was underneath the bottom layer of clouds he pulled the four-line jettison, enabling him to steer and control where he was drifting.

The first thing he saw was a town (Ruma) about 5.5 km to the north. This was connected to another town about 2.5 km behind him by a two-lane road, running roughly north-south. There was quite a bit of traffic on the road. He was drifting north/northeast. As far as he could see the terrain was open, flat sections of farm fields separated by sparse shrub lines or irrigation ditches; not ideal for concealment. There was also a major four-lane highway to the north of his position running north-west to south-east (Belgrade–Zagreb).

With some aggressive steering he was able to crab into the wind and land on an open ploughed farm field some 40 metres west of the road he had seen, next to what seemed at the time to be a T intersection leading east. Although he landed softly, there was a stiff wind, so he was dragged a little bit. He was able to deflate the parachute canopy, then he stayed still for about a minute.

Before he touched down he picked out a spot just west of the road some 250 m away which he hoped to be able to use as an initial hole-up site. He thought it was a drainage or irrigation ditch. He got busy securing the landing area. He pulled in the parachute, took off his helmet and harness as well as any hardware items that could catch the light and give his position away. He wanted to get away from spot where he landed as fast as possible. So he put everything he didn't need in the bottom of a ploughed furrow and then put the dark green one-man life raft on top. He packed dirt around the edges and on top of the raft so that the wind wouldn't flip it over and expose everything. He was very cautious to minimize disturbance of the top of the furrows. That would have been easy to spot from the road, particularly with the near-full moon. As he moved towards his chosen initial hole-up spot he was careful to step only in the bottom of the furrows so that he wouldn't disturb the neatly groomed surface and give away his direction of travel. One of the first things he did in the hole-up site was to grab some moist dark Serbian soil and do a bit of expedient combat camouflage to cover all his exposed skin. An hour later he took off his gloves and applied 'soil camouflage' to his wrists and hands. This is when he noticed that the back of his right hand was caked in blood from the scratch he got during the ejection.

It was a wet and cold night. He had on four layers of clothes, with the top layer being a winter flight jacket, as well as three pairs of socks – two thin cotton and one high-quality woolen ski sock. This kept him fairly comfortable through the night. It was important to be well hydrated: he had brought along at least 12 extra flex packs of water besides the 12 normally placed in the survival kit by the life support professionals in Aviano. Water helps to reduce potential shock, it raises alertness and provides strength and endurance to the body and senses. A good dinner before the flight provided him with complex carbohydrate energy. He also had four power bars in his pocket. But nothing can prepare a downed pilot for every circumstance.

Pilots are trained in survival courses to meticulously assess and adapt to the situation. As soon as he was in the hole he made a quick check of all the equipment he had: a survival vest, seat kit and hit-and-run pack. The seat kit is like a little backpack containing survival/evasion equipment. If you land and don't have time or the means to take much, you can sling the hit-and-run pack over your shoulder and take off. Shaped almost like a banana pack, it has the essential items you may need to survive and evade.

In the first hour after he landed, still holed up in the shallow irrigation ditch, Zelko detected and began monitoring Yugoslav search activity close to where he was. The Yugoslavs knew they had shot down an aircraft and were at the wreckage site quickly, probably within 15 minutes of the crash. They certainly realised that they had shot down an F-117A. Next they would do whatever it took to capture the pilot. So they unleashed a manhunt which involved the military, police, and villagers in the area. The letter brought hunting guns and dogs, but the police asked them to 'restrict' their actions because there was a danger of fighting and there could be casualties. If the pilot was captured by local hunters he might not have been treated according to the Geneva Convention.

> I also experienced a little bit of the receiving end of our own actions when I was in my hole-up site. At first I didn't quite know what it was, but remembering the Air Tasking Order, I quickly realized it was the B-2s that were to bomb targets in the general Belgrade area

after us. Although a safe distance away, the bombs hit close enough that the compression and shock waves that went through the air over me in my hole-up site were significant – they got my attention.

The pilot claims to describe shockwaves from the bombs dropped from B-2s which flew after him, but this is highly unlikely because all missions were cancelled after Vicenza command realized that a F-117 was down. Even if the bombs had been dropped, his position was very far away from the targets near or in Belgrade.

All through the night, I was trying to stick as close as possible to my pre-planned EPA [Evasion Plan of Action]. Of course, war fighting is fluid; it's moment by moment, routinely demanding flexibility and improvisation. One dilemma for an evader is how to be as predictable as possible for rescue forces and as unpredictable as possible for the adversary. As soon as I was relatively comfortable with my state of concealment, I took out my hand held GPS. Shortly before we deployed to Aviano, our squadron life support shop had bought, with our own squadron money, a series of basic and inexpensive hand held GPS sets. It came in extremely handy that night.

Before I turned it on, though, I made a rough guess of where I was. I had briefed extensively with our squadron Intel specialists and familiarized myself with the area I'd be operating in before going into combat. I had a very good idea where I was. So I was facing north, and mentally visualized myself with my Intel folks in the squadron briefing room, standing in front of the AOR [Area of Responsibility] map. Before calling up the GPS, I guessed where I was in relationship to some predetermined references. Hunkered down, I couldn't raise enough satellites and had to expose myself somewhat to where I could hold out my arm and a portion of my body over the shallow curve of the ditch to get the best line of site with the horizon. I had my guess of my position and wanted to confirm it with what the GPS indicated, ensuring the machine was giving me accurate information. It was essential that I not pass bogus information to our rescue guys. The GPS data was right where I had guessed! The first time I made voice contact on the ground was after about an hour and twenty minutes. I passed my position to one of our Command and Control assets. That was the first and only time I talked to him.

I didn't realize it then, but even after my immediate contact under the canopy and this initial contact on the ground, there was a great deal of confusion and uncertainty throughout the night as to my location and authenticity.

The pilot minimized his physical activity as much as possible. About three and a half hours into the event he detected what seemed like search dog activity south of his position, and shortly afterwards he had a visitor – a hunting-size dog walking along deliberately and purposefully, seemingly looking for something. Suddenly the dog stopped and looked interested in exactly the place where the pilot had been perhaps 18 m away. Possibly the dog had the pilot's scent. The moon was now low on the western horizon and the pilot could see the dog clearly as he approached the hiding place, silhouetted against the illumination. The dog stood for some time, then turned and left.

> All along, I had thought that if it was my fate to be captured, I'd rather be found by police or Serbian military, rather than by villagers who would likely be less charitable during capture. During the few minutes of my dog visit, not only did I hope to not have to tangle with the dog, I also imagined, still in a light humorous way, what would happen to me if I harmed the dog and ended up captured by the villagers who owned it! I had a 9 mm pistol with me but of course I never considered using it because of the noise. To this day I don't know if it was a military or police trained search dog, or perhaps a villager's dog sent out to try and alert on something.

During the night, cloud rolled in and some pretty heavy rain started to fall. The darkness and poor weather made everything more difficult for the CSAR Task Force. However, it worked against the Serbs as well. Although it added an extra challenge for the CSAR team, in the end the darkness, thick clouds and rain were probably more of a help than a hindrance, providing valuable cover and concealment.

The next time Zelko talked to anybody, after initial contact with the rescue team on the ground, was a little over three hours, when the 'Sandy' pilots arrived on the scene. 'Sandy' was the call sign introduced during the Vietnam war for the CSAR mission pilots and the name stuck. Zelko established and remained in radio contact with them for the rest of the event.

Throughout the night there had been uncertainty as to the pilot's authenticity. Was he really Vega-31 or was this a Serbian trick? There were many uncertainties. Throughout the evening numerous different sets of coordinates were produced from various sources indicating Vega-31's position. These were filtered down and approximately six sets of coordinates made their way to the Sandys and rescue helicopters. The helicopters had begun to execute and push into Serbia several times but were called off. There was repeated authentication throughout the evening and the Sandys managed it skillfully. Any airman behind enemy lines prepares some general information about himself, which is kept closely-guarded, to be used only if needed. Authentication that night was effective and essential to the CSAR success (**Figure 8-45**).

The rescue helicopters faced their own problems. Visibility was poor and deteriorating and the lead helicopter in the final push into Serbian airspace barely avoided some high voltage power lines, seeing them only seconds before.

Helicopters were supported by sorties of A-10 airplanes whose main task was to eliminate all ground threats. Not less than ten airplanes were engaged. The proximity of Batajnica airport, the base of the Serbian MiG squadrons, added to their stress as F-15 fighter jets needed to cover the Serbian fighter threat. They also needed to keep F-16s in the air armed with HARM to attack any detected Serbian SAM batteries. The overall battle space was controlled by the NATO Sentry airborne control centre. There was no USAF AWACS in the area because they were engaged in the Middle East and Persian Gulf.

Pilots and aircraft crews reported that they were illuminated a few times with Serbian engagement and fire control radars, but this is highly unlikely because the 3rd Battalion switched off all their radars and started relocation immediately after the F-117A was shot down. Not even the radar imitator was on. There were no low-altitude surveillance radars such as 'Giraffe' available. The only illumination that airplanes might have got was from distant P-15 radars. Serbian air defence was silent immediately after the F-117A was shot, and official records do not show any SA-6 radar in operation at that time.

Thirty minutes before pick-up the Sandys authenticated Zelko once again, because at that point they still were not sure if they were going to proceed with the mission.

> At that moment they asked of me the hardest thing I had to do that night: 'Vega-31, is it alright to come in there?' As soon as I heard that I thought to myself: 'Ahhh, don't ask me that! Don't make me take that decision!' Over a minute went by and I still couldn't answer. Finally, one of the Sandy pilots came back on the radio, and this time he sounded just like a mom: 'Now Vega- 31, if you don't answer us, we're going to have to come back and do this a little bit later.' Another 20 seconds went by until I finally said: 'Ok. Go for it. Let's do it!' The reason it was so gut-wrenching to make that decision was that… I had limited awareness of precisely the extent and nature of surrounding enemy activity, or their capabilities.
>
> There were search forces within several hundred yards of me, and had been for most of the night. I could not confidently assess the risk of bringing those guys into what could develop into a very harmful situation for them. I just could not answer them. The reason

I ultimately gave the go-ahead was that I felt fully confident my situational awareness was high enough that if capture was imminent, I'd be able to call off the CSAR and take care of a few essentials that I didn't want compromised. Even though the Sandy traditionally would have solid awareness of the objective area and be the one to make the continuous assessments and decisions, I still had rehearsed, throughout the night, a radio call I'd use, as well as the actions I'd take, for calling it all off. It was unexpected to be asked if it was ok to execute. When they were fifteen minutes out the Sandys authenticated me again, reaffirmed if OK to come in, and told me to prepare my infrared strobe – my only covert signalling device. And again, I had a tough time answering.

It wasn't until this point that I first started to think: 'You know, they may actually try something tonight.' Up until then, although I never gave up hope or backed off my fierce determination, I was also a realist and did not expect a rescue attempt to be tried that night, if at all. I thought: 'These guys would be out of their minds to try and come in where I am.' I was mentally and emotionally well prepared for capture. Those CSAR professionals are simply astonishing. Ten minutes after this authentication I started hearing a helicopter approach from the west – it wasn't until later that I realized there was more than one involved in the rescue attempt, in fact there were two MH-53s and one MH-60. I was prepared to try to get them to land on the western field because that would have been a little further from the road.

The Sandys had already established an authentication code that would alert the pilot to activate the strobe. Zelko was busy tracking the helicopter sound starting to go a bit towards the north of his position when he heard the signal to activate the strobe. Zelko came out of his hole-up site just enough to hold it slightly off the ground. Keeping low profile was essential. He still needed to maintain as low a 'signature' as possible as this was the most dangerous moment of all and things could instantly go bad.

He activated the strobe, all the while monitoring the radio, with time clicking by and no word from anyone. Then the Sandy came up and said, 'We're not getting your strobe.'

When Zelko heard that call he slid back down into the best hiding position possible, cautiously examined the strobe and determined it was not working. There was no backup covert device. He made a radio call that the strobe was inoperative, then Sandy came up and said, 'Well, can you see the helicopters? Can you give them a vector?'

They were north of his positioned and Zelko radioed back: 'Yeah, I think you guys are north of me a couple of miles, come right, come south.'

And it was then that he noticed that there was other airborne activity in the area. With a search light on! He saw the Serbian airborne search activity more or less in the same area where he was tracking the CSAR helicopter.

This was very weird because there were no confirmed Serbian air activities in the area. Serbs did not have helicopters with night flight capabilities. To fly in the zone of potentially active enemy airplanes was highly unlikely. Most likely Zelko got confused by a light reflection or illumination from the helicopter blades.

> That threw me off for a moment and it wasn't until I heard the sound of the helicopters moving away from where the slow-moving airborne spotlight was that I knew for certain the light was not from a friendly. I heard Sandy on the radio once again: 'Vega- 31, give us a pen gun flare.'

This device was developed in the Vietnam era to penetrate foliage. It shoots up 250-400 m. But he hadn't prepared the one that was in his evasion kit. He reached it in few seconds. It was extremely well packed and while he unwrapped the packaging the thought came into his mind that he wasn't comfortable firing a flare 300 m up in the air because it would compromise his position. But then he decided: 'This needs to happen now.'

The co-pilot of the lead MH-53 came on the radio and said, 'Hey Vega-31, if we're this close, just go overt.'

Zelko replied, 'How about a regular flare?'

He had that flare out and prepped in about four seconds. These are the standard ones, with a day end and a night end. As he was prepping the flare he wondered which end to use. The day end is smoke, the night end is flame. With the day end there's little flame, but the smoke could be picked up by the night vision devices the helicopter pilots were likely using. Zelko opted for the night end and popped it. Just in case, he stayed at ground level with his body half protected by the sloping side of the embankment where it was coming up to the flat part of the field. He held the flare just above the dirt and let it burn for about two seconds and then snuffed it out in the soil.

The helicopters instantly saw the flare and had eyes on the pilot. They made an immediate radio call for the pilot to 'put out the flare' because in that darkness it was 'blooming' their night vision devices making it hard to see. Zelko didn't receive that radio call because he was using the radio's earpiece which kept popping out with any head or arm movement. But it didn't matter as Zelko had killed the flare quickly anyway. The helicopters were probably 1.5 km away from his position when they saw the flare, and they decide the MH-60 would try to make a quick grab and go. They were monitoring the considerable amount of Serbian search activity in the area, almost on top of the downed pilot, and were still not 100 per cent certain it was the real Vega-31. Just in case, several gun sights were trained on the pilot during pickup.

Normally even helicopters like to set up an approach, but that crew decided there was no time for that. The flying skills and nerve of rescue helicopter crews are extraordinary. USAF CSAR pilots are the cream of the force. They auto-rotated into the black hole of nothing. In a situation like that there is no depth perception, there is no horizon; they had a difficult time even judging distance and closure rate to the ground. The MH-60 peeled off and landed pretty much where the pilot hoped they would. The helicopter came down just to the west of him, about a rotor arc away. It was so dark that Zelko couldn't see them until they settled and the very top of the helicopter became barely illuminated by static electricity generated from dust hitting the rotors. The PJs (Para-rescuemen/Para Jumpers) came out while Zelko waited in a low crouch, non-threatening position. Two non-distinct shapes appeared out of the blackness, approaching from his left. Zelko didn't see them until they were maybe three metres away. To him they looked like aliens with their helmets, night vision devices and weapons. The PJ team leader came up to the pilot, grabbed him by the upper left arm and pulled him towards him. He was doing a visual identification of Zelko's profile. That was the final authentication. Finally, they were certain it was Vega-31 and not a trap. The PJ yelled to the pilot, 'How're you feeling Sir?'

Zelko yelled back, 'Great! Let's get out of here!'

The PJ gave Zelko a tug and said, 'Your PJs are here to take you home.'

Zelko followed them to the chopper. They all jumped in and off they went. From eyes on the survivor, to auto-rotate into the black hole, PJs out and all of them back in and flying, took ninety seconds. Forty-five seconds on the ground… that was fast.

But from the time Zelko pulled his ejection handles to five minutes out of Tuzla, rescue team base in Bosnia, just west of the Serbian border and the same place when they landed, almost eight hours had elapsed. From a CSAR perspective, that was a very long time.

Nobody in NATO command expected that any of their airplanes would be shot down so there were no prior search and rescue plans available (NATO arrogance!). There was not even a CSAR team near Yugoslav territory. The nearest was in Brindizi, Italy. The Vega-31 event was a wake-up call for everyone involved in Operation Allied Force.

The post-rescue debriefing by the JPRA (Joint Personnel Recovery Agency) team was a place to put all thoughts of what went wrong and what went right. Overall communications were enormously frustrating for everyone, from very limited or no SATCOM capability to almost non-existent secure voice capability.

CSAR had rehearsed nothing of that nature before. It was put together and executed ad hoc and on the fly.

From the evader point of view there was also much learned. During Zelko's debrief with JPRA, they asked what three things he would have liked to have had. Zelko responded without hesitation:

1. STU-III phone,
2. Night vision device, and
3. A one-day shopping spree at LL Bean!

The STU-III would have given him over-the-horizon secure voice and situational awareness of what the CSAR's plan was. The night vision device would have also given him enhanced situational awareness. As for LL Bean, that is a civilian outdoor store reckoned to have a better supply of survival equipment than the one used by the military.

The survivor/evader is a vital part of the CSAR team and can have an enormous impact on the success, or failure, of the rescue. Another lesson learned: training and preparation. In this scenario there was not the luxury of time, there was little time to think and no time to reference the manual.

The Mystery of the Radar Warning Receiver (RWR)

In interviews after the war, on the question did he ever get any warning about the illumination on his fire control radar, now retired Colonel Zelko never gave any direct answer, always replying that that was in the domain of the operational abilities of the airplane and that he couldn't discuss it further, or he simply changed the subject. One can only guess whether there was an RWR installed in F-117A.

The F-117A continues to be one of the most intriguing aircraft ever built, even a decade after it was officially retired, and more than thirty years after it was first unveiled to the public. Maybe one of the most obscure and enigmatic details of the 'Black Jet' is an elusive component called the Radar Locating System (RLS). For an aircraft that survives on its stealthy shape and coatings, these flip-down antenna arrays seem to deviate drastically from the F-117's modus operandi. But then again, the impetus for their existence may make more sense than not – that is if they ever existed at all.

The F-117's Radar Locating System consists (as far as is known from one publicly available drawing) of a pair of small planar antenna farms located under the aircraft's wings, about three metres from the wing roots, near their leading edges. The idea behind the system seems to have been that the F-117 pilot, who would normally retract all the jet's antennas when moving into hostile territory to minimize its radar reflectivity, could activate the system and its antennas would pop down into the airstream. Once deployed, they would work as a radar homing and warning receiver (RHWR or RWR), not only notifying the pilot of an enemy radar's presence and type, but also its direction and maybe even its general location (**Figure 7-20**).

Based on some accounts, the RLS seems to have been more about using the F-117 for a destruction of enemy air defences (DEAD) role than just avoiding enemy emitters and was possibly part of a programme that aimed to see the F-117A dynamically go after radar and SAM sites as a secondary mission set. Based on the information available, it may have also had a recording function and could have given the aircraft a secondary signals intelligence collection capability as well.

According to one source, the array appears to be set up for spiral omni-directional electronic support measures (ESM) antennas, roughly 50 mm in diameter, which are typical for 0.2-18 GHZ surveillance coverage, and they can be specifically tuned to different bands. Because of their wide spacing on each side of the jet's wings, the two sensor blocks/arrays coupled with the forward motion of the jet would provide direction finding ability. In other words, at least the threat emitter's bearing could be identified, and possibly its range. This would be especially useful for finding and attacking newer mobile SAM systems like the S-300 that were emerging at the same time the F-117A was operating under high secrecy in the Nevada desert.

Today some of the most powerful capabilities that a combat aircraft possesses, especially the stealth kind like the F-22 and F-35, are their abilities to detect, classify and geolocate threat emitters and other components of an enemy's integrated air defence systems (IADS). This is done via antennas placed all around the aircraft, under its stealthy skin. These conformal arrays are tied to high-speed computers that use interferometry, a large threat library, and other methods to give pilots – and even other aircraft connected via data-link within the battlespace – a real-time tactical 'picture' of the electronic order of battle around them. RLS seems like a very early and somewhat poorly conceived attempt to give the F-117A a fraction of this capability. Because conformal arrays and their composite coverings were not available at the time, the flip-down method was probably used.

The likely problem with the system was that it drastically increased the F-117's radar cross section when in use, as its flip-down antennas compromised the jet's smooth surface. This is an especially bad attribute when it comes to maintaining a very low radar cross section for the critical forward hemisphere of the aircraft. The likely result was the F-117's radar signature bloomed drastically when the RLS was activated. As such, the system would not only blow the Nighthawk's cover, but it would also turn it into a target. Not just that, but it would have only offered a 'snapshot' of the electronic threat environment around the F-117A at any given time. That's because the system would need to be retracted quickly, or it would turn the jet into a sitting duck while operating in enemy airspace.

By most accounts, it seems that the system was either just part of a test series or was only used for a very limited amount of time operationally, and how many jets it was installed on remains unknown – that is if it ever existed at all.

Some veteran F-117A maintainers seem to remember the quirky RLS trap-doors pretty well. They have even mentioned that they were known to sag, which would not only hurt the jet's stealth capabilities, but on dark nights that often were prime operations time for F-117 missions, partially opened RLS doors could be a hazard for maintainer's foreheads.

Not just that, but the RLS is prominently featured in the F-117's 'Dash One' operating manual. It is not only mentioned, and its abandoned control panel identified, but its location is also shown clearly in a diagram of the jet. It has been noted that by 2006 the system was not listed in official hazard and crash responder's documents. The diagram showing the RLS doors are still there, but it does not identify it as being something that is accessible like the rest of the aircraft's retractable antenna, so it seems as if the doors were permanently sealed or filled in at some point in time. This could have occurred during a depot overhaul or upgrade.

It seems that the Radar Locator System's existence is still highly doubted by some – including the man who largely oversaw the development of the jet – senior Skunk Works engineer and F-117 programme manager Alan Brown. There is a possibility that the USAF made the modification themselves without Lockheed's knowledge, but really that is not possible, knowing how well the manufacturer followed up with the airplane in the field. Lockheed Skunk Works always had a cradle-to-grave philosophy in terms of follow-up with its products in service.

F-117 programme manager Sherm Mullin, who took over the F-117 programme, stated that RLS 'was never put on the F-117A'. Although he did mention that it could have been a concept from a study that occurred from 1984 to 1985 that apparently went off the rails conceptually and was disbanded.

During roughly that same time period it is known, although not well documented publicly, that the F-117A was tested with some fairly elaborate modifications. This supposedly included a handful of sensor systems in addition to the jet's stock Infrared Acquisition and Designation System (IRADS). It is known that passive electronically scanned array (PESA) radar was flown on one F-117A in a specially-built radome fitted on the Nighthawk's wedge-like nose. Maybe RLS was one of the other mods that was deemed successful, and was accommodated for in some of the F-117s built but never fully installed. The reader can refer to **Figure 7-14** in the previous chapter to get an insight into the F-117A cockpit.

As there is much contradictory information in the available literature, the authors invite the reader to reach his/her own conclusions as to whether the F-117A which flew into combat over Yugoslavia had RWR installed or not.

Combat Search and Rescue (CSAR)

NATO air planners were concerned about the possibility of allied aircraft being shot down. They recalled how several NATO aircraft had been shot down in earlier Balkans operations. On 16 April 1994, a British Sea Harrier was downed by an SA-7 missile near Gorazde, Bosnia. A year later, on 2 June 1995, a Serbian SA-6 brought down a USAF F-16 pilot, Scott O'Grady, over western Bosnia. Both the British and American pilots were rescued. On 30 August 1995 near the town of Pale, Bosnian Serbs employing a surface-to-air missile scored against a French Mirage 2000K. US aircraft flew ninety-two dedicated sorties in support of recovery efforts for two pilots until officials confirmed that the Serbians had captured the two-man crew.

On the night of 27 March a 20th Special Operation Service (SOS) crew including Captain Cardoso as flight leader for the rescue package took off in an MH-53M. Their call sign was Moccasin 60. One wingman, Moccasin 61, was an MH-53J from the 21st SOS. The other wingman was Gator 07, an MH-60G from the 55th SOS. As directed, some other special tactics personnel were dispersed among the three aircraft.

As the flight of three helicopters proceeded to Tuzla from Brindisi during the day, the crews checked in with the NATO E-3 Sentry airborne radar on station overseeing the strikes that evening. The weather over the region was poor, with mixed rain showers and low visibility, and many strikes had been cancelled. Cardoso and his group landed at Tuzla and taxied to the refueling pits to fill their tanks. As they were doing so, the crews aboard Moccasin 61 and Gator 07 heard a Mayday call on the UHF 'Guard' (military aircraft emergency) frequency.

Immediately, aircraft commanders went into the Tuzla command centre to determine what was going on. There they were told that an F-117A had gone down in Serbia. They quickly began to formulate a recovery plan and tasked intelligence for the most accurate location of the pilot. What was in the minds of the crews was: 'a Stealth just got shot down and now [they] want us to go in there???' While the immediate plan was not clear, the crews knew what they had to do and would figure out a way to get the pilot out of Serbia. The requested information promptly flowed into the command centre. Intelligence sources indicated that Vega-31 was down near Novi Sad, Serbia, an estimated 145 km from Tuzla. Those sources also reported that the Serbs realized they had shot down an F-117A and were scrambling to capture the pilot. Several flights of

A-10s and other supporting aircraft including F-16CJ, F-15 and E-6 were being launched to assist in the rescue.

With that information, Lieutenant Colonel Laushine, commander of 55 Special Operation Service and rescue mission commander, directed his task force to take off and head north to set up a rendezvous with the A-10s near Osijek in north-east Croatia. The three helicopters quickly launched and headed north. In this area, at least, the air was clear, and night visibility was good, although the moon was slowly setting. En route though they had difficulties establishing communications with the A-10s and other support aircraft as Laushine tried to organize the recovery effort.

Meanwhile Zelko had been able to determine his location and had securely passed it to a C130 orbiting over Kosovo. The C130 crew quickly forwarded it through intelligence channels to Laushine. The reported position, validated by the A-10 flight lead, Captain John Cherrey, who had established radio communications with and authenticated the survivor, indicated that Vega-31 was on the ground just south of Ruma, 40 km further south. This was much closer to Belgrade, the heavily defended Serbian capital, and necessitated a complete rework of the recovery plan as the helicopter crews quickly entered Zelko's reported GPS location into their navigation systems.

To save fuel, Cardoso directed his flight crews to land their helicopters and dismount some ODA troops to provide site security. Meanwhile Cardoso and his team built a new route to the survivor while the crew of Moccasin 61 coordinated for a MC-130P to refuel the helicopters. Once that was worked out, the helicopters relaunched, quickly rendezvoused with the tanker, just 250 m above the ground, and took on fuel as ground fog and low clouds were forming in the area. They repositioned to a holding point west of Ruma but still in Bosnian airspace and awaited the arrival of Cherrey's flight, which would escort them in to the survivor and provide top cover against any threats that challenged them.

Finally the approval to enter Serbian airspace came and, descending to 15-20 m above the terrain, the CSAR three-ship proceeded inbound towards the pilot location. Several times Cardoso increased his altitude to 30 m to avoid obstacles and populated areas. Throughout the night the helicopters had been operating mostly in clear air. As they turned inbound to Zelko though, they encountered a layer of low-hanging clouds, fog, and rain. As visibility rapidly deteriorated, Cardoso and his crew, already wearing night vision goggles, began using the forward-looking infrared radar (FLIR) system to proceed (**Figure 8-46**).

As they entered the low scud, A-10 flight could no longer see the helicopters to provide direct fire support. They themselves were being engaged (as they claimed) by SA-6 missile batteries. The authors do not have any information that any of the Serbian mobile batteries had been detected or engaged by the airplanes. Also, an F-16 launched a HARM missile towards one of Serbian

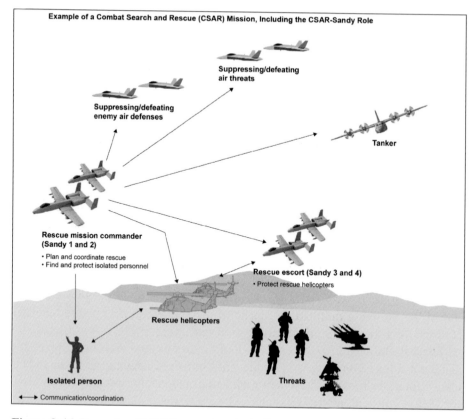

Figure 8-46: Example of CSAR operation, including the CSAR Sandy role. (USAF)

radars (unconfirmed from the Serbian side). That may be the light that was seen by Zelko, describing the 'search light' looking for him. As confirmed, there were no Serbian aircraft in the air that night. Entering the scud at about 20 m above the ground, the two other helicopters held tactical formation on Moccasin 60 so that they did not get separated while so dangerously close to the ground. On board all three helicopters, gunners and flight engineers were scanning for immediate physical threats such as trees, towers, or power lines – anything that could damage or destroy a helicopter – as well as Serbian forces. Suddenly one of the crew members spotted an uncharted power line in the haze, just ahead and level with the helicopters. He shouted, 'Wires! Climb! Climb!' Captain Cardoso immediately reacted and pulled back on the controls, flying his helicopter up and over the threatening wires. The other two crews maintained formation and also avoided the threat. Once clear of the wires, Cardoso descended back down to about 30 m and proceeded towards Lieutenant Colonel Zelko.

Approaching Zelko's location, the helicopters encountered Serbian spotlights looking for them. There is no confirmed information from the Serbian side that any of the units in the vicinity used any search lights. About 5 km from Vega-31, the CSAR team spotted three Serbian trucks evenly spaced on a road. Three km from Vega's location the rescuers contacted the survivor, but they could not see him. Vega's infrared strobe was inoperable and he couldn't locate his pen-gun flares. Cardoso's team told him to fire his overt flare. Vega did so, as we saw from Zelko's description. The rescue team saw the flare and immediately flew into position and the PJs picked up Zelko.

The MH-60G and the 53s flew a different route leaving Serbia than on the ingress. As they approached the border with Bosnia they observed Serbian anti-aircraft fire in the vicinity of their previous flight path. Without being able to see the aircraft, the estimate of the crew was that the Serbians appeared to be firing volleys in hopes that the helicopters were flying the same route as before. After the five and a half hour mission, Cardoso's team landed safely at Tuzla at 03:54 **(Figure 8-47)**.

The US rescue team reported that the search light was 'like in the Second World War'. Serbia didn't have that kind of equipment, except in museums. If there were any lights, they might have been vehicles' high-beam lights or powerful flashlights.

The 3rd Battalion were not active again that night after downing the F-117. Other battalions possibly used their radars to illuminate the airspace in search of enemy airplanes but in general on the

Serbian side all was quiet. Some of the army air defence units with triple 20 mm cannons occasionally opened fire if something suspicious was in the air,

Figure 8-47: CSAR team which rescued Lieutenant Colonel Zelko. (USAF)

and some infantry units with their heavy machine guns may also have opened fire, but there is no official record of any of the units firing that night. In the area of crash, some units of the Serbian 453rd Armoured Brigade were located but they were not involved in any fire reported by the rescue mission. Military police from the armoured brigade and police searched the area and found items that Zelko left behind.

In some local sources there was a report that during the rescue mission one of the CSAR team members was accidentally left on the ground and the helicopter had to go back and search for him. The authors were unable to confirm this story, but it may have happened.

Many books, publications and documentaries of the time described Serbian air defence as integrated, modern and formidable, and Serbian airspace as the 'most heavily defended space on earth'. Later, however, it was said that NATO airplanes were easily able to 'deal' with obsolete Serbian SA-2 and SA-3 units. Perhaps by exaggerating the opponent's capabilities NATO wanted to raise their own achievements.

One thing is evident: the Serbian side did not expect to down an enemy airplane and a pilot to land on their territory. There were no plans how to react or how to organize search forces. Searches were organised only on a local level. Serbian intelligence had some knowledge of CSAR procedures, but it was not widely distributed among field units. Local army units in the vicinity searched the terrain, assisted by local police, and police were tasked to prevent locals searching on their own. The Serbian concern was that if the pilot was captured by local civilians then the Geneva Convention would not protect him, and that in case of a shootout with the rescue team there might be unnecessary casualties.

The Serbian side learned from the experience. US CSAR manuals and procedures were studied, teams were formed based on territorial locations, including the regular army, and state security forces and police formed local hunter groups.

F-16CG

May 2

From Aviano base a group of two pairs of two F-16CGs entered Yugoslav airspace from the Croatian side. The group leader call sign for the mission was Hammer Three-Four (3-4). From west-north-west another group of four planes also entered Yugoslav airspace. Two groups of airplanes, approaching from different bases, formed a dynamic combat group whose main task was to search and destroy missile batteries in the northern part of Serbia, the batteries which defended the approaches to the capital. The F-16CG group from Aviano, as per intelligence reports obtained before the mission, would try to enter the destruction envelopes of missile batteries previously identified and provoke the batteries to turn on engagement and fire control radars. This would be detected by the SEAD group which would launch anti-radiation missiles. Emissions of the fire control radars would be recorded and exact locations of the units pinpointed so that the airplanes could attack with laser guided bombs. This is basically standard counter SAM and SEAD tactics.

Third Battalion was in the area. That night the combat crew in the UNK consisted of Major Bosko Dotlic, commander; Sub-Lieutenant Miodrag Stojanovic, deputy; Major Milorad Roksandic, missile battery commander; Sub-Lieutenant Tiosav Jankovic, missile guidance officer; Sergeant Igor Radivojevic, manual tracking officer on F1; Warrant Officer Dragan Matic, manual tracking officer on F2; and Private Sead Ljajic, manual plotting operator. That night the radar emission imitator was connected and ready for use (**Figure 8-48**, **Figure 8-52**). It is interesting to mention that just before taking their shift, the whole crew spent time in the local village pub. Slightly before 20:00 the battalion security officer with an officer from brigade HQ entered the pub. That HQ officer was surprised when he saw the complete shift there and protested to the shift commander asking why his shift was not resting before combat duty. The security officer told him: 'let them stay, maybe it's their last time'. It was black humor but everybody laughed.

About thirty minutes before midnight, P-18 surveillance radar detected the target in the distance for which the crew turned on the fire control radar for ten seconds to illuminate it. It was evident that there was activity in the air. One of the missile battery's tasks is also to try to illuminate aerial targets to 'scare' them and chase them out of protected airspace. After receiving the signal that it was illuminated by the fire control radar, the aircraft quickly changed direction and flew away. Most likely the pilot informed his control centre about the radar. This was unpleasant news that Major Dotlic's crew got when they took their shift at midnight: their position may be compromised. Slightly after the midnight, General Velickovic, from air-force headquarters, made an appearance. Major Dotlic told him that they were expecting airplanes around 02:00.

After the general and his team departed about 02:00, the shift commander noted six to eight blips on the VIKO display, scattered in small groups on azimuth 300 at distance 80-100 km. A smaller group had been detected in the area of Valjevo, to the south. For a moment the group that was north-west of the battery disappeared from the screen. Shortly after, one of the planes appeared on azimuth 310 at about 30 km distance.

Major Dotlic ordered reposition on the radar search antenna to azimuth 310. The crew was calm but everyone felt that 'something and somebody out there' was hunting for them. The hunters approached in pairs from three different directions trying to provoke the battalion to turn on fire control radar and disclose

its location – classic SEAD tactics. Major Dotlic didn't allow the rest of the crew to look at his screen. He wanted them to concentrate on their tasks.

After a few antenna turns, he saw that one of the planes was holding a stable course with relatively small parameters right towards the battalion position. He immediately issued orders to correct the antenna position +/-2 to 5 degrees left/right from the existing position. At moment later he said: 'This one is going to get in!' He then ordered: 'Preparation 1!'

With the target at 17-18 km he ordered: 'Turn the High On! Distance 17 km!... Search!'

Figure 8-48: Part of Major Dotlic's crew. (Author's archive)

At the same time, the command was issued to the radar emission imitator to turn on as well. Major Roksandic, missile battery commander, quickly turned the control wheels on UK-31 in an attempt to direct the missile guidance office by azimuth and elevation. At that moment, Low Blow radar was turned on. The distance and angle were preset to 16 km and the instruments showed altitude of 6 km. Missile guidance officer Sub-Lieutenant Jankovic rapidly moved his control wheels positioning the antenna in the target direction. He saw the target on his screens and at the moment when one of the tracks started to fade from the screen, he noted a smaller one, slightly right from the screen marker, with RCS similar to a MiG-29 fighter. He quickly realized that both were on the same course and altitude and that the second one, which was slightly closer, was the real one and the other one was a decoy. Jankovic knew that NATO airplanes used AN/ALE-50 towed decoys. He quickly put the marker crosshair on the target on his screens in preparation for transfer to manual tracking, and handed over to the manual tracking operators on F1 and F2. The manual tracking operators reported stable target tracking and Jankovic's instruments showed target speed was about 250 m/s with parameter 4. He didn't have time to properly report parameters when the target was 14-15 km away, Major Dotlic yelled an order to launch two missiles with three point guiding: 'Launch!'

A loud bang followed by blast-off from the launching platform. The second missile, as in the case of F-117A, didn't acquire the target on the second channel and went on ballistic trajectory. This was the second time it had happened, which was a worry. Something was wrong with the guidance blocks and coordinate system. It is standard procedure that when the new crew take the shift, the missile guidance officer checks the functionality of the station. All parameters so far were satisfactory and there were no indications pointing to any equipment malfunctioning. But something was wrong because the missile was not able to 'take' the guidance commands.

Dotlic followed the missile on his F2 screen: 'At the moment the missile reached the target, I saw a conical shape which covered the target, which corresponded to the warhead explosion in the target proximity.' (**Figure 8-35**)

The missile guidance officer reported: 'Target destroyed, distance 11-12 km!...'

It was a textbook example of a warhead explosion in the proximity of the target. The conical shape on the radar screen corresponded with the warhead fragments covering the target. At that moment VIKO showed the target still in the air and manoeuvring, heading east. The target was not destroyed!

Major Dotlic ordered the fire control radar turned off. Only the radar imitator was still on. From the brigade command post it was observed that the target changed direction rapidly, taking a course westward, towards Bosnia. Obviously the airplane had sustained damage: it had a long black smoke trail behind it. Now it was trying to escape Yugoslav airspace. The whole crew hoped it would not reach Bosnian airspace and that it would crash on Serbian territory. If it did, it would be second material proof that an enemy airplane was downed. Five minutes after the hit, Major Stankovic from brigade HQ said in a cheerful voice: 'Bole![13] he crashed!!!'

Not long after, the crew got confirmation that the plane crashed near Nakucani village not far from the city of Sabac – in Serbian territory (**Figure 49, Figure 8-53, Figure 8-54**).

The missiles fired by the 3rd Battalion were called *Natalia* and *Zivadinka*. After the first downing, the crew decided to give every missile a female name – the name of spouses, girlfriends... Natalia, 5V27D missile, launched from the 5P73 s/n. 13013, had a 'hot date' with the US pilot. This time it was with Lieutenant Colonel David Goldfein F-16CGs, who then commanded the 555th Fighter Squadron and led the first of many missions of Operation Allied Force over Serbia. Goldfein's family is strongly related to the Air Force as both his father and brother are high ranking officers. At the time of writing, he was a four-star general and Chief of Staff in USAF (**Figure 8-50**).

---

13. Dotlic's nickname

Figure 8-49: F-16CG on Aviano base tarmac. (USAF)

Figure 8-50: General David Goldfein. At the time he was shot down over Serbia, he was 555th Squadron Commander. (USAF)

During the engagement, the radar imitator was on, constantly covering the 'Low Blow' radar, providing protection and cover against HARMs. After the engagement, two HARMs were found not far from the battalion radar post. The SAM launch sites had proved to be a constant threat in Serbia, disappearing and reappearing. NATO was never sure how many of them were actually operable at any given time.

Hammer Three-Four

The SAM launch sites had proved to be a constant threat in Serbia, disappearing and reappearing. NATO was never sure how many of them were operable at any given time, even though they claimed that a significant number had been destroyed. This one, which appeared right under the 555th Squadron's route as it flew into Serbia, on a night mission to destroy enemy air defences, belonged to the battle-hardened 3rd Battalion.

The tactic applied was to pinpoint SAM site location provoking the radar emission, than as soon as the site is located, HARMs may be launched from the F-16CJ and F-16CG with the laser bombs will attack the position. This is classic SEAD procedure.

When the missile proximity fuse detonated, the cone of steel shrapnel heavily damaged the airplane's engine and some of the avionics but the airplane was still flyable. The pilot reported the damage to his command and changed course towards Bosnia. In F-16 CG pilot Lieutenant Colonel David Goldfein's own words, it wasn't an easy task:

CHAPTER EIGHT

I became a very expensive glider pretty quick. My first reaction
was: 'Shoot!' The second was disgust and frustration.[14]

Over the radio, he told the other jets in the area that he was going to continue to
glide as long as he can. Then he said he would try shutting down the engine and
restarting. Once it was obvious that the engine would not restart, he focused on
getting out alive and without giving his position.

He saw the flak clouds from the anti-aircraft fire that was trying to zero in
on his damaged plane. One shoulder-launched SA-7 missile had also been fired
on him. His airplane was crippled and he would soon have to eject, either over
Serbian territory or over 'friendly' Bosnian territory.

He felt a stinging sensation on his hand and looked down to find blood welling
from a minor shrapnel injury.

He waited as long as possible to eject so he would have just enough time for
his parachute to deploy while spending as little time as possible as a floating
target. On the radio he asked his rescuers to start looking for him and received
assurances that they had a lock on his position. He made one last transmission:
'I'm out.' The ejection mechanism worked flawlessly.

I knew the race was on as soon as I pulled the handles and I wanted
to be in the lead of that race for as long as it took to get picked up...
Ejecting was a loud explosion, then a feeling like someone kicking
me in the backside as hard as you can possibly kick.
    That's when your training kicks in. It was a full-moon night. You
don't want to be highlighted [in the sky] too long.

After landing in a 'perfectly plowed field', he rolled and popped off his parachute.
Helmet still on, he grabbed his things and headed for a ravine. The ravine sloped
down at a steeper angle than he had expected from his hasty survey, and he
tripped and fell face first.

My stuff was like a raft in front...I was riding it like Indiana Jones
down to the bottom.

He collected himself together and then made radio contact with the fighters still
circling above. He was located at 03:55.

---

14. Based on D. Goldfein interview to *AF Magazine*, September 2016.

My first call was answered by my buds who were with me. There wasn't a minute I didn't hear jets overhead, and that was very comforting. There was absolutely no question in my mind I was getting out that night.

As his training had taught him, he dumped anything shiny that would reveal his location, and traveled along the edge of the plowed field. If the field had land mines, he thought, the farmers would already have dug them up (a strange thought to have: why would Serbs have mined the field when there was no danger of land attack?)

The countryside looked a lot like Indiana or Ohio farmland. There were lots of dogs and roosters up and awake and sounding off at 2 am.

After walking about three kilometres, he found a relatively remote cleared area.

I had to find a good spot to stay hidden and coordinate the rescue…It was just…Don't screw it up; don't get in the way.

He once again communicated his position, and then, from his hiding spot, heard a rustling sound and looked in the direction of the noise.

Whatever it was, it reared up on its hind legs ... I saw beady eyes… I say it was a Serbian tiger, but my buds said it was probably a field mouse.

He ran for a distance, which turned out to be a good move because he found a better landing spot.

In the meantime, the rest of the airplanes from his group left Serbian airspace for refuelling over Bosnia. A rescue mission was scrambled right away. The CSAR team was supported by scores of combat F-16, EA-6B, A-10 and support aircraft. When the rescue helicopters arrived, they attracted Serbian small arms fire.

Some locals opened small arms fire from carbines and assault guns but they were no match for the machine-gun fire from the helicopters. Within seconds of its arrival, Goldfein was in the helicopter. He was in Tuzla airport at 4:45. A later inspection revealed five bullet holes in the helicopter fuselage. In an *Air Force Magazine* interview, some of the participants in the rescue mission explained that they were under a 'heavy barrage of surface-to-air missile, artillery fire and

Figure 8-51: F-16 CG jet engine. (Zastava Film)

Figure 8-52: Major Dotlic (third from the left) and his combat shift which downed F-16 CG flown by 555th squadron commander Lieutenant Colonel Goldfein, later 4 star USAF general. (Author's archive)

Figure 8-53: Lieutenant Colonel Goldfein's helmet and parachute. (Zastava Film)

Figure 8-54: Hammer Three-Four's tail in Belgrade Aeronautical Museum. (Authors)

small arms fire.' This is an exaggeration: the only fire was sporadic small arms fire from a few military rifles and hunters' carbines. Goldfein said he wanted to fly immediately afterwards, but his commanders told him to wait a day. Although he flew the next day, he points out that pilots in Vietnam often flew the same day they were rescued, and they didn't even receive a hero's welcome when they returned home.

Something VERY BIG was in the air...

19/20 May
Lieutenant Colonel Anicic and his crew took the afternoon shift at 16:00 on 19 May. That day Russian envoy Victor Chernomirdin was visiting Belgrade to discuss the situation with Serbian president Milosevic. Indications were that it would be a quiet day. Around 22:30 Chernomirdin left. The crew had been at readiness No. 2 since 22:50, meaning no immediate danger. The crew took off their flak jackets and helmets because it got warm in the UNK cabin. It seemed strange to the shift commander that Readiness No. 2 was declared when most of the previous day it was Readiness No. 1 in expectation of a NATO strike (**Figure 8-55**).

Figure 8-55: The combat shift that hit 'something big'. (Author's archive)

The Serbs developed an ingenious way to 'upgrade' the capacity of their light AA systems. The M53/59 Praga is a Czechoslovak self-propelled anti-aircraft gun developed in the late 1950s. It consists of a modified Praga V3S six-wheel-drive truck chassis, armed with a twin 30 mm AA automatic cannon mounted on the rear. The system is optically aimed and can only be used effectively during the day in good weather conditions; for night operation it was basically useless. However, the technical department decided to combine the obsolete AA system with the short-range missiles from a MiG-29. A rail was mounted on the top of the truck and a MiG short range IR missile was fixed to it (**Figure 8-56**). What it meant was that the battalion had the support of additional firepower without the need of fire control radar because the missile was guided by the heat emission of the jet engine. It was like having a shoulder-launched platform but with a range of 20 km. An improvised solution, but effective if employed correctly.

Lieutenant Colonel Anicic and Lieutenant Colonel Milenkovic developed the tactic to use this modified Praga in ambush. As Praga doesn't have radar and the missile is passive there is no danger that it can be detected and jammed before launching.

Figure 8-56: Praga with R-73 air-to-air missile installed. (Author's archive)

CHAPTER EIGHT

On the night of 19 May, the modified Praga defended the area in azimuth 100-120 degrees. In USAF jargon, this kind of action is known as a 'snake in the grass'.

During the previous days the battalion had had difficulty preparing combat positions because of rain and mud. That night readiness was No. 2, which was not usual. The combat shift used the opportunity to relax a bit. Suddenly, at 11:00, the brigade command post ordered Readiness No. 1 and the crew quickly took their positions ready for engagement. Anicic ordered P-18 surveillance radar to be turned on. The VIKO screen showed numerous targets at 10-12 km distance – very close! Obviously a massive attack was on the way.

Fire control radar was not fully ready – that old technology needs some time to 'warm up'. As the radar was not ready, the first 'ring' was not engaged. The second 'ring' was about 25 km away.

The target blips on the radar screen are specific. By now operators and commanders had learned how a real aircraft looked, how a towed decoy looked and how a radar decoy looked, but now there was a new blip they had never seen before. It was triangular.

In the UNK, tension mounted.

'Azimuth 180…Search!' Anicic orders a radar search on azimuth 180. Target is 17-18 km away.

'High [voltage] – Up!'

'Antenna!'

The target is 15-16 km away.

Within a few seconds missile guidance officer Jankovic finds the target. With a little turning of the wheels by azimuth and angle the target is in the crosshairs. The target is manoeuvring; he must have detected radar emission and know he is in the fire control radar sight.

One click of the wheels, pushed away from the operator, towards the station, means that now the manual tracking operators have the target on their F1 and F2.

A few seconds later Anicic orders: 'Target destroy with two missiles!…three point guidance!!!'

Loud hissing, missile booster motors ignition…and start…first missile blasts off from the ramp, five seconds later the next.

The missile guidance officer reports the parameters: height, velocity…first missile, *Tanya* acquires the target…second missile, *Ivana*, acquires the target… guidance normal on both channels… distance to target 14 km. It was textbook shooting.

Suddenly the manual tracking operator on F1 says, 'What the f..k!!!…What the f..k is this?!!!'

The blip on the screen was enormous; it took almost the entire screen.

The first missile exploded in the vicinity of the target... then a second... 13 km distance, azimuth 180 degrees. A bright explosion in the sky. The target was hit at 00:11.

'Target hit...both missiles!' the operator reported.

'Take the high down!... Equivalent!' Anicic ordered.

The next shift, which was waiting outside the UNK, knocked on the van door. It was slightly after midnight. As the combat engagement was in progress there was no shift change. It is not a good situation: with two combat shifts at the site one well-placed bomb or missile could eliminate both!

The second shift observed the whole engagement visually from outside... the missile launch...the explosion in the distance. The modified Pragas also launched their AA heat seeking missiles.

Information from brigade operation centre is there are helicopters in the air. Everybody thinks: 'Something happened...something big... otherwise why would they launch helicopters?'

There are planes in the air from three directions...swarms of them. After the launch the UNK has an indication that the missile ramp is not functioning.

Something has happened. As the two missiles were launched at high elevation, the blasts have made a crater. From the force the 13-ton platform has moved 20 cm from its original position and one of the missiles has fallen off its launching beam (**Figure 8-57**, **Figure 8-58**).

Figure 8-57: High elevation, ready for launch. (Author's archive)

Figure 8-58: The 5V27D that fell from the launcher. (Author's archive)

The airplanes seem to sense the situation and a major attack comes from azimuth 205. The UNK can't launch in that direction from the other platforms because it is a 'forbidden zone' – the blast will damage their own equipment. One of the strongest attacks since the beginning of the war and one of the ramps is out of service! From azimuths 300-330 and 150-180 there are numerous airplanes. Anicic orders his deputy to emit from the radar imitator. Commands are short… the radar imitator performs emission in short bursts, switching from one target to another. Radar emission is very short – 5 seconds, then switching to the next target. The planes in the air know they are illuminated but they don't know if it is by real fire control radar or an imitator. While the fire control radar illuminates one group of attacking airplanes, the radar imitator illuminates the other one which comes from the 'forbidden launch cone'. The third group of aircraft is not covered because there are not enough imitators.

In the meantime, brigade HQ phones inquiring about the engagement and how the radar picture of the target looks. They have seen the whole engagement on their P-18 radar but they are interested how it looks on Low Blow radar. Anicic transfers that task to the missile guidance officer.

Anicic orders a search one more time and detects a pair 14-18 km away, heading out of range. On the other side, from behind, a plane is entering the zone, distance 15 km. There is no time to launch and engage departing targets… the next target is the approaching one.

As soon as the target is illuminated, the screen shows a lot of clutter… jamming. The missile guidance officer reports that he can't see the target anymore. Anicic orders to turn off the fire control radar. For the rest of the night only radar imitator is used. There were airplanes in the air but they didn't enter the destruction envelope (**Figure 8-59**).

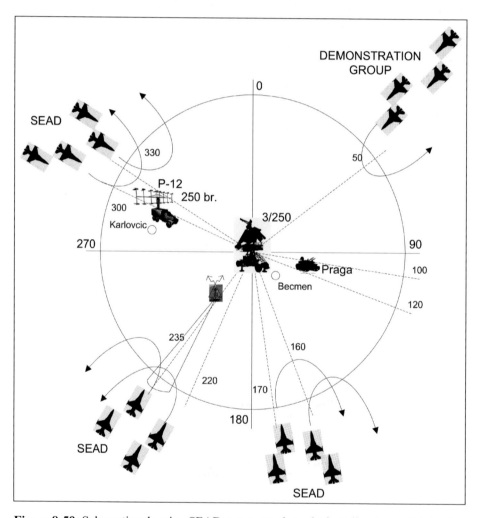

Figure 8-59: Schematics showing SEAD group attack on the battalion immediately after launching at the large target. Three SEAD groups simultaneously approaching from different azimuths and one demonstration group from the north-east. (Authors)

CHAPTER EIGHT

Something important happened that night… so many attempts to attack the unit, like never before. The sky 'cleared' at 01:30 and the combat crew ended their shift.

Walking towards the unit camp, Anicic went over what happened. How come that during all the engagement not a single HARM missile was launched? The radar emission was very short. From the moment of locking onto the target, launch and hit, the target flew only 4 km. The key was to let the target come as close as possible, lock onto it, and launch, with a high probability of hit before the HARM shooters had time to acquire the direction of the signal and launch missiles.

So what was hit that night? Was it the towed decoy or a radar target or a real airplane; and if an airplane, then which one? There are many speculations about this and in the following paragraphs we will consider them.

In one of analyses, Colonel Vladimir Neskovic PhD, information systems expert in the military technical institute, provided the combat engagement parameters analysis and calculations (**Figure 8-60**, **Figure 8-61**)

In the Serbian press it was reported that a B-2 had been hit and crashed in the area of Spacvan forest, on the Croatian side, about 15 km from the Serbian border.

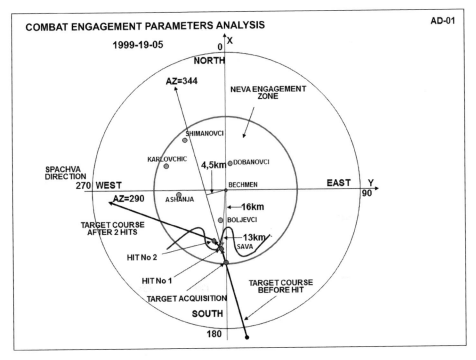

Figure 8-60: Combat engagement analysis. (V. Neskovic)

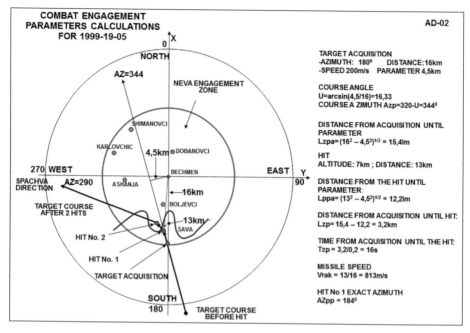

Figure 8-61: Combat engagement calculation. (V. Neskovic)

The fact is, there is no material evidence that anything crashed. No publicly available photos, no video, no audio records. However, there are strong indications that something did happen that night.

We believe that it was an aerial target that night which was engaged and hits observed. However, the following are the facts and readers may draw their own conclusions.

- The crew had no idea what type of the aircraft was in the air. For them it was just one of the targets they picked up.
- Can a B-2 be detected on SA-3 radar systems? The answer is yes. Though a huge airplane, the RCS of a B-2 is less than 0.1 m². But that is within the RCS detection capabilities of the Neva system. (See **Figure 1-20** for B-2 RCS).
- The F1 screen showed a very large radar blip. Could it have been from a real aircraft? The answer is yes. Could it have been from a towed decoy? The answer is also yes, but not likely.
- The aerial speed of the target, height and direction was a classic evasive path after a bombing mission and aerial hit.
- Immediately after the hit, position lights were observed in the air in the vicinity of the border with Croatia. It is not common practice that aircraft in the vicinity of enemy airspace turn on position lights.

- A crash was recorded at 00:23 on the Croatian side. Captain Ilija Vuckovic, radar operator on P-12 surveillance radar, under the 250th Brigade command, in position in the village of Karlovcic, was able to track the aerial target until it disappeared from the screen at a distance of 105 km and azimuth 275-280. From Karlovcic to the Spacvan forest is approximately 100 km.
- There were unusually fierce attacks from multiple directions immediately after. The battalion had never been engaged before in coordinated attacks from different directions.
- Helicopters were reported in the air immediately after, but without entering Serbian airspace.
- Radio amateurs reported an unusually loud noise similar to grinding, the explosion and a large fire on the Croatian side. They were particularly active all through the war and were a valuable source of information for the Serbian side.
- Croatian Zupanja radio and TV station broadcast that something crashed in the forest, then suddenly all reports of that stopped. There is no taped or recorded report or hard copy on the Serbian side.
- The next edition of *Voice of Zupanja* newspaper published that a large airplane had crashed in their area, but promptly all copies were removed from the news kiosks. The whereabouts of all issues are unknown to this day.
- The local fire department was urgently sent to extinguish a fire in the forest. Firefighters reported something big on the ground, no tail, no markings, burning. One firefighter reported that it looked like a spaceship, but the name of the firefighter is unknown to the authors.
- Local police were called to secure the perimeter.
- NATO and SFOR increased activities from Bosnia to Croatia. This was reported by multiple sources and confirmed by radio amateurs.
- The area of the possible crash site was 'sanitized' for the next few months, with nobody unauthorised allowed in. Local police provided outer perimeter protection.
- Heavy trucks with closed cargo space were observed moving in and out from the area. This was reported to Serbian intelligence by multiple sources.
- There was increased flight of transport airplanes from Tuzla airport, as reported by local residents and observed by surveillance radars.
- After the war, at the alleged crash site in the forest, a small pond appeared, not recorded before the war on any map. Satellite photos of the area taken after the war show that beside the dense forest where there are few available local roads there are large gaps in the tree lines with traces of heavy vehicles visible on the ground (**Figures 8-64**, **Figure 8-65**).
- No B-2 missions over Yugoslavia were conducted for the rest of the war, though combat sorties of other aircraft were intensified. The deputy commander of 509th Bomber Wing, Steven Bashen, in an interview for

an aviation magazine confirmed that B-2s were withdrawn from combat against Yugoslavian targets after 21 May, the day after the engagement. The same was confirmed in *B-2 Spirit Units in Combat* by Thomas Withington on page 43. US commanders in the theatre stated that the Serbian sky was still dangerous to the last day. Was that because there were no valuable targets for them or because they feared losing valuable airplanes after the engagement from the night before?

- Serbian security forces recorded emissions on emergency radio frequencies between a pilot and the command centre with the request to eject. The request was denied until Serbian airspace cleared. The record of this 'disappeared' from the secret service after the government changed in Serbia. The authors have been told that the whereabouts of the transcript is unknown. Serbs definitely had the ability to record the conversation on unscrambled links, but this can be 'fabricated', as proved later in the 'fake' and 'fabricated' radio transmissions in the so-called 'B-52 downing'.
- B-2s were in the air that night, bombing targets in Belgrade. Call signs for two airplanes were Stub 1 and Stub 2. This information is not verified. It is possible that Serbian side didn't record the correct names.
- A local communications employee in Tuzla said he heard the crew request to eject which was not granted until they cleared Yugoslav airspace, but the name of the employee was never published and is still unknown.
- The annual US air force inventory report didn't list *Spirit of Missouri*. US officials claimed that was typo or editorial mistake. The name of B-2 *Spirit of Missouri* appeared in a later edition.
- The Pentagon does not officially announce the loss of an airplane in a combat mission until the other side possesses material evidence such as a wreck or pilots. If the plane is damaged and crashed after or during the mission on 'friendly territory' it is considered lost due to mechanical or human error. That is the truth if we pretend the missile hit was a 'mechanical problem'. If readers refer to Chapter Seven: Stealth Development, they will see that when F-117 no. 792 crashed on 11 July 1986 outside the US zone of control and available to the general population, the entire area was cordoned off until the very last piece of wreckage was removed. The analogy is here…to think about.
- Register numbers and marks of the airplanes are recycled. In example, F-16CG from the 555th squadron which was downed over Yugoslavia appeared on the other similar airplane. B-2 with the identical number and name 'Spirit of Missouri' was recorded during the initial campaign against Iraq in 2003,
- The brigade officially recognized the shooting down of a B-2 on 20 May 1999. The victory silhouette mark of the downed airplane appeared on the UNK cabin door, beside F-117 and F-16 marks, and as of the time of writing is still there (**Figure 8-62**). It is also recorded that the higher commander

ordered the victory signs to be removed (as 'not appropriate' as per service regulations – ???) but the order created a protest from battalion members and the signs were returned to the cabin door.

- After the overthrow of the Milosevic regime, government changes in Serbia, and the normalization of the relationship with NATO and the US, the US officially asked Serbia four questions which show their interest in Serbian abilities to detect the stealth. Lieutenant Colonel Anicic had an opportunity to look at the original questions in English. For this book that copy is not available but as an illustration there is a Serbian language response to every question with the author's translation (**Figure 8-63**).
- A US delegation visited the combat crew which downed F-117A in 2005. During the conversation, Warrant Officer Matic, F2 operator (then retired), showed them photos of the B-2 victory mark on the UNK door. Matic asked them about the downing of the B-2. The US representative was caught and simply couldn't look Matic in the eye and answer his question. He changed the subject.
- The alleged crash site in Spacvan forest: the azimuth of the cleared space more or less corresponds with the recorded azimuth of the crash (**Figure 8-64**, **Figure 8-6**5).

1. Колико су били важни визуелни осматрачи на терену за Ф-117 и за Б-2?

Битно је нагласити за визуелно извиђање да су авиони углавном коришћени ноћу, а Б-2 и на врло великим висинама, те није видљив визуелним осматрачима.

2. Путање сипања горива за Б-2 – где је сипано гориво? Б-2 користи много другачији начин сипања горива од Ф-117. Да ли сте могли распознавати понашање Ф-117 од понашања Б-2 ?.

3. Основно питање за Б-2 је.Да ли сте препознавали овај авион при прелету преко ваше зоне?.

Према нашим сазнањима Б2 је полетао из базе Вајтман из САД у пратњи обезбеђења ловачке заштите пуњења у ваздуху. Летео је на висинама преко 40.000 фита, чиме је могао избећи дејство ПВО. Како смо га ми откривали, слушали... Као и сваки авион мора да се пријави некој контроли летења када долази у тај реон. Имао је специфичне позивне знаке, изваредно јаку радио-станицу и летео је искључиво ноћу. Пријављивао се контроли летења Бриндизи. Долетео је са севера и дејствовао северно од 45 паралеле у рејону Београда, по унапред задатим специфичним циљевима: кинеска амбасада, зграда Муп-а, зграда МО. Регистровано је више од 10 авионолета.

4. Да ли можете пратити тај авион? Да ли можете идентификовати тај авион?

Можемо пратити циљеве до 18.000 метара те можемо идентификовати и овај авион.

Above left: **Figure 8-62**: Kill marks on UNK cabin door. (Author's archive)

Above right: **Figure 8-63**: Translated US questions. (Authors)

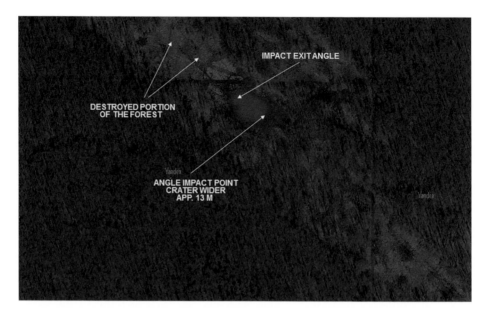

Figure 8-64: The alleged crash site. Photo taken from Yandeks as it has higher resolution than Google maps. (Yandeks, modified by authors)

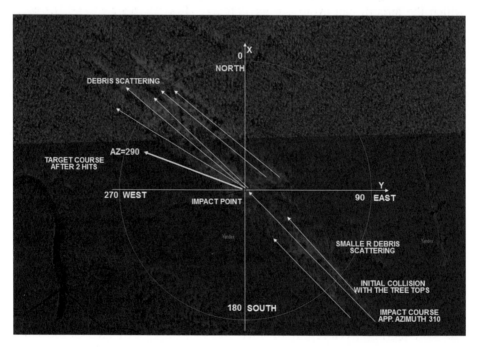

Figure 8-65: Impact angles. Note the similarity with the target departure azimuth after the engagement in **Figures 8-60** and **Figure 8-61**. (Yandeks maps, modified by authors)

Questions and answers
Question 1: What was the importance of the field visual observers for F-117 and B-2?

Answer: It is important to point out, as regards visual observation, that the aircraft mostly flew during the night, and the B-2 at very high altitudes, meaning that it was not visible to visual observers.

Question 2: The B-2 uses a very different refuelling system from the F-117. Have you been able to distinguish between F-117 and B-2 aerial refuelling?

Answer: Not provided in this document. The answer may well be in other documents. An aerial tanker has a large RCS; it may create a single blip on surveillance radar and the aircraft refuelling may be 'masked' by it. Modern radars can tell the difference.

Question 3: Where were you able to recognize and track the B-2 during flyovers of your territory?

Answer: According to our information, the B-2 took off from the USA and was escorted by fighters during air refuelling. Typical altitude was 40,000 feet, at which the aircraft can avoid our air defence. How we detected and 'listened' to it?… Like every other aircraft, the aircraft must report to his own command when he enters into the combat zone. Every airplane had a specific call sign, extraordinarily powerful radio, and only flew at night. The aircraft reported to flight command in Brindizi. Typically it approached from the north and fulfilled its missions north of the 45th parallel in the Belgrade zone as per defined targets such as the Chinese embassy, Interior ministry building, Defence ministry buildings, etc. We registered more than ten missions.

Question 4: Can you track the B-2, and can you identify it?

Answer: We can track targets up to 18,000 m altitude and we can identify the B-2.
    As previously mentioned, there is much speculation, but little direct evidence from the US side, that a B-2 was lost. But for the sake of clarity, there is evidence that something was hit that night… something really big. What it was, and did it crash or not? These are subjects for further research.

'Intelligence Games and Throwing Dust in Eyes'

The smouldering wreck near Budjanovci was soon being scavenged for souvenirs. The 3rd Battalion men took, of course, many souvenirs for themselves. The locals, especially gypsies, brought carts to salvage material they thought would sell for cash. To their disappointment, local scrap yards didn't want to buy composite material! They were interested only in metal. So they used it to cover their pigsties and outhouses! (**Figure 8-66**, **Figure 8-67**).

Engines, canopy, parts of wings were collected and most of what was left after the war is now in storage in the Belgrade Airspace Museum. The canopy and one wing are on public display. Some parts were handed over to the Russians and Chinese. Everything was shrouded in secrecy and there are no officially published documents about this, but it is certain that the Russians got parts interesting for them and the Chinese also got 'their share'.

Figure 8-66: Picking up F-117 souvenirs. (Media Centre Odbrana)

Figure 8-67: ...and useful parts for the pigsty and outhouse roofs. (Media Centre Odbrana)

After the war it was observed that the area of downing and the village of Budjanovci was frequently visited by Chinese 'tourists' who bought from locals whatever they could find that belonged to the F-117A. Intelligence reports confirm it. Even a pilot's oxygen mask hose, which collected dust for years in a farmer's barn, was sold to a Chinese 'collector' for the price of a new wood stove! There is no doubt that the Chinese got parts which were thoroughly analyzed and the knowledge used in the development of their own stealth airplane. The Russians also analyzed the coatings. Some of the parts are now on internal display in Institute No. 2 for radio electronics. The Russians wanted to confirm that their estimates of radar absorption characteristics were correct during RCS testing for their stealth models.

More importantly, Russian delegations were at the command post of 3rd Battalion observing tactical procedures which were implemented in the new combat engagement procedures. Straight after the briefings with the missile crew and step by step analyses, Colonel Victor (Russian military observer, second name not disclosed) sent his notes to Moscow through the Russian embassy in Belgrade. The Russians thoroughly analyzed the information and their reaction was very fast: the combat engagement of the 3rd Battalion was used as an amendment package which was promptly implemented in the missile battalion tactics. One can be sure that all interested parties, such as Iraqis, North Koreans, Syrians and Iranians, now possess all this knowledge… NATO too probably.

Colonel Dani after the war placed calculated disinformation in the documentary movie *21 seconds* that he modified the search radar so that it could detect the stealth airplane far away. Also, ordinary kitchen microwaves were used to confuse the HARM missiles because they have similar frequencies to the target and missile guidance radars. However, there were no technical modifications to the radar nor were microwaves ever used by 3rd Battalion for that purpose.

USAF officials immediately after the downing came up with multiple theories how it happened. Some reports spoke of prearranged flight paths and that Serbs somehow found the pattern. Serbian spies tracked F-117 from its take-off, through Hungary and during target approach. Serbian command used optical cables and mobile phones to transfer the information to the specific designated unit which would launch the missiles. One report spoke of a lucky shot, that Serbians randomly fired missiles and scored. Another guessed that Serbs were able to penetrate the radio communications between airplanes and command centres and pinpoint the individual plane location. There was also a report that Serbs are believed to have plugged powerful computers into their air defence radar system that helped to reveal the flight paths from the faint stealth radar signatures; that a Czech company produced the radar system that could pick up electronic emissions from the stealth airplane, but it went bankrupt and Serbia somehow got possession of their 'Tamara' systems. This is nonsense and pure fantasy!

SHOOTING DOWN THE STEALTH FIGHTER

There is a short text which Rand Corporation wrote in their analyses after the war, blaming procedural errors for the stealth downing (the following is an extract from Rand Corporation *NATO's Air War for Kosovo, a Strategic and Operational Assessment.*

At least three procedural errors were alleged to have contributed to the downing. The first was the reported inability of ELINT collectors to track the changing location of the three or four offending SAM batteries. Three low-frequency Serb radars that at least theoretically could have detected the F-117's presence were reportedly not neutralized because U.S. strike aircraft had earlier bombed the wrong aim points within the radar complexes. Also, F-16CJs carrying HARMs and operating in adjacent airspace could have deterred the SA-3 battery from emitting, but those aircraft had been recalled before the F-117 shootdown. The second alleged procedural error entailed an EA-6B support jammer that was said to have been operating not only too far away from the F-117 (80 to 100 miles) to have been of much protective value, but also out of proper alignment with the offending threat radars, resulting in inefficient jamming.

Last was the reported fact that F-117s operating out of Aviano had previously flown along more or less the same transit routes for four nights in a row because of a SACEUR ban on overflight of Bosnia to avoid jeopardizing the Dayton accords. That would have made their approach pattern into Yugoslav airspace predictable. Knowing from which direction the F-117s would be coming, Serb air defenders could have employed low-frequency radars for the best chance of getting a snap look at the aircraft. Former F-117 pilots and several industry experts acknowledged that the aircraft is detectable by such radars when viewed from the side or from directly below. U.S. officials also suggested that the Serbs may have been able to get brief nightly radar hits while the aircraft's weapons bay doors were fleetingly open.

Heated arguments arose in Washington and elsewhere in the immediate aftermath of the shootdown over whether USEU-COM had erred in not aggressively having sought to destroy the wreckage of the downed F-117 in order to keep its valuable stealth technology out of unfriendly hands and eliminate its propaganda value, which the Serbs bent every effort to exploit. Said a former commander of Tactical Air Command, General John M. Loh: 'I'm surprised we didn't bomb it, because the standing procedure has always been that when you lose something of real or perceived value – in this case real technology, stealth – you destroy it.' The case for at least trying to deny the enemy the wreckage was bolstered by Paul Kaminski, the Pentagon's former acquisition chief and the Air Force's first F-117 programme manager during the 1970s. Kaminski noted that although the F-117 had been operational for 15 years, 'there are things in that airplane, while they may not be leading technologies today in the United States, that are certainly ahead of what some potential adversaries have.' Kaminski added that the main concern was not that any exploitation of the F-117's low-observable technology would enable an enemy to put the F-117 at greater risk, but rather that it could help him eventually develop his own stealth technology in due course. Reports indicated that military officials had at first considered attempting to destroy the wreckage but opted in the end not to follow.

Regarding the Rand analysis about ELINT picking up radar emissions, it is interesting to recall what happened that afternoon just before the engagement. There was intensive action on the Serbian side which simulated radar emission with the radar emission imitators on azimuths and locations which were, by coincidence or not, almost the same as those followed by the F-117A that night. It is hard to believe that prolonged radar emissions on those frequencies were not picked up by ELINT aircraft which flew in the vicinity.

It is true that the Serbian side used a wide network of informers and sympathizers, even some people who were positioned inside the base and had up-to-date information. In the book *Stealth Down* there is a short description of the 'aircraft spotters' behind the fence who took photographs of planes taking off and landing. Some were Serbian. One of the authors knew someone who was there every night, and as soon as the planes took off he sent information to air defence: take-off time, type, direction of flight. Field tactical units however were never directly connected with any of the sources. Even the media, such as CNN or RAI, covered planes taking off from different NATO bases; the Serbian side closely followed the news. Flight paths through Slovenia and Hungary were monitored. Airplanes made plenty of noise, and contrails in the sky above those countries provided clear vectors. Radio amateurs in the region were a valuable information source. The Serbians would calculate the flight time to estimate when the aircraft would be approaching the target. This sounds easy, but in practice it was not. Some of the information received definitely helped the Serbian side, but none was indispensable to the downing of the stealth.

The truth is that an old Soviet P-18 radar can detect an F-117 at least 30 km away. Fire control radar can also track a stealth airplane even with electronic jamming. The F-117A was not invisible to radar… just the signature is not high. A well trained and organized crew can routinely detect and recognize a typical RCS 20 km away or more. That night, two other radar blips were on the screen. What they were is not known at the time of writing.

The Americans also put part of the blame on the mission planners using predetermined paths in and out of Yugoslav airspace. The F-117A was flying alone without any fighter or EW-capable airplane to mask it. In the post-F-117A phase of the war, NATO extensively used these tactics, in most cases successfully blocking Serbian air defence, but not without casualties. There are two F-117As which were most likely damaged during the missions. One landed at Zagreb's Pleso airport with significant but not catastrophic damage. After the war, two airplanes, unidentified by serial number, were disassembled, packed into transport planes and returned to US. Why would anybody return airplanes this way? Either they were not able to cross the ocean on their own, or they were not airworthy due to damage sustained. On their return they were assessed and as repair was not feasible they were placed in a holding ground and eventually scrapped.

How were the parts handed over to the Russians and Chinese? High-ranking US officials were not overwhelmingly concerned about this possibility because F-117 was very well known and many publications and articles were available at that time. Burned wreckage and destroyed electronics were not a major cause for concern. For the USAF it was yesterday's technology. The Serbian side never published details of what had been found and what was 'delivered' to other countries.

Russian officials admitted in 2001 that they used remains from the USAF stealth fighter shot down over Yugoslavia to improve their air defence systems. Acknowledging that researchers had access to the remains of the F-117, a senior Russian aerospace official said that they were able to test their system against the broken pieces. Of course, Russia will never say what information they were able to get and are likely to try to mislead and downplay what they recovered. The fact is, anti-stealth radars were rapidly developed afterwards. The early Nebo VHF radar at MAKS in 2001 was the ancestor of the huge active electronically-scanned array shown in 2013. Stealth modifications to tactical aircraft were confirmed a couple of years later when engineers from Moscow's Institute for Theoretical and Applied Electromagnetics spoke at a London conference about radar cross-section (RCS) reduction work on the Sukhoi Su-27 family.

The Russian Defence Ministry's 2nd Central Scientific & Research Institute (2nd TzNII) and its facilities, in Tver, tested RCS models of the F-117, B-2, and many other aircraft (**Figure 8-68**, **Figure 8-69a** and **Figure 8-69b**). Parts of the F-117A are on internal exhibition there. That research led to the development of the Sukhoi Su-57, the first Russian stealth plane.

China has a history of being accused of stealing military aircraft technology. The Croatian intelligence service and the admiral who was Croatia's chief of staff during the Kosovo war, Admiral Domazet-Lošo, said he believes that China formulated the technology for its J-20 jet from an American F-117A. This was based on reports which Croatian intelligence gathered about Chinese activities in the area where the F-117A crashed.

Figure 8-68: CNII VKKO radar research institute. (Voenaya Priemka)

Figure 8-69a: CNII VKKO B-2
scale model for RCS testing.
(Voenaya Priemka)

The bombing of the Chinese embassy in Belgrade and hangars at Belgrade's civilian airport during the NATO air campaign where parts of the F-117A allegedly were stored, may be considered as a deliberate warning to the Chinese not to try to remove airplane parts. Of course, NATO will never acknowledge that.

Manipulations started immediately after the aircraft was downed. They started with the NATO press conference under PR agent Jamie Shein. NATO PR stated that the video clips and photos on Serbian TV were Serbian propaganda. Then they announced that the aircraft crashed because of a technical malfunction. They also tried to 'buy time' while the rescue operation was underway. It was questionable why the smouldering wreck was not bombed the same night and obliterated.

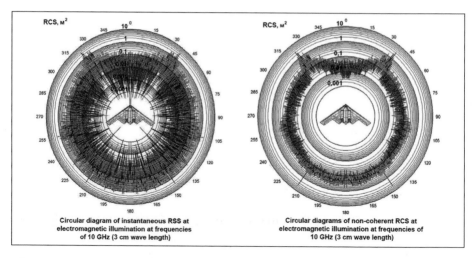

RCS, м²

Circular diagram of instantaneous RSS at electromagnetic illumination at frequencies of 10 GHz (3 cm wave length)

Circular diagrams of non-coherent RCS at electromagnetic illumination at frequencies of 10 GHz (3 cm wave length)

Figure 8-69b: B-2 circular RCS for 10 GHz/3cm radar which is a common frequency in fire control radars. (Raseyanie Elektromagnetnih Voln, modified by authors)

On the Serbian side, after the initial euphoria and celebrations, some started to play their own games. Unfortunately, from one extraordinary event the seeds of division were planted. Lieutenant Colonel Dani started to behave as if he alone downed the stealth. A missile crew is a team – no one member can say that he downed a plane. Immediately after the downing he and a few other crew members were promoted, but brigade HQ, the air defence directorate and high command, in the humble opinion of one of the authors, didn't adequately reward all participants. The brass explained that there are no service regulations which say that everyone must be rewarded. This created tension within the battalion. But it did not negatively affect the unit's performance. As we have seen, the battalion had more successful engagements.

The key players in the events retired a few years later. Some others stayed with the military and at the time of writing are still there.

After the war the 3rd Battalion ceased to exist as a unit. The whole of 250th Brigade was reorganized, merging the few remaining SA-3 battalions with their surviving equipment with the SA-6 battalions forming a new formation with the same designation.

Dani retired in 2004 and started his own bakery business in his village. Anicic retired at his own request after the military couldn't find a position adequate to his rank and achievements. He then decided to write a book based on the diary he wrote during the war. His diary is officially classified as a military document. Some were upset by his observations and comments. In his own words, he couldn't wait to be discharged from the military. That was the consequence of the stresses and strains imposed on him.

Chapter Nine

Aftermath

The Yugoslav Air Defence System survived the NATO air campaign to force the removal of Serbian forces from Kosovo, which ran from 24 March to 9 June 1999 and at its height involved over 1,000 aircraft. Survival of the IADS was achieved by employing three different methods to negate NATO's air power. The NATO decision not to use ground forces certainly made Serb defensive measures much easier. By deliberately not employing all their defence assets at once, known as the strategy of withholding military force, the Yugoslavs could move their mobile surface-to-air missiles about to ensure they could not be targeted.

A defending ground force needs to be forced to expose itself, thus allowing it to be attacked by air power. A major lesson NATO learned was that an opposing force must be driven out from cover. One option is to stage an attack that is designed to compel a defending force to react. To enable air power to hunt down and destroy targets requires robust Intelligence, Surveillance and Reconnaissance (ISR) systems and Precision Guided Munitions (PGM). Terrain masking and deception measures by small forces in complex terrain, such as hilly and/or jungle terrain, as occurred in Kosovo and in the various conflicts in South East Asia, often negate the use of ISR systems, presenting difficulties in locating and positively identifying targets.

The aim of Operation Allied Force was 'to stop Serbian forces attacking' ethnic Albanians and eject them from Kosovo through the application of air power alone. This was to reduce casualties on the NATO side, but it made life for the Serbian forces in Kosovo easier as there were no ground troops to worry about, except KLA separatists and a few NATO special forces either fighting with the KLA or independently. By withholding military force the Serbs avoided having their air defence and field units destroyed in the first days of the air campaign. They had absorbed the lessons of Operation Desert Storm and preserved their assets for the long haul. This was a successful strategy: Serb forces were still firing surface-to-air missiles on the last day of Operation Allied Force. Employing passive systems such as electro-optical tracking equipment further enhanced the survivability of IADS components, by not creating an emission signature that NATO defence suppression aircraft could lock on to.

Bad weather and the 'rigid' insistence on avoiding collateral damage and casualties to the attack force dogged NATO planners. It led to an over-reliance on Precision Guided Munitions (PGMs). In the first three weeks of Allied Force there were only seven days of favourable weather for air operations and ten days on which fifty per cent of the strikes had to be cancelled for fear of collateral damage.

Ninety per cent of the ordnance dropped was PGMs which had their own problems. GPS-aided munitions, the only affordable all-weather munitions, can be inaccurate due to the cumulative effect of numerous errors, as well as small inaccuracies in the targeting aircraft, maps and the munition itself. This is called the 'sensor-to-shooter error budget' in US parlance. Further, the amount of cloud over Kosovo caused many laser-guided bombs (LGBs) to 'lose lock' and 'go rogue' often landing kilometres away from their intended target or hitting civilian targets.

The reliance on GPS guided bombs caused a shortage that became so acute in late April that the GPS guided Joint Direct Attack Munitions (JDAM) were available for only the B-2A Spirit bomber. By late April the ratio of PGMs to unguided munitions used had dropped to 69 per cent. Many of the targets struck by PGMs in Kosovo were not judged to be worth the cost of US$12,000 per Paveway II bomb kit (the price tag at the time), and could have been hit safely by unguided ordnance. The fire control avionics fitted to most NATO aircraft enabled very accurate bombing using 'dumb' bombs, albeit with a necessary reduction in bombing altitude.

Serbian ground forces were hard to locate due to their small unit size and movement, generally being company-sized units of 80 to 150 personnel and around six armoured vehicles, operating autonomously or semi-autonomously of each other. Using the woods and mountains, and by not being a large target or moving in a set direction, prevented the building up of an intelligence picture and thus made these forces difficult to locate from the air.

The air campaign over Kosovo severely affected the readiness rates of the USAF's Air Combat Command during that period. Units in the United States were the most badly affected, as they were stripped of their personnel and spare parts to support ACC (Air Combat Command) and AMC (Air Mobility Command) units involved in Operation Allied Force. The Commander of the USAF's Air Combat Command, General Richard Hawley, outlined this in a speech to reporters on 29 April 1999. Further, aircraft would have to be replaced earlier than previously planned, PGM inventories would need to be restocked, and the war-stock of AGM-86C Conventional Air-Launched Cruise Missiles dropped to 100 rounds or fewer. Of the more than 25,000 bombs and missiles expended, nearly 8,500 were PGMs, with the replacement cost estimated at $US1.3 billion.

Thus the USAF suffered from virtual attrition of its air force without having scored a large number of kills in theatre. Even if the US's best estimates of Serbian casualties are used, the Serbians left Kosovo with a large part of their armoured forces intact.

Successful Deception Measures

Sun Tzu wrote that all warfare is based on deception. Serbian deception measures were very successful. Decoys were a real problem for strike aircraft, as loitering over an area at low altitude made them targets for MAN-PADS, infrared guided point defence SAMs such as the SA-9 Gaskin and SA-13 Gopher, and SPAAGs such as the BOV-3/30 series and the Praga M53/59. Hundreds of decoys were hit that were thought to be real targets. Some decoys were hit multiple times. Pilots would not loiter over them trying to discriminate between them and real targets. Air forces have not always invested sufficiently in sensors to counter deception and camouflage techniques, and the Serbs exploited this quite successfully; this was noted in the post-Allied Force after-action study.

NATO flew approximately 30,000 sorties during the war, and just under 2,000 of these saw ordnance expended. These sorties were claimed at the time to have destroyed 93 tanks and 153 armoured personnel carriers (APCs) out of the approximately 350 tanks and 440 APCs believed to have been in Kosovo. NATO also claimed to have hit 339 military vehicles and 389 artillery pieces and mortars. These figures were wide of the mark, as General Clark, the Operation Allied Force commander, agreed, conceding that not all targets hit were destroyed, and that only twenty-six vehicles could be confirmed as kills.

In a *New York Times* article, there was an interesting view immediately after the war:[15]

> Towards the end of the Balkans air war, rarely a day passed when NATO did not triumphantly declare that allied warplanes had destroyed several more Yugoslav tanks or artillery pieces with precision-guided bombs or missiles.
>
> Now it turns out that a significant fraction of those weapons that looked fearsome from 15,000 feet up may have been nothing more than artfully designed decoys meant to fool allied pilots. Indeed, the Serb military, outgunned by a technologically superior foe, proved to be a master of camouflage, concealment and deception. Yugoslav commanders built 'tanks' of wood and plastic sheeting, sometimes draping them with camouflage netting. To trick thermal sensors,

---

15. Eric Schmidt, 'The World; Bombs Are Smart, People Are Smarter', *New York Times*, 4 July 1999.

they put metal tape or plates on some decoys and even set trays of water inside them that heated up in the sun, just like a real tank would.

Some suspected artillery revetments turned out to be disguised pits, empty but for a long tube protruding towards the sky. And to the dismay of the NATO air commanders, several Yugoslav MiG-21 fighter jets emerged from hidden caves once the war was over.

Of course, the air campaign's overall results were still devastating and no doubt instrumental in forcing the Yugoslav President Slobodan Milosevic to cry uncle and withdraw his forces from Kosovo.

But the phony targets have become a sore point with NATO's military commander, General Wesley K. Clark, who now says the alliance destroyed only 110 of the roughly 300 tanks that Yugoslavia poured into Kosovo, not the 150 tanks NATO initially thought it blasted into scrap.

'For the most part, our pilots recognized those decoys,' General Clark bristled last week. 'There is a concerted disinformation campaign underway by the Government of Yugoslavia to protect the reputation of its armed forces and to diminish the reputation of NATO's air power campaign.'

Yet one of the emerging lessons from the air war is that low-technology countermeasures can still fool high-technology weaponry and sensors enough of the time to make a difference. 'The history of warfare suggests there are always countermeasures, and human ingenuity will find its way,' said Eliot A. Cohen, a professor at Johns Hopkins who directed the Air Force's definitive study of the 1991 Persian Gulf war.

'One of the big surprises was the extent to which the Yugoslav military was able to use ground decoys to cause us to strike targets that weren't real,' said one senior Defence Department official.

Serbian techniques included constructing false bridges, fake artillery pieces made of long telephone poles painted black with old truck wheels, anti-aircraft missile launchers constructed of old milk cartons, wooden mock-ups of MiG-29 aircraft, self-propelled artillery vehicles constructed on old vehicle shells and chassis from the scrapyards, radar reflectors and special camouflage nets (developed by one of the authors) around the real military equipment, extensive use of field camouflage, to name but a few. Some of the ingenious deceptions included cow manure in combination with metal plates to attract NATO thermal guided missiles. Manure naturally radiates heat similar to the heat radiation signature of a tank engine. Real tank engines were often covered with mattresses soaked with water to lower the thermal radiation. One of the authors designed thermal sleeves for artillery and tank cannons to prevent thermal emission detection after firing (**Figure 9-1**, **Figure 9-2**, **Figure 9-3**, **Figure 9-4**, **Figure 9-5**). To quote a NATO

Figure 9-1: Dummy 'armoured vehicle' made from scrapped Zastava 101 car. (Author's archive)

Figure 9-2: Old Sherman tank used as a decoy. (Author's archive)

Figure 9-3: Field camouflage for UNK and Low Blow radar. (Author's archive)

Figure 9-4: Dummy MiG-29 in Belgrade Aeronautical Museum. (Author's archive)

Figure 9-5: P-18 radar masked at the combat position. (Author's archive)

officer who performed field assessments after the war: 'Our guys in Kosovo have found hundreds of imitation tanks, trucks, artillery pieces, missiles and missile launchers, roads and even bridges that NATO aircraft and cruise missiles had "destroyed". From up close they look like junk, but from three miles up, they'd look like the real thing.'

In particular, radar imitators played a crucial role in the survival of the missile battalions, and in cooperation with fire control radar emission successfully defended the missile battalion when under attack. In today's air defence, radar imitators are standard issue for every missile battalion. Russian battalions may use six or more imitators per unit.

Fixed Air Defences Damaged but Mobile Air Defences Survived

NATO air planners were certainly concerned that not as many Serbian SAM batteries were destroyed as they would have liked, with the then commander of the USAF in Europe acknowledging the success of Serbian SAM battery shoot-and-scoot operational tactics.

Mobile systems suffered few casualties, but the fixed defences were badly damaged. Two of Serbia's three static S-75 Dvina/SA-2 Guideline SAM battalions and seventy per cent of their static S-125 Neva/SA-3 Goa SAM sites were hit and most taken out of action. Some of the systems were damaged but repaired after. Only three mobile 9M9 Kvadrat/SA-6 Gainful SAM systems were hit and damaged (**Figure 9-6**, **Figure 9-7**, **Figure 9-8**).

Serbia certainly left Kosovo and suffered a tremendous amount of damage to its infrastructure, but Serbian combat power remained substantially intact. Even if the Milosevic regime did not achieve its political objectives Serbia retained its ground combat strength in the face of overwhelming air power, and the Kosovo Liberation Army was 'disarmed' as part of the political settlement. intact. Even if the Milosevic regime did not achieve its political objectives Serbia retained its ground combat strength in the face of overwhelming air power, and the Kosovo Liberation Army was 'disarmed' as part of the political settlement.

Figure 9-6: Laser guided bomb craters after attack on UNK. (Author's archive)

Figure 9-7: Equipment burning just after attack on UNK. (Author's archive)

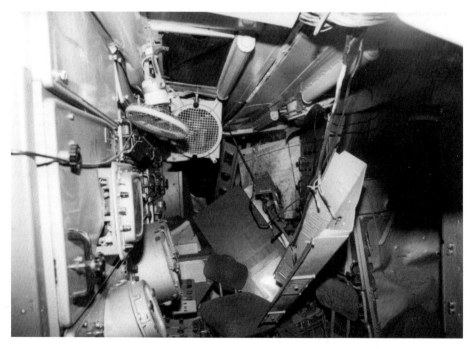

Figure 9-8: Heavily damaged UNK cabin. (Author's archive)

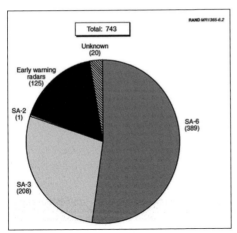 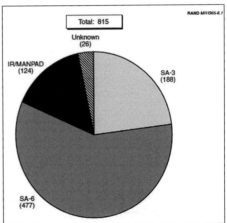

Above left: **Figure 9-9**: NATO expended a total of 743 AGM-88 HARM anti-radiation missile rounds, launched by EA-6B Prowlers, F-16CJ Weasels and Tornado ECRs. The most notable aspect of this chart is that more than 50 per cent of HARMs were fired at mobile SA-6 batteries, which suffered the lowest attrition of any Serbian radar guided SAM type. At least twenty-two HARM missiles were launched against the 3rd Battalion without any hit.

Above right: **Figure 9-10**: As per NATO statistics a total of 815 SAMs were fired at NATO aircraft, of which 665 were radar guided SA-3 and SA-6 rounds. Out of them, F-16CG and F-117A were downed and several other aircraft sustained damage through hit or near miss. Many SAM shots were unguided due to the radar shutting down to avoid HARM shots. (AWOS Fact Sheet via www.ausairpower.net). NATO and Serbian sources about the quantity of missiles launched are very different:[16] the Serbian side launched a total of 163 SA-3 and SA-6 missiles (according to the material lists of expended ammunition). The Serbs also launched 168 missiles from portable shoulder launchers (MANPAD).

F-117A Retirement and Beyond

F-117 went into 'retirement' in 2008. The most common explanation why F-117A was withdrawn from service is the introduction of the F-22 Raptor. According to the US Air Force, when the Nighthawk was retired it was mandated that it be kept in 'Type 1000' storage. Aircraft in Type 1000 storage are to be maintained until recalled to active service, should the need arise. Type 1000 aircraft are termed inviolate; meaning they have a high potential to return to flying status and no parts may be removed from them. These aircraft are 're-preserved' every four years. It can take 30-120 days, depending upon how long the aircraft has been in Type 1000 storage, for it to become flyable again.

---

16. NATO believes that the Serbs launched missiles randomly in attempt to 'scare' their airplanes.

Since retirement from active flying status in 2008, the USAF's F-117 Nighthawks have been maintained in their original, climate-friendly hangars at the Tonopah Test Range Airport in Nevada. Given the cost of establishing secure storage facilities at the Aircraft Maintenance and Regeneration Center (AMARC at Davis-Monthan AFB), the Air Force chose instead to store the F-117s at Tonopah. Some of the F-117 aircraft are occasionally flown. One pre-production example was scrapped (**Figure 9-11**). The stored aircrafts' systems are 'mummified' and their wings removed so that up to five aircraft can fit into a single hangar instead of two.

Since the F-117 officially stopped flying, the black jet has been spotted on numerous occasions. But keeping even a small force of F-117s flying is not a cheap or easy task. The knowledgeable maintenance personnel have to keep working; the temperamental radar absorbent material needs constant care; the pilots have to manage without the simulators and training regimes that once existed for the aircraft.

There were some speculations that the F-117 could be used as a 'flying measuring platform' for evaluating a radar system's ability to detect and track low-observable flying objects. Or it could be used as a surrogate to test new radar absorbent materials and coatings applied to its surface that was originally built to accept such applications.

By using the F-117, defence programme managers could have a control variable, in this case the F-117's well documented radar cross section, infrared and visual signature, to test upon, that independent variable being an experimental

Figure 9-11: F-117A scrapping. (techsob.com)

radar absorbent material or other signature control application. The F-117 is a near-perfect low-observable aircraft to test everything from ground-based radars and SAM systems, to AWACS modifications, fighter radars and even infrared search and track systems. Measuring radar cross sections of aircraft flying under real world conditions may be an entirely worthwhile reason to keep a small cadre of F-117s operational for calibrating and improving the DYCOMS array at Groom Lake.

As one confirmed F-117 was shot down during Operation Allied Force over Serbia, and its wreckage evaluated by America's military technology competitors, the technological risk of using such a modified platform in future conflict seems negligible. In fact, it would probably be much lower than using a new drone featuring the latest in stealth, sensor and automated technologies.

The rest of the world is increasingly catching up with the US's once exclusive monopoly on 'stealth' technology. Fighters such as the Russian Sukhoi Su-57 and the Chinese Chengdu J-20 are well on their way to becoming potential challengers to American and allied air supremacy. Furthermore, stealthy unmanned aerial vehicles and cruise missiles are even easier to develop than their manned counterparts. So, it would make sense for the USA and other allied nations to begin training against low-observable adversary aircraft, especially in the realm of detecting, intercepting and engaging them. With all of this in mind, it could make sense for the USAF to field the F-117s as stealth aggressors, even though the aircraft is well over thirty years old.

As non-American stealth platforms hit the skies operationally around the world, the US is going to have to begin fielding some sort of low-observable aggressor aircraft for large air warfare exercises. Red Flag, the largest aerial wargame of its kind, happens to take place right where the remaining F-117s are based, either at Tonopah Test Range Air Base, or at Groom Lake, otherwise known as Area 51.

In April 2016 lawmakers appeared ready to 'remove the requirement that certain F-117 aircraft be maintained in a condition that would allow recall of those aircraft to 'future service', which would move them from storage to the aerospace maintenance and regeneration yard in Arizona to be scavenged for hard-to-find parts, or completely disassembled.

On 11 September 2017 it was reported that in accordance with the National Defence Authorization Act for Fiscal Year 2017, signed into law on 23 December 2016, 'the Air Force will remove four F-117s every year to fully divest them – a process known as demilitarizing aircraft.' At time of writing (2019), this is still in force.

On the other hand, SAM-3 is still in use in many countries worldwide. As we saw in the Chapter Four, numerous S-125 upgrades are available. Since Russia replaced all of its S-125 sites with SA-10 and SA-12 systems, they decided to upgrade the S-125 systems being removed from service to make them more attractive to export customers.

Figure 9-12: Modernized towed Low-Blow (UNV-125). (Almaz-Antey)

Figure 9-13: Mounted Low-Blow radar. (Cenrex)

Figure 9-14 (above): Polish Newa SC Anaconda launcher based on T-55 chassis. (Cenrex) **(right)**: Cuban SA-3 TELs. (Vestnik PVO)

In 1999, a Russian-Belarus financial-industrial consortium called Oboronitelnye Sistemy (Defence Systems) was awarded a contract to overhaul Egypt's S-125 SAM system. These refurbished weapons have been reintroduced as the S-125 Pechora 2M (**Figure 9-12**, **Figure 9-13**).

In 2001, Poland began offering an upgrade to the S-125 known as the Newa SC (**Figure 9-14** above). This replaced analogue components with digital ones, mounted the missile launcher on a WZT-1 tank chassis, and added IFF capability and data-links. Radar is mounted on an 8-wheeled heavy truck chassis (formerly used for Scud launchers). Serbian modifications include terminal/camera homing from radar base and digital displays.

Cuba developed a similar upgrade to the Polish one, mounted on T-55 chassis, which was displayed in La Habana in 2006 (**Figure 9-14** right).

There is a version of the S-125 available from Russia with the warhead replaced with telemetry instrumentation, for use as target drones.

In October 2010, Ukrainian Aerotechnica announced a modernized version of S-125 named S-125-2D Pechora. As of 2018 according to the UkrOboronProm, the SA-3/S-125 surface-to-air missile underwent an integrated modification of all elements.

It is obvious that the SAM-3 passed through a rebirth and for years to come it will continue to be in use with constant modifications and upgrades.

Future of SAM vs Stealth

We have already discussed some implications of the first stealth downing in combat. Both sides in the conflict learned hard lessons. Tactics and procedures for the attackers were improved; counter-stealth measures for the defenders were also improved. Some of the manuals have been rewritten and corrected. SAM-3 has been improved with new technical developments injecting new life into the old-timer so it will serve well into the twenty-first century. F-117A, now officially retired (since 2008), was a revolutionary airplane which pushed the boundaries of aerodynamics and stealth into new areas. New stealth airplanes have been developed, and they are and will be involved in conflicts and wars to come. Air defence has also evolved; there are constant improvements with new systems introduced. It is a never-ending process. There are three major fields where these technologies clash:

- Stealth aircraft
- Counter-stealth detection and tracking
- Air defence missiles

Stealth Aircraft

The F-117A, B-2 and B1-B can be regarded as the three emblematic low-observability aircraft of the late 80s. Having realized the capabilities offered by low-observability technology, the US went on developing a number of stealth jet fighters, such as the F-22A Raptor (first flight in 1997, production ended in 2011, 195 planes built). Lockheed Martin was the prime contractor and Boeing the main partner (**Figure 9-15**, **Figure 9-16**).

The Lockheed Martin (LM) F-35 Lightning II (**Figure 9-17**) is a general fighter with stealth capabilities currently in production (first flight 2006). There are three variants, the F-35A CTOL (Conventional Take-Off and Landing), the F-35B STOVL (Short-Take Off and Vertical-Landing), the F-5C CV (Carrier Variant). The F-35 is based on the Joint Strike Fighter (JSF) programme, which started in the mid '90s. In 2001 the LM X-35 won the JSF competition over the Boeing X-32. Consequently LM was awarded the System Development and Demonstration contract to develop the F-35, based on X-35. The development of the F-35 is funded primarily by the US but also by several other partner nations. F-35's first foreign buyer was Israel.

Figure 9-15: F-22 Raptor. (USAF)

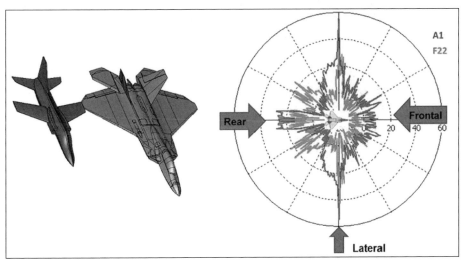

Figure 9-16: Comparison of the sizes of the AMX-A1 and the F-22 (left). Monostatic RCS plot of both planes, at the frequency of 10.5GHz (right). (Radar Cross Section of a stealthy aircraft using electromagnetic simulation in the X and in VHF/UHF Bands, IJRAME)

It is claimed that the F-35 fuselage design was a compromise between cost and requirements and some capabilities were 'sacrificed': RCS is really low in the X-band (8-12 GHz) and in the Ku-band (12-18 GHz), while it is not so low at lower frequency bands. The aim is the breaking of the killing chain:[17] even if the F-35 is detected by surveillance radar, it may not be easy to engage it with a fire control radar, which usually operates in the X or Ku bands. The F-22, on the

_____

17. The killing chain refers to the sequence of detection, tracking, locking onto target, launching, guiding and hitting. If any of these parts can be eliminated or obscured, the airplane has a chance of avoiding being hit.

Figure 9-17: F-35 Lighting II. (USAF)

other hand, presents a lower RCS from all aspects and at more frequency bands, of course at a considerably higher cost.

The production F-35 presents a slightly higher RCS than the prototype X-35 since more volume was required for internal equipment and armament bays. The curves of the redesigned fuselage will incur an RCS increase from some certain directions. It was calculated that the RCS would remain very low from the frontal sector – to be precise, from a sector of 29° in front of the aircraft. However, the RCS will not be so low from the lateral aspect or the rear. The researchers at Air Power Australia created a 3-D model of the underside of the fuselage and tried to calculate the RCS using the POFACETS algorithm developed at the Naval Postgraduate School of the USN.

In any case, there is no doubt that the F-35 exhibits stealth capabilities, maybe not as good as the F-22 but probably better than any other aircraft. To estimate the maximum detection range for the F-35, first there should be an estimation of the F-35 RCS, and then a calculation, using the radar equation and the logic mentioned before, with respect to the detection range for a standard target used for comparison purposes. As a 'standard target' for the comparison, a 1 m² RCS target is used. A target of 1 m² RCS corresponds to a small fighter, such as the Northrop T-38 Talon. Simulated RCS is shown in **Figure 9-18**.

CHAPTER NINE

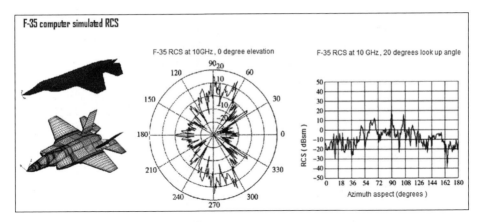

Figure 9-18: F-35 simulated RCS. (www.ausairpower.net).

The detection range for a search radar 64N6E of the S-300 PMU-1 system (Almaz-Antey) operating in the S-band with a maximum range of 300 km (162 nm), for a 1 m² RCS target is calculated to be 110 nautical miles. For engagement radar 30N6E1 of the same system operating in the X-band, with a maximum range of 150 km (81 nm), the detection range for a 'standard target' is 55 nm.

Boeing proposed a low-observability (LO) variant of its proven fighter F-15E, designated F-15SE Silent Eagle. Initially Boeing declared that the F-15SE would exhibit an LO level comparable to that of a 5th generation aircraft, implying the F-35. A Boeing spokesman clarified that they meant that 'the Silent Eagle could meet the level of stealth approved by the US government for release to international customers', a point still reflected in their most recent description of F-15SE. Also, Boeing had extensively applied LO techniques on the F/A-18E/F Super Hornet. Furthermore, in August 2013, Boeing started flight-testing the 'Advanced Super Hornet', a new variant of the F/A-18E/F Super Hornet, with conformal fuel tanks, an enclosed weapons pod and 'signature enhancements' designed to substantially increase the range and reduce the radar signature.

Russia developed their stealth programme with the PAK FA which is now renamed Su-57, being developed by Sukhoi. Its prototype, T-50, flew for the first time in 2010. The PAK FA is a 5th generation, multirole, twin-engine jet fighter which will replace a number of older Russian fighters. The expectation is that the PAK FA will reach the stealth levels of the F-22 and outperform it in other aspects. Sukhoi offered a partnership with HAL (Hindustan Aeronautics Limited), the 'Fifth Generation Fighter Aircraft' (FGFA) for India, but it has not yet materialized (**Figure 9-19**).

On 21 February 2018 two Su-57s were spotted landing at the Russian Khmeimim air base in Syria. They were deployed with four Sukhoi Su-35 fighters, four Sukhoi Su-25s, and one Beriev A-50 AEW&C. Three days later two more

297

Figure 9-19: Su-57.
(Vitaly Kuzmin)

Figure 9-20:
Eurofighter Typhoon.
(RAF)

Su-57s were reported to have arrived in Syria. According to the Russian press, the Su-57s have 'excellently' carried out their mission in Eastern Ghouta. On 1 March 2018 the Russian Defence Minister confirmed that the two Su-57s spent two days in Syria and successfully completed a trials programme, including combat trials during which parameters of weapons work were monitored. On 25 May 2018 the Russian Defence Ministry revealed that during the February 2018 deployment to Syria a Su-57 fired a Kh-59MK2 cruise missile in combat.

China is developing the Chengdu J-20 (first flight in 2011) and more recently the smaller Shenyang J-31 (first flight in 2012), both twin-engine. It is speculated that the Chinese used parts of the downed F-117A to reverse engineer the structure and stealth coating of their planes.

In Europe, LO techniques have been applied to Rafale (Dassault Aviation) and Eurofighter Typhoon (EADS), reducing drastically their radar signatures, even though technically they are not stealth aircraft. Rafale is supposed to employ active techniques to hide from enemy radars, using its advanced countermeasures suite (**Figure 9-20**, **Figure 9-21** and **Figure 9-22**).

Figure 9-21: Eurofighter
RCS. (Harakteristiki
Radiolokacionih
Zametnosti Letalnih
Aparatov)

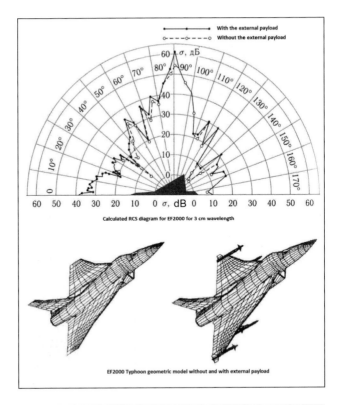

Figure 9-22: Dassault
Raphale. (Author's
archive)

On the subject of LO aircraft, one should also mention the TF-X, a 5th generation fighter being developed by Turkish Aerospace Industries in partnership with SAAB AB, according to the Turkish press. The first flight is scheduled for 2023. In the next decade, more than 250 TFX are expected to serve alongside the 100 F-35s which Turkey intends to procure. At the time of writing, there is ongoing dispute between Washington and Ankara about the purchase of the Russian S-400 system, which may delay or cancel the Turkish F-35 programme.

Counter-Stealth Radar Systems

The US approach to stealth has seen a combination of technologies employed, to produce the overall effect of 'stealth'. Active emissions by aircraft radar and data-links have been reduced by the adoption of what are termed 'low probability of intercept' or LPI techniques. LPI techniques typically rely on the use of very wideband frequency hopping techniques, noiselike waveform modulations, and sometimes pseudorandom scan patterns, to made radar and data-link/network emissions very hard to detect. A modern AESA (active ellectronicaly scanned array) radar with the ability to hop across a gigahertz or more of bandwidth, using spread spectrum modulated pulse trains, will be all but invisible to the crystal video receiver technology radar threat warning systems of the late Cold War era. The radar signatures of aircraft and missiles present a much more challenging problem, for a variety of good reasons. The most prominent of these is that threat radars may be operating across a range of wavelengths, from around ten metres down to less than a centimetre. This has important implications for the two primary technologies employed in producing VLO capability. The two primary technologies used in airframe radar cross section reduction are shaping and materials.

Materials are often touted as the solution by parties who do not understand the physics well. For example, 'apply this magical coating and your aircraft will vanish off their screens'. The reality is that coatings and materials are usually only effective over a fairly narrow band of frequencies, and often to get good effect considerable depth or thickness is required, resulting in weight and volume penalties. Central to the difficulties with radar-absorbent and lossy materials is the 'skin effect', where radio-frequency electrical currents induced by an impinging wave tend to concentrate in the surface of an object. With highly conductive materials like aluminium skins, this layer is extremely thin for most frequencies of interest, making such skins excellent reflectors. Absorbent or lossy coatings, however, must be much less conductive to produce effect, and this results in much greater skin depth. As a result, a very thin coating or laminate which might be highly effective against a 10 GHz radar is apt to be ineffective against a 10 MHz or 100 MHz radar as the skin depth becomes many millimetres or centimetres deep.

The most common approach to this problem is the use of radar-absorbent structures, an example being the leading edge on the B-2A 'batwing' bomber, which has the depth to accommodate complex absorbent structures which are highly effective over a very large bandwidth. This is a more difficult problem for fighters, as volume and weight are critical problems. Airframe shaping is however where the biggest gains are to be had in making aircraft stealthy; in fact the rule of thumb is that the first one hundredfold reduction in radar signature is produced by smart airframe shaping, and the remaining 'fuzzball' of minor reflections is then soaked up by absorbent or lossy materials.

For example, a conventional fighter design might have a radar cross section of 1 m^2 in the centimetre wavelength band, but an equivalent design with proper stealth shaping might be only 0.01 m^2. Further application of absorbent materials in the right places then drives that down to 0.001 to 0.0001 m^2.

The effectiveness of shaping is, like the effectiveness of materials, dependent upon the wavelength of the threat radar. Where the flat area, facet or leading edge is much larger in dimensions than the wavelength of the radar, the rules of geometrical optics apply, and reflections can be very precisely bounced away from the threat radar. The aligned leading edges, aligned planforms and facets or flat areas seen in the F-117A, B-2A and F-22A are all extremely effective down to wavelengths of the order of tens of centimetres, or in the instance of the B-2A down to metres. In frequency terms, fighters are stealthiest in the X-band and S-band, while the B-2A is stealthy down to the VHF band.

Where the shaping features are comparable in dimensions to the wavelength of the radar, an effect called 'resonance' occurs, resulting in the induced electrical charges in the skin of the target running back and forth and waves then re-radiating from edges, tips, or other prominent shapes. For fighter-sized aircraft the resonance region is primarily in the UHF frequency band. In this so-termed 'resonance scattering region' it becomes very difficult to control the direction and shape of reflections. Some techniques using for instance resistive and magnetic materials along edges are often used, but in general fighter-sized targets are no longer marble- or golf-ball-sized reflectors.

This effect becomes exacerbated as the wavelength reaches a metre or more, where the radar signature becomes effectively proportional to the physical size of the reflecting feature. This is termed the 'Raleigh Scattering Region'. VHF band radars which operate typically between three and one metre in wavelength occupy this region for typical fighter-sized targets.

Historically, stealth designers have focused their efforts in the centimetre and decimetre bands, since these are where most fire control, engagement, air intercept and missile battery acquisition radars operate. The aim of the stealth effort was thus to disrupt the 'kill chain' by denying opportunities to launch and guide missiles, or frustrating the missile seekers and thus disrupting terminal missile guidance. If we look at operating bands for typical Soviet-era missile battery engagement guidance and illumination radars, we find the following: SA-2's SNR-75 Fan Song in the upper S-band or lower X-band; the SA-3's SNR-125 Low Blow in the X-band; the SA-4's 1S32 Pat Hand in the X-band; the SA-5's 5N62 Square Pair in the S-band; the SA-6's 1S91 Straight Flush and the SA-8's Land Roll radars in both the X- and S-bands, and finally the SA-10's 30N6 Flap Lid and SA-12's 9S32 Grill Pan in the X-band.

Where a defender is reliant on search and acquisition radars operating in the S-band, examples including the widely used Soviet/Russian P-30 Big Mesh, P35/37 Bar Lock, P-40 Long Track, 19Zh6/36D6 Tin Shield, 64N6 Big Bird, or US AN/TPS-43 and AN/SPY-1 Aegis, then a byproduct of good stealth is surprise as beyond some detection range the stealth aircraft is invisible. Operators of Russian air defence equipment will be willing customers for upgrades to legacy systems that were considered ineffective against stealth aircraft. Upgrade packages are on offer for the VHF band P-14 Tall King and P-18 Spoon Rest D, the UHF band P-15/15M/19 Flat Face and Squat Eye, and customers can also purchase a range of new-build VHF radars, including the 55Zh6-1 Nebo UE Tall Rack, the 5N84AE Oborona-14 Tall King, the 1L13-3 Nebo SV, the 1L119 Nebo SVU, and the Vostok E. The latter two are entirely new post-Cold War designs. The trusty Flat Face/Squat Eye UHF radars remain in production in digital solid-state form, as the 39N6E Kasta 2E1 and 2E2. The Chinese have followed this trend and are actively marketing the JY-27 VHF radar, similar but larger than the 1L13 Nebo SV, and have displayed another smaller type which remains to be identified.

Many of the new Russian designs are phased arrays, and at least two of the VHF designs are active phased arrays (AESA) dispensing completely with all vacuum tube technology, and embedding Transmit Receive Modules in the antenna subsystem. Typically the computers and software used for digital signal and data processing in these radars are Commercial off the Shelf, no different from than their Western counterparts, even using large LCD display panels. Russian literature claims the use of the latest Space Time Adaptive Processing algorithms for clutter rejection, which given the known skills base in mathematics and physics in Russian research institutes, is a credible claim. If a Western manufacturer were asked to design a VHF radar, the technology and components it would be built from would be much the same.

Russia is leading the counter-stealth development programmes. Russian marketing literature and numerous interviews with chief designers or senior design engineers invariably focus on the issue of counter-stealth capabilities in these radars. Key points raised repeatedly in interviews are Raleigh and resonance mode scattering versus geometrical optics scattering, and skin depth impairing the performance of radar absorbent coatings. These are precisely what radio frequency physics and the extensive unclassified US engineering literature on stealth identify as key limitations. More than one Russian designer has publicly commented on the F-117A, famously known in the West as a 'ball bearing sized target' in the S-band and X-band, as a 'one half square metre' sized or beach-ball sized radar target in the VHF band. Likely this claim is the result of detailed scientific analysis of radar tapes from the Allied Force campaign. Russian and Belarus designers have claimed detection ranges of up to 180 nautical miles against fighter-sized stealth aircraft, claims consistent with cited range specifications for these radars.

The flagship of the Russian counter-stealth radar effort is the digital 55Zh6M Nebo-M radar (**Figure 9-23**, **Figure 9-24**) system. This design is a genuine three-dimensional active array radar system (AESA), with three individual networked radars on three separate high mobility BAZ-6909 8x8 vehicles, and a fourth vehicle which performs data fusion from the three radars, and target tracking. One radar operates in the VHF-band, one in the L-band, and one in the S or C-band. The VHF-band RLM-M radar is the largest mobile 3D VHF-band radar ever built anywhere. The design could accommodate configurations with different mixes of radars such as replacing the C or S-band RLM-S component with an L-band RLM-D or VHF-band RLM-M. The use of networked data fusion permits this system to cue the RLM-S and RLM-D components to stealth targets detected initially by the RLM-M component.

Figure 9-23: NEBO-M new Russian counter-stealth radar (side view). (Vitaly Kuzmin)

Figure 9-24: NEBO-M new Russian counter-stealth radar (front view). (Vitaly Kuzmin)

The Nebo-M evolved in part from the earlier 1L117 Nebo SVU mobile VHF-band radar, at least one example of which was sold to Iran some years ago. The Nebo SVU included some sophisticated anti-jamming features. Curiously the Nebo-M's numerical designation is based on the very different 55Zh6UE Nebo U/UE Tall Rack, a gargantuan fixed 3D VHF-band radar with a characteristic and unique T-shaped antenna. These systems are supplemented by the Rezonans N/NE marketed by Rosoboronexport as a 'Stealth Air Target Early Warning Radar'. It is a large multi-static relocatable VHF-band radar system, carried on several vehicles. Technical disclosures have been scarce.

China's CETC/CPMIEC has also been very active in this area, following their earlier YJ- 27 VHF-Band radar. The recently disclosed VHF-band HK-JM with cited 300 km range, and the HK-JM2 with cited 500 km range, are genuine mobile radars with integrated telescoping and elevating mast systems.

The third player in this market is Belarus, where KB Radar are selling the modern digital solid state Vostok D and E VHF-band radar, a high mobility design which can stow and deploy in six minutes, almost as quickly as a SAM battery. The Chinese HK-JM series is modelled in part on the Vostok series, but using older antenna technology than the innovative Belarus design.

Counter-Stealth Concepts
Counter-Stealth or Counter-Very Low Observable (CVLO) techniques encompass possible techniques that overcome the effects of stealth design methods. While many technologies and techniques have been proclaimed to be CVLO panaceas,

closer examination suggests otherwise. Broadly, there are two approaches in overcoming a stealth design. One is the brute force approach of finding ways of making a sensor that is much more sensitive, able to find a much fainter target; the other is to build a sensor that can see the stealth design in some area in which it was not designed to be stealthy.

The brute force approach in radar design usually involves increasing the peak and average microwave power the radar produces. This is usually not cheap, and often introduces other problems such as providing enough power to drive the radar, getting rid of waste heat from the radar, and making sure key components in the radar are not overstressed electrically or thermally. This is a commonly favoured approach in land based or naval radars, as the requirements can be challenging for compact airborne radars. Due to the inverse square law behaviour of radars, maintaining detection range against a target which reflects 1/100th of a conventional target requires a 100-fold increase in radar emitted power. While doubling or quadrupling power output in a radar may be feasible, increasing it tenfold or a hundredfold usually is not.

Two techniques which can alter the radar's 'duty cycle' are to increase the density of pulses the radar emits, and to increase its 'dwell time' or how long it spends looking in a given direction. The former inevitably increases the power requirement, while the latter increases search times. Since the aim of radars is to find and track targets, increasing dwell times can seriously degrade effectiveness. Mostly, the brute force approach is a loser's game, especially against highly stealthy targets like the B-2A and F-22A. Much less stealthy targets yield some payoff.

The alternative of building sensors that can see the aircraft from directions or at wavelengths where it was not designed to be very stealthy is a much better game plan, and this is also where most current investment by the Russians and Chinese is visible.

There are numerous ways in which this game can be played, and combinations of multiple techniques can be quite effective, especially against designs with poor or otherwise limited stealth performance. A technique that is often overstated in effectiveness is the use of networked radars and data fusion techniques, similar to the US Navy Cooperative Engagement Capability (CEC) system. CEC collects and simultaneously fuses tracking data from multiple shipboard search radars, the intent being to share tracking data across the fleet even if some targets are too distant to cleanly track for some radars, or below the radar horizon for others. In the CEC system a target blip might be a fusion of intermittent or partial tracks from half a dozen different radars.

Defeating stealth targets using networking and data fusion presupposes that some radars can see the target some of the time, also that the target's stealth is poorer from some directions and aspects than others. Suffice to say, a vehicle with excellent 'all aspect' stealth such as a B-2A will not be susceptible to this technique, since all of the radars in the network are equally blind. Even the F-22A is not particularly exposed, as its weakest areas in the beam aspect are not exposed long enough to seriously matter. Much more exposed are the compromised J-20, Su-57 and F-35, as their side and rear aspects present many more tracking opportunities. In some of designs, the frontal hemisphere of an airplane is stealthy but the rear hemisphere is not.

A networked data fusion system is thus not a panacea, but is potentially quite effective against stealth designs that do not have genuine 'all aspect' stealth capability. There are technical challenges in designing such systems, as the constituent radars must be built to not discard poor quality radar returns from point targets, in typical radars automatically rejected as 'false alarms'. Also, a lot of computing power is needed to sift and sort the collected data to determine which returns amount to a real target track. To date only the US and Russia have demonstrated the ability to build such a system.

The alternative game plan to exploiting aspect limitations in target stealth shaping is to exploit wavelength limitations. This area has been the focus of most Russian and Chinese activity in CVLO systems design. It relies on the basic physics of stealth shaping, where a straight edge or flat facet can only reflect sharply in one direction, and if its geometrical size is larger than two or more wavelengths. A straight edge or flat facet which reflects the radar illumination away in a tight beam (technically a 'lobe') must be many wavelengths in size. If not, its reflection smears out over a wide range of angles, making it easier to detect.

In stealth fighters this effect is most prominent, as their size puts hard limits on the wavelengths where their forward and aft fuselages can still cleanly bounce illumination away. Typically performance that is reasonable in the 3 GHz decimetre wavelength S-band degrades with varying rapidity as the wavelength increases through the L-band, UHF-band down to the metre wavelength VHF-band.

Anti-Antiradiation Missile Techniques

We already saw in Chapter Five what are the major trends in the development of anti-radiation missiles and some basics in protection against them. To summarize, there are few countermeasures available against ARMs.

From the radar point of view, the best ECMs against an ARM are:

- Extremely low peak power, so that the aircraft is forced to launch the ARM from short range, thus exposing itself to anti-aircraft defences. This mean to get the ARM shooter as close as possible so that it can be targeted and destroyed with higher probability,

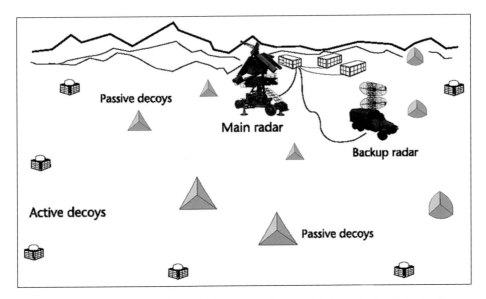

Figure 9-25: Anti-anti-radiation missile battery layout. (Filippo Neri – Introduction to Electronic Defense Systems, modified by authors)

- Well-randomized parameters, and therefore frequency agility, change of Pulse Width, and change of Pulse Repetition Frequency (PRF)
- Extremely low sidelobes so the signal can't be detected on the far distance.

At a radar site, ECCMs (electronic counter-counter measures) can be organized into:

- Highly reflective points to generate false targets credible to the ARM, for example use of passive decoys

- Decoys simulating radar emission to confuse the ARM (**Figure 9-25**) as we already saw the role of radar emission imitators.

Air Defence Systems[18]

S-500 Prometei (Prometheus)/Triumfator
The S-500 Prometheus/55R6M Triumfator-M is a new Russian surface-to-air missile system for which a development S-400 system is used. In comparison to

---

18. Information from www.ausairpower.net and Almaz-Antey.

the S-400, it is designed for intercepting and destroying intercontinental ballistic missiles, as well as hypersonic cruise missiles and aircraft, for air defence against Airborne Early Warning and Control and for jamming aircraft. With a planned range of 600 km for anti-ballistic missile (ABM) and 400 km for the air defence, the S-500 would be able to detect and simultaneously engage up to ten ballistic targets flying at a speeds of 5,000 m/s up to a limit of 7 km/s (25,000 km/h). It also aims at destroying hypersonic cruise missiles and other aerial targets at speeds of higher than Mach 5, as well as spacecraft. The declared altitude of a target engaged can be as high as 180-200 km. It is effective against ballistic missiles with a launch range of 3,500 km and the radar reaches a radius of 3,000 km for an RCS of 0.1 m^2. Other targets it has been announced to defend against include: unmanned aerial vehicles, low earth orbit satellites, and space weapons launched from hypersonic aircraft, drones, and hypersonic orbital platforms.

The system is highly mobile and will have rapid deployability. Its capabilities can affect enemy intercontinental ballistic missiles at the middle and end portions of flight. System developer Almaz-Antey declared that the external target-designation system (RLS Voronezh-DM and missile defence system A-135 radar Don-2N) was capable of mid-early flight portion interceptions of enemy ballistic missiles, which is one of the final stages of the S-500 project.

In 2009 the system was under development at the design stage at Almaz-Antey and had been planned to be completed in 2012. In February 2011 it was announced that the first S-500 systems should be in production by 2014. Two plants were developed to produce the S-500 by 2015. Under the State Armament Programme 2020 (GPV-2020), the plan is to purchase ten S-500 battalions for Russian Aerospace Defence (Vozdushno Kosmiceskaya Oborona – KO).

The main components of the S-500 are (for now):

- Launcher/Transport vehicle 77P6, based on the BAZ-69096 10x10 truck,
- Command posts 55K6MA and 85Zh6-2 on BAZ-69092-12 6x6,
- Acquisition and battle management radar 91N6A(M), a modification of the 91N6 (Big Bird) towed by the BAZ-6403.01 8x8 tractor,
- 96L6-TsP acquisition radar, an upgraded version of the 96L6 (Cheese Board) on BAZ- 69096 10x10,
- Multi-mode engagement radar 76T6 on BAZ-6909-022 8x8,
- ABM engagement radar 77T6 on BAZ-69096 10x10,
- System response time for up to ten missiles: less than 4 seconds (Compared to the S-400's 10).

Although sharing a similar designation, the relationship between this new S-500 and the S-500U project of the 1960s is unclear. The S-500U multichannel anti-aircraft system was a 1968 initiative by the Soviet Air Defence Forces, Soviet

Navy, Ministry of the Radio Industry (Ministerstvo Radio Promyshlennosti SSSR), and Ministry of the Shipbuilding Industry, to create a unified complex for the National Air Defence Troops, Navy and Army. Missiles of the S-500U complex were supposed to engage enemy aircraft at a range of up to 100 km. The S-500U SAM complex project was rejected by the Soviet Army, which had a requirement to engage not only enemy aircraft but also short-range ballistic missiles. Consequently the S-300 family (SA-10 and SA-12) was developed instead.

Five batteries of S-500 missiles are planned to be in service by 2020. The S-500s will work with S-400s and are planned to together replace S-300 air defence missiles systems. The first units are planned to be deployed around Moscow and the country's central area. A naval version is the likely armament for the new Lider-class air-defence destroyers due to enter service in 2023-25.

Triumf (Triumph)/SA-21
In the late 20th and early 21st century the following trends became apparent in the development of air and space attack weapons:

- Development of low and extremely low flight altitudes, sharp reduction in their visibility in the basic physical fields through the integrated use of stealth technology
- Increase in the number of air threats in air defence weapons operations areas through the use of unmanned vehicles
- Equipping all air attack weapons with highly effective EW equipment and use of precision guided weapons
- Growth in production and adoption of non-strategic ballistic missiles, primarily tactical and theatre missiles, as well as the assimilation of production of medium-range ballistic missiles by some countries.

An opportunity to analyze the potential of the most effective air attack weapons became available also as a result of their use during operations in Iraq and Yugoslavia. The need to effectively accomplish the aerospace defence missions in these circumstances became the focal point in developing the new generation.

All assets of the Triumph system are mounted on self-propelled wheeled all-terrain chassis, have built-in self-contained power supply, orientation and survey control, communications and life support systems. In addition, provision is made for using ADMS assets in specialized shelters, with removal of equipment containers of the multi-functional radar, command and control post, and radar system from their self-propelled chassis.

Time to deploy from marching position to operational readiness is 5 to 10 minutes. The prime developer of the Triumph ADMS is Almaz-Antey. Among

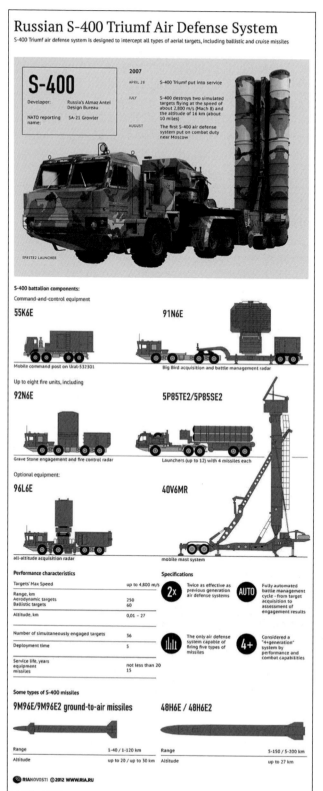

Figure 9-26: S-400/SA-21. (Almaz-Antey)

its other developers are Fakel Design Bureau (missiles development); Research Institute of Instrumentation (acquisition radar system for the command post), and Special Engineering Design Bureau (launchers developer).

S-400 Triumf/SA-21 (**Figure 9-26**, **Figure 9-27**), mobile multi-channel air defence missile system is a system of a new generation to effectively engage practically all the modern and future air attack weapons, including medium range ballistic missiles.

The system interacts with other air defence missile complexes, air defence missile systems and air defence missile/gun complexes in a complicated tactical situation as well as with the S-400 Triumf.

S-400 Triumf incorporates:

- 30K6E – an administration system which manages eight battalions
- The 55K6E – a command and control centre based on the Ural-532301
- The 91N6E – a panoramic radar detection system (range 600 km) with protection against jamming which is mounted on an MZKT-7930. The S-band system can track 300 targets. Six battalions of 98ZH6E surface-to-air missile systems (an independent combat system) can track no more than six targets on their own, with an additional two battalions if they are within a 40-km range
- The 92N6E (or 92N2E) – a multi-functional radar with a 400-km range which can track 100 targets
- The 5P85TE2 launcher and the 5P85SE2 on a trailer (up to 12 launchers)
- The 48N6E, 48N6E2, 48N6E3, 48N6DM, 9M96E, 9M96E2 and the ultra-long-range 40N6E, authorized by a Russian presidential decree.

Figure 9-27: S-400/SA-21 components. (Almaz-Antey)

According to the Russian government, the S-400 uses an active electronically scanned array. The first combat deployment of the system is in Khmeimim air base, Syria (**Figure 9-28**). Optional elements of the S-400 (98ZH6E) include the 15I6ME-98ZH6E, with coverage of 30, 60 and 90 km beyond the 30K6E coverage. The 96L6E has a 300 km detection range. The 40B6M is housing for the 92N6E or 96L6E radar. The Protivnik-GE is an anti-stealth UHF radar with a 400 km range. The Moscow-1 passive sensor is 2½ times more effective than the Protivnik, with a 400 km range. Orion for a target-designation on-the-air defence system, and the Avtobaza-M and Orion+ Avtobaza, add high-precision detection. The 1RL220BE versions are reportedly used for jamming. The 400 km range S-200D Dubna (SA-5c) missiles and S-300 P-family radar systems can be used without additional command-and-control centres. S-300 (SA-20A, SA-20B) missiles may also be guided. A-50 and A-50U aircraft provide early warning and command-and-control target designation.

The 30K6E control system can be integrated with the S-400 Triumph 98ZH6E system; the S-300PMU2 (through the 83M6E2 control system); the S-300PMU1 (through the 83M6E control system); the Tor-M1 through the Ranzhir-M battery-command post; the Pantsir-S1 through the lead battery vehicle. The Protivnik-GE and Gamma-DE radars, integrated with the 92H6E radar system, enables communication between each battery with Baikal-E senior command posts and similar types; nearby 30K6E, 83M6E and 83M6E2 administration systems; the Polyana-D4M1 command post; fighter-aircraft command post, and mobile long-range radars. The Nebo-M system is designed to hunt the F-35 joint-strike fighter. The system's VHF component provides sector search and tracking, with the X and L band components providing fine-tracking capability. Good placement of the radars relative to the threat axis enables the L- and X-band components to illuminate the incoming target from angles where the target RCS is sub-optimal. Attempts to jam the Nebo-M would be problematic since all the radars have passive angle track capability against jammers; jamming permits passive triangulation of the target using three angle-track outputs. The RLM-S and RLM-D have better elevation-tracking accuracy than the RLM-M, and the Nebo M should be capable of producing high-quality tracks suitable for mid-course guidance of modern surface-to-air missiles and trajectory guidance of legacy SAMs.

The Gamma-C1E SHF mobile radar station has a 300 km detection range. The Nebo VHF mobile radar station and the Resonance-NE radar station have a detection range of 1,200 kilometres and 65 kilometres to a height of 500 metres. All Nebo-family locators are doubled for army air defence. During the 1970s, the long-range mobile UHF 5H87 and SHF 5H69 low-altitude locators were used. A 1980s goal was detection at a height of 10 metres at a distance of 40 km.

For export to foreign customers, with the purpose of integrating existing customer air defence systems, additional work on improvement of the 30K6E administration system is in progress at the time of writing.

Figure 9-28: S-400/SA-21 in Khmeimim air base, Syria. (Vadim Savitsky/Russian Defence Ministry Press Service)

Additional equipment includes the external power supply facilities, group SPTA sets, radar 96L6E, training/operating missiles, towers for the antennas of the multifunction radars, 96L6E radar to improve detection of low-altitude targets, maintenance complex incorporating an air servicer, a unified compressor station, a mobile vehicle-mounted repair workshop and other equipment.

One system, comprising up to 8 battalions, can control up to 72 launchers, with a maximum of 384 missiles. The missiles are fired by a gas system from the launch tubes up to 30 metres into the air before the rocket motor ignites, which increases the maximum and decreases the minimum ranges. In April 2015 a successful test firing of the missile was conducted at an airborne target at a range of 400 km; TELs carrying the long-range 40N6 may only be able to hold two missiles instead of the typical four due to its larger size. Another test recorded a 9M96 missile using an active radar homing head reaching a height of 56 km. All the missiles are equipped with directed explosion warhead, which increases the probability of complete destruction of targets.

In 2016, Russian anti-aircraft missile troops received new guided missiles for S-300 and S-400 defence systems. An anti-aircraft missile system designed to destroy aircraft, cruise and ballistic missiles, it can also be used against ground objectives. The S-400 is able to intercept cruise missiles out to a range of about 40 km due to their low altitude flight paths.

S-400 ammunition includes 48N6E3 and 48N6E2 air-to-surface missiles. The 48N6E surface-to-air may be also used. The 48N6E and 48N6E2 missiles are similar to those the Favorit air defence missile system employs.

A new 48N6E3 SAM has been developed by upgrading the 48N6E2 SAM. Upgrade of the engine by using a solid propellant grain with higher energetic characteristics offered an opportunity to expand the engagement zone at the outer boundary and to increase the employed engagement zones of ballistic missiles.

Upgrade of the missile payload, i.e. a radio fuse with the controlled warhead, has enhanced the effectiveness of high-speed, small, manoeuvring targets, also providing for high probability of initiation of the high-explosive war payload of ballistic targets, including medium-range ballistic missiles flying at up to 4,800 m/s.

In November 2015 the deployment of S-400 was reported in Syria, along with a contingent of Russian troops and other military hardware in the air campaign conducted by Russian forces on the side of the Syrian government. The first S-400 system was reportedly installed at Khmeimim Air Base in Latakia Governorate. Between April and July 2017, a second S-400 system was deployed 13 km north-west of Masyaf, Hama Governorate.

S-300/SA-10

The origins of this system date back to the 1960s. Anti-aircraft missile systems developed by that time suffered many flaws: insufficient range, poor target kill effectiveness; and engagement of aircraft, whose capabilities grew almost every year, was becoming increasingly difficult. This was confirmed during actions in Vietnam and the Middle East, where Soviet SA-2/S-75 and SA-3/S-125 passed the most severe test in extreme climatic conditions while repelling real air attacks.

A comprehensive assessment of the air threat growth prospects carried out by experts from leading research institutes and design bureaus in the mid-1960s led them to conclude that an all-new air defence missile system was required, capable of simultaneously firing at several targets flying in a wide range of speeds and altitudes, repelling massive air attacks from different directions.

By the late 1960s, these searches helped define the basic requirements for a system, which later received the designation S-300P/SA-10 (**Figure 9-29, Figure 9-30, Figure 9-31**). These requirements included the engagement and destruction of new generation aircraft, cruise missiles and tactical ballistic missiles. On 27 May 1969 the CPSU Central Committee and USSR Council of Ministers passed a resolution authorizing the beginning of this work, whose degrees of novelty and promise were at the level of the most significant Soviet military-technical programmes.

The main developer was Central Design Bureau (CDB) ALMAZ (general designer B.V. Bunkin) and missile developer was Fakel (general designer P.D. Grushin). First assessments showed that the system was possible only through the assimilation of new materials and technologies, widespread use of electronic

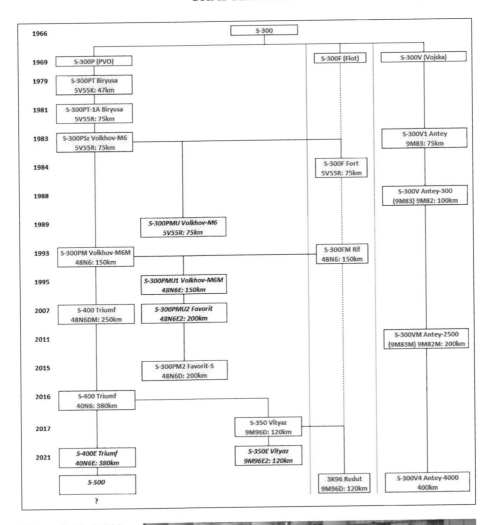

1966		S-300	
1969	S-300P (PVO)	S-300F (Flot)	S-300V (Vojska)
1979	S-300PT Biryusa 5V55K: 47km		
1981	S-300PT-1A Biryusa 5V55R: 75km		
1983	S-300PSz Volkhov-M6 5V55R: 75km		S-300V1 Antey 9M83: 75km
1984		S-300F Fort 5V55R: 75km	
1988			S-300V Antey-300 (9M83) 9M82: 100km
1989	S-300PMU Volkhov-M6 5V55R: 75km		
1993	S-300PM Volkhov-M6M 48N6: 150km	S-300FM Rif 48N6: 150km	
1995	S-300PMU1 Volkhov-M6M 48N6E: 150km		
2007	S-400 Triumf 48N6DM: 250km	S-300PMU2 Favorit 48N6E2: 200km	
2011			S-300VM Antey-2500 (9M83M) 9M82M: 200km
2015		S-300PM2 Favorit-S 48N6D: 200km	
2016	S-400 Triumf 40N6: 380km		
2017		S-350 Vityaz 9M96D: 120km	
2021	S-400E Triumf 40N6E: 380km	S-350E Vityaz 9M96E2: 120km	
	S-500	3K96 Redut 9M96D: 120km	S-300V4 Antey-4000 400km
	?		

Figure 9-29: S-300 development. (Almaz-Antey)

Figure 9-30: S-300/SA-10 on Moscow V-E parade. (Vitaly Kuzmin)

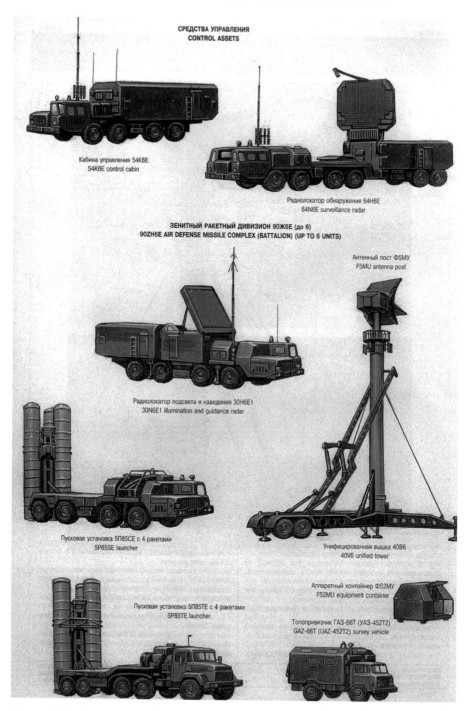

Figure 9-31: Components of an early S-300/SA-10. (RosOboronEksport)

integrated circuits and digital technology, and maximum automation of the basic combat functions. To be capable of tracking and destroying several targets at the same time (for example to provide multi-channel operation as opposed to the single-channel S-75 and S-125) required the use of a multifunction phased array radar and multiple missile launchers. There was also a requirement to keep costs down.

The 5V55 missile developed for the S-300P fully met these criteria.

A number of innovative technical solutions were used during the development of the 5V55, for example the use of a transport & launch container (TLC), in which the whole life-cycle of the missile was to take place, from assembly at plant to launch. The requirement for a high rate of fire led to a number of decisions aimed at minimizing the duration of pre-launch operations and time to target. Central among these was the use, for the first time for this type of missiles, of a forced vertical launch from TLC. This helped greatly increase the rate of fire of the system, since in this case all the missiles were directly on the launcher and ready for immediate launch; this allowed effective all-around engagement of enemy aircraft and missiles flying in from different directions.

With such a launch, the sustainer engine of the 5V55 starts at an altitude of 20 to 25 metres. This minimizes the erosive effects of the gas jet on the nearby components of the system. For a quick turn towards a target after engine start, the missile is equipped with a special gas dynamic system. The first variant of the S-300 entered service with the Air Defence Forces in 1979. A more improved version designated S-300 PMU was adopted in the mid-1980s. Increased cross-country capacity was one of its features. In this version all the system components were carried by a MAZ-543M tractor truck and their deployment from marching order to ready-for-launch took 5 minutes.

In the mid-1980s, the S-300PMU was one of the most advanced weapons in the world. However, the progress achieved by this time in electronic technology, the emergence of new materials at the disposal of designers and process engineers made possible a significant increase in system performance. Of particular significance was the possibility of an almost twofold increase in engagement range against aerial targets, with virtually the same missile dimensions and launch weight.

The missile for the new S-300 PMU1 version received the designation 48N6E and was capable of effectively engaging almost all existing aircraft and helicopters, cruise missiles, air-to-surface missiles, and short-range ballistic missiles.

Favorit Air Defence Missile System

The Favorit mobile multi-channel air defence missile system (**Figure 9-32**) incorporates one 83M6E2 control element and up to six S-300PMU2 air defence missile systems. It can interact with other weapons, control systems and information equipment.

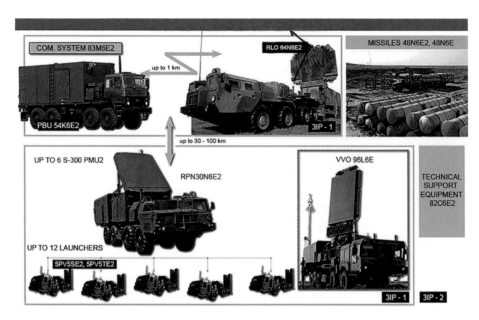

Figure 9-32: Favorit system components. (RosOboronEksport, modified by authors)

Favorit retained the basic principles of the S-300PMU1 ADMS and 83M6E control system (CS). It was created after upgrade of its predecessors S-300 PMU1 ADMS and 83M6E CS, and 48N6E2 SAM with updated payload and new radar systems.

The Favorit 83M6E2 control system controls the combat activities of the S-300PMU2 air defence system. The 54K6E2 combat control point automatically processes and displays the radar reconnaissance data, selects targets for engagement, generates and transmits target designation data to the air defence systems, controls their combat actions, documents the combat actions of the air defence missile and control systems in real time, transmits information to the higher control equipment and interacts with adjacent control systems and command posts.

The 83M6E2 control system includes:

- Combat control centre 54K6E2
- Acquisition radar 64N6E2
- Maintenance facilities including the SPTA sets, external power supply sources and vehicles
- Supplementary equipment including the antenna-mast assemblies and repeaters to extend a radio communication range.

S-300PMU2 ADMS/SA-20

The S-300PMU2/SA-20 mobile multi-channel air defence missile systems can destroy air attack weapons both using data from the 83M6E2 control system and when operating independently.

Each S-300PMU2 air defence missile system includes combat assets, maintenance facilities and supplementary equipment.

Combat assets incorporate:

- One illumination and guidance radar 30N6E2 (IGR),
- Up to 12 launchers 5P85SE2 (chassis mounted) or launchers 5P85SE2 (trailer-mounted with a prime mover),
- Surface-to-air missiles (SAM) 48N6E2 and 48N6E in the container-launchers.

Maintenance facilities include operation and missile storage equipment, SPTA sets and sets of operational documentation, external power supply, sources of illumination, guidance radar and control point, soft mock-ups and training/operating missiles and vehicles.

The supplementary equipment includes the 96L6E radar (all-altitude radar), mobile towers for the illumination and guidance radar (IGR) antenna posts, 96L6E radar antenna devices (to improve acquisition of low-altitude targets), and maintenance and repair facilities for the air defence missile systems, vehicles, survey vehicle, unified compressor station and air servicer and cable-laying vehicle.

30N6E2 IGR is the main radar element in the S-300PMU2 ADMS. It performs automatic radar search for a target either against the target designation data or independently (also using all-altitude radar), acquisition, identification, classification, lock-on and automatic tracking of targets, automatic solution of the launch tasks, placing missiles for preparation, automatic lock-on and tracking of the targets in response to the radio signals of the airborne transponders and their guidance towards the tracked targets. The IGR also provides for detonation of the warheads and automatic assessment of the combat operation's results.

Missiles are launched on commands from the illumination and guidance radar. A missile is guided at a target by the 'track-via-missile' method. Once locked on by the IGR, the missile is automatically guided at its initial phase at a target by the radio command method, and at its final phase by the semi-active radar homing using the data of the target tracked by the missile radar direction finder that receives the signals of the target illuminated by the IGR. These target data are transmitted from the SAM to the IGR to be correlated there with the data of the same target that the IGR tracks. After correlation of data, the IGR forms and transmits control commands to the missile to correct its flight trajectory.

The SAM warhead is detonated by the semi-active radio fuse in response to the special return signal from the target illuminated by the IGR. The ballistic missile warhead detonation is initiated in this case and the aerodynamic target is destroyed. The ADMS combat assets are mounted on a cross-country wheeled chassis. They are equipped with navigation, survey control and orientation, autonomous power supply, tele-code and voice communication, and life support equipment.

S-300V/SA-12

The 9K81 S-300V Antey-300 (Russian 9K81 C-300B Антей-300 – named after Antaeus, NATO reporting name SA-12 Gladiator/Giant) varies from the other designs in the series. This complex is not part of the S-300; it is designed by another developer. It was built by Antey rather than Almaz, and its 9M82 and 9M83 missiles were designed by NPO Novator. The V suffix stands for Voyska (army – ground forces). It was designed to form a top tier army air defence system providing defence against ballistic missiles, cruise missiles and aircraft, replacing the SA-4 Ganef. The 'Gladiator' missiles have a maximum engagement

Figure 9-33: S-300V/SA-12 army tracked mobile air defence system of 202 brigade. (Vitaly Kuzmin)

range of around 75 km while the 'Giant' missiles can engage targets out to 100 km and to altitudes of around 32 km. In both cases the warhead is around 150 kg. The S-300VM (Antey 2500) is an upgrade to the S-300V. It consists of a new command post vehicle, the 9S457ME and a selection of new radars. These consist of the 9S15M2, 9S15MT2E and 9S15MV2E all-round surveillance radars, and the 9S19ME sector surveillance radar. The upgraded guidance radar has index 9S32ME. The system can still employ up to six TELARs, the 9A84ME launchers (up to 4×9M83ME missile) and up to six launcher/loader vehicles assigned to each launcher (2×9M83ME missile each). An upgraded version, dubbed S-300V4, was delivered to the Russian army in 2011 (**Figure 9-33**).

The Antey-2500 complex is the export version developed separately from the S-300 family and has been exported to Venezuela for an estimated price of 1 billion dollars. The system has one type of missile in two versions, basic and amended with a sustainer stage that doubles the range (up to 200 km or according to other data up to 250 km) and can simultaneously engage up to 24 aircraft or 16 ballistic targets in various combinations (**Figure 9-34**).

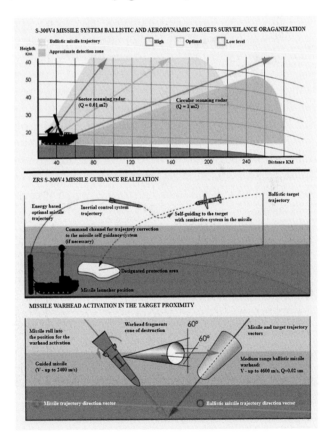

Figure 9-34: S-300V ballistic missile engagement. (Vozdushokosmicheskaya sfera No 2, 2017 with authors' modification)

S-350 Vityaz

The S-530E Vityaz (50R6) is a new mobile surface-to-air missile system designed, developed and manufactured by Almaz-Antey. Development began in the early 1990s. There was speculation that the system was mainly aimed at the export market, designed to complement the S-300/S-400 missile family. However, after successful trials, the Russian armed forces have adopted the new system. South Korea is developing a simplified version of the Vityaz called Cheolmae-2 with the help of the Almaz Central Design Bureau. The Vityaz is expected to replace, at the time of writing, the older S-300PS systems. Vityaz has a more advanced radar and a launcher with sixteen missiles compared to only four on the S-300. The system was unveiled to the public for the first time at the MAKS Air Show in Moscow, August 2013. According to the developer, Vityaz could replace older SAMs like the venerable S-125 while adding multiple-target and anti-missile capabilities. It can be considered a 'budget' option instead of S-300.

The system can be delivered in two configurations: a version optimized for protecting against high-precision weapons (cruise missiles, ARMs, smart bombs and tactical UAVs) able to simultaneously engage up to eight targets; or a multi-role version. In the former configuration the battery consists of a radar and up to four launchers with thirty-two 'small' missiles each, while in the latter the heart of the battery is a mobile command post linked to one or two radars and up to eight launchers. The missile is the 9M96 guided missile which was originally designed for the S-400 system. On 23 December 2019 it was announced by Almaz-Antey that Russian troops had received the first set of the advanced S-350.

The S-350E Vityaz (50R6) missile system is mounted on an 8x8 truck chassis, under the technical name of 50P6. It is a dual missile system whereby each of the standard containers can be replaced by a pack of four smaller and shorter weapons. The vertical launcher truck carried twelve tubular containers, in two lines of six.

Each S-350E Vityaz typically includes:

- Three launcher trucks 50P6;
- Fire control system with target and surveillance radar 50N6A;
- Command and control vehicle 50K6;
- Communication relay station.

9K37 BUK/SA-11, SA-17

Development of the Buk (9K37)/SA-11 & SA-17 (**Figure 9-35**) battlefield self-propelled SAM system commenced in accordance with the Resolution of the CPSU Central Committee and USSR Council of Ministers dated 13 January 1972

Figure 9-35: BUK M1.
(Wikipedia)

and provided for cooperation between the main developers and manufacturers that had earlier developed the Kub system.

The Buk missile system was designed to surpass the 2K12 Kub in all parameters, and its designers, including its chief designer Ardalion Rastov, visited Egypt in 1971 to see Kub in operation. Both the Kub and Buk used self-propelled launchers developed by Ardalion Rastov. As a result of this visit, the developers came to the conclusion that each Buk transporter erector launcher (TEL) should have its own fire control radar, rather than being reliant on one central radar for the whole system as in Kub. The result of this move from TEL to transporter erector launcher and radar (TELAR) was the development of a system able to shoot at multiple targets in multiple directions at the same time.

In 1974 the developers determined that although the Buk missile system is the successor to the Kub missile system, both systems could share some interoperability. The result of this decision was the 9K37-1 Buk-1 system. Interoperability between Buk TELAR and Kub TEL meant an increase in the number of fire control channels and available missiles for each system, as well as faster entry of Buk system components into service. The Buk-1 was adopted into service in 1978 following completion of state trials, while the complete Buk missile system was accepted into service in 1980 after state trials took place between 1977 and 1979.

Another modification to the Buk missile system was started in 1992 with work carried out between 1994 and 1997 to produce the 9K37M1-2 Buk-M1-2, which entered service in 1998. This modification introduced a new missile, the 9M317, which offered greater kinematic performance over the previous 9M38, which could still be used by the Buk-M1-2 (**Figure 9-36**, **Figure 9-37**).

Such sharing of the missile type caused a transition to a different GRAU (Russian Main Missile and Artillery Directorate) designation 9K317, which has been used independently for all later systems. The previous 9K37 series name was also preserved for the complex, as was the Buk name. The new missile, as well as a variety of other modifications, allowed the system to shoot down ballistic missiles and surface targets, as well as enlarging the 'performance and

Figure 9-36: BUK M2. (Almaz-Antey)

Figure 9-37: BUK M2 (front) and S-300 launchers (rear) in Moscow Patriot park. (Vitaly Kuzmin)

engagement envelope' (zone of danger for potential attack) for more traditional targets like aircraft and helicopters. The 9K37M1-2 Buk-M1-2 received a new NATO reporting name distinguishing it from previous generations of the Buk system: SA-17 Grizzly. The export version of the 9K37M1-2 system is called 'Ural'; this name has also been applied to M2, at least to early, towed, export versions.

9K317M – BUK M3

The latest modernization of the BUK family is 9K317M (**Figure 9-38**), or the Buk-M3 also nicknamed Viking. A medium-range surface-to-air missile system, it is a modernized version of the Buk-M2, features advanced electronic components and a deadly new missile and could be regarded as a completely new system. The system is designed, developed and manufactured by the Russian Defence Company Almaz-Antey. The Buk-M3 system boasts a new digital computer, high-speed data exchange system, and a tele-thermal imaging target designator instead of the tele-optical trackers used in previous models. A battery of Buk-M3 missiles can track and engage up to 36 targets simultaneously, while its advanced 9R31M missile is capable of knocking down all existing flying objects, including highly manouevrable ones, even during active electronic jamming. The Buk-M3 can launch vertically and can engage sea and land targets.

Figure 9-38: 9K317M (BUK M3) in Moscow Patriot park. (Vitaly Kuzmin)

A Buk-M3 Viking missile battery consists of two TELAR 9A317M (Transporter Erector LAuncher and Radar) and one TEL 9A316M (Transporter Erector Launcher) vehicle. The TELAR is based on the GM-569 tracked armoured chassis, and carries six ready-to-fire missiles mounted on a turntable that can traverse a full 360°. The turret of the Buk-M3 TELAR includes fire control radar at the front and a launcher with six ready-to-fire missiles on top. In August 2018, at Army-2018 International Military Technical Forum in Moscow, the latest variant of the Buk-M3 was shown for the first time to the public with a new launcher turret equipped with two rows of three missile containers. The reloader vehicle of the Buk-M3 Viking is equipped with two blocks of six missiles using the same tracked chassis as the previous version of the Buk family.

The Buk-M3 Viking uses the new 9R31M missile radar-guided surface-to-air missile. The Buk-3M's target-destruction probability has been tested to 0.9999. It is able to destroy any type of air targets from a range of 2.5 to 70 km, with a speed of 3,000 m/s at altitudes of 15 metres up to 35 km. The Buk-M3 missile has been optimized for the interception of low-flying cruise missiles. The missile system includes a high-speed data exchange system and a thermal target imaging designator replacing optical trackers on previous Buk models. The 9R31M missile is fitted with a high-explosive fragmentation warhead.

BUK Combat Service

Abkhaz authorities claimed that Buk air defence system was used to shoot down four Georgian drones at the beginning of May 2008. Analysts concluded that Georgian Buk missile systems were responsible for downing four Russian aircraft – three Sukhoi Su-25 close air support aircraft and a Tupolev Tu-22M strategic bomber – in the 2008 South Ossetia war. US officials have said Georgia's SA-11 Buk-1M was certainly the cause of the Tu-22M's loss and contributed to the losses of the three Su-25s. According to some analysts, the loss of four aircraft is surprising and a heavy toll for Russia given the small size of Georgia's military. Some have also pointed out that Russian electronic countermeasures systems were apparently unable to jam and suppress enemy SAMs in the conflict and that Russia was unable to come up with effective countermeasures against missile systems that it had designed. Georgia bought these missile systems from Ukraine which had an inquiry to determine if the purchase was illegal.

The system was used in the downing of Boeing 777 Malaysia Airlines Flight 17 on 17 July 2014 in eastern Ukraine which resulted in 298 fatalities. Evidence included pieces of warhead stuck in the wreckage, some with serial number remnants, and missile fragments recovered from the bodies of the flight crew.

On 14 April 2018, American, British, and French forces launched a barrage of 105 air-to-surface and cruise missiles targeting eight sites in Syria. According to

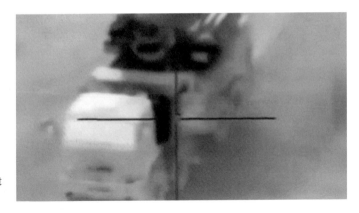

Figure 9-39: Israeli Air Force missile attack on Syrian/Iranian SA-22/Pantsir S1 truck. During the attack and based on the missiles position the vehicle was not at combat readiness and the crew was not inside. (IDF)

a Russian source, twenty-nine Buk- M2E missiles launched in response allegedly destroyed twenty-four incoming missiles. However, the American Department of Defence stated no Allied missiles were shot down (*déja vu* in previous conflicts).

In May 2018, during Operation House of Cards, the Israeli Air Force allegedly hit a Syrian Buk system. No independent source confirmed this. However, Israeli military published a video of an attack on a Syrian/Iranian SA-22/Pantsir S1 vehicle which was not manned by the crew at that time (**Figure 9-39**).

Soviet/Russian Missile Systems in the West

It is well known that the USA and some other western countries possess Soviet/Russian missile systems. The Israelis were the first to capture almost intact Soviet-made air defence systems during the Six Day War. They captured SA-2 equipment including launchers with the missiles, radar systems and command and control centres. These captured systems were thoroughly examined and from them Israelis developed their own tactics and procedures to combat them (**Figure 9-40**).

In one daring operation, Operation Rooster 53, during the War of Attrition, Israelis were able to capture and bring to Israel an intact Soviet-made P-12 radar. The mission was launched at 21:00 on 26/27 December 1969. A-4 Skyhawks and F-4 Phantoms began attacking Egyptian forces along the western bank of the Suez Canal and Red Sea. Hidden by the noise of the attacking jets, three Aérospatiale Super Frelon helicopters, carrying a force from the 35th Paratroopers Brigade, led by Lieutenant Colonel Arie Sidon and his deputy Doron Rubin, made their way west towards their target on the Egyptian side. Approaching carefully so as not to be spotted, the paratroopers overwhelmed the light security contingent at the radar installation and quickly took control of the site. By 02:00 on 27 December, when the paratroops had taken apart the radar station and prepared the various parts for the CH-53s, the two helicopters were called in from across

Figure 9-40: Israeli soldiers looking at a SAM-2 missile. (GPO)

Figure 9-41: Israeli soldiers on SA-3 system missile transport truck. (GPO)

the Red Sea. One CH-53 carried the communications van and the radar antenna, the other took the heavier, four-ton radar itself. The two helicopters made their way back across the Red Sea to Israeli-controlled territory.

During the Yom Kippur war, after crossing the Suez Canal, Israelis were able to get to the Egyptian air defence units providing a shield to the forces at Sinai, and with lighting strikes eliminate and capture entire Egyptian battalions. Into Israeli hands fell missiles, launchers, radars and other equipment (**Figure 9-41**).

CHAPTER NINE

After the collapse of the Soviet Union there was plenty of military hardware for sale and the US military got possession of the most advanced Soviet military hardware. Air defence systems were of particular interest. In the murky world of arms deals, the collapse of the Soviet Union opened the door for various deals in which the US was more than happy to take part.

In one case a company whose chairman was once the US Secretary of Defense teamed up with a Canadian arms dealer and some enterprising officials in the former Soviet republic of Belarus in a most unusual arms deal, financed in secret by the Pentagon. The deal came to light when a Russian-made transport plane parked within sight of an interstate highway in Huntsville, Alabama. Its cargo was the components of the S-300. The buyer was the Defence Intelligence Agency, the Pentagon's chief military intelligence branch. The broker was a company called BDM International, whose chairman is one of Washington's most powerful government officials-turned-businessmen, Frank C. Carlucci, a Secretary of Defense and national security adviser under President Reagan. The operation to obtain the S-300 was a secret mission paid for with classified financing, said government officials, arms dealers and military analysts.

In 1994 a Russian-made An-124 aircraft delivered its special cargo, the components of an S-300P. The system included a missile launcher, radars and missiles. The USA wanted to buy Russian weapons, a former American intelligence official said, to 'figure out what they are, how they work and what to do about them'. He said that taking the weapons apart and seeing how they tick helps to evaluate how good they are and the threat they might pose to American forces in the future, should the technology fall into the hands of an enemy of the United States. Also, American officials want to see if there are any especially good elements in the S-300 that might improve the Patriot. They also want to test the S-300 against the Patriot, and use the results to prove the Patriot's superiority to sell the system to other nations.

BDM apparently got one by acquiring components in Belarus. The President of Belarus, Aleksandar Lukashenko, confirmed that the former Soviet republic had sold one of the S-300 systems; although to whom, for what price and on what basis remained unsaid. The secrecy of the deal left many unanswered questions. How much of the system had the Pentagon acquired? Did the seller know that the buyer was the Pentagon?

The effort to acquire the S-300 infuriated some Russian military and political officials, who saw the purchase as a theft of Moscow's defence secrets. They also saw it as an attempt to encroach on Russia's share of the market for military equipment in Middle Eastern and Asian nations. For example, the government of Kuwait purchased both the Patriot and the S-300, and Russian generals tried to argue that their system was superior.

SHOOTING DOWN THE STEALTH FIGHTER

A number of recent reports have indicated that at least one S-300PT surface to air missile system has been delivered to the United States for testing. Satellite images at an American military testing site show a 30N6 fire control system and 5P85 transporter erector launchers, though the time of delivery as of yet remains uncertain (**Figure 9-42**). The acquisition of the S-300 system by the US Military is far from unprecedented, with a long history of acquisitions of Soviet aerial warfare systems for performance evaluation since the early days of the Cold War. These previously included, among other examples, MiG-21 and MiG-23 third generation fighters, an S-75, a 2K12 KUB air defence platform acquired from Egypt in the 1970s, a MiG-29 and Su-27 fourth generation fighters acquired from Moldova and Belarus respectively in the 1990s, and even Chinese manufactured J-7 fighters sold by the Chengdu Aircraft Corporation – sought out for their close similarly to the Soviet MiG-21. While a number of US defence clients in Europe operate or have previously operated older variants of the S-300, including Bulgaria with the S-300P, Slovakia with the S-300PS and Greece with the S-300PMU-1, Ukraine is almost entirely unique for its access to the PT variant which is believed to have been delivered to the US. With Ukraine having previously demonstrated its willingness to cooperate closely with Western states and share sensitive technologies inherited from the Soviet Union, including providing full access to its elite Su-27 air superiority fighters, and in light of reports that NATO pilots had been allowed to train against Ukrainian S-300 systems in the country, it is likely that Kiev would be a willing supplier of the S-300PT to the United States.

Given the limited similarity of the S-300PT to current systems deployed by potential US adversaries, the value of studying the platform remains somewhat limited. While Russia does deploy a number of newer S-300PS systems which are similar to the PT variant – having entered service in 1985 – these currently fulfill a very limited role in its air defence network and are soon set to be replaced by the more modern and sophisticated medium ranged platform. The S-300PT represents a very different kind of air defence system to even the 1990s platforms developed by Russia, such as the S-300PMU-2 which are designed for wide ranging anti access area denial rather than short ranged point defence and are capable of engaging dozens of targets simultaneously at hypersonic speeds and at extreme ranges almost three times that of the S-300PT. The sensors, electronic warfare systems and munitions used by these 1990s platforms are all well ahead of their Soviet predecessors. The discrepancy is greater still when considering platforms which entered service in the mid-2000s such as the S-300VM currently operated by Venezuela, and the S-400, or the S-300V4 of the following decade. Trying to evaluate modern Russian long range air defences such as the S-400 or S-300V4 through study of the S-300PT, a platform at least three generations behind, would be like evaluating America's F-35 based on the F-5A Freedom

330

Figure 9-42: Satellite imagery shows Russian S-300 missile defence systems in the US. (https://defence-blog.com)

Fighter which the USSR acquired from Vietnam – both unspecialised light fighters but of the second and fifth generations respectively. Whether the US Military will be able to gain access to more modern Russian air defence technologies, possibly the S-300VM and complementary R-77 and R-27ER missiles which are likely to be transferred if efforts to overthrow the Venezuelan government are successful, remains to be seen.

Interest in the newest Russian missile systems in the west is increasing with the tension in the Middle East. In the Libyan civil war, a few Pantsir-S gun-missile systems were captured by Turkish backed GNA forces. It is sure that these captured units will have been thoroughly examined by NATO experts. The deal that Turkey signed with Russia for the procurement of S-400 started much controversy. There is a proposal in the US Senate for an amendment to the 2021 National Defense Authorization Act that would allow the purchase of S-400 from Turkey to be made using the US Army's missile procurement account. The move comes a year after the US expelled NATO ally Turkey from the multinational F-35 programme because it received the S-400 in a multi-billion dollar deal. The US routinely buys foreign technology and could both exploit the S-400's technology and test US tactics. What will happen with this amendment is yet to be seen.

Appendix

NATO Codification System

- SA-1 'Guild' (S-25 Berkut)
- SA-2 'Guideline' (S-75 Dvina/Volkhov/Desna)
- SA-3 'Goa' (S-125 Neva)
- SA-4 'Ganef' (9M8 Krug)
- SA-5 'Gammon' (S-200 Volga)
- SA-6 'Gainful' (3M9 Kub/Kvadrat)
- SA-7 'Galosh' and 'Grail' (9K32 Strela-2)
- SA-8 'Gecko' (9K33 Osa)
- SA-9 'Gaskin' (9K31 Strela-1)
- SA-10 'Grumble' (S-300P/PS/PT)
- SA-11 'Gadfly' (9K37 Buk)
- SA-12 'Gladiator' and 'Giant' (S-300V)
- SA-13 'Gopher' (9K35 Strela-10)
- SA-14 'Gremlin' (9K36 Strela-3)
- SA-15 'Gauntlet' (9K330/9K331/9K332 Tor)
- SA-16 'Gimlet' (9K310 Igla-1)
- SA-17 'Grizzly' (9K37 Buk-M1-2)
- SA-18 'Grouse' (9K38 Igla)
- SA-19 'Grison' (2K22 Tunguska)
- SA-20 'Gargoyle' (S-300PM/PMU Favorit)
- SA-21 'Growler' (S-400 Triumf)
- SA-22 'Greyhound' (Pantsir-S1)
- SA-23 'Gladiator/Giant' (S-300VM 'Antey-2500')
- SA-24 'Grinch' (9K338 Igla-S)
- SA-25 (9K333 Verba)
- Viking (9K317 BUK M3)
- S-500 Prometheus

APPENDIX

The US DoD has different designations for naval surface-to-air missiles (SAN series) with Soviet designations. However, these are not standard NATO names. NATO uses the regular SA series for naval SAM. The US DoD refers to them by these names:

- SA-N-1 Goa (4K90 Volna) [SA-3]
- SA-N-2 Guideline (M-2 Volkhov-M) [SA-2]
- SA-N-3 Goblet (4K60/4K65 Shtorm)
- SA-N-4 Gecko (9M33 Osa-M) [SA-8]
- SA-N-5 Grail (9K32 Strela-2) [SA-7]
- SA-N-6 Grumble (S-300F Fort) [SA-10]
- SA-N-7 Gadfly (9M38/9M38M Uragan)[[SA-11]
- SA-N-8 Gremlin (9K34 Strela-3) [SA-14]
- SA-N-9 Gauntlet (3K95 Kinzhal) [SA-15]
- SA-N-10 Grouse (3M38 Igla) [SA-18]
- SA-N-11 Grison (3M87 Kashtan) [SA-19]
- SA-N-12 Grizzly (3K37 Smerch/Shtil) [SA-17]
- SA-N-14 Grouse (9K38 Igla) [SA-18]
- SA-N-20 Gargoyle (S-300FM) [SA-20]

Glossary

Glossary and Abbreviations

The following are typical terms used in radar, electronic warfare, stealth and air defence. Often, abbreviations are used immediately after the full meaning.

Not all the terms in this list are used in this book, but it is worth having them all in one place as it may help the reader to understand the meaning of abbreviations and terminology often used in these fields.

Absorption – Dissipation of energy of electromagnetic waves, sound, and light waves into other forms of energy because of interaction with matter. Absorption characteristics of specific materials are used as blankets, coatings, or structural and surface materials for aircraft to reduce effective radar cross-sections.

Acoustic jamming – The deliberate radiation of mechanical or electro-acoustic signals with the objective of obliterating or obscuring signals which the enemy is attempting to receive, and of deterring enemy weapon systems.

Active homing guidance – A system of homing guidance in which both the source for illuminating the target, and the receiver for detecting the energy reflected from the target as the result of illumination, are carried within the missile.

Airborne early warning and control – Air surveillance and control provided by airborne early warning vehicles that are equipped with search and height finding radar and communications equipment for controlling weapons.

Airborne Interceptor (AI) – A manned aircraft used for identification and/or engagement of airborne objects. (An AI may or may not be equipped with radar to assist in the interception.)

Airborne Warning and Control System (AWACS) – An aircraft suitably equipped to provide control, surveillance, and communications capability for strategic defence and/or tactical air operations.

GLOSSARY

Air defence – All defensive measures designed to destroy attacking enemy aircraft or missiles in the earth's envelope of atmosphere, or to nullify or reduce the effectiveness of such attack.

Air Surveillance Radar (ASR) – A radar displaying range and azimuth that is normally employed in a terminal area as an aid to approach and departure control.

Air-to-air missile (AAM) – A missile launched from an airborne carrier at a target above the surface.

Air-to-surface missile (ASM) – A missile launched from an airborne carrier to impact on a surface target.

Amplifier – An electronic circuit usually used to obtain amplification of voltage, current, or power.

Angle jamming – A deception jamming technique used to deny azimuth and elevation information to a TTR by transmitting a jamming pulse similar to the radar pulse, but with modulation information out of phase with the returning target azimuth modulation information.

Antenna – A device used for transmitting or receiving RF energy. The function of the antenna during transmission is to concentrate the radar energy from the transmitter into a shaped beam that points in the desired direction. During reception, or listening time, the function of the antenna is to collect the returning radar energy, contained in the echo signals, and deliver these signals to the receiver. Radar antennas are characterized by directive beams that are usually scanned in a recognizable pattern. The primary radar antenna types in use today fall into three categories: parabolic, Cassegrain, and phased array antennas.

Anti-aircraft artillery (AAA) – Guns used to shoot unguided projectiles at airborne aircraft. Usually used in the air defence system.

Anti-radiation missile (ARM) – A missile that homes passively on a radiation source.

Area defence – The concept of locating defence units to intercept enemy attacks, remote from, and without reference to, individual vital installations, industrial complexes, or population centres.

Automatic gain control (AGC) –

1. A feature involving special circuitry designed to maintain the output of a radio, radar, or television receiver essentially constant, or to prevent its exceeding certain limits, despite variations in the strength of the incoming signal. In a radio receiver in particular, though something of a misnomer, also known as automatic volume control.

2. A self-acting compensating device that maintains the output of a transmission system constant with narrow limits, even in the face of wide variations in the attenuation of the system.

3. A radar circuit that prevents saturation of the radar receiver by long blocks of receiver signals, or by a carrier modulated at low frequency.

4. Automatic search jamming – An intercept receiver and jamming transmitting system that automatically searches for and jams enemy signals of specific radiation characteristics.

5. Automatic tracking – Tracking in which a system employs some mechanism, e.g. servo or computer, to automatically follow some characteristics of the signal.

Azimuth –

1. the direction of a celestial object from the observer, expressed as the angular distance from the north or south point of the horizon to the point at which a vertical circle passing through the object intersects the horizon.

2. the horizontal angle or direction of a compass bearing.

Azimuth – Search – Command to start searching with the tracking and/or fire control radar in a designated direction.

Azimuth resolution – The ability of a radar to distinguish two targets in close azimuth proximity and distance.

Backlobe – The portion of the radiation pattern of an antenna that is orientated 180° in relation to the main beam. The antenna backlobe is a result of diffraction effects of the reflector and direct leakage through the reflector surface.

Bandwidth – The range of frequencies within which performance, with respect to some characteristics, falls, with specific limits (i.e., the width of frequency of a barrage noise package).

Beam rider – A missile guided by an electronic beam.

Beamwidth – The width of a radar beam measured between lines of half-power points on the polar pattern of the antenna. This width is measured at the 3 dB points.

Bistatic radar – A radar where the transmitting and receiving antennas are separated by a considerable distance. Bistatic operation provides several advantages for its user. The covert positioning of the receivers poses problems for a potential attacking force since ELINT techniques locate the transmitter not the receiver. The proper placement of jamming assets is difficult, since the receiving sites are unknown. In addition, if a stand-off jammer is directed at the transmitter, its effectiveness in the direction of the covert receiver is diminished.

Jammers not in the same beam as the wanted targets will be attenuated by the receiver's sidelobe protection and these targets will be more readily detected.

CFAR – Constant false alarm rate detection refers to a common form of adaptive algorithm used in radar systems to detect target returns against a background of noise, clutter and interference.

Chaff – Ribbon-like pieces of metallic materials or metalized plastic that are dispensed by aircraft to mask or screen other aircraft or to cause a tracking radar to break lock. The foil materials are generally cut into small pieces for which the size is dependent on the radar interrogation frequency (approximately half the wavelength of the victim radar frequency). Being half a wavelength long, chaff acts as a resonant dipole and reflects much of the energy back to the radar.

Chaff corridor – Operational technique of dropping large quantities of chaff for a continuous period of time. This results in a 'ribbon' or 'stream' of returns many kilometres long on radar scopes. The penetrating strike force can then use the resulting chaff corridor to mask its penetration.

Circular scan – The pattern generated by an antenna that is continuously rotating in one direction.

Clutter – Unwanted signals, echoes, or images on the face of a scope that interfere with the observation of desired signals. Also called noise. This tends to mask the true target from detection or cause a tracking radar to break lock.

Clutter elimination – The clutter eliminator circuit discriminates against any target echo that exceeds three times the transmitted pulse width, and will not display it on the indicator. It is normally employed on the lower beams of a high frequency radar. This will allow targets above a preset signal strength to be presented, while the clutter (land) will be eliminated.

Command and control warfare (C2W) – The integrated use of operations security (OPSEC), military deception, psychological operations (PSYOP), electronic warfare (EW), and physical destruction, mutually supported by intelligence to deny information, influence, degrade, or destroy adversary C2 capabilities while protecting friendly C2 capabilities.

Command, control, communications, and computer systems (C4) – The process of, and means for, the exercise of authority and direction by a properly designated commander over assigned forces in the accomplishment of the commander's mission.

Command guidance – A guidance system in which intelligence transmitted to the missile from an off-board source causes the missile to traverse a directed flight path.

Communications intelligence (COMINT) – Intelligence derived from the interception of enemy communications signals.

Communications security (COMSEC) – The protection resulting from all measures designed to deny unauthorized persons information of value that might be derived from the possession and study of telecommunications, or to mislead unauthorized persons in their interpretation of the results of such possession and study. COMSEC includes: 1. Cryptosecurity; 2. transmission security; 3. emission security; and 4. physical security of communications security material and information.

1. **Cryptosecurity** – The component of communications security that results from the provision of technically sound cryptosystems and their proper use.
2. **Transmission security** – The component of communications security from which all measures designed to protect transmissions from interception and exploitation by means other than cryptoanalysis.
3. **Emission security** – The component of communications security that results from all measures taken to deny unauthorized persons information of value that might be derived from intercept and analysis of compromising emanations from crypto equipment and telecommunications systems.
4. **Physical security** – The component of communications security that results from all physical measures necessary to safeguard classified equipment, material, and documents from access thereto or observation thereof by being within a friendly power.

Conical scan (CONSCAN) – A type of scanning in which the axis of the RF beam is tilted away from the axis of the reflector and rotated about it, thus generating a cone.

Cross-eye – A jamming technique used to produce angular errors in monopulse and other passive lobing radars. A jammer is a two-source interferometer that causes the phase front of the signal reaching the radar to be highly distorted. With such a technique it is difficult for the radar to determine the points from which the transmissions are originating. Requires a high jam-to-signal ratio or the skin echo will show up in the pattern nulls.

Cross-gated – A CFAR technique employed to achieve the fast switching required for an optimum combination of normal and MTI modes. Here, the MTI video signals are used to 'gate' on the normal video when the MTI indicates a target in clutter. CFAR action is achieved by the wideband as in the zero-crossing and Dicke fix CFARs.

CW jamming – The transmission of constant-amplitude, constant-frequency, unmodulated jamming signals to change the signal-to-noise ratio of a radar receiver.

GLOSSARY

Data-link – A communications link which permits automatic transmission of information in digital form.

Deception – Those measures designed to mislead the enemy by manipulation, distortion, or falsification of evidence to induce him to react in a manner prejudicial to his interests. (See Electronic Deception, or Manipulative Deception.)

Deception jamming – Any means of jamming consisting of false signals that have similar characteristics to the victim radar thereby deceiving the operator into erroneous conclusions.

Decibel (dB) – A dimensionless unit for expressing the ratio of two values, the number of decibels being 10 times the logarithm to the base 10 of a power ratio, or 20 times the logarithm to the base 10 of a voltage of current ratio. A power increase by 3 dB indicates a doubling of the original power.

(dBm) – Same as dBw except the reference level is one milliwatt instead of one watt.

(dBw) – Unit used to describe the ratio of the power at any point in a transmission system to a referenced level of one watt. The ratio expresses decibels above and below the reference level of one watt.

Defence suppression – A term applied to weapons systems that are intended to eliminate or degrade enemy detection, acquisition, or tracking equipment.

Doppler (effect) – Continuous wave (CW) Doppler radar modules are sensors that measure the shift in frequency created when an object moves. A transmitter emits energy at a specific frequency which, when reflected, can indicate both speed and direction of the target. When objects move closer to the Doppler source, they increase in shift (positive value), and when they move further away, they decrease in shift (negative value).

Doppler radar – A radar system that measures the velocity of a moving object by the apparent shift in carrier frequency of the returned signal as it approaches or recedes.

Downlink – The signal from a transponder beacon located on a surface-to-air missile (SAM) used to provide a traceable radar return for missile guidance.

Downlink jamming (DLJ) – Some command guidance missiles carry a beacon (downlink) which is used by the parent radar to track the missile. If this beacon reply can be hidden from the parent tracking radar, the missile guidance solution can be defeated. Hence, downlink (beacon) jamming is intended to screen the missile beacon signal from the parent radar's view.

Ducting – The bending of radar rays due to atmospheric conditions. Ducting can either extend radar coverage beyond normal line of sight or it can deny the radar picture above a duct. Ducting is also called Anomalous Propagation.

Dummy antenna – A device that has the necessary impedance characteristics of an antenna and the necessary power-handling capabilities, but does not radiate or receive radio waves. Note: In receiver practice, that portion of the impedance not included in the signal generator is often called a dummy antenna.

Dummy load (radio transmission) – A dissipative but essentially non-radiating substitute device having impedance characteristics simulating those of the substituted device. This allows power to be applied to the radar unit without radiating into free space.

Duplex – In radar, a condition of operation when two identical and interchangeable equipments are provided—one in an active state, and the other immediately available for operation.

Duplexer – A switching device used in radar to permit alternate use of the same antenna for both transmitting and receiving.

Duty cycle – The ratio of the time the transmitter is actually on versus the time it could be on in a given transmission cycle.

Dynamic range –

1. The difference, in decibels, between the overload level and the minimum acceptable signal level in a system or transducer. Note: The minimum acceptable signal level of a system or transducer is ordinarily fixed by one or more of the following: noise level, low-level distortion, interference, or resolution level.
2. Ratio of the specified maximum signal level capability of a system or component to its noise or resolution level, usually expressed in decibels.

Early warning radar – A radar set or system used near the periphery of a defended area to provide early notification of hostile aircraft approaching the area.

EA pod – A jamming system that is designed to be carried externally on an aircraft. Effective radiated power (ERP) – Input power to antenna time multiplied by the gain of the antenna, expressed in watts.

Electromagnetic interference (EMI) – Any electromagnetic disturbance that interrupts, obstructs, or otherwise degrades or limits the effective performance of electronic systems. EMI can be induced intentionally, by way of jamming, or unintentionally because of spurious emissions and modulations.

Electromagnetic pulse (EMP) – The generation and radiation in a transmission medium of a very narrow and very high-amplitude pulse of electromagnetic noise. The term is associated with the high-level pulse because of a nuclear

GLOSSARY

detonation and with an intentionally generated narrow, high-amplitude pulse for EA applications. In nuclear detonations, the EMP signal consists of a continuous spectrum with most of its energy distributed throughout the low frequency band of 3 to 30 kHz.

Electromagnetic radiation – Radiation made up of oscillating electric and magnetic fields and propagated with the speed of light. Includes gamma radiation, x-rays, ultraviolet, visible and infrared radiation, plus radar and radio waves.

Electromagnetic spectrum – The total range of frequencies (or wavelengths) over which any form of electromagnetic radiation occurs.

Electronic attack (EA) – The use of electromagnetic energy, directed energy, or antiradiation weapons to attack personnel, facilities, or equipment with the intent of degrading, neutralizing, or destroying enemy combat capability. Action taken to reduce the enemy's effective use of the electromagnetic spectrum. EA is a division of electronic warfare (EW).

Electronic combat (EC) – Action taken in support of military operations against the enemy's electromagnetic capabilities. EC is task-oriented and includes electronic warfare (EW), command and control warfare (C2W), and suppression of enemy air defences (SEAD).

ECM – Electronic countermeasure.

Electronic protection (EP) – Active and passive means taken to protect personnel, facilities, and equipment from any effects of friendly or enemy employment of electronic warfare that degrade, neutralize or destroy friendly combat capability. EP is a division of electronic warfare (EW).

Electromagnetic deception – The deliberate radiation, reradiation, alteration, absorption, or reflection of electromagnetic radiations in a manner intended to mislead an enemy in the interpretation of, or use of, information received by his electronic systems. There are two categories of electronic deception:

1. **Manipulative deception** – The alteration or simulation of friendly electromagnetic radiation to accomplish deception.
2. **Imitative deception** – The introduction of radiations into enemy channels that imitate his own emissions.

Electronic intelligence (ELINT) – The intelligence information product of activities engaged in the collection and processing for subsequent intelligence purposes of foreign, noncommunications, electromagnetic radiations emanating from other than nuclear detonations or radioactive sources.

Electronic jammers –

1. Expendable – A transmitter designed for special use such as being dropped behind enemy lines.
2. Repeater – A receiver-transmitter device that, when triggered by enemy radar impulses, returns synchronized false signals to the enemy equipment. The returned impulses are spaced and timed to produce false echoes or bearing errors in the enemy equipment. See Expendable and Repeater Jammers.

Electronic jamming – The deliberate radiation, reradiation, or reflection of electromagnetic energy with the object of impairing the use of electronic devices, equipment, or systems.

Electronic order of battle – A listing of all the electronic radiating equipment of a military force giving location, type function, and other pertinent data.

Electronic reconnaissance – Specific reconnaissance directed towards the collection of electromagnetic radiations. Examples:

COMINT Communications Intelligence

ELINT Electronic Intelligence

OPINT Optical Intelligence

RINT Radiated Intelligence

SIGINT Signal Intelligence

Electronic warfare (EW) – Military action involving the use of electromagnetic energy and directed energy to control the electromagnetic spectrum. EW has three divisions: electronic attack (EA), electronic protection (EP), and electronic warfare support (ES).

Electronic warfare support (ES) – Actions taken to search for, intercept, identify, and locate sources of intentional radiated electromagnetic energy for the purpose of immediate threat recognition. Surveillance of the electromagnetic spectrum that directly supports an operational commander's electromagnetic information needs. ES is a division of EW.

Electro-optics (EO) – The interaction between optics and electronics leading to the transformation of electrical energy into light, or vice versa, with the use of an optical device.

Electro-optic counter-countermeasures (EOCCM) – Actions taken to ensure the effective friendly use of the electro-optic spectrum despite the enemy's use of countermeasures in that spectrum.

GLOSSARY

Emission control (EMCON) –

1. The management of electromagnetic radiations to counter an enemy's capability to detect, identify, or locate friendly emitters for exploitation by hostile action.
2. Controlling the radiation of an active system to minimize detection by enemy sensors.

Emitter Identification Data (EID) – A list of identified electronic emitter, typically related to enemy radars.

Endgame – The period of military engagement 3-5 seconds before missile impact.

Endgame countermeasures (EGCM) – Actions taken to defeat a tracking missile. This includes expendables, decoys, and manoeuvres.

EO – Electro-Optics

Equivalent – The command 'Equivalent' is to 'turn off' the high frequency energy emission into the space, but not turn off the radar.

EW – Electronic warfare

Expendable jammer – A nonrecoverable jammer. Early expendables were limited to chaff and flare deployments; however, various radiating jamming systems exist that use noise or repeater techniques. These are dispensed by aircraft or other delivery systems and are designed to disrupt or deceive a victim radar for a short period of time.

Extremely high frequency (EHF) – Frequencies in the range of 30 to 300 GHz.

False target – A radiated bundle of electromagnetic energy that is displaced in time from the echo that creates a response in the receiver where no reflecting surface exists.

False target generator – Device for generating electromagnetic energy of the correct frequency of the receiver that is displaced in time from the reflected energy of the target.

Field of view (FOV) – The maximum solid angle visible by an optical or electrooptic system.

Field (near/far) – regions of the electromagnetic field (EM) around an object, such as a transmitting antenna, or the result of radiation scattering off an object.

Fire control radar – Specialized radar systems used to locate and track airborne and surface targets, compute an optimum weapons firing point, and control the firing and sometimes guidance of its weapons.

FM-by-noise modulation – A method of frequency modulating with an effective jamming method against AM and fix-tuned FM receivers. Not very effective against continuously tunable PFM receivers; careful tuning can defeat a great portion of the jamming signal. For this reason FM-by-noise is not considered optimum as a type of modulation for jamming FM receivers.

FM jamming – A technique consisting of a constant amplitude RF signal that is varied in frequency around a centre frequency to produce a signal over a band of frequencies.

Frequency spectrum – The entire range of frequencies of electromagnetic radiation.

G, g – Acceleration due to gravity (32.2 ft/sec^2).

Gain (manual) – The receiver gain control allows the operator to vary the receiver sensitivity. It is not designed as an AJ feature; however, when properly employed it may greatly reduce the effects of jamming. The radar detection capability is also reduced by an equal amount.

Gain (transmission gain) – The increase in signal power in transmission from one point to another under static conditions. Note: Power gain is usually expressed in decibels.

Gated – Term used in electromagnetism meaning a pulse which is 'confined'.

Get the High Down – This command means that the high voltage is turned off but the emitter is still working in normal mode but there is no high energy emission into space.

GRAU – Main Missile and Artillery Directorate of the Ministry of Defence of the Russian Federation.

Ground controlled intercept (GCI) – Vectoring an interceptor aircraft to an airborne target by means of information relayed from a ground-based radar site that observes both the interceptor and target.

Guidance system (missile) – A system that evaluates flight information, correlates it with target data, determines the desired flight path of the missile, and communicates the necessary commands to the missile flight control system.

Guided missile – An unmanned vehicle moving above the surface of the earth whose trajectory of flight path is capable of being altered by an external or internal mechanism.

Height finder – A radar used to detect the angular elevation, slant range and height of objects in the vertical sight plane. An air defence ground radar used specifically to accurately determine aircraft altitude for tracking and ground controlled intercepts.

GLOSSARY

Hertz (Hz) – The unit of frequency, equal to one cycle of variation per second. It supersedes the unit cycle per second (cps).

High frequency (HF) – Frequencies from 3,000 to 30,000 kHz.

Home-on-jam (HOJ) – A missile mode of operation in which a jamming signal is used to develop steering information for the missile to home in on the jamming source.

Homing guidance – A system by which a missile steers itself towards a target by means of a self-contained mechanism which is activated by some distinguishing characteristics of the target.

Identification, friend or foe (IFF) – A system using radar transmission to which equipment carried by friendly forces automatically responds, for example, by emitting pulses, thereby distinguishing themselves from enemy forces. It is the primary method of determining the friendly or unfriendly character of aircraft and ships by other aircraft and ships, and by ground forces employing radar detection equipment and associated identification, friend or foe units.

IGR – Illumination and Guidance Radar.

Image frequency – An undesired input frequency capable of producing the selected frequency by the same process. NOTE: An image frequency is a frequency which differs from, but has a certain symmetrical relationship to, that which a superheterodyne receiver is tuned. Consequently, the image frequency can be mistakenly accepted and processed as a true frequency by the receiver.

Image jamming – Jamming at the image frequency of the radar receiver. Barrage jamming is made most effective by generating energy at both the normal operating and imaging frequency of the radar. Image jamming inverts the phase of the response and is thereby useful as an eagle deception technique. Not effective if the radar uses image rejection.

Imitative deception – The introduction of radiations into enemy channels which imitates their own emissions.

Imitative jamming – The jamming technique of transmitting a signal identical to the original guidance signal.

Infrared (IR) – That portion of the frequency spectrum lying between the upper end of the millimetre wave region and the lower (red) end of the visible spectrum. In wavelength, the IR lies between 0.78 and 300 microns; in frequency, it lies between one and 400 terahertz (THz).

Infrared counter-countermeasures (IRCCM) – Actions taken to effectively employ our own infrared radiation equipment and systems in spite of the enemy's actions o counter their use.

Infrared countermeasures (IRCM) –

1. Countermeasures used specifically against enemy threats operating in the infrared spectrum.

2. Actions taken to prevent or reduce the effectiveness of enemy equipment and tactics employing infrared radiation.

Intercept point – A computed point in space towards which an interceptor is vectored to complete an interception.

Interference (electronic) – An electrical or electromagnetic disturbance that causes undesirable responses on electronic equipment. Electrical interference refers specifically to interference caused by the operation of electrical apparatus that is not designed to radiate electromagnetic energy.

Intermediate frequency (IF) –

1. A fixed frequency to which all carrier waves are converted in a super-heterodyne receiver.
2. A frequency to which a signaling wave is shifted locally as an intermediate step during transmission or reception.
3. A frequency resulting from the combination of the received signal and that of the local oscillator in a superheterodyne receiver.

Intermediate frequency jamming – Form of CW jamming that is accomplished by transmitting two CW signals separated by a frequency equal to the centre frequency of the radar receiver IF amplifier.

Interrogator – A device used to transmit pulse-coded challenges to an IFF transponder and then evaluates the pulse-coded reply for identification purposes.

Intrapulse modulation repeater – A classified deception jamming technique.
Intrusion – the intentional insertion of electromagnetic energy into transmission paths in any manner with the objective of deceiving operators or causing confusion.

Intrusion –

1. The entry of a non friendly aircraft or system into friendly air space.
2. The intentional interference in a communication system by which the intruder attempts to confuse, delay, or cause error by the selective introduction of additional data.

IRST – Infra Red Search and Track

GLOSSARY

Jammer – A device used to deprive, limit, or degrade the use of communications or radar systems. Radio frequency jammers include noise, discrete frequency repeater, and deceptive equipment.

Jamming-to-signal (J/S) ratio – The relative power ratio of jamming to the radar return signal at the radar antenna. The inverse of the signal-to-jamming ratio.

Jamming – the deliberate radiation, reradiation, or reflection of electromagnetic energy with the intent of impairing the use of electronic devices, equipment, or systems being used by the enemy.

Jam strobe – Also called JAVA (jamming amplitude versus azimuth). A circuit that generates a marker on the PPI to indicate signal strength as a function of bearing. It does this by sampling the jamming intensity once each repetition period. Besides showing the direction of the jammer, it also indicates the severity of main beam and sidelobe jamming.

Jet engine modulation (JEM) – Modulation present in the radar returns received from a jet aircraft, caused by the rotation of the fan or turbine blades of the aircraft's engines.

Klystron – A very stable microwave amplifier that provides high gain at good efficiency. This is accomplished by velocity modulating (accelerating a beam of electronics flowing from its cathode to its anode.

Laser target designation – The use of a laser to direct a light beam onto the target so that appropriate sensors can track or home on the reflected energy.

Light amplification by stimulated emission of radiation (LASER) – A process of generating coherent light. The process uses a natural molecular (and atomic) phenomenon whereby molecules absorb incident electromagnetic energy at specific frequencies. It then stores this energy for short but usable periods, then releases the stored energy as light at particular frequencies, and in an extremely narrow frequency band.

Lobe – One of the three-dimensional sections of the radiation pattern of a directional antenna bounded by 1-2 cones of nulls.

Lobe-on-receive-only (LORO) – Mode of operation consisting of transmitting on one antenna system and receiving the reflected energy on another system (TWS, conical, or monopulse).

Look-down, shoot-down – Refers to an air interceptor (AI) equipped with a pulse Doppler radar, or a radar that has a moving target indicator (MTI) feature, that can detect and lock-on to a target within ground return clutter enabling the AI to track and shoot the target.

Look-through –

1. When jamming, a technique by which the jamming emission is interrupted irregularly for extremely short periods to allow monitoring of the victim signal during jamming operations.
2. When being jammed, the technique of observing or monitoring a desired signal during interruptions in the jamming signals.

Low frequency (LF) – Frequencies from 30 – 300 kHz.

Low power spread spectrum radar – A low power, high duty cycle radar whose spectrum is spread 100 MHz or more. Since this radar has a broad output spectrum and a high duty cycle, neither time nor frequency can be effectively used to resolve these signals. This leaves direction as the prime method of resolution. The spectrum of these radars is spread over the bandwidth by any of the pseudo random noise modulating techniques commonly used in communications. Techniques such as bi-phase modulation, quaternary phase modulation, chirp, random frequency jumping, etc., may be used to spread either a CW signal or a very high duty cycle signal. Such signals have a very good range resolution—approximately equal to the reciprocal of the bandwidth.

LPI – Low Probability Intercept

Magnetron – A radar microwave device whose operation is based on the motion of electrons (AC) under the influence of combined electric and magnetic fields.

Mainlobe – The lobe of a transmitting or receiving antenna centred on the directivity axis of the antenna.

Manipulative deception – The alteration or simulation of friendly electromagnetic radiations to accomplish the deception.

Medium frequency (MF) – Frequencies from 300 to 3,000 kHz.

Micron – A unit of length equal to a micrometre (10^{-6} metres).

Microwave amplification by stimulated emission or radiation (MASER) – A low noise, radio-frequency amplifier. The emission of energy stored in a molecular or atomic system by a microwave power supply is stimulated by the input signal.

Microwave communications – Line-of-sight communications, the frequency of which is higher than 300 MHz.

Millimetre waves – Frequencies (30 GHz to 300 GHz) in the millimetre portion of the electromagnetic spectrum.

Miss distance – The distance measured between the closest paths of a target and interceptor (i.e., aircraft and missile). One objective of self-protection jamming systems is to increase the miss distance to avoid destruction if missile launch cannot be prevented.

Missile approach warning system (MAWS) – A system used to detect and provide warning of approaching missiles. MAWS may be partitioned into active MAWS and passive MAWS.

1. Active missile approach warning system (AMAWS) – Generally employs pulse Doppler radar as its sensor. This radar is able to discern a moving target in stationary or slow- moving background clutter.
2. Passive missile approach warning system (PMAWS) – An ultraviolet (UV) or infrared based detector system with the ability to detect and distinguish threat missiles from surrounding clutter and non-lethal missiles.

Modulation – The variation of amplitude, frequency, or phase of an electromagnetic wave by impressing another wave on it.

Modulator – A device (such as an electron tube) for modulating a carrier wave or signal for the transmission of intelligence of some sort.

Monopulse – A method of pulse generation that allows the simultaneous determining of azimuth, elevation and range, and/or speed from a single pulse.

Monopulse radar – A radar using a receiving antenna system having two or more partially overlapping lobes in the radiation patterns. Sum and difference channels in the receiver compare the amplitudes or the phases of the antenna outputs to determine the angle of arrival of the received signal relative to the antenna boresight. A well-designed monopulse tracking system will achieve a more accurate track under conventional jamming techniques than on the skin return. Certain monopulse trackers are susceptible to angular jamming techniques such as skirt and image jamming. Techniques such as 'CROSS EYE' are designed to attack all monopulse tracking systems. Monopulse deception is a major area of advanced R&D with no clear 'best technique' yet in sight.

Moving target indicator (MTI) – A radar presentation that shows only targets that are in motion. Signals from stationary targets are subtracted out of the return signal by the output of a suitable memory circuit.

Multiband radar – Radar that simultaneously operates on more than one frequency band through a common antenna. This technique allows for many sophisticated forms of video processing and requires that a jammer must jam all channels simultaneously.

Noise –

1. Any unwanted disturbance within a dynamic electrical or mechanical system, such as undesired electromagnetic radiation, and any transmission channel or device.
2. Uncontrolled random disturbances that arise in a guided missile system because of various physical phenomena.

Noise jamming – Direct (straight) AM or FM noise on a carrier frequency that has a highly variable bandwidth for the purpose of increasing (saturating) the radar receiver's noise level.

Oscillator – Electronic circuit or device capable of converting direct current (DC) into alternating current (AC) at a frequency determined by the inductive and the capacitive constants of the oscillator.

Over-the-horizon radar – A radar system that makes use of the ionosphere to extend its range of detection beyond line-of-sight. Over-the-horizon radars may be either forward scatter or backscatter systems.

Passive detection and tracking – By combining azimuth data on jamming strobes from several stations, intersections are obtained which indicate the position of the jammers. The number of ghosts can be reduced by increasing the number of friendly stations and obtaining elevation angles of strobes when available.

Passive electronic countermeasures – Electronic countermeasures based on the reflection, absorption or modification of the enemy's electromagnetic energy. This distinction between active and passive countermeasures is not currently used, but is based on the presence or absence of an electronic transmitter.

Passive homing guidance – A system of homing guidance in which the receiver in the missile uses radiations only from the target.

Phased array radar – Radar using many antenna elements that are fed out-of-phase to each other. The direction of the beam can be changed as rapidly as the phase relationships (usually less than 20 μsec). Thus, the antenna remains stationary while the beam is moved electronically. The use of many antenna elements allows for very rapid and high directivity of the beam(s) with a large peak and/or average power.

Point defence – The defence of specified geographical areas, cities, and vital installations. One distinguishing feature of point defence missiles is that their guidance information is received from radars located near the launching sites.

Polarization – The direction of an electrical field is considered the direction of polarization. When a half-wave dipole antenna is horizontally oriented, the emitted wave is horizontally polarized. A vertical polarized wave is emitted when the antenna is erected vertically.

Pulse Doppler radar – A highly complex radar system that employs a very high pulse repetition frequency (usually 10,000 PPS or higher) to reduce 'blind speeds' and measure the Doppler frequency shift to resolve target velocity. Pulse Doppler is applied principally to radar systems requiring the detection of moving targets in a ground clutter environment. It uses pulse modulation to achieve higher peak power, greater range, less susceptibility to unfriendly detection, and enhanced range resolution.

Pulse duration – The time in microseconds that the radar set is transmitting RF energy. Generally, the greater the pulse duration, the higher the average power, but the poorer the range resolution. Also known as pulse width. More technically, it is the time interval, measured at the half-amplitude points, from the leading edge to the trailing edge of a pulse.

PVO – Yugoslav/Serbian abbreviation for Air Defence (Protiv Vazdusna Odbrana)

Radar absorbent material (RAM) – Material used as a radar camouflage

device to reduce the echo area of an object.

Radar beacon – A receiver-transmitter combination that sends out a coded signal when triggered by the proper type of pulse enabling determination of range and bearing information by the interrogating station or aircraft.

Radar cross section – The equivalent area intercepted by a radiated signal and, if scattered uniformly in all directions, produces an echo at the radar receiver equal to that of the target. Typical radar cross sections of aircraft vary from one to over 1,000 square metres. The RCS of ships may exceed 10,000 square metres.

Radar definition – The accuracy with which a radar obtains target information such as range, azimuth, or elevation.

Radar homing – Homing on the source of a radar beam.

Radar homing and warning (RHAW) – Typically consists of an airborne, wideband video receiver designed to intercept, identify, and display the direction to pulsetype emitters.

Radar resolution – A measure of a radar's ability to separate targets that are close together in some aspect of range, azimuth, or elevation into individual returns.

Radar warning receiver (RWR) – A receiver onboard an aircraft that analyzes the hostile radar environment and determines radar threat by type, frequency, relative bearing, and relative distance. The threat is displayed to the aircrew by means of display lights, video symbols, and aural tones.

Radio frequency (RF) – Electromagnetic energy radiated at some frequency.

Radio frequency interference – An unintentional interfering signal capable of being propagated into electronic equipment, usually derived from sources outside the system.

Range – The distance from one object to another.

Range tracking – Pulse radars measure the time difference between radar pulse transmission and echo reception. The range gate is positioned at a range where the target is expected. The receiver is blanked off except during the period where the range gate is positioned. Range tracking may occur at the leading edge of the return pulse or between ON and OFF gates.

Resolution – The ability of a system to distinguish between two adjacent objects and to display them separately.

SAM – Surface-to-air missile.

Scan – The process of directing a beam of RF energy successively over a given region, or the corresponding process in reception.

Scan interval – The time interval from the peak of one mainlobe in a scan pattern to the peak of the next mainlobe.

Scan period – The time period of basic scan types (except conical and lobe switching) or the period of the lowest repetitive cycle of complex scan combinations. The basic unit of measurement is degrees/mils per second or seconds per cycle.

Scan type – The path made in space by a point on the radar beam, for example, circular, helical, conical, spiral, or sector.

Search –

1. A term applied to that phase of radar operation when the lobe, or beam of radiated energy, is directed in such a way to search for targets in the area.
2. A systematic examination of space to locate and identify targets of interest.

Sector scan – A scan in which the antenna sweeps back and forth through a selected angle.

Self-protection jamming – Jamming to protect the vehicle upon which the jammer is deployed.

Semiactive radar homing – Semiactive homing guidance combines principles from both the beam rider and the active radar homing missile. Track on the target is established by the AI's radar; the missile is launched when the target comes within its effective range. During missile flight, the Al maintains track on the target. Radar returns from the target are received by the missile. Guidance commands are generated within the missile from the radar returns.

Sidelobe – Part of the beam from an antenna, other than the mainlobe. Sidelobe gain is usually less than mainlobe gain. Given that the mainlobe radiates most of the power at zero degrees azimuth, sidelobes inherently radiate significant power in the direction of +20°, 90°, and 150° relative to the mainlobe.

Sidelobe jamming – Jamming through a sidelobe of the receiving antenna in an attempt to obliterate the desired signal received through the mainlobe of the receiving antenna at fixed points.

Sidelobe suppression – The suppression of that portion of the beam from a radar antenna other than the mainlobe.

Signal intelligence (SIGINT) – Intelligence derived from the interception of enemy communications and noncommunication signals. A generic term that includes both COMINT and ELINT.

Signal-to-jamming ratio (S/J) – The ratio of the signal power to the jamming power or intentional interference at some point in the system. This ratio is often expressed in decibels.

Signal-to-noise ratio (S/N) – Ratio of the power of the signal to the power of the noise. Signature – The set of parameters that describes the characteristics of a radar target or an RF emitter and distinguishes one emitter from another. Signature parameters include the RF of the carrier, the modulation characteristics (typically the pulse modulation code), and the scan pattern.

SLCM – Sea launched cruise missile

SPAAG – Self propelled anti aircraft gun

Super high frequency (SHF) – Frequencies from 3 to 30 GHz.

Support jamming – A tactic by which aircraft carrying electronic jamming equipment orbit at a safe distance from the enemy threat defences or fly escort with the strike force for the primary purpose of screening them from the threat radars.

Suppression of enemy air defences (SEAD) – That activity which neutralizes, destroys, or temporarily degrades enemy air defence systems in a specific area by using physical attack, deception, and/or electronic warfare.

Surface-to-air missile (SAM) – A missile launched from a surface launcher at a target above the surface.

Sweep jammer – Electronic jammer that sweeps a narrow band of electronic energy over a broad bandwidth.

Synthetic aperture radar (SAR) – A high-resolution ground mapping technique in which advantage is taken of the forward motion of a coherent pulsed radar to synthesize the equivalent of a very long side looking array antenna from the radar returns received over a period of up to several seconds or more.

Target acquisition – The detection, identification, and location of a target in sufficient detail to permit the effective employment of weapons.

TELAR – Transporter, Erector LAuncheR – acronym for the mobile launchers.

Terminal guidance –

1. The guidance applied to a guided missile between mid-course and arrival in the vicinity of the target.
2. Electronic, mechanical, visual, or other assistance given to aircraft pilots to facilitate arrival at, operation within or over, landing upon or departure from an air landing or air drop facility.

Terminal threat – The weapon systems, generally near a target, used to directly engage an aircraft in order to destroy it.

Terrain-avoidance radar – An airborne radar that provides a display of terrain ahead of low-flying aircraft to permit horizontal avoidance of obstacles.

Terrain-following radar (TFR) – An airborne radar that provides a display of terrain ahead of low-flying aircraft to permit manual control, or signals for automatic control to maintain constant altitude above the ground.

Threshold – The minimum value of a signal that can be detected by a system or sensor under consideration.

Time-of-arrival (TOA) – A method of locating a distant pulse emitter by measuring the difference in the time-of-arrival of its pulses at three separate locations. This method is also called Inverse LORAN.

Track –

1. A series of related contacts displayed on a plotting board.
2. To display or record the successive positions of a moving object.
3. To lock onto a point of radiation and obtain guidance from it.
4. To keep a gun properly aimed, or to continuously point a target-locating instrument at a moving target.
5. The actual path of an aircraft above, or a ship on, the surface of the earth. The course is the path that is planned; the track is the path that is taken.

GLOSSARY

Tracking – The continuous monitoring of range, velocity, or position of a target in space from a reference position. This is accomplished via radar and/or optical means.

Tracking radar – A radar that measures the range, azimuth, elevation, and/or velocity of the target and provides data that may be used by the fire control computer to determine the target path and predict its future position.

Track-on-jam – A method of passive target tracking using the jamming signal emitted by the target.

Track-while-scan (TWS) radar – Although it is not really a tracking radar in the true sense of the word, it does provide complete and accurate position information for missile guidance by using two separate beams produced by two separate antennas on two different frequencies. The system uses electronic computer techniques whereby raw data are used to track an assigned target, compute target velocity, and predict its future position while maintaining normal sector scan.

Ultra high frequency (UHF) – Frequencies from 300 to 3,000 MHz.

Very high frequency (VHF) – Frequencies from 30 to 300 MHz.

Very low frequency (VLF) – Frequencies from 3 to 30 kHz.

Video frequency –

1. A band of frequencies extending from approximately 100 Hz to several MHz.
2. The frequency of the voltage resulting from television scanning. Range from zero to 4 MHz or more.

VIKO – name for the detached radar screen located in the UNK cabin of SA-3/S-125 system.

Warning receiver – A receiver with the primary function of warning the user that his unit is being illuminated by an electromagnetic signal of interest.

WO – Warrant officer

XO – executive officer

Further Reading and Bibliography

1999 F-117A Shootdown, Wikipedia: en.wikipedia.org/ wiki/1999_F-117A_ shoot- down

Adamy, David L. (2011), Electronic Warfare Pocket Guide, Scitech Publishing

Advanced Anti-radiation Guided Missile (AARGM) (2009) NDIA guns and missiles conference

Air Force Magazine, September 2016

Air Power Over Serbia (2014), Air Power History, Fall 2014 issue

Airpower Australia, http://www.ausairpower.net, miscellaneous articles

Allen Patrick, Special Forces Aviation, MBI Publishing Company

Andersen. Yu. A., Drozhkin A. I., Lozik P.M. (1979) Protivvozdushnaya Oborona Suhoputnih Voisk, Voeno Izdatestvo Ministerstvo Oboroni SSSR, Moskva

Andrea De Martino, (2012) Introduction to Modern EW Systems, Artech House

Anicic, Djordje. (2009), Smena – Ratni Dnevnik (The Shift – War Diary)

Anil K Maini (2018), Handbook of Defense Electronics and Optronics, Wiley

Arhangelski I. I., (2001) Proektirovanie Zenitnih Upravlyaemih Raket, Moskovskii Aviacioni Institut (MAI)

Aviation Classics F-16 Fighting Falcon

Aviatsia i Kosmonavtika (1999-2018)

Balajrishnan R., (1998), Guided Weapon System Design, DRDO, India

Balkani 1991-2000, Voina v Vazduhe 10

Banjac Dusan (1986): Elektronska Borba u Protivvazdusnoj Odbrani, Vojno Tehnicki Izdavaci Centar, Beograd

Barton D.K. (2012), Radar Equations for Modern Radar, Artech House.

Barton, D.K. (1972-1978), Radars Volumes 1–7, Artech House.

Ben Rich, Leo Janos (1996) Skunk Works: A personal memoir of my years in Lockheed

Bipin Kumar Jha, Mayur Somnath Aswale (2016) Mechanical Aspects in Stealth Technology: review, IJETR, Volume 4

Blast from the Past – Interview of Col. Dale Zelko to Carlos Lorch, Director and Chief Editor of the 'National Brazilian Air Force Magazine, Volume 5, Issue 1

Bowdoin Van Riper, A. Rockets and Missiles, (2004) Greenwood Press

FURTHER READING AND BIBLIOGRAPHY

Cadirci, Serdar (2010) Atmospheric Effects on Communication and Electronic Warfare Systems Within Turkey and Surrounding Areas, Naval Postgraduate School, Monterey, California

Charvat, G.L. (2014), Small and Short-Range Radar Systems, CRC Press.

Crickmore, Paul (2000), Lockheed's Blackworld Skunk Works, Osprey Publishing

Crickmore, Paul (2016) Lockheed F-117 Nighthawk Stealth Fighter, Osprey Publishing

Dan Hampton (2015), The Hunter Killers, William Morrow (An imprint of Harper Collins)

Davies, Peter (2017) F-105 Wild Weasel vs SA-2 Guideline SAM, Osprey Publishing

Davis, Larry (1993) Wild Weasel, Squadron Signal Publishing

Dobrinkin, V.D, Kupriyanov A. I., Pomomarev V, G., Shustov, L.N. (2007) Radiolektronaya Borba, Vuzovskaya Kniga, Moskva

Dr Carlo Kopp, (2009) The Collapse of American Air Power: The proliferation of Counter-Stealth Systems, airpoweraustralia.com

Dwight Zimmerman, (2014) Area 51, Graphic History, Zenith Press

Eaves, J.L. and Reedy, E.K. (2011), Principles of Modern Radar, Springer.

Electronic Warfare and Radar Systems (1913) Engineering handbook, Naval Air Warfare Center Weapon Division, Point Mugu, California

Electronic Warfare Fundamentals (2000), student supplementary text, Det 8, ACC TRSS, Nellis AFB

Eugene F. Knott; Radar Cross Section (2006), SciTech Publishing

F-16.net, Holloman commander recalls being shot down in Serbia

Faulconbridge, I. (2002), Radar Fundamentals, Argos Press.

Fuhs, Akken (1983) Radar Cross Section Lectures, Naval Postgraduate School, Monterey, California

Ganin Sergei, Korovin Vladimir, Karpenko Aleksanr, Angelyskii Rostislav, (2003) Sistema 125, Tehnika i Voruzhenie No. 5,8,9

Ganin, S.M, Karpenko, A.V. (2001) Zenitnaya Rketnaya Sistema S-300, Bastion Press St. Petersburg

Georg M. Siouris, (2004), Missile Guidance and Controls Systems, Springer

Grant, Rebecca (1998) The Radar Game, Next American Century Series, IRIS Independent Research

Griffiths, H.D. (2014), Stimson's Introduction to Airborne Radar, SciTech Publishing.

Haave Christopher, (2003) A-10s over Kosovo, Air University Press

History of the Electro-Optical Guided Missile (2016) Hpasp Ver. 1.01

http://simhq.com/forum/ubbthreads.php/topics/3900842/1

Jeffrey, T.W. (2008), Phased Array Radar Design, SciTech Publishing.

Jenkins Daniel (1999) Lockheed Martin F-117, Warbird Tech Volume 25

Jenn, D.C. (2005), Radar and Laser Cross section Engineering, AIAA.

Jenn, David (2005) Radar and Laser Cross Section Engineering, AIAA Education Series

Jianbin Z., Kai G., Eryang Z. Research on Angle measurements of Anti-radiation Missile, Przeglad Elektrotechniczny (Electrical Review)

Kapur, Vivek (2014), Stealth Technology and Its Effect on Aerial Warfare, IDSA Monograph Series No. 33

Knott, E.F., Shaeffer, J.F. and Tuley, M.T. (2004), Radar Cross section, SciTech Publishing.

Knyazkov, V.S., Rozhkov, V.V. (1977) Boevie Raketi, DOSAAV, Moskva

Konstantinos Zikidis, Alexios Skondras, Charisions Tokas (2014) Low Observable Principles, Stealth Aircraft and Anti-Stealth Technologies, Sciencepress Ltd.

Koran Frantishek, Bouchal Tomash, Horak Jan (2005) SA-6 Gainful in Detail

Korovin, V. (2003) Raketi fakela (fakel Missiles), MKB Fakel

Korovin, V.N, Afanasyev P.P, Svetov V.G. (2011) Petr Grushin, Znameniti Konstruktori Rossii, Politehnika, St. Petersburg

Kulikov A. I. (2006) Voenoe Iskustvo v Lokalnih Voinah, Ministerstvo Oboroni RF

Lambert Benjamin (2001): NATO Air War for Kosovo, RAND Corporation

Leonov, A.P. and others (2015) Voiskovaya Protivvozdushanay Oborona 1915-2015, Zbornik

Levanon, N. (1988), Radar Principles, Wiley-Interscience.

Lockheed F-117 Nighthawk, Wikipedia: en.wikipedia.org/wiki/ Lockheed_F-117_ Nighthawk

Lynch, David (2004) Introduction to RF Stealth, Scitech Publishing

Mark A. Richards, James A. Scheer, William A. Holm, Principles of Modern Radar: Basic Principles (2010), SciTech Publishing

Mark Johnson USMC, Jessica Meyeraan, USAF, (2003), Military Deception, Joint Forces Staff College

Mihajlovic Mihajlo, Arsic Stanislav (2003) Specijalne Snage Sveta (World Special Forces) Novinsko Izdavacki Centar Vojska, Beograd

Mihajlovic, Mihajlo, (1994) Proporcionalno vodjenje – Proportional Guidance), Faculty of Technical Sciences (Fakultet Tehnickih Nauka) Novi Sad, Serbia

Miller, Jay Skunk (1995) Works, Aerofax, Midland Publishing

Narcelo B. Perotoni, Luiz Aleberto de Andrade, Mirabel Cerqueria Rezende, Radar Cross Section of a stealthy aircraft using electromagnetic simulation in the X and in VHF/UHF bands, Researchgate

Naval Training Command Gunner's Mate, NAVTRA 10200-8 www. mycitymiltary.com

Nepokoev, F. K. (1991) Strelba Zenitnim Raketami, Voenoe Izdateltvo, Moskva

Nerri, Filippo (2006), Introduction to Electronic Defense Systems, Artech House

FURTHER READING AND BIBLIOGRAPHY

Nicolaescu, I (2006) Radar Absorbing Materials Used for target Camouflage, Military Technical Academy, Bucharest, Romania

O'Donnell, Robert, Radar System Engineering lectrures, IEEE New Hampshire Section

Osnovi Postroenia Zenitnogo Rakenogo Kompleksa S-125M, (1973) Ministry of Defence USSR

Pace, Steve (1999) F-22 Raptor, McGraw-Hill

Palumbo, Neil (2010), Basic Principles of Homing Guidance, John Hopkins Technical Digest, Vol 29

Peebles, P.Z. (1998), Radar Principles, Wiley-Interscience.

Pervov, Mikhail (2012) Raskazi o Ruskih Raketah, Stolicnaya Enciklopedia, Moskva

Peyton Z. Peebles jr., (1998) Radar Principles, John Wiley & Sons Inc

Poisel, Richard (2013), Information Warfare and Electronic Warfare Systems, Artech House

Pokorni, Slavko (2001), Tendencije Razvoja Pasivnih Mamaca, Vojno Tehnicki Glasnik, Serbia

Pyotr Ufimtsev, (2007) Fundamental of the Physical Theory of Diffraction, Wiley-Interscience

Radic Aleksandar, (2012) Vazduhoplovstvo i Protivvazdusna Odbrana Vojske Srbije, Medija Centar Odbrana, Beograd

Richards, M.A. (2005), Fundamentals of Radar Signal Processing, McGraw Education.

Richards, M.A., Scheer, J.A. and Holm, W.A. (2010), Principles of Modern Radar-Basic Principles, SciTech Publishing.

Richardson Doug, (2001) Stealth Warplanes, MBI Publishing Company

Roger N. McDermott (2017) Russia's Electronic Warfare Capabilities to 2025, Estonian MoD

Ross Simpson, (2002), Stealth Down, Narwhal Press

S-125 Neva/Pechora Wikipedia: en.wikipedia.org/wiki/S-125_ Neva/Pechora

SAM Simulator, https://sites.google.com/site/samsimulator1972/home

Scott Bill (1991) Inside the Stealth Bomber, The B-2 Story, TAB Aero

Shaefer, John, Understanding Stealth, Marietta Scientific Inc.

Singh, Mohinder (1988), Electronic Warfare, DESIDOC, India

Skolnik, M.I. (2002), Introduction to Radar Systems, McGraw-Hill Education.

Skolnik, M.I. (2008), Radar Handbook, McGraw-Hill Education.

Stanicaya SNR-125M1, Tehnicekoe Opisanie I, II, II, IV (1982), Voenoe Izdatelstvo MO SSSR

Stealth Special (2017) Aviation news December 2017

Steven J. Zaloga, (2000) The Evolving SAM Threat: Kosovo and Beyond, Journal of Electronic Defense, May 2000,

Sukharevsky O., (2009) Raseyanie Elektromagnetnih Voln Vozdushim I Nazemnim Radiolokacionim Obyektam, Kharkiv Air Forces University

Sweetman Bill, Goodal James, Lockheed F-117A (1990), Haynes

T.O.GR1F-16CJ-1-1 Flight Manual F-16C/D (2003)

T.O.GR1F-16CJ-34-1-1 Avionics and Nonnuclear Weapons Delivery Flight Manual, F-16C/D (1997)

Taktika Zenitnih Raketnih Voisk, Uchebnik (1969) Ministerstvo Obo- roni SSSR

Tehnika i Voruzhenie (1999-2018)

Teperin L.L., Vozhdaev V. V. (2018) Kharakteristiki Radiolokatsionnoy Zametnosti Letatelnih Aparatov, FizMatLit, Moskva

The Soviet SA-3 Missile System (1965) Scientific Intelligence Report, Office of Scientific Intelligence

Toomay, J.C. (2004), Radar Principles for Non-specialist, SciTech Publishing.

Tuzlukov, V. (2012), Signal Processing in Radar Systems, CRC Press.

Vakin, Sergei A., Shustov, Lev N., Dunwell, Robert H. (2001), Fundamentals of Electronic Warfare, Artech House

Video material: Discovery

Video Material: Dozvolite

Video Material: RTS

Video material: Sdelano v SSSR

Video material: TV Zvezda, Voenaya Priyomka Video material: Samiy-Samiy

Video material: Udarnaya Sila

Video material: Zastava Film

Voruzhenie PVO I RES Rossii (Air Defence Weapons and Electronic Systems of Russia) (2011) Rosoboronexport, Moskva

Vozusno Kosmicheskaya Oborona 2007-2015

Warren J. Board, John B. Hoffman (2016), Air and Missile Defense System Engineering, CRC Press

Whitcomb, Darrel (2014), Team Sport Combat Search and Rescue over Serbia 1999, Air Power, Fall 2014

William D. Hartung,(2011) Prophets of War, Lockheed Martin and the Making of the Military-Industrial Complex, Nation Books

Yanushevsky, Rafael, (2011) Guidance of Unmanned Aerial Vehicles, CRC Press

Zenitni Raketni Kompleksi PVO Suhoputniy Voisk, (1997), Tehnika i Voruzhenie

Zhirkov V.M. (2003) Analiz Konstruktivniih Osobenosti i Ocenka Effikasnosti Boevogo Primenenia Razlichnih Modifikacii ZRK Tipa S-125, CNII MO RF

ZRK Kub, Ruskie Tanki, (2013) Eaglemoss Collection

Index

INDEX